MW00579631

DISPENSATIONALISM REVISITED

A TWENTY-FIRST CENTURY RESTATEMENT

EDITED BY

KEVIN T. BAUDER

&

R. BRUCE COMPTON

CENTRAL SEMINARY PRESS

FOR THE CHURCH. FOR THE GOSPEL.

PLYMOUTH, MN

Dispensationalism Revisited: A Twenty-First Century Restatement
©2023 Central Baptist Theological Seminary of Minneapolis

Published by:
Central Seminary Press
900 Forestview Ln N
Plymouth, MN 55441
763-417-8250

Printed by:
Nystrom Publishing Company, Inc.
9100 Cottonwood Lane North
Maple Grove, MN 55396

ISBN: 978-1-7363064-1-3
LCCN: 2023903499

"Scripture quotations taken from the (NASB®) New American Standard Bible®, Copyright © 1960, 1971, 1977, 1995, 2020 by The Lockman Foundation. Used by permission. All rights reserved. lockman.org."

Editors: Kevin T. Bauder and R. Bruce Compton
Design & Layout: Chris Hartzler (mindsquall.com)

Cover Image: The cover of this book features a detail from a dispensational chart painted by H. H. Wagner of Bible School Park, New York in 1945 (copyrighted by the artist and reproduced by permission). Such charts were a significant way that various versions of dispensationalism were propagated. They also illustrate some of the ways in which dispensationalism has changed. For example, few if any contemporary dispensationalists accept Wagner's appeal to Luke 13:24–27 as a proof text to show that the door of grace permanently closes at the Rapture. Indeed, most believe that an innumerable multitude will be saved during the Tribulation.

Printed in the United States of America
All rights reserved

Authors

William D. Barrick is retired from teaching at The Master's Seminary. He earned a ThD at Grace Theological Seminary.

Kevin T. Bauder is research professor of systematic theology at Central Baptist Theological Seminary of Minneapolis. His PhD is from Dallas Theological Seminary.

Roy Beacham is professor of Old Testament at Central Baptist Theological Seminary of Minneapolis. He earned his ThD at Grace Theological Seminary.

Douglas Brown is the dean of Faith Baptist Theological Seminary. He earned his PhD at Trinity Evangelical Divinity School.

R. Bruce Compton is professor of biblical languages at Detroit Baptist Theological Seminary. He holds a ThD from Grace Theological Seminary.

W. Edward Glenny is professor of New Testament studies and Greek at the University of Northwestern. He has earned a ThD from Dallas Theological Seminary and a PhD from the University of Minnesota.

O. Andrew Hudson is the pastor of Westside Baptist Church in Janesville, Wisconsin. He holds a PhD from Central Baptist Theological Seminary of Minneapolis.

Ryan Martin is the pastor of Columbiaville Baptist Church in Columbiaville, Michigan. His PhD is from Central Baptist Theological Seminary of Minneapolis.

Larry Pettegrew is research professor of theology at Shepherd's Seminary. He earned his PhD at Dallas Theological Seminary.

Jonathan Pratt is academic vice president of Central Baptist Theological Seminary of Minneapolis. He holds a PhD from Dallas Theological Seminary.

Contents

Abbreviations

Note: Unless otherwise noted, all Scripture quotations are from the New American Standard Bible®, Copyright © 1960, 1971, 1977, 1995, 2020 by the Lockman Foundation. All rights reserved.

AB	Anchor Bible (Commentary)
AF	J. B. Lightfoot, ed. The Apostolic Fathers. New York: Macmillan, 1898.
ANF	Roberts, Alexander, James Donaldson, and A. Cleveland Coxe, eds. The Ante-Nicene Fathers. 10 Vols. Buffalo, NY: Christian Literature Company, 1885.
BDAG	Bauer, W., F. W. Danker, W. F. Arndt, and F. W. Gingrich. A Greek-English Lexicon of the New Testament and Other Early Christian Literature. 3d ed. Chicago: University of Chicago Press, 2000.
BECNT	Baker Exegetical Commentary on the New Testament
BSac	Bibliotheca Sacra
CTJ	Conservative Theological Journal
DBSJ	Detroit Baptist Seminary Journal
EBC	Expositor's Bible Commentary
EDNT	Balz, Horst, and Gerhard Schneider. Exegetical Dictionary of the New Testament. 3 vols. Grand Rapids: Eerdmans, 1994–2000.
EMBC	Everyman Bible Commentary
EvQ	Evangelical Quarterly
IVPNTC	IVP New Testament Commentary Series
JBL	Journal of Biblical Literature
JSNT	Journal for the Study of the New Testament
LSJ	Liddell, Henry George, and Robert Scott. A Greek-English Lexicon. Revised and augmented throughout by Sir Henry Stuart Jones with the assistance of Roderick McKenzie. Oxford: Clarendon Press, 1996.
LXX	Septuagint
MT	Masoretic Text
NAC	New American Commentary

NCB	New Century Bible
NDBT	Alexander, T. Desmond, and Brian S. Rosner, eds. New Dictionary of Biblical Theology. Downers Grove, IL: InterVarsity, 2000.
NICNT	New International Commentary on the New Testament
NIDOTTE	Van Gemeren, Willem A., ed. New International Dictionary of Old Testament Theology and Exegesis. 5 vols. Grand Rapids: Zondervan, 1997.
NIGTC	New International Greek Testament Commentary
NPNF 1	Schaff, Philip, ed. A Select Library of the Nicene and Post-Nicene Fathers of the Christian Church. First Series. Buffalo, NY: Christian Literature Company, 1887.
NPNF 2	Schaff, Philip, and Henry Wace, eds. A Select Library of the Nicene and Post-Nicene Fathers of the Christian Church. Second Series. New York: Christian Literature Company, 1895.
NT	New Testament
OT	Old Testament
PNTC	Pillar New Testament Commentary
SJT	Scottish Journal of Theology
SWJT	Southwestern Journal of Theology
TMSJ	The Master's Seminary Journal
TNTC	Tyndale New Testament Commentaries
TrinJ	Trinity Journal
TWOT	Harris, R. Laird, Gleason L. Archer, Jr., and Bruce K. Waltke, eds. Theological Wordbook of the Old Testament. 2 vols. Chicago: Moody Press, 1999.
TynBul	Tyndale Bulletin
WBC	Word Biblical Commentary
WUNT	Wissenschaftliche Untersuchungen zum Neuen Testament
ZAW	Zeitschrift für die alttestamentliche Wissenschaft
ZNW	Zeitschrift für die neutamentliche Wissenschaft
ZECNT	Zondervan Exegetical Commentary on the New Testament

Preface

Festschriften (collections of essays that honor particular individuals) have gone out of style, at least as far as the major publishers are concerned. Publishers print books to make money. Festschriften tend to sell mainly among the friends of the individual to whom the volume is dedicated, and hardly anybody has enough friends to make a book like that profitable. Publishing such books is usually bad for business.

Furthermore, dispensationalism is thought to be nearly obsolete by the academy. A generation or so ago, it was a dominant way of reading the Bible in North America; now it is decidedly a minority view, though varieties of it are still influential at the popular level. Consequently, the mainstream publishers are no more interested in books about dispensationalism than they are Festschriften.

Yet here we are, a group of academic authors publishing a Festschrift in honor of Charles A. Hauser, Jr. What is more, the book is devoted to a restatement of dispensational theology. Why would we do such a thing? To this question I respond with four reasons.

The first reason is that we (the editors and authors) have all been affected by the ministry of Charles Hauser, and we all wish to render honor to whom honor is due. He did not influence us all in the same way, a fact that is illustrated by the various names that people called him. To his students he was always Dr. Hauser. To his colleagues he was Charles, Charlie, or even Chuck. To his family he was Chick. Whomever he touched, however, carried the marks of the encounter. He impressed people by his gentleness, kindness, forbearance, and devotion to Christ. Those who labored with him in the academy also saw him as a careful thinker.

Some of the authors in this book were his students. Some were his colleagues. Some (including my coeditor, Bruce Compton) were both. As for me, I was both his student and his colleague. Besides that, I was his employee (he was my supervisor at Denver Baptist Bible College and later at Central Baptist Theological Seminary). Later still, when I became the president of that seminary, I was his boss. All the authors of this book agree: here was a man of God who loved the Word of God and who, through exposition and example, brought it to bear upon the lives of God's people. Consequently, we have included in this volume a section of tributes from people whose lives he touched.

The second reason is because dispensationalism, like all theologies, requires fresh articulation. Certainly, Charles Hauser recognized this need. Dispensationalism was one of his most important theological emphases, but he was prepared to distance himself from some aspects of older dispensational theories. While not highly theologically inventive, Hauser labored to relieve certain tensions within dispensationalism. His rethinking of dispensational theology sometimes brought him into intellectual conflict with his peers, and such conflict invariably drove him toward greater precision and clarification, just as it moved him to seek a deeper understanding of Scripture.

Some of the older criticisms of dispensationalism were answered, either by argument or by example, years ago. We are past the day when a responsible critic can claim that dispensationalism teaches multiple ways of salvation, that it is anti-cultural (as if such a thing were possible), or that it squelches social and political activity. We have no reason to devote space to those complaints in this volume.

Nevertheless, new and more sophisticated criticisms of dispensationalism have been offered. A new generation of covenant theologians has abandoned the old canards but still considers dispensationalism an opposing theology. New covenant theology and its twin sister, progressive covenantalism, have brought their own criticisms. Furthermore, the development of progressive dispensationalism has raised new issues within the dispensational camp. For these reasons, we believe that a restatement of dispensational thought can incorporate the best of new developments while responding to the more recent criticisms.

We do not claim that we will address every dispensational development or issue in this volume. Each writer has a particular purpose and, in the editors' judgment, fulfills that purpose. Because of the limitations of space and interest, however, these writers may not address some closely related issues. Consequently, this book aims to be one voice for dispensationalism at one point in the conversation. We have not tried to answer every question or to solve every problem.

We have tried to avoid debate over intramural disputes that arise within the dispensational camp. Progressive dispensationalism became a distinct influence within dispensationalism during the 1980s, engendering significant internal controversy. This present book includes writers who represent some version of traditional dispensationalism, and it probably tilts in that direction (which is only fair, since Charle Hauser argued for traditional dispensationalism). Yet the book also includes authors who have contributed to progressive dispensationalism. We lament that adherents of these two positions have sometimes positioned themselves as theological opponents speaking against one another rather than allies conversing with each other.

The essays are ordered around a structure. The first essays deal with three *sine qua nons* of dispensationalism. Doug Brown writes about the glory of God. Roy Beacham offers an extended explanation and defense of literal hermeneutics in the interpretation of prophecy, defending the proposition that what the prophet says is exactly what God says. My own essay attempts to clarify the nature of the distinction between Israel and the church, arguing that these are only two of the many peoples of God that will populate God's kingdom.

The next three essays deal with broad topics within dispensationalism. Bill Barrick shows how dispensationalists view the relationship between the biblical covenants and the dispensations. Bruce Compton addresses the nature of the kingdom of God, a key concept in dispensational thought. Then Larry Pettegrew wrestles with a question from history: why did Israel disappear so quickly from the thinking of the early Church Fathers?

The last four essays deal with more specific topics in dispensational thought. Andy Hudson offers a dispensationalist reading of the book of Acts, explaining why dispensationalists understand that book to be transitional. Ryan Martin wrestles with the question of what Romans 9–11 teaches about the future of Israel. Ed Glenny examines Revelation 20 to discover whether it really teaches a premillennial second coming. Finally, Jonathan Pratt offers a defense of a pretribulational rapture of the church.

Whether you are a dispensationalist or not, our authors hope that you will find this volume to be a helpful tool for understanding dispensational theology as it currently exists. We understand as well as anyone that dispensationalism as a theological position is not a slam dunk. Rather, different theological systems and various readings of the Bible are more or less probable. As with every intellectual construct, some evidence points toward dispensationalism, and some points against it. Our job is to help you see the evidence that explains our position while explaining the evidence that doesn't seem to fit. Defenders of alternative positions also perform this same task with respect to their systems. We think that the evidence that appears to favor dispensationalism is stronger than the evidence that seems to point against it, and we think that the evidence pointing against it is more easily explained than the evidence that points against the alternative theories. We hope that this book will help you to understand why we see it that way.

A third reason we are offering this book is because we find many popular presentations of dispensationalism to be irresponsible and misleading. Too many broadcasters and popular authors are too eager to draw lines directly from newspaper headlines to supposed fulfillments of biblical prophecy. They keep banging on about supposed signs of the rapture that they see in current events, and some of them see what they think is a "convergence" (their word) of these signs that virtually assures a rapture in the immediate future.

The authors of this book hold to the doctrine of imminency (i.e., that the rapture could occur at any moment), but we are not looking for signs. We don't believe that the Bible gives any signs that need to be fulfilled before the rapture occurs. Jesus may return in the air for his church at any moment. That event may be in the immediate future, but it may also be delayed longer than we might wish. Scripture simply does not give us any mechanism for discovering the timing of the rapture from our point of view.

We believe that preoccupation with the timing of the rapture is a distraction. It keeps people from focusing on the more important issues that dispensationalism addresses. In this book we intend to discuss those important matters, matters that are genuinely definitive for dispensationalists. Furthermore, while we hope that some in the academy will read this book, we are not writing for the academy. We are writing for intelligent but nontechnical readers. We are trying to write in ordinary language. Where we use technical terms, we try to define them. We do not quote Greek or Hebrew in the main text (though we do in the footnotes).

If we have to refer to a Greek or Hebrew word, we transliterate it into English letters.

In other words, we want ordinary Christians to be able to read and to profit from this book. We recognize that it is a big book, and we are aware that the average church member would rather watch a video or listen to a podcast. But we encourage the average pastor, deacon, or Sunday school teacher to work through the first three chapters. These are the heart of the book, and together they explain what dispensationalism is. Once you have mastered those, the remaining chapters will help you to refine your dispensationalism. We are writing for the church, and we will be disappointed if only professors read our book.

We also have a fourth reason for publishing this volume, and specifically for publishing it through Central Seminary Press, namely that generous donors have contributed to making this publication possible. Among them are Jim Hunter, Henry and Grace Tsuei, and especially Bob Freiberg. Without their material help, this book could not have seen the light of day. Special mention should also be made of Debbie Bauder and Laura Glassel, who proofread every chapter, of Dennis Cone, who did the final copyediting, and of Nystrom Publishing, which has printed this and many other volumes for Central Seminary Press.

One more thing—in preparing the volume for publication, we chose to cite the New American Standard Bible throughout. We had two reasons. One is the readability and exactness of the translation. The other is that the NASB was Charles Hauser's favorite version of the Bible and the one that he used exclusively in his seminary classes. It should be noted, however, that some authors used the 1995 edition, while other authors employed the 2020 edition.

Kevin T. Bauder
Central Baptist Theological Seminary
December 1, 2022

The Glory of God and Dispensationalism: Revisiting the *Sine Qua Nons* of Dispensationalism

Douglas Brown
Faith Baptist Bible College & Theological Seminary
Ankeny, Iowa

In 1965, Charles Ryrie published *Dispensationalism Today*. In this influential volume, Ryrie attempted to explain, systematize, and defend the dispensational approach to the Scriptures. His most notable contribution was arguably the three *sine qua nons* of dispensationalism: First, a dispensationalist consistently keeps Israel and the church distinct. Second, a dispensationalist consistently employs a literal system of hermeneutics (i.e., what Ryrie calls "normal" or "plain" interpretation). Third, a dispensationalist believes that the underlying purpose of the world is the glory of God.[1]

The acceptance of Ryrie's *sine qua nons* of dispensationalism has varied within dispensational circles. In general, traditional dispensationalists have accepted and used them as a starting point to explain the essence of dispensationalism.[2] In contrast, progressive dispensationalists have largely rejected Ryrie's proposal and have explored new ways to explain the essential tenets of dispensationalism.[3] Despite criticisms leveled by progressive dispensationalists, Ryrie reaffirmed the *sine qua nons* when he revised and expanded his book in 2007.[4] It is remarkable that after more than fifty years dispensational advocates continue to affirm, debate, and dispute Ryrie's *sine qua nons* of dispensationalism.

This study is primarily concerned with Ryrie's third essential aspect, the glory of God. On balance, dispensational scholarship has focused more on

---

[1] Charles C. Ryrie, *Dispensationalism Today* (Chicago: Moody Press, 1965), 43–47.

[2] See, for example, Renald Showers, *There Really Is a Difference*, 12th ed. (Bellmawr, NJ: Friends of Israel Gospel Ministry, 2010), 52, 53; Rolland McCune, *A Systematic Theology of Biblical Christianity*, vol. 1 (Allen Park, MI: Detroit Baptist Theological Seminary, 2009), 112–15; Christopher Cone, ed., *Dispensationalism Tomorrow and Beyond: A Theological Collection in Honor of Charles C. Ryrie* (Fort Worth: Tyndale Seminary Press, 2008), passim.

[3] Craig A. Blaising and Darrell L. Bock, *Progressive Dispensationalism: An Up-to-Date Handbook of Contemporary Dispensational Thought* (Wheaton: Bridgepoint, 1993), 9–56, see esp. endnote 8, pp. 304–5; Robert L. Saucy, *The Case for Progressive Dispensationalism: The Interface Between Dispensational and Non-Dispensational Theology* (Grand Rapids: Zondervan, 1993), 19–29; John S. Feinberg, "Systems of Discontinuity," in *Continuity and Discontinuity: Perspectives on the Relationship Between the Old and New Testaments*, ed. John S. Feinberg (Wheaton: Crossway, 1988), 67–85; Michael Vlach, *Dispensationalism: Essential Beliefs and Common Myths* (Los Angeles: Theological Studies Press, 2008), 13–31.

[4] Charles C. Ryrie, *Dispensationalism*, rev. ed. (Chicago: Moody Press, 2007), 45–48.

the other two distinctives, the distinction between Israel and the church and a consistent literal hermeneutic. Elliott E. Johnson correctly observed, "In this author's view dispensationalists have not always given adequate attention to the glory of God in their teaching on dispensationalism. Yet the Bible repeatedly focuses on this aspect of God's program." [5] I have divided this study into three parts. First, I will explain the controversy surrounding the glory of God as a distinguishing mark of dispensational thought. Second, I will attempt to develop an outline for a biblical theology for God's glory based on Scripture. Third, I will draw some conclusions about the validity of using the glory of God as a unifying principle for dispensationalism.

The Controversy Concerning God's Glory within Dispensationalism

A short historical overview is in order to help understand the controversy related to the glory of God and dispensationalism. [6] Classical dispensationalists such as C. I. Scofield and Lewis Sperry Chafer taught that God had two separate redemptive purposes for Israel and the church. Israel was seen as the earthly people of God through whom God would fulfill an earthly redemption. The church was seen as the heavenly people of God through whom God would fulfill a heavenly redemption. These two divine purposes were eternally separate and helped to explain why God instituted different dispensations. Critics from covenantal theology, such as O. T. Allis, charged dispensationalists with undermining the unity of the Bible and Reformed theology, especially the covenant of grace and the Westminster Confession. [7] For Allis and other covenant theologians, the unifying theme of redemptive history is soteriological, grounded in the covenant of grace.

In response to these criticisms, dispensational scholars searched for a unifying theme within the dispensational theology. John Walvoord responded to these charges by affirming that there is one overarching purpose of Scripture—the glory of God:

All the events of the created world are designed to manifest the glory of God. The error of covenant theologians is that they combine all the many facets

---

[5] Elliott E. Johnson, "A Biblical Theology of God's Glory," BSac 169 (2012): 403. Stanley Tousaint remarks, "Of these three [*sine qua nons*], undoubtedly the most important is the distinction between Israel and the church" ("Israel and the Church of a Traditional Dispensationalist," in *Three Central Issues in Contemporary Dispensationalism: A Comparison of Traditional and Progressive Views*, ed. Herbert W. Bateman IV (Grand Rapids: Kregel, 1999), 227.

[6] See the helpful summaries by Craig A. Blaising, "Contemporary Dispensationalism," SWJT 36 (1994): 5–10 and "Development of Dispensationalism by Contemporary Dispensationalists, Part 2," *BSac* 145 (1988): 266–69.

[7] Oswald T. Allis, "Modern Dispensationalism and the Unity of Scripture," *EvQ* (1936): 22–35.

of divine purpose in the one objective of the fulfillment of the covenant of grace. From a logical standpoint, this is the reductive error—the use of one aspect of the whole as the determining element.[8]

Ryrie followed Walvoord's lead and incorporated the glory of God in his *sine qua nons* of dispensationalism.

Decades later, controversy continues to swirl around the proposal that the glory of God is a distinguishing mark of dispensationalism. Herb Bateman IV summarizes the criticisms under two questions. He asks, "First, do all dispensationalists agree that the self-glorification of God is the unifying theme of Scripture?"[9] Bateman notes that prior to Walvoord and Ryrie there was a lack of consensus among classical dispensationalists such as Chafer, who evidently proposed no overarching principle. In addition, contemporaries of Ryrie argued for other unifying principles. For example, Alva McClain and Dwight Pentecost argued respectively that the unifying theme of Scripture is the mediatorial kingdom or theocratic kingdom of God.[10] To this list, one should add progressive dispensationalists. Blaising states, "For progressive dispensationalism, the kingdom of God is the unifying theme of the history of divine revelation, and Jesus Christ is the apex of that kingdom, the agent and mediator through whom it is brought to fulfillment, and the focal point of divine revelation."[11]

The second question Bateman raises is "whether the doxological principle is a unique or distinguishing feature of dispensationalism."[12] To this inquiry, he responds negatively as well. In other words, dispensationalists are not the only theologians who see God's glory as the ultimate purpose for creation. Covenant theologians enjoy a rich heritage of celebrating the glory of God. One could look to the Westminster Shorter Catechism or Jonathan Edwards's treatise, *The End for Which God Created the World*.[13] Ryrie (and Walvoord), however, knew about this emphasis and even acknowledged that covenant theologians

[8] John F. Walvoord, *The Millennial Kingdom* (Findlay, OH: Dunham Publishing Co., 1959), 92.

[9] Bateman IV, "Introduction: Dispensationalism Yesterday and Today," in *Three Central Issues in Contemporary Dispensationalism*, 36.

[10] Alva J. McClain, *The Greatness of the Kingdom: An Inductive Study of the Kingdom of God* (Winona Lake, IN: BMH Books, 1992), 4–5; J. Dwight Pentecost, *Things to Come: A Study in Biblical Eschatology* (Grand Rapids: Zondervan, 1964), 433.

[11] Blaising, "Contemporary Dispensationalism," 12. Thus also Saucy, *The Case for Progressive Dispensationalism*, 27–29.

[12] Bateman, "Dispensationalism Yesterday," 36.

[13] The catechism asks as Question 1: "What is the chief end of man?" Answer: "Man's chief end is to glorify God and to enjoy Him forever."

recognize the ultimate end of God's glory.[14]

The doxological principle in dispensationalism is part of a much larger discussion than merely recognizing God's glory. It relates to one's philosophy of history. Ryrie articulates three elements needed to establish a philosophy of history: (1) "a proper concept of the progress of revelation in history; (2) the unifying principle; and (3) the ultimate goal of history."[15] Ryrie does a commendable job explaining the differences not only between covenant theology and dispensationalism, but also between progressive dispensationalism and traditional dispensationalism as they relate to their philosophies of history.[16] Their views of progressive revelation are different, their unifying principles are different, and their ultimate goals are different as well.

Before attempting to outline the biblical theology of God's glory, one more topic needs to be discussed, namely, the problem of finding a unifying center. Both systematic and biblical theologians have long recognized the difficulty of finding one center that provides an adequate foundation for all other truth.[17] James Hamilton describes a biblical theological center as follows:

> This centre of the Bible's theology acts as the centre of gravity for all of its other themes, it undergirds biblical wisdom, and it presents itself as the apex of the purposes of the God who speaks and acts from creation and redemption to judgement and consummation. . . . Moreover the centre of biblical theology is the theme which all of the Bible's other themes serve to exposit.[18]

The Case for a Dispensational Understanding of God's Glory

Attempting to develop a biblical theology of God's glory is an immense undertaking. Such an endeavor is complicated by the fact that we are finite and God is infinite, so there is always more about God to know and to learn. Even for all of eternity, the redeemed will grow in their understanding of the glory of God. Pentecost comments, "A finite mind could no more

---

[14] For example, see Ryrie's comments about Charles Hodge and William G. T. Shedd in *Dispensationalism*, 108.

[15] Ryrie, *Dispensationalism*, 21.

[16] Ibid., 20–23, 103 109. See also Showers, *There Really Is a Difference*, 49–52.

[17] James Hamilton, "The Glory of God in Salvation through Judgment: The Centre of Biblical Theology?" *TynBul* 57 (2006): 59–62; Gerhard F. Hasel, "The Problem of the Center in the OT Theology Debate," *ZAW* 86 (1974): 65–82; McCune, *Systematic Theology*, 1:135; Craig L. Blomberg, "The Unity and Diversity of Scripture," *NDBT*, 66–69.

[18] Hamilton, "The Glory of God in Salvation through Judgment," 59, 61.

comprehend His glory than one can compress the ocean into a bucket. All eternity will be spent learning more and more about how great, how good, and how glorious God is." [19] So the following is just the start of a biblical theology of God's glory, especially as it relates to dispensationalism. The outline progresses through seven premises that build on each other.

Premise One: God is a glorious God.

What exactly is the glory of God? Christians speak frequently about God's glory and glorifying God, but few have considered what it is. Unfortunately, many systematic theologies do not directly discuss the issue.

Perhaps the best place to start is with the terms most frequently used for glory in the Old and New Testaments. In the Old Testament, the Hebrew term *kābôd* (used 376 times along with its derivatives) is used most frequently of God's glory. [20] When it is used in a context not directly related to God, *kābôd* can refer to (1) a weight or burden (1 Sam 4:18; Isa 2:24); (2) possessions (Gen 31:1) or impressive appearance (Gen 45:3); (3) splendor, magnificence (Hag 2:3); or (4) distinction, respect or a mark of honor (1 Kgs 3:13; Prov 26:8). [21] When used in relation to God, *kābôd* refers to the manifestation of his being. "Over against the transience of human and earthly glory stands the unchanging beauty of the manifest God (Ps 145:5). In this sense the noun *kābôd* takes on its most unusual and distinctive meaning. Forty-five times this form of the root relates to a visible manifestation of God and whenever 'the glory of God' is mentioned this usage must be taken account of."[22] R. B. Gaffin states that "the phrase 'glory of the LORD' (*kebôd yhwh*) occurs frequently in the OT; it is virtually a technical term (e.g., Exod 16:7; 1 Kgs. 8:11; Ps 63:2). God's glory is His visible and active presence."[23]

The most common New Testament term related to God's glory is *doxa* (used 166 times). In secular Greek, *doxa* is most frequently used to refer to one's "opinion" or "view"; surprisingly this usage is absent from biblical Greek (both the LXX and NT). [24] The Septuagint translators shaped the biblical use of *doxa*

---

[19] J. Dwight Pentecost, *The Glory of God* (Portland: Multnomah, 1978), 97.

[20] *TWOT*, s.v. "כָּבֵד."

[21] William Lee Holladay and Ludwig Köhler, *A Concise Hebrew and Aramaic Lexicon of the Old Testament* (Leiden: Brill, 2000), s.v. "דּוֹבָך."

[22] Oswalt, "943 כָּבֵד," 1:427.

[23] Richard B. Gaffin, Jr., "Glory," *NDBT*, 507.

when they used it to translate *kābôd*. In the New Testament, *doxa* has four basic meanings: (1) the condition of being bright or shining, *brightness, splendor, radiance* (Acts 7:55); (2) a state of being magnificent, *greatness, splendor* (Mark 6:29); (3) honor as enhancement or recognition of status or performance, *fame, recognition, renown, honor, prestige* (2 Pet 1:17); and (4) a transcendent being deserving of honor, a majestic being (2 Pet 2:10). [25] The two key ways New Testament writers use *doxa* in relation to God are to either display his visible radiance or uphold and spread his reputation and honor. [26] At times, it is hard to distinguish which meaning a particular author is using in any given context. The glory of God goes beyond lexical studies. How do we understand the glory of God theologically? Several theologians make a helpful distinction between the intrinsic and extrinsic glory of God. [27] The intrinsic glory of God relates to the very essence or being of God. Glory is not merely an attribute of God. Rather, it is the sum total of all his attributes. John Walvoord defines God's glory as "the manifestation of God's infinite perfections."[28] J. Dwight Pentecost concurs, "The glory of God is the sum total of all His perfections as revealed to men."[29] Scripture presents many of God's attributes and works as glorious, because they reflect the intrinsic glory of God. God is a glorious God. The extrinsic glory of God relates to the manifestation or revelation of God's intrinsic glory. Wayne Grudem defines God's glory as "the created brightness that surrounds God's revelation of himself." He further comments, "It is very appropriate that God's revelation of himself should be accompanied by such splendor and brightness, for this glory of God is the visible manifestation of the excellence of God's character." [30] Many scholars link the display of God's glory to his presence, both

---

[24] *EDNT*, 1:345; LSJ, s,v, "δόξα."

[25] BDAG, s,v, "δόξα."

[26] See the very helpful summary in Richard Bauckham, *The Gospel of Glory: Major Themes in Johannine Theology* (Grand Rapids: Baker, 2015).

[27] See the survey in Christopher W. Morgan, "Toward a Theology of the Glory of God," in *The Glory of God*, ed. Christopher W. Morgan and Robert A. Peterson, Theology in Community (Wheaton: Crossway, 2010) 165–67. So also John MacArthur, Jr., *God: How to Know and Glorify Him* (Panorama City, CA: Word of Grace Communications, 1982), 56–62; John D. Hannah, *How Do We Glorify God?* Basics of the Faith Series (Phillipsburg, NJ: P&R, 2000), 10–11. Lewis Sperry Chafer distinguishes between the essential (i.e., intrinsic) and declarative aspects to "the boundless glory of God" in *Systematic Theology*, vol. 7 (Dallas: Dallas Theological Seminary, 1948), 172–73.

[28] John F. Walvoord, *The Prophecy Knowledge Handbook* (Wheaton: Victor, 1990), 476.

[29] Pentecost, *The Glory of God*, 123.

[30] Wayne Grudem, *Systematic Theology: An Introduction to Biblical Doctrine* (Grand Rapids: Zondervan, 1994), 220–21.

in the world and among his people (John 1:14). [31] In many respects, the Bible's story line is the progressive revelation of God's extrinsic glory.

Premise Two: The ultimate goal of all creation is the glory of God.

Romans 11:36 states, "For from Him and through Him and to Him are all things. To Him be the glory forever. Amen." This doxology (along with many other doxologies in the Bible) captures the key purpose for which God created the world—for his own glory. The three prepositional phrases in this verse describe the comprehensive scope of God's purpose. "From Him" (*ek autou*) explains that God is the creator. God made the universe and everything in it. "Through Him" (*di autou*) explains that God is the sustainer. By his eternal power and wisdom, God sustains the universe and directs its course. "To Him" (*eis auton*) explains that God himself is the goal of creation. This telic use of the preposition eis reveals that the universe is inherently God-centered. He is the first and last cause of "all things" (*ta panta*). [32] This theological reality cannot be overemphasized. A God-centered approach to theology radically affects how one understands and applies Scripture. The doxological conclusion of Romans 11:36, "To Him be the glory forever," summarizes the proper response all creation should have toward the one true God. Ephesians 1:3–14 confirms that every facet of God's eternal plan (1:11) is ultimately accomplished "to the praise of God's glory" (1:6, 12, 14). J. D. Hannah states it this way: "What is the chief end or purpose of God? Why did God create the world and mankind? I answer: God's chief end is to be known in all his glory."[33] H. C. Thiessen and V. D. Doerksen concur:

> Though God sincerely seeks to promote the happiness of his creatures and to perfect the saints in holiness, neither of these is the highest possible end. The end is his own glory. All his works in creation (Ps. 19:1–6; Prov. 3:19), preservation (Neh. 9:6; Rev. 4:11), providence (Ps. 33:10f.; Dan. 4:35; Eph. 1:11), and redemption (1 Cor. 2:7; Eph. 3:10f.) have this end in view. [34]

A God-centered view of reality is what John Piper calls a "continental divide

---

[31] Gaffin, "Glory," 507–9.

[32] See similar ideas in Col 1:16 and 1 Cor 8:6.

[33] Hannah, *How Do We Glorify God?* 11.

[34] Henry Clarence Thiessen and Vernon D. Doerksen, *Lectures in Systematic Theology* (Grand Rapids: Eerdmans, 1979), 82, see also 100, 103, 111, 118, 126.

in theology. If you really believe this, all rivers of your thinking run toward God. If you do not, all rivers run toward man. The theological and practical implications are innumerable." [35]

This observation raises a theological paradox that is interesting to unwind. Is God selfish or sinful for seeking his own glory? [36] The answer to this question rests ultimately in the perfections of God's essence and character. If the God of the Bible is the one true God, then for him to seek some other end outside himself would be absurd. God is the highest entity in the universe and has infinite value. There is nothing greater to seek. For God to create the world for himself demonstrates the reality that he is indeed God. If God called creation to seek something other than his own glory, he would be calling people to idolatry. In contrast, calling people to recognize and understand his glory is an act of love and is in no way selfish or sinful.

Premise Three: God wants every creature to glorify him.

If God is a glorious God, and he has created the world for his own glory, the next logical question is, how does one glorify God? Christians speak of glorifying God on a regular basis. Yet the true meaning of this familiar phrase seems lost to the contemporary church.

Let us first consider what glorifying God cannot mean. First, glorifying God does not mean that God is deficient of glory. Second, glorifying God does not mean that God is part of creation. Third, glorifying God does not mean that God is dependent on creation. To the contrary, God is eternally perfect, and his glory is neither deficient nor incomplete. Chafer states, "As for that glory which is called intrinsic or essential, it may be observed that, regardless of any recognition of it on the part of creatures, God is Himself a glorious being." [37] In addition, God is completely separate from and transcendent above creation. God is not dependent upon creation for anything—he is self-existent. Psalm 115:3 states, "But our God is in the heavens; He does whatever He pleases." Therefore, no creature can add to or diminish God's intrinsic glory.[38] This conclusion raises another paradox related to God's glory. On the one hand,

---

[35] John Piper, *God's Passion for His Glory: Living the Vision of Jonathan Edwards* (Wheaton: Crossway, 1998), 141n21.

[36] See Jonathan Edwards, "The End for Which God Created the World" in Piper, *God's Passion for His Glory*, 168–76; Hannah, *How Do We Glorify God?* 15–16.

[37] Chafer, *Systematic Theology*, 7:172.

[38] See Morgan, "Towards a Theology of the Glory of God," 167–69.

God's glory is perfect and complete; on the other hand, God still receives glory and praise from creatures. Both concepts are true. The genuine reception of praise and honor does not diminish God's full and complete intrinsic glory.

Now let us consider positively what glorifying God does mean. The Greek verb *doxazō* (used sixty-one times in the NT) has two basic meanings: (1) "to influence one's opinion about another so as to enhance the latter's reputation, *praise, honor, extol*;" and (2) "to cause to have splendid greatness, *clothe in splendor, glorify*." [39] In the New Testament, the second meaning of *glorify* is an activity reserved exclusively for God (Acts 3:13, Rom 8:30). Only God can cause one to have splendid greatness. The first definition, however, captures the main thrust of how creatures can glorify God—to influence people's opinion about God so as to enhance his reputation throughout the world. Scripture articulates this concept in passages such as Matthew 5:16, "In the same way, let your light shine before others, so that they may see your good works and give glory to your Father who is in heaven." First Peter 2:12 echoes the same theme: "Keep your conduct among the Gentiles honorable, so that when they speak against you as evildoers, they may see your good deeds and glorify God on the day of visitation."

The biblical idea of glorifying God comprises three principal activities. First, glorifying God involves primarily the *revelation* of the one true God. When God reveals himself, he is glorified. When people come to know God, God is glorified.

Second, glorifying God involves the spread of the *reputation* of the one true God. When the true reputation of God spreads and people begin to honor and respect him, God is glorified. One way the spread of God's reputation occurs in Scripture is through the spread of God's name. When God called Moses, Moses's task was to remind the nation of God's name: "God, furthermore, said to Moses, 'Thus you shall say to the sons of Israel, "The LORD, the God of your fathers, the God of Abraham, the God of Isaac, and the God of Jacob, has sent me to you." This is My name forever, and this is My memorial-name to all generations'" (Exod 3:15). In the Lord's Prayer, Jesus's first request is that God's name would be hallowed throughout the world (Matt 6:9).

Third, glorifying God relates to the *pleasure* of the one true God. Hannah asserts,

> To state it succinctly, God is only pleased with that which is in perfect agreement with his perfections. God is only glorified in himself

---

[39] BDAG, s.v. "δοξάζω.".

24

either in beholding his innate triune perfections with his own being or observing himself through his creation. Truly pleasing God from the creature's perspective means being like God in moral and spiritual qualities.[40]

Therefore, whatever pleases God is also what glorifies him. Here are just a few things that please God: the spread of the gospel, the salvation of the lost, the sanctification of believers, the bearing of spiritual fruit, and the genuine offer of praise, thanks, and worship.

Premise Four: Glorifying God is bound to God's self-disclosure.

Foundational to glorifying God is the self-disclosure of God.[41] "Revelation is thus God's disclosure to man, in which He reveals truth about Himself that man would not otherwise know."[42] God has chosen to reveal himself through various means. First, God has revealed his glory through *general revelation* to all humanity. God has revealed his glory in creation: "The heavens are telling of the glory of God; and their expanse is declaring the work of His hands" (Ps 19:1). In Romans 1, Paul explains that creation reveals the invisible attributes of God, including his eternal power and divine nature, so that all of humanity is without excuse (Rom 1:19–21). Those who reject God foolishly "exchange the glory of God" for idolatry (Rom 1:23). God also reveals himself generally through the conscience (Rom 2:14–15) and through divine providence (Acts 14:15–17; Matt 5:45).

Second, God has revealed his glory in *special revelation*. The scope of special revelation is narrower than general revelation since not all people may receive the message. It is special because it reveals more information about God and his will for humanity through a variety of means (Heb 1:1). Salvation is possible only through special revelation (Rom 10:17). We will focus on just two avenues of special revelation: the Word of God and the Son of God. Scripture was inspired by God and is capable of equipping believers for every good work (2 Tim 3:16). It is through the pages of Scripture that we learn of God, his glory, and his eternal plan. John Piper states, "The whole Bible, properly understood, has this divine purpose to communicate or display the glory of God. And this pervasive aim of the Scriptures to glorify God,

---

[40] Hannah, *How Do We Glorify God?* 26.

[41] See esp. Hamilton, "The Glory of God in Salvation through Judgment," 57–84, and Pentecost, *The Glory of God*, passim.

[42] Paul P. Enns, *The Moody Handbook of Theology* (Chicago: Moody, 1989), 186.

in what they teach and how they teach it, reveals the handiwork of God in the writing of the Bible." [43] Jesus Christ is the climax of God's revelation (John 1:1, 18; Heb 1:1–4). God manifested his glory in Jesus's first advent (John 1:14) and will manifest it again in the second advent (Matt 24:30).

Premise Five: God has chosen to reveal his glory progressively and systematically through redemptive history (i.e., through every dispensation).

Under the previous premise, I asserted that God reveals his own glory. Under this premise, I am asserting that God reveals his glory progressively and systematically throughout redemptive history. Dispensationalists recognize that God has chosen to reveal himself progressively in each dispensation. A proper view of progressive revelation is foundational to the proper understanding of Scripture. Ryrie summarizes the issue well:

> Progressive revelation views the Bible not as a textbook on theology but as the continually unfolding revelation of God given by various means throughout the successive ages. In this unfolding there are distinguishable stages of revelation when God introduces new things for which man becomes responsible. These stages are the economies, stewardships, or dispensations in the unfolding of His purpose. Dispensationalism, therefore, recognizes both the unity of His purpose and the diversity in the unfolding of it. [44]

Throughout the dispensations, God specifically reveals more about his glory. The following are just a few highlights of the progressive revelation of God's glory. This survey takes special note of God's display of brightness and light as well as explicit statements about His own glory.[45] As already noted, creation declares the glory of God and his invisible attributes (Ps 19:1–6; Rom 1:19–23). God created humans in his own image and crowned them in glory (Gen 1:26–28; Ps 8:3–5; Heb 2:5–9). The Lord revealed his own glory and name to Moses at the burning bush (Exod 3). On Mount Sinai when God gave the law, God revealed his glory to his servant Moses (Exod 33–34). Both the apostles John and Paul allude to this famous event in the life of Moses when

---

[43] John Piper, *A Peculiar Glory: How the Christian Scriptures Reveal Their Complete Truthfulness* (Wheaton: Crossway, 2016), 195.

[44] Ryrie, *Dispensationalism*, 39.

[45] See similar surveys in Gaffin, "Glory," 507–11; Morgan and Peterson, *The Glory of God*, passim; Edwards, "The End for Which God Created the World," 183–251; Pentecost, *The Glory of God*, passim.

they compare the glory under the law to the glory of the New Covenant (John 1:14–18; 2 Cor 3:13–18). Throughout the exodus and wilderness wanderings God's presence was with the Israelites through the Shekinah glory—a cloud by day, a pillar of fire at night, and a cloud of glory within the tabernacle (Exod 40:34–38; Lev 16:2). The glory of the Lord filled the first temple until the days of Ezekiel (1 Kgs 8:10–14; Ezek 9–11). God displayed his glory repeatedly in his judgment of the nations and of Israel (Exod 14:4, 17). At least three Old Testament prophets had the privilege of seeing prophetic visions of the glory inside the very throne room of God—Isaiah (Isa 6), Ezekiel (Ezek 1), and Daniel (Dan 7).

In the New Testament, God revealed his glory in the life and ministry of Jesus. The incarnation of Jesus showed the glory of God (John 1:14). Jesus is the light of the world (1:4; 8:12; 9:5). The brightness of God's glory lit up the night sky when the angels announced Jesus's birth to the shepherds (Luke 2:8–14). The miracles of Jesus displayed the glory of God (John 2:11; 9:1–4; 11:4, 40). The transfiguration of Jesus gave Peter, James, and John an eyewitness experience of the glory of Jesus, which was otherwise veiled during his first advent (Matt 17:1–13; 2 Pet 1:16–18). The passion and death of Jesus revealed God's glory as Jesus was lifted up (John 13:31–32). After Jesus's resurrection and ascension, God restored the glory of Jesus (John 17:5; Acts 2:32, 33; 13:13–15; Heb 2:5–9). The church displays the glory of God in many different capacities (Eph 1:22, 23; 3:20, 21; 1 Cor 10:31). The church's gospel ministry is characterized by a greater glory than that under the law (2 Cor 3). Both Paul and John saw visions of the glorious throne room in heaven (2 Cor 12:1–4; Rev 4–5). Paul identifies the rapture of the church as the "appearing of the glory of our great God and Savior Jesus Christ" (Titus 2:13). The second coming of Christ will display the glory of God before the entire world (Matt 24:30). All will acknowledge the lordship of Jesus and witness his exaltation (Phil 2:9, 10). Jesus will manifest the glory of God throughout the millennial kingdom (Isa 24:23).

Premise Six: The climax of God's glorification in human history will occur at the second coming and during the millennium.

The climax of God's glorification in human history is the second coming of Christ and the reign of Christ during the millennium. The millennium is the final dispensation; it represents the culmination of progressive revelation and goal of eschatology. Ryrie calls the millennium the eschatological goal of dispensationalism. The unifying theological principle is doxological, but the goal of history is Christ's rule on earth in the kingdom. Ryrie states, "Concerning the goal of history, dispensationalists find it in the establishment of the millennial kingdom on earth. . . . They insist that the display of the glory of the God who is sovereign in human history must be seen in the present heavens and earth." [46]

Scripture anticipates and predicts this future display of God's glory in many places. Here are just a few examples. In the Lord's Prayer, Jesus articulated the future coming kingdom when he prayed, "Our Father who is in heaven, hallowed be Your name. Your kingdom come. Your will be done, on earth as it is in heaven" (Matt 6:9–10). The ultimate time and place God's name will be hallowed is when God's kingdom is established on earth. Disciples of Jesus are to pray for the coming of Christ and the future millennium. In the Olivet Discourse, Jesus explains that the Son of Man's return will be glorious: "For just as the lightning comes from the east and flashes even to the west, so will the coming of the Son of Man be" (Matt 24:27). He continues, "And then the sign of the Son of Man will appear in the sky, and then all the tribes of the earth will mourn, and they will see the SON OF MAN COMING ON THE CLOUDS OF THE SKY with power and great glory" (Matt 24:30).[47] The manner of Christ's second coming is radically different from the first coming. Jesus's first advent was marked by humility, coming as a babe in the manger. Jesus's second advent is marked by a glorious and powerful display of might, descending from heaven with the hosts of the redeemed (Rev 19:11–16). After the second coming, Christ will rule on earth for a thousand years (Rev 20:1–7). His dominion will be the entire earth; all humanity will submit to Christ's glorious rule (Ps 2:6–9; Ps 110; Dan 7:14). Addressing the conditions of the millennial kingdom, Walvoord states, "The kingdom will be a glorious kingdom, in which the glory of God will find full manifestation." [48]

Premise Seven: The ultimate completion of God's glorification before all creation will occur only as he fulfills the national promises to Israel in the millennium.

Recognizing Christ's earthly rule as the climax of God's revelation of his glory is essentially a premillennial position. It is not distinctively dispensational since historic premillennialists would agree to the same premise. So what makes a dispensational understanding of God's glory different? What is distinctive about dispensationalism? The main difference is that dispensationalists see the millennium as the restoration of the theocratic kingdom to the nation of Israel.

---

[46] Ryrie, *Dispensationalism*, 21.

[47] See Matt 16:27; 24:64; 2 Thess 1:7; Rev 1:7.

[48] J. Dwight Pentecost, *Things to Come*, 488. Showers notes, "The Scriptures repeatedly associate the glory of God with His sovereign rule," *There Really is a Difference*, 50.

At this point, a dispensational explanation of the kingdom of God might be helpful.

God's kingdom program is one of the most important themes in Scripture. Dispensationalists have consistently seen different aspects to God's rule. [49] First, God rules sovereignly over all creation at all times. This aspect of God's kingdom is the *universal kingdom* of God. The Scriptures reflect God's universal rule in verses such as Psalm 103:19, "The LORD has established His throne in the heavens, and His sovereignty rules over all," and Psalm 145:13, "Your kingdom is an everlasting kingdom, and Your dominion endures throughout all generations." God's omnipotent rule over creation is unshakeable despite the enemies of God.

Second, God will rule beyond time as we know it into eternity. This aspect of God's kingdom is the *eternal kingdom*. In eternity, God will vanquish all the enemies, both on the earth and in the angelic realm. God will completely reverse the curse of sin on creation as he creates a new heaven and new earth (Rev 22).

Third, God at various times has manifested his rule on the earth through a mediator or representative. This aspect of God's kingdom is the *theocratic* or *mediatorial kingdom*. The theocratic rule of God started in Eden with Adam as God's image bearer (Gen 1:26–28). Adam's sin and subsequent fall ruined humanity's mediatorial rule over creation and allowed Satan to implement his kingdom (Gen 3). God instituted his theocratic rule again with the nation of Israel at Sinai (Exod 19). Though limited in scope and imperfect in its implementation, Israel's theocracy lasted from Sinai until the departure of the presence of God's glory at the time of the exile (Ezek 10). The reinstatement of God's theocratic rule on earth will take place at Christ's second coming and the establishment of the millennium (Matt 25:31). As the God-man, Jesus Christ will restore humanity's rightful place to rule over creation (Ps 8; Heb 2:5–9). As the Messiah, Jesus will rule God's theocratic kingdom over all nations of the earth from David's throne in Jerusalem (2 Sam 7:14; Isa 11:1–5). The millennium will restore the nation of Israel's kingdom for one thousand years (Rev 20).

---

[49] See, for example, McClain, *The Greatness of the Kingdom*; J. D. Pentecost, *Thy Kingdom Come* (Wheaton: Victor, 1990); Arnold. G. Fruchtenbaum, Israelology: *The Missing Link in Systematic Theology*, rev. ed. (Tustin, CA: Ariel Ministries, 1994), 604–11; Showers, *There Really is a Difference*, 155–67. Dispensationalists continue to debate the relationship of the church to the kingdom. While this issue is worthy of consideration, it is not essential to the argument in this discussion. For a basic introduction to the issues, see Stanley D. Toussaint, "Israel and the Church of a Traditional Dispensationalist," in Bateman, *Three Central Issues in Contemporary Dispensationalism*, 227–62; J. Lanier Burns, "Israel and the Church of a Progressive Dispensationalist," in ibid., 263–306.

The establishment of Israel's theocratic kingdom will fulfill the covenants God has made with Israel: the Abrahamic Covenant (Gen 12:1–3), the Palestinian Covenant (Deut 30:1–10), the Davidic Covenant (2 Sam 7:16), and the New Covenant (Jer 31:31–34). All the promises and prophecies God made with Israel will come to fulfillment in the millennium. Only through the completion of God's program with the nation of Israel will God's full measure of glory be manifested. Isaiah 24:23 states, "Then the moon will be abashed and the sun ashamed, for the LORD of hosts will reign on Mount Zion and in Jerusalem, and His glory will be before His elders." Christ will rule in Jerusalem, and he will radiate forth glory so bright that the moon and sun will fade by comparison (see also Isa 30:26). Isaiah 65 is an exemplary passage in which God promises to restore the nation of Israel with abundant blessing. This was Paul's hope and expectation for Israel in Romans 9–11. He succinctly states, "All Israel will be saved" (Rom 11:26). Showers summarizes this expectation well:

> The dispensations progressively move history toward the fulfillment of its God-intended climax. In the final "dispensation of the fullness of times" (Eph. 1:9–10), God will fully glorify Himself by crushing Satan and his kingdom (Rom. 16:20; Rev. 20:1–3), restoring His own Kingdom rule to earth through Jesus Christ (Rev. 11:15; 20:4–6), and reversing the tragic consequences of man's rebellion (Mt. 19:28; Acts 3:19–21).[50]

Both the Old Testament and the New Testament are full of similar promises and prophecies about Israel. All these expectations reflect the wisdom and sovereignty of God to the praise of his glory. Any other theological or hermeneutical system that fails to acknowledge the fulfillment of God's covenants, promises, and prophecies to Israel diminishes God's glory. Only a dispensational understanding of the millennium captures the full expression of God's glory within human history.

Conclusion

The glory of God is a great theme throughout Scripture and a watershed issue among theological systems. All genuine Christians, regardless of their theological system, should recognize the doxological purpose of God and its implications for scholarship and the church. The glory of God affects hermeneutics; biblical,

---

[50] Showers, *There Really Is a Difference*, 51.

systematic, and practical theology; and, of course, Christian living. I will draw a few conclusions based on this study.

First, the Scriptures clearly teach that the glory of God is the overarching purpose of God. God is a God of glory. His glory is intrinsic to his essence, and it is the first and last cause of why God created the world. God has progressively revealed and expressed his glory throughout each dispensation. The ultimate end of all humanity is to glorify God by recognizing and reflecting his glory.

Second, the doxological purpose of creation is a shared belief among theological systems. Dispensationalists need to do a better job recognizing that other theologians with other theological systems (such as covenant theology and progressive covenantalism [51]) do uphold God's glory as creation's chief end. The doxological purpose of creation is not unique to dispensationalists. This point has been a source of much confusion both within and outside dispensational circles. This is why virtually all progressive dispensationalists and even some traditional dispensationalists have abandoned the glory of God as a defining mark of dispensationalism. Since the glory of God is not unique to dispensationalism, it is assumed that it cannot be a *sine qua non* of the system. But is this abandonment necessary? I would argue, "No." Dispensationalism should retain the glory of God as its unifying principle.

Third, the dispensational view of God's glory is unique. What distinguishes a dispensational view of God's glory from other theological systems is the complete manifestation of God's glory in the millennium—that is, the theocratic kingdom restored to national Israel. Any theological system that undermines the completion of God's program with Israel diminishes God's glory. This argument has the advantage of uniting dispensationalists, especially those who see kingdom as the unifying principle of Scripture. God's glory and the kingdom are thematically united in God's purposes. This is a mediating position. My hope is that it could help dispensationalists present God and his glory to future generations and help unite the movement.

---

[51] Stephen J. Wellum and Brent E. Parker, eds., *Progressive Covenantalism: Charting a Course between Dispensational and Covenant Theologies* (Nashville: B&H Academic, 2016).

Literalism and the Prophets:
The Case for a Unified Hermeneutic

Roy E. Beacham
Central Baptist Theological Seminary
Plymouth, Minnesota

Introduction

The hermeneutical rubrics for interpreting the Old Testament prophets have long stood as a key point of controversy between two of the most common forms of evangelical Bible interpretation: dispensationalism and covenant theology. Dispensationalism has historically followed a single or unified hermeneutic with regard to predictive prophecy. Dispensationalists embrace the idea that God intended all prophetic foretelling in Scripture to be understood literally and only literally.[1] On the other hand, historic forms of covenant theology have fundamentally denied a single or unified hermeneutic. They have disavowed the consistent literal interpretation and fulfillment of Old Testament prophecy.[2] In their view, the self-same prophetic discourse might contain some predictive propositions that God intended to fulfill literally, while at the same time God intended other prophetic pronouncements in that discourse to find accomplishment in some other, nonliteralistic way.[3]

Numerous hermeneutical systems, overarching presuppositions, and intricate

---

[1] It seems unprofitable to quibble about the term *literal interpretation*. In this study the terms *literal* or *literalistic* describe the idea of the consistent, strict interpretation and fulfillment of all true predictive prophecy in precise accord with the original author's intent as stated in the historical context of his foretelling. In the legal debate surrounding the interpretation of the United States Constitution, this literalistic or authorial-historical approach is called *foundationalism* or *originalism*. The judicial analyst of the Constitution, by engaging this method, seeks to discover the meaning of the framers, given the historical, literary, and political context of the document's original writing. See Mark Snoeberger, who adopts the nomenclature of *originalist* or *foundationalist* in his essay "Traditional Dispensationalism," in *Covenantal and Dispensational Theologies: Four Views on the Continuity of Scripture*, ed. Brent E. Parker and Richard J. Lucas (Downers Grove, IL: InterVarsity Press, 2022). It is also broadly recognized that the idea of literalism in no way precludes the use of any number of figures of speech, from *abusio* (Hos 14:2) to *zeugma* (Isa 2:3) and multiple forms between. See Ethelbert William Bullinger, *Figures of Speech Used in the Bible* (London; New York: Eyre & Spottiswoode; E. & J. B. Young & Co., 1898, repr., Grand Rapids: Baker, 1968) 674, 131 et al. The often "exaggerated" nature of the language of biblical prophecy was addressed by literalists as early as the turn of the twentieth century. See R. B. Girdlestone, *The Grammar of Prophecy* (London: Eyre & Spottiswoode, 1901). It is granted, of course, that not all traditional dispensationalists will agree on the specific outworking of their views of consistent literal fulfillment. The fact that there is no monolithic application of the idea does not negate the idea itself.

[2] A prolific and scholarly proponent of historic covenant theology framed the distinction as follows: "The (dispensational) theory is based on a literal interpretation of the prophetic delineations of the future of Israel and of the Kingdom of God, which is entirely untenable. . . . Jesus never had in mind the re-establishment of the OT theocracy, but the introduction of the spiritual reality, of which the OT kingdom was but a type." Louis Berkhof, *Systematic Theology* (Grand Rapids: Eerdmans, 1938), 712–14.

[3] See, for example, Bruce Waltke, "Kingdom Promises as Spiritual" in *Continuity and Discontinuity: Perspectives on the Relationship Between the Old and New Testaments*, ed. John Feinberg (Wheaton: Crossway, 1988), 282. Further, the use of the term *proposition(s)* in this study refers to the process of verbal communication by means of sentences (subject/predicate).

textual arguments have been forwarded in support of various forms and relative degrees of nonliteral fulfillment. These systems, presuppositions, and arguments may all seem formidable and even convincing. Yet their lines of reasoning can be challenged, significantly, when exposed to explicit textual data stated directly by God in reference to his purpose for and delimitations of this prophetic genre. That exposure constitutes the goal of this study. To suppose that historic theological preunderstandings and/or later biblical writings can negate these foundational definitive statements is to suppose too much. According to the primary affirmations of God in Scripture with regard to this genre, it is arguable that predictive prophecy was intended by God to be literally and only literally understood, interpreted, and fulfilled. God's own declarations, delimitations, and descriptions plead the case. All other biblical texts, hermeneutical preunderstandings, exegetical analyses, and theological schemes should find ground on God's clear prescriptions with regard to prophetic foretelling, and those prescriptions are copious.[4]

Of course, there is incontrovertible evidence and, thus, universal recognition that *some* of the predictions of the Old Testament were intended by God to find exacting fulfillment with unmodified, literalistic precision because many prophecies have already been fulfilled in precisely this way. The foretold birth of Messiah in Bethlehem of Judea happened exactly there, not somewhere else. No evangelical covenant theologian would deny the hermeneutic of prophetic literalism; they only deny its consistent application. In concert with the evidence of already-fulfilled prophecy, however, dispensationalism asserts that God intended *all* prophecy to follow the same rubric; he intended *all* prophecy to be understood, interpreted, and fulfilled literally, in perfect accord with these already

---

[4] There is, of course, a hermeneutical spiral in the formation and implementation of any interpretational scheme. Nevertheless, it is both widely accepted and inherently logical that in the process of biblical studies, hermeneutical rubrics precede exegetical analysis and, in turn, that exegetical analysis precedes theological postulates. I have dealt with this concern in "Exegesis: The Focal Point of Textually Based Theological Education, A Preliminary Study" (paper at Bible Faculty Leadership Summit, Summer, 2000). Since hermeneutics logically precedes exegesis, then any preunderstanding that asserts that predictive prophecy can find fulfillment in some other way than literally will greatly affect the exegesis of prophetic texts. Likewise, the preunderstanding of consistent, literal fulfillment will greatly affect that interpreter's exegesis of predictive prophetic texts. Further, since both hermeneutics and exegesis logically precede theology, then predetermined theological systems should never serve as the *crux* of hermeneutical, and thus exegetical, constructs. The arguments regarding the interpretation of predictive prophecy must begin with the hermeneutical presuppositions that are brought to the interpretation (exegesis) of this controversial genre, not with the interpretation of the prophecies themselves, and certainly not with some overarching theological paradigm. The arguments must examine the scriptural foundation for asserting those hermeneutical preunderstandings. They should focus on texts that are descriptive and prescriptive of the genre. They cannot rest solely on the exegesis of specific, predictive texts or citations thereof and, thus, upon interpretations that have already applied the interpreter's hermeneutical preconditions, much less his or her theological biases. Likewise, this logical and biblical spiral must rely on the clearest, most unambiguous, and most self-evident texts of Scripture over against those that are more unclear, relative, and controversial in nature. For this reason, this study focuses on explicit prescriptive and descriptive statements by God with regard to the purpose, ground, nature, function, and test of true predictive prophecy, not on the prophecies themselves. The question becomes this: in the exegesis of any prophetic prediction, is it more tenable to presuppose that *every* predictive prophecy will be fulfilled literally, in exacting accord with its original pronouncement, or is it more tenable to presuppose that *some* predictive prophecies will be fulfilled with exacting literalness, while others will be fulfilled nonliterally, in a manner divergent from exacting correspondence? This study examines these questions and argues for the first position, consistent literalness, based on the foundational prescriptions of God in Scripture with reference to his conception and use of this unique revelatory method.

established norms.

In the view of historic dispensationalism, God did not commingle two diverse interpretational schemes into one revelational genre. Historic covenant theology, however, *must* embrace a dual hermeneutic with respect to the prophets: partial literalism interlaced with partial nonliteralism.[5] Numerous elements of their theological construct have, from the beginning, necessitated such a view hermeneutically, most particularly their understanding of the nature both of national Israel and of the church. In the system of historic covenantalism, it is impossible to believe that all of God's predictions regarding the eschatological future of national Israel will be literally fulfilled. Partial nonliteral fulfillment is a fundamental tenet of historic covenantal theology.[6] That theological system cannot stand if all God's forecasts are fulfilled literally. In turn, this partial nonliteralism persists in the hermeneutical systems of more contemporary permutations of covenantalism. A growing movement within covenant theology, most recently called progressive covenant theology or progressive covenantalism, continues to embrace partial nonliteral fulfillment.[7]

Dispensationalism itself has not escaped the prophetic controversy. Progressive dispensationalism from its inception (ca. 1980) rejected this long-standing tenet of more traditional forms[8] of dispensationalism: the solely literal interpretation of

---

[5] Throughout this study the description "nonliteral fulfillment" will always assume a nexus with "partial nonliteral fulfillment" since no orthodox interpreter would espouse consistent nonliteralism.

[6] These theological and hermeneutical tenets within historic forms of covenant theology are well established. Berkhof's representation above (see note 2) is characteristic.

[7] Progressive covenantalism grew out of the earlier new covenant theology. See Dennis M. Swanson, "Introduction to New Covenant Theology," *TMSJ* (Fall 2007): 149–63. For an overview of the nonliteralistic interpretive preunderstandings of progressive covenantalism, see Peter J. Gentry and Stephen J. Wellum, *Kingdom through Covenant* (Wheaton: Crossway, 2018), 107–58. The label "progressive covenant theology" will be used herein to include the earlier "New Covenant Theology" (35). In light of progressive covenantalism's clear presuppositional approach to hermeneutics, exegesis, and theology, it seems an unfortunate choice of words in their *magnum opus* to claim that "care has been taken to let the Scripture speak for itself" (Gentry and Wellum, *Kingdom through Covenant*, preface to the first edition, republished in the second edition, p. 19). While it should be allowed that any one text in its original context can "speak for itself" in accord with the original author's intent, it is ill-advised for any interpreter—covenant, dispensational, or otherwise—to imagine that his overall exegetical analyses and systemized theological structures stand without presuppositional bias (see note 4 above). In that light, the claim of allowing Scripture to "speak for itself" is usually unhelpful. Nevertheless, that and similar terminology is used throughout Gentry and Wellum's work in a highly stylized way to refer to their own complex hermeneutical schematic. In their view, it is only through engaging their exclusive interpretational system (p. 87) that the Scripture can be read "on its own terms" (Gentry and Wellum, *Kingdom through Covenant*, 127n50, 157, and throughout).

[8] In this study, no distinction will be made between what some have labeled *classical dispensationalism* over against an asserted *revised dispensationalism*. See Craig A. Blaising, "The Extent and Varieties of Dispensationalism," in Darrel L. Bock and Craig A. Blaising, *Progressive Dispensationalism* (Wheaton: Bridgepoint/Victor, 1993), 22. The distinction itself is dubious per Mike Stallard, "Emile Guers: An Early Darbyite Response to Irvinism and a Precursor to Charles Ryrie," *CTJ* 1 (April 1997): 31–46. The appellation *traditional* or *historic* dispensationalism is used throughout this study to refer to that general form of dispensationalism that preceded and survives the development of what came to be called progressive dispensationalism. Progressive dispensationalism, then, is contrasted throughout with traditional and historic dispensationalism. For an early analysis of progressive dispensationalism, see Roy E. Beacham, "Progressive Dispensationalism: An Overview and Personal Analysis," *DBSJ* 9:1 (Fall 2004): 5–32. The term *traditional dispensationalism* in this study will also exclude what is commonly called *hyper-dispensationalism*, though some of that persuasion might agree with many, if not all, the hermeneutical arguments herein associated with more traditional forms of dispensationalism.

prophecy.[9] One common thread that unites progressive dispensationalism with current expressions of covenant theology is the presupposition of inaugurated eschatology.[10] All three of these methodologies—traditional covenant theology, progressive covenant theology, and progressive dispensationalism—embrace the preunderstanding that predictive prophecy can be, has been, and is being fulfilled in some other way than literally.[11] In fact, this hermeneutic is intrinsic to each of these systems since none of their theological constructs could exist apart from the idea of partial nonliteral fulfillment. Historic dispensationalism, in contrast, believes that all the predictive prophecies of Scripture were meant by God to be understood, fulfilled, and thus interpreted literally and only literally, exactly as foretold. Traditional dispensational methodology, exegesis, and eschatology are founded on this premise.

Clearly, then, the controversy in view here centers on the interpretation of the prophets. The biblical term *prophet* finds broad engagement in Scripture to include anyone who received and/or in some way communicated revelation from God either by word, by experience, or simply by virtue of their heritage or the office that they held. Besides the best known examples of prophets, the Scriptures place men such as Abel (Luke 11:49–51), Abraham (Gen 20:2–7), and the high priest Caiaphas (John 11:49–51) in this category. The poets David and Asaph were also deemed prophets (Acts 2:30–31 referring to Ps 16:10; Matt 13:35 referring to Ps 78:2) along with the king and wisdom writer Solomon (Acts 7:48 referring to 1 Kgs 8:27). In fact, all the Old Testament Scriptures were broadly labeled as prophetic (consider the appellation "the Law and the Prophets," Matt 7:12; Matt 22:40; Luke 16:16, et al.) since even the law was penned by a prophet, Moses (Deut 18:15; 34:10), and Jesus himself stated that "the Law prophesied"

[9] Charles C. Ryrie expressed the idea of literalism as a *sine qua non* in terms of "consistently literal," "normal," or "plain" interpretation" in *Dispensationalism,* rev. ed. (Chicago: Moody, 1995), 40. Craig Blaising, in the earliest published book on progressive dispensationalism, unambiguously disowned this method. See Craig A. Blaising, "Dispensationalism: The Search for a Definition" in *Dispensationalism, Israel and the Church: The Search for a Definition,* ed. Craig A. Blaising and Darrell L. Bock (Grand Rapids: Zondervan, 1992), 26, 30–32.

[10] The idea of inaugurated eschatology was popularized in America by George Eldon Ladd in his adaptation and publication of select pulpit and conference lectures in the book *The Gospel of the Kingdom* (Grand Rapids: Eerdmans, 1959), followed by numerous, more scholastic works by Ladd on the topic. Ladd was a covenant premillennialist. Inaugurated eschatology was decisively incorporated into covenant amillennialism by Anthony Hoekema in *The Bible and the Future* (Grand Rapids: Eerdmans, 1979), see especially, Part One: "Inaugurated Eschatology," 1. Progressive dispensationalism was born through the aegis of inaugurated eschatology as this popular eschatological presupposition was adopted by and incorporated into this developing movement within dispensationalism. See Darrell L. Bock, "The Reign of the Lord Christ" in Bock and Blaising, *Dispensationalism, Israel and the Church,* passim but especially 46ff. Bruce Waltke, in "A Response" appended to Bock and Blaising, *Dispensationalism, Israel, and the Church,* 347, begins his analysis as follows: "This book signals a significant restructuring of dispensationalism within the framework of inaugurated eschatology."

[11] Although progressive dispensationalism has adopted a nonliteralistic (complementary) view of prophetic fulfillment in the present age, the movement still gives lip service to the future literal fulfillment of God's forecasts, especially those concerning national Israel. However, their view of the continuance of the body of Christ, the church, on earth throughout the tribulation and millennial kingdom becomes highly problematic to the idea of a return to eschatological literalism with regard to national Israel (see Waltke's analysis in "A Response," 354).

(Matt 11:13).

The topic of study at hand, however, specifically deals with prophecy that is directly predictive.[12] Much could be gleaned by a wider survey of prophetic biblical literature in its most inclusive sense. Likewise, the false presupposition that typology constitutes a form of prophecy deserves much more attention than can be afforded here.[13] Under consideration in this study, however, are direct, divine prophetic pronouncements that foretell future events as otherwise known only by God.[14] These direct prophetic predictions lie at the core of traditional dispensational interpretation, exegesis, and theology, and distinguish traditional dispensationalism from traditional covenantalism, progressive covenantalism, and progressive dispensationalism. *The purpose of this study is to reaffirm and to defend biblically the idea that all genuine prophetic foretelling in Scripture is intended by God to be understood literally, fulfilled literally, and therefore interpreted literally and only literally.* There is no formidable biblical, exegetical, or hermeneutical reason to abandon this standard tenet of traditional dispensationalism. Each assertion in this study deserves a much fuller treatment than is possible here, and the implicit outworking of each assertion would demand a substantial volume (if not volumes) of biblical analysis. Nonetheless, direct arguments from God's own prescriptive statements about his intent in the use, delimitation, and meaning of predictive prophecy will serve to sustain the thesis in this brief study.[15]

---

[12] Of course, God through his prophets never merely "predicts" the future in the popular sense of the term; he actually foretells the future (formally *praedictiō*: "to speak beforehand"). In any case, the term *predictive*, in its various permutations, will be engaged throughout this study to refer to God's direct foretelling of the future. Similarly, any reference to a human prophet's *predicting* assumes the prophet's service simply as God's agent of divine foretelling.

[13] The study of directly predictive prophecy is greatly obfuscated by many who assert that biblical typology is predictive and, thus, hermeneutically and exegetically interchangeable with actual prophetic foretelling. This comparison is both false and misleading. Although God certainly intended some historic persons, places, and events (e.g., Melchizedek, the tabernacle, animal sacrifice, etc.) to be engaged, later, as analogical to other persons, places, and events, the recognition and application of types (better, analogies) in Scripture can only be drawn in retrospect. The original person, place, or event predicted nothing because no human in that context could, would, or even should have anticipated some future antitype. As will be demonstrated, God's actual revelatory forecasts were intended first to be *known* as predictions by the original audience and then to demonstrate his veracity when fulfilled in perfect accord with the details of the original, known prediction. As a means of divine revelation, all true predictions categorically point forward; typology as a revelatory tool can only point backward. The logical and hermeneutical fallacy of categorizing types as predictive stands at the foundation of many, if not most, nonliteralistic systems currently in vogue. Gentry and Wellum, for example, base their entire progressive-covenantal system on this premise: "Typology is *prophetic* and *predictive* [emphasis theirs]. . . . Typology ought to be viewed as a subset of predictive prophecy" (Gentry and Wellum, *Kingdom through Covenant*, 131). Having turned typology, categorically, into predictive prophecy, these (and other) nonliteralists then turn predictive prophecy into typology, thus deriving the notion of the typological fulfillment of predictive prophecy. This circular hermeneutical recategorization is certainly parsed by Gentry and Wellum with elaborate complexity (128–37), but both its accuracy and its logic fail. The premise itself (that typology is predictive) stands as categorically false. See especially David L. Baker, "Typology and the Christian Use of the Old Testament," *SJT* 29 (April 1976): 137–57, esp. 149. Furthermore, even if typology were a subset of predictive prophecy, which it is not, subsets neither define nor govern sets. This study wholly rejects the idea of typology as predictive.

[14] Excluded from the idea of "directly predictive," herein, are most psalms commonly categorized as "messianic" and any other analogical connections drawn in Scripture including the analogies commonly labeled as "types" (see previous note).

[15] It is clearly impossible to address every proposed argument for partial nonliteralism and every Old Testament or New Testament citation engaged by partial nonliteralists in defense of their dual-hermeneutical systems. It can only be adduced here that other well-reasoned arguments can be and have been forwarded that challenge these systems, and that exegetically defensible

Why would traditional dispensationalism tenaciously espouse the consistent, exclusive, literalistic view of God's foretelling? In this study, five biblically perspicuous reasons are advanced as grounds to the claim. A solely literalistic approach to the foretelling of the prophets finds basis in the *purpose, ground, nature, function,* and *test* of divinely appointed predictive prophecy as described by God himself. In the end, it seems both logically and theologically untenable to espouse any form of other-than-literal, less-than-literal, or more-than-literal interpretation of prophetic predictions,[16] while at the same time giving full credence to God's stated prerequisites with regard to this genre. In other words, the specific texts examined here seem unequivocal in their demand for a consistent and exclusive literalistic methodology for interpreting all prophetic foretelling.

The Purpose of Predictive Prophecy

Why did God engage the genre of directly predictive prophecy? There need be no debate on this question since the Scriptures respond explicitly. Predictive prophecy was designed by God as a revelatory apologetic. By this means he intended to evidence his singularity (i.e., to prove that he alone is the one true God). The apologetic nature of God's singular ability to foretell the future finds specific expression in the repeated testimony of God himself. God, through Isaiah, the prophet most vocal in defense of the uniqueness of God (i.e., his holiness),[17] states the case most clearly and most often. The gods of human invention are powerless and, therefore, bogus, and one unassailable evidence of their impotence is this: Yahweh God alone can foretell the future.

---

explanations have long been advanced that interpret all these Old and New Testament texts in concert with the tenet of consistent literalism.

[16] This terminology ("other-than-, less-than-, and more-than-literal interpretation") is used herein to encapsulate the multiple methods that have been espoused to describe all kinds of nonliteral fulfillment. Note, for example, William W. Klein, Craig L. Blomberg, and David L. Hubbard, Jr., *Introduction to Biblical Interpretation*, 3rd ed. (Grand Rapids: Zondervan, 2017), especially in the section entitled "Many Ways of Fulfillment," 482–86. According to these authors, some prophetic predictions are fulfilled in a "surprising," reinterpreted sense, amassing "new meaning" that differs from that of the original prediction ("other-than-literal," 484). Further, in their view, some predictions are brought to completion in a "less-than-literal way," entailing a more symbolic or "figurative fulfillment" than that of the original prediction ("less-than-literal," 483). Still other prophecies, as they describe them, will find a more expansive sense that "exceed(s) the expectations of (God's) ancient words" ("more-than-literal," 485). Numerous nonliteralistic theories and explanations find various categorical labels, often overlapping, thus the need to characterize them *in toto* by a general, all-encompassing description.

[17] Holiness, in reference to God, describes much more than his purity or sinlessness. Rather, it references God's essential and absolute uniqueness, his "God-ness," ultimately in contrast to everything that is creaturely, common, or ordinary (i.e., profane). A. B. Davidson summarizes this truth succinctly when he says: "It seems clear, therefore, that *Kadosh* [holiness] is not a word that expresses any attribute of deity, but deity itself." Andrew Bruce Davidson, *The Theology of the Old Testament*, ed. S. D. F. Salmond (New York: Scribners, 1906), see "The Holiness of God," 144–53, esp. 152). The book of Isaiah refers to God as "the Holy One of Israel" twenty-five times, and once more Isaiah engages this descriptor in his words recorded in 2 Kgs 19:22. It should be no surprise that Isaiah championed God's holiness because the prophet himself uniquely experienced the glory of God enthroned in heaven (Isa 6:1–5).

Isaiah 41:21–24, 26

[21] "Present your case," the LORD says.

"Bring forward your strong *arguments*,"

The King of Jacob says.

[22] "Let them bring forth and declare to us what is going to take place;

As for the former *events*, declare what they *were*,

That we may consider them and know their outcome.

Or announce to us what is coming;

[23] Declare the things that are going to come afterward,

That we may know that you are gods;

Indeed, do good or evil, that we may anxiously look about us and fear together.

[24] Behold, you are of no account,

And your work amounts to nothing;

He who chooses you is an abomination. . . .

[26] Who has declared *this* from the beginning, that we might know?

Or from former times, that we may say, '*He is* right!'?

Surely there was no one who declared,

Surely there was no one who proclaimed,

Surely there was no one who heard your words."

Isaiah 42:8–9

[8] "I am the LORD, that is My name;

I will not give My glory to another,

Nor My praise to graven images.

[9] Behold, the former things have come to pass,

Now I declare new things;

Before they spring forth I proclaim *them* to you."

Isaiah 44:6–8

[6] "Thus says the LORD, the King of Israel

And his Redeemer, the LORD of hosts:

'I am the first and I am the last,

And there is no God besides Me.

[7] And who is like Me? Let him proclaim and declare it;

Yes, let him recount it to Me in order,

From the time that I established the ancient nation.

And let them declare to them the things that are coming

And the events that are going to take place.
⁸ Do not tremble and do not be afraid;
Have I not long since announced *it* to you and declared *it*?
And you are My witnesses.
Is there any God besides Me,
Or is there any *other* Rock?
I know of none.'"

Isaiah 45:18, 20–21
¹⁸ For thus says the LORD, who created the heavens
(He is the God who formed the earth and made it,
He established it *and* did not create it a waste place,
But formed it to be inhabited),
"I am the LORD, and there is none else. . . .
²⁰ Gather yourselves and come;
Draw near together, you fugitives of the nations;
They have no knowledge,
Who carry about their wooden idol
And pray to a god who cannot save.
²¹ Declare and set forth *your case*;
Indeed, let them consult together.
Who has announced this from of old?
Who has long since declared it?
Is it not I, the LORD?
And there is no other God besides Me,
A righteous God and a Savior;
There is none except Me."

Isaiah 48:3–5
³ "I declared the former things long ago
And they went forth from My mouth, and I proclaimed them.
Suddenly I acted, and they came to pass.
⁴ Because I know that you are obstinate,
And your neck is an iron sinew
And your forehead bronze,
⁵ Therefore I declared *them* to you long ago,
Before they took place I proclaimed *them* to you,

So that you would not say,

'My idol has done them,

And my graven image and my molten image have commanded them.'"[18]

Clearly, God purposed to use the genre of prophetic foretelling as absolute, unimpeachable evidence of his exclusivity. This verification of his sole claim to deity was, and continues to be, conclusive. The true God, Yahweh God alone, can announce beforehand, with specificity and precision, that which will transpire both in the near and distant future. He alone has caused former events to happen, many of which he foretold. He alone will bring yet future events to pass, including those announced decades, even millennia, ahead of time. Only the God of Israel, the one and only true God, can proclaim in prospect that which will be verified in retrospect. The Creator of the material world is the sovereign of the temporal: past, present, and future. The evidence is both empirical and incontrovertible. His sole deity cannot be doubted. His exclusive, sovereign control over time is confirmed by the express fact that he declares the events of the distant future from the vantage point of the ancient past.[19]

It appears intuitive, then, that the evidentiary purpose of divine prediction in Scripture finds validity only if *everything* that God foretells actually comes to pass precisely as foretold. Every detail of the outcome must correspond with every detail of his foretelling, or his purpose is thwarted. One cannot claim sovereign omnipotence as evidenced by absolute omniscience unless there is perfect, self-evident parity between every forecast of future events and every outcome of each event. True and absolute prescience is evidenced by clear and detailed prediction followed by exacting and indisputable accomplishment in every respect and all the time. God's argument stands only by means of consistent literal fulfillment. Apart from consistent literal fulfillment, the evidence crumbles. Any alternative outcome places him on equal ground with the false gods of the masses.[20]

---

[18] See also Isa 43:9–10; 46:9–13, et al.

[19] Even the most extremely cryptic form of prophetic foretelling, apocalyptic, does not disparage literalistic interpretation and exacting future fulfillment. Some of the most picturesque prophetic representations forecast the most literal of realities since many of the outcomes of those picturesque predictions have already been fulfilled with absolute precision (see, e.g., Dan 7:2–7 and Dan 8:1–14, the literal fulfillment of which causes many liberal interpreters to postdate them or to view them as *ex eventu* and, thus, a pious fraud).

[20] Much has been written and much could be said about conditional prophecy, which some have adduced as a foil to consistent literal fulfillment. The prototypical text for describing this phenomenon is Jer 18:1–10. See D. Brent Sandy, *Plowshares and Pruning Hooks: Rethinking the Language of Biblical Prophecy and Apocalyptic* (Downers Grove, IL: IVP Academic, 2002), 47, 160. Sandy both queries and then seems to assume the conditional nature of all predictive prophecy on the basis of this text. This current study, however, finds no reason for apprehension about either the existence or the nature of conditional prophecies. Clearly, conditional prophecies exist, some being explicitly conditional (Mal 3:10–12) and others being only implicit (2 Kgs 20:1; Jonah 3:4). The existence of conditional prophecy in no way either disproves literalism or argues for nonliteralism. All conditional prophecies were intended to be understood and interpreted literally;

In light of God's universal challenge to non-gods, and his evidential purpose for predictive prophecy as categorically stated in Scripture, should we suppose that God intended only some of his predictive prophecies to be fulfilled literally, precisely as originally stated, while at the same time he intended others of his pre-announcements (even those spoken by the same prophets in the same discourse) to find other-than-, less-than-, or more-than-literal fulfillment?[21] Does Isaiah, or Ezekiel, or any other prophet or unambiguous text of Scripture allow for, much less assert, two diverging purposes or resignified outcomes of God's evidentiary foretelling? Any hermeneutical viewpoint that espouses any form of other-than-, less-than-, or more-than-literal fulfillment of God's foretelling negates the declared purpose and evidentiary worth of this genre as attested by God. According to God's bold and frequent challenge to false gods, nonliteral fulfilment of predictive prophecy only proves pseudo-deific ignorance and impotence, not absolute deific omniscience and omnipotence. False deities spawned amorphous fulfillments; not so the true God of heaven.[22] All genuine predictive prophecy, through its persistent, exacting outcomes, gives evidence to the sole deity of Yahweh God. The divinely stated purpose of predictive foretelling, all predictive foretelling, argues for the consistent literal interpretation and fulfillment of that genre.

The Ground of Predictive Prophecy

If the *purpose* of predictive prophecy, literally fulfilled, displayed the exclusive deity of God, the *ground* of predictive prophecy displayed the absolute perfections

---

otherwise, the conditions (stated or unstated) were meaningless and could not be met, nor the outcome mitigated. On the other hand, the fact that conditional predictions existed in no way proves that *all* predictions were conditional. In fact, numerous forecasts were framed by divine oath as irrevocable and, thus, inexorable (e.g., Isa 14:24–27). Most evident in that regard were the forecasts of God with reference to the New Covenant that he will assuredly ratify with national Israel in the eschaton. Forecasts about this future kingdom-covenant often contained overtly indubitable, God-sworn promises that included not only so-called spiritual benefits but also detailed physical, geographical, national, geopolitical, and agricultural provisions (see, especially, the *locus classicus*, Jer 31:27–40, esp. vv. 35–37). Even the greatest curse against Israel for the nation's disobedience will be mitigated by God's eschatological blessing upon a divinely promised remnant that will ultimately experience all the predicted blessings of a future, final, national-political covenant and kingdom (Ezek 11:14–21). This future, final restoration of national Israel's remnant under the New Covenant is not dependent on its own effort and agency but is sworn to come about on the basis of God's own person, in vindication of the holiness of his great name for his own glory (Ezek 36:17–38). It is fallacious to imagine, much less to assert, that the idea of conditional prophecy argues *for* nonliteralism or in any way argues *against* the literal fulfillment of God's sworn promises to national Israel or to anyone else, for that matter. Every forecast that God fulfills in accordance with his divine will and word, he fulfills literally, only and always.

[21] See, for example, Waltke, who says of God's foretelling, "I argued in 'Kingdom Promises as Spiritual' that prophecies finding fulfillment up to the ascension of Christ, such as his birth in Bethlehem, will have an earthly, visible fulfillment, and those pertaining to the church formed with the coming of the Spirit at Pentecost from Christ's heavenly Davidic throne will have an invisible, spiritual fulfillment." Waltke, "A Response," 355.

[22] The Oracle at Delphi provides the classic example of prognostic obfuscation when the pythoness prophesied on behalf of Loxias (Apollo) regarding the potential engagement of Croesus in opposition to Cyrus of Persia. See Herodotus, *Herodotus, with an English Translation*, trans. by A. D. Godley (Medford, MA: Harvard, 1920) 1:91:1–6. Nebuchadnezzar well understood this kind of prophetic doubletalk (Dan 2:8–9). See also the many biblical descriptions of such prophetic fabrication and duplicity (e.g., Isa 41:27–29; Jer 14:14; 23:32; Lam 2:14; Ezek 12:24; 13:7–16; 21:23, 29; 22:28; Acts 13:6–10).

of God: God's immutable person and efficacious speech. God intended *all* his prophetic pronouncements to find inalterable accomplishment in exacting accord with his essential holiness, unchangeable character, and unfailing words. God himself links the integrity of his being with the efficacy of his foretelling. Because of his divine person and perfections, his speech itself will produce the absolute accomplishment of his preannounced plans. In fact, he attests to this connection by his self-sworn oath.

Embedded in God's revelatory purpose statement cited above (Isa 45), God defends his creative authority over matter and his sovereign rule over time by affirming the following with regard to his prophetic words:

Isaiah 45:18–19

[18] For thus says the LORD, who created the heavens
(He is the God who formed the earth and made it. . . .)
"I am the LORD, and there is none else.
[19] I have not spoken in secret,
In some dark land;
I did not say to the offspring of Jacob,
'Seek Me in a waste place'; I, the LORD, speak righteousness,
Declaring things that are upright."

God concludes this affirmation as follows:

Isaiah 45:22–25

[22] "Turn to Me and be saved, all the ends of the earth;
For I am God, and there is no other.
[23] I have sworn by Myself,
The word has gone forth from My mouth in righteousness
And [that word] will not turn back,
That to Me every knee will bow, every tongue will swear *allegiance*.
[24] They will say of Me, 'Only in the LORD are righteousness and strength.'
Men will come to Him,
And all who were angry at Him will be put to shame.
[25] In the LORD all the offspring of Israel
Will be justified and will glory."

In 45:22–25, God speaks of distant and final future events. He links the accomplishment of these distant and final future events to his own oath and personal righteousness in both 19c and 23a. The ground of God's self-revelation through prophetic foretelling is his own name: his divine person and essential nature. His prophetic revelation is neither disguised (spoken in "secret," 45:19) nor shadowed (shrouded "in darkness," 45:19). He swears to the details of his future actions on the basis of his own being ("by myself," 45:23) and his word brooks no divergence ("[it] will not turn back," 45:23). His prophetic speech accords with his divine perfections ("righteousness" [*tsedeq*], 45:19, cf. 45:24) and his futuristic declarations are without deviation ("straightforward" or "right" [*meyshar*; LXX *aletheia*, "true"], 45:19). If God is God, his foretold plans will come to pass fastidiously, exactly as spoken. *All* his forecasts are of one voice, determinative, and efficacious, without variance, in rigorous accord with his unique essence and unwavering perfections. Exactly what he says is precisely what he does because of who he is.

On the basis of God's direct portrayal of his prophetic speech, it seems incongruous, at best, to believe that he foretells the future univocally in one proposition and equivocally in another. According to his own sworn testimony, none of his spoken words will deviate ("turn"); all of them will be accomplished in fixed accord with their originally stated purpose (cf. Isa 55:10–11). His pre-declared plans involving specific peoples who will experience specific events that occur at specific times in specific locations are not mutable and malleable. They are not intended to find actualization with different peoples at alternate times and restaged places in resignified ways. In these texts, all of God's declarations are as axiomatic as his attributes. If he is God, each and every one of his affirmations, specifically his affirmations that foretell the future, will come about exactly as stated. According to his own testimony, he does not employ any single forecast to inhere pliable meanings with diverse interpretations in the accomplishment of disparate fulfillments. His overarching temporal plan, diachronically, *has* conformed to and *will* conform to all his stated propositions synchronically.[23]

---

[23] For a survey of God's overarching plan, diachronically, from a more traditional dispensational perspective, see Alva J. McClain, *The Greatness of the Kingdom: An Inductive Study of the Kingdom of God* (Chicago: Moody Press, 1968, repr., Winona Lake, IN: BMH Books, 1974) and, more recently, Michael J. Vlach, *He Will Reign Forever: A Biblical Theology of the Kingdom of God* (Silverton, OR: Lampion, 2017). These authors accept as foundational the tenet that the literalistic interpretation of divine foretelling should be applied to *all* prophecy (consistent literalism), not just some prophecy (partial nonliteralism). They present a coherent, reasonable, and defensible story line grounded on belief in the fixed nature of divine propositions and the unitary, literal fulfillment of divine foretelling. See McClain, *Greatness of the Kingdom,* Ch. XII, 2 "The Interpretation of Kingdom Prophecy," 139–46, and Vlach, *He Will Reign Forever,* Ch. 2, "Proper Starting Points for Understanding the Kingdom," 31–51. For a comprehensive theology grounded on a traditional dispensational hermeneutic, see Rolland McCune, *A Systematic Theology of Biblical Christianity,* vols. 1–3 (Allen Park, MI: Detroit Baptist Theological Seminary, 2009–10).

Time does not alter God, and time does not alter God's truth-claims.[24]

In this same prophetic complex (Isa 44–48),[25] God foretells the coming of a distant, divinely anointed servant whom he calls by name:

Isaiah 44:24–28

[24] Thus says the LORD, your Redeemer,

and the one who formed you from the womb,

"I, the LORD, am the maker of all things,

Stretching out the heavens by Myself,

And spreading out the earth all alone,

[25] Causing the omens of boasters to fail,

Making fools out of diviners,

Causing wise men to draw back,

And turning their knowledge into foolishness,

[26] Confirming the word of His servant,

And performing the purpose of His messengers.

It is I who says of Jerusalem, 'She shall be inhabited!'

And of the cities of Judah, 'They shall be built.'

And I will raise up her ruins *again*.

[27] *It is I* who says to the depth of the sea, 'Be dried up!'

And I will make your rivers dry.

[28] *It is I* who says of Cyrus, '*He is* My shepherd! And he will perform

---

[24] Gentry and Wellum, *Kingdom Through Covenant*, concur with Michael Scott Horton, *Covenant and Eschatology: The Divine Drama* (Louisville: Westminster John Knox, 2002), concerning divine truth-claims and time-deferred meaning. They do not view the revelatory statements of Scripture as cognitive: God, as agent, expressing propositions as knowable, objective, and fixed truth-claims in-and-of themselves. Rather, they see the revelatory statements of Scripture as dramatic: God, as narrator, expressing propositions that are open to fuller, exchangeable, "progressive" meanings as transmuted diachronically throughout the passing millennia of history in an ever-evolving story line (Gentry and Wellum, *Kingdom Through Covenant*, 117–18, cf. 111–12). To Gentry and Wellum, interpreting the Bible on the basis of the fixed nature of divine propositions constitutes "prooftexting" (118–19). Having championed, then, the malleable nature of divine speech over against the fixed nature of divine propositions, Gentry and Wellum construct an intricate hermeneutical system (107–58) which, to them, is exclusively "biblical"; it is a system that "is *not* an optional way to interpret Scripture" but is "*demanded* by the nature of Scripture" itself (emphasis theirs, 113). In their words, "*Not* to read Scripture in this [dramatic, evolving] way is to fail to interpret Scripture correctly and is to be less than 'biblical'" (emphasis theirs). This exclusive, expansive, and fluid reading of the text is what they mean by reading Scripture "on its own terms" (45, 110, 115, 117, et al.). Clearly, though, their reading of Scripture "on its own terms" is far from straightforward. Overtly and without apology, this complex textual overlay (progressive covenantalism) thoroughly infuses the reading of Scripture "on its own terms" with the presuppositions of the soteriological *mitte* of God's purpose (redemptive history), hermeneutical Christo-centrism, New Testament interpretational priority, inaugurated eschatology, "three horizon" literary theory, segmented authorial intent, canonical deferment (time-suspended truth), typological recategorization, typological fulfillment of predictive prophecy, and a complex of other methodological strictures. All these strictures rest upon, necessitate, and drive the overarching presupposition of partial nonliteralism. These interpreters, foundationally, hold to a covenantalist form of biblical theology and theory that must, by nature, embrace a nonliteral hermeneutic to exist as a system. Belief in consistent literalism and absolute, fixed truth-claims would wholly contravene their theological superstructure.

[25] See J. Alec Motyer, *The Prophecy of Isaiah: An Introduction and Commentary* (Downers Grove, IL: InterVarsity, 1993), where he groups Isa 38–55 as a major Isaianic book, "The Book of the Servant" (287) including the subsection of 44:24–48:22 as a unit titled "The Great Deliverance" (352).

all My desire.' And he declares of Jerusalem, 'She will be built,' And of t he temple, 'Your foundation will be laid.'"

Isaiah 45:1–7

¹ Thus says the LORD to Cyrus, His anointed,
Whom I have taken by the right hand,
To subdue nations before him,
And to loose the loins of kings;
To open doors before him so that gates will not be shut:
² "I will go before you and make the rough places smooth;
I will shatter the doors of bronze and cut through their iron bars.
³ I will give you the treasures of darkness,
And hidden wealth of secret places,
So that you may know that it is I,
The LORD, the God of Israel, who calls you by your name.
⁴ For the sake of Jacob My servant,
And Israel My chosen *one*,
I have also called you by your name;
I have given you a title of honor
Though you have not known Me.
⁵ I am the LORD, and there is no other;
Besides Me there is no God.
I will gird you, though you have not known Me;
⁶ That men may know from the rising to the setting of the sun
That there is no one besides Me.
I am the LORD, and there is no other,
⁷ The One forming light and creating darkness,
Causing well-being and creating calamity;
I am the LORD who does all these.

It seems to be self-evident that if God, through Isaiah, predicts that a man named Cyrus will someday "perform all [God's] desire" (Isa 44:28) and will "subdue nations" (45:1), then Isaiah's audience should expect that God, at some appointed time, would raise up a man named Cyrus who would "perform all [God's] desire" and would "subdue nations." It should be no surprise, then, that a man named Cyrus did exactly that, a century and a half later, precisely as foretold by God. Embedded throughout this same Isaianic prophecy, one that forecasts God's sworn, predetermined plans for Cyrus, are found specific, sworn, predetermined plans for national Israel—plans associated with an eschatological New Covenant—plans that far surpass the achievements of Cyrus both in scope and in time:[26]

Isaiah 44:1–5

[1] "But now listen, O Jacob, My servant,
And Israel, whom I have chosen:
[2] Thus says the LORD who made you
And formed you from the womb, who will help you,
'Do not fear, O Jacob My servant;
And you Jeshurun whom I have chosen.
[3] For I will pour out water on the thirsty *land*
And streams on the dry ground;
I will pour out My Spirit on your offspring
And My blessing on your descendants;
[4] And they will spring up among the grass
Like poplars by streams of water.'
[5] "This one will say, 'I am the LORD'S';
And that one will call on the name of Jacob;
And another will write *on* his hand,
'Belonging to the LORD,'
And will name Israel's name with honor."

Isaiah 44:21–23

[21] "Remember these things, O Jacob,
And Israel, for you are My servant;
I have formed you, you are My servant,
O Israel, you will not be forgotten by Me.
[22] I have wiped out your transgressions like a thick cloud
And your sins like a heavy mist.

---

[26] These coming blessings, embedded in the unified prophecy of Isa 44–48, are part of a larger complex of New Covenant provisions that are promised unequivocally and repeatedly to restored national Israel in the eschatological last days of earth history. See David Fredrickson, "Which Are the New Covenant Passages in the Bible?" in *Dispensational Understanding of the New Covenant*, ed. Mike Stallard (Arlington Heights, IL: Regular Baptist Books, 2012), 47, 61–63. These predicted, sworn benefits attend the ratification of Israel/Judah's New Covenant, and are distinct from but concurrent with the apogee of the Abrahamic and Davidic covenants in their fulfillment. These sworn benefits include the agency of the Spirit of God in enacting and enabling the covenant, the internal spiritual transformation of every individual ethnic Israelite at the time of covenant ratification, the physical regathering of the Jewish nation to its promised homeland along with the full and final restoration of Israel's political, international, civil, economic, ceremonial, military, geographical, and agricultural status as God's favored kingdom-nation, all without interruption (see also Jer 31:31—40; Mic 4:1–8).

Return to Me, for I have redeemed you."

[23] Shout for joy, O heavens, for the LORD has done *it*!

Shout joyfully, you lower parts of the earth;

Break forth into a shout of joy, you mountains,

O forest, and every tree in it;

For the LORD has redeemed[27] Jacob

And in Israel He shows forth His glory.

Isaiah 45:11, 14, 17, 25

[11] Thus says the LORD, the Holy One of Israel, and his Maker:

"Ask Me about the things to come concerning My sons,

And you shall commit to Me the work of My hands." . . .

[14] Thus says the LORD,

"The products of Egypt and the merchandise of Cush

And the Sabeans, men of stature,

Will come over to you and will be yours;

They will walk behind you, they will come over in chains

And will bow down to you;

They will make supplication to you:

'Surely, God is with you, and there is none else,

No other God.'. . .

[17] Israel has been saved[28] by the LORD

With an everlasting salvation;

You will not be put to shame or humiliated

To all eternity. . . .

[25] In the LORD all the offspring of Israel

Will be justified and will glory."

God, in one unified prophecy (Isa 44–48) and in unequivocal terms, announced that he, the sovereign of the created order, had planned a future for a conqueror named Cyrus and that he, the sovereign of the created order, had planned a future for a nation called Israel. There is no compelling reason—hermeneutical, exegetical, or theological—to question either of God's propositions. There is no inherent evidence for accepting one as literal while, at the same time, asserting

---

[27] The verb here stands in the suffixed or perfect conjugation. In this prophetic context its nuance is doubtless indicative of a future event that is certain. See Bruce K. Waltke and Michael Patrick O'Connor, *Introduction to Biblical Hebrew Syntax* (University Park, PA: Eisenbrauns, 1990), 30.5.1e, 38, 39.

[28] Again, the verb here is a suffixed perfect (see preceding note)

that the other will come to pass through different events in a modified location with another people-group at an altered time.

Why would any interpreter of Scripture believe God's literal forecast through Isaiah that "all the ends of the earth" should "turn to [the LORD] and be saved" (45:22), that "every knee will bow, [and] every tongue will swear *allegiance*" to Yahweh God (45:23), and that "all who were angry at him will be put to shame" (45:24), yet at the same time disbelieve the literalness of the ensuing prediction that "all of the offspring of Israel will be justified and will glory" (45:25)? Why would anyone suggest that when God says "all of the offspring of Israel will be justified," God does not *really* mean that every living descendant of ethnic/national Israel will experience personal justification (salvation/regeneration) at some appointed time in the future (Isa 45:25, cf. 45:17; see also Deut 30:1–6; Isa 44:3, 59:20–21; 60:21; Jer 31:33–34; Ezek 37:21–28; Rom 11:26–29, et al.)? Why interpret every one of the preceding divine affirmations literally, then interpret this last divine affirmation nonliterally? Why agree that the prophecy regarding King Cyrus would actually be fulfilled by King Cyrus but then assert that the prophecy regarding national Israel would actually be fulfilled by someone else—for example, by the church?[29]

It seems apparent that the only impetus to forward such a drastic and non-self-evident bifurcation of this otherwise unified prophecy would find cause in theological preunderstandings and ensuing hermeneutical complexities that are forced upon the text from without. The prophecy itself gives neither the original hearers nor the ensuing readers any indication that God intended some of these sworn forecasts to be fulfilled exactly as stated, while others he intended to resignify, typologize, expand, and/or spiritualize. In fact, in this very prophecy

---

[29] Motyer agrees that this entire predictive complex (Isa 45:14–45) is spoken by God in absolute fidelity. From v. 19 he observes: "[God's] word is a plain word and not intrinsically puzzling. It is certainly not misleading, nor does it deal in deceitful commands or promises whereby people would follow them and end up in a maze of 'meaninglessness' (*tohu*, 'vain'). The Lord's word is not shifting sand but solid ground. He speaks *truth/'righteousness'* and *what is right/'plain/ straightforward things'*. The former is the content of the divine word (truth in conformity to an absolute norm); the latter is the expression of the truth plainly and without duplicity" (Motyer, *Isaiah*, 364–65). In conjunction with his strong affirmation of God's verbal fidelity, Motyer believes that the "bowing" of "every knee" (v. 23) will indeed occur exactly as God swore: "'I myself have spoken' . . . *in all integrity* 'in righteousness' . . . the word which *will not be revoked* . . . which will not fail to complete its allotted task" (p. 366). But when it comes to the ensuing words from God in reference to national Israel ("All the offspring of Israel will be justified and will glory" [v. 25]), Motyer immediately equivocates. He cites Westermann who says that a "crucial change is made in the concept of the people of God . . . a final break . . . between the people of God and any form of existence as a political entity" (ellipses Motyer's, 366–67). Without any evidence other than his *ipse dixit*, Motyer concludes that "a merely national [or literal] significance of *Israel* would make nonsense of the whole argument of this passage [Isa 45:22–25]. . . . The honoured name [Israel] now casts its mantle over a world-wide confessional community [the church]" (367). Motyer's hermeneutical retreat should be no surprise. He earlier described Israel "in Isaiah's time (as) the people of God, his 'church,' [that] was constituted a nation among nations" (363); yet in the future, after Isaiah's time, Motyer says, "The great name Israel must now include the saved of the Gentile world" (p. 364). Thus, Motyer contends that "world-wide salvation" in this prophetic resignification (Isa 45:25) means "the world Israel'" (364). In Motyer's covenantalist view, the "church" of the Old Testament (national Israel) is infused into the "church" of the New Testament (spiritual Israel) and literalism, therefore, must be forfeit in select parts of God's otherwise "plain and not intrinsically puzzling" words. Motyer's citation of Westermann is from Claus Westermann, *Isaiah 40–66: A Commentary*, trans. David M. G. Stalker (Philadelphia: Westminster, 1969), 176.

God categorically swears by himself that his words, *all his words*, will come to pass efficaciously, exactly as spoken, always, without change, in fixed accord with his immutable essence and his righteous perfections (Isa 45:18–23). Why not, rather, believe exactly that in *every* case rather than only in some?

Similar affirmations of the ground of predictive prophecy, God's immutable person and efficacious words, are embedded by God in other texts cited above that speak of God's singular ability to foretell the future. Here is an example:

Isaiah 46:9–11

[9] "Remember the former things long past,

For I am God, and there is no other;

I am God, and there is no one like Me,

[10] Declaring the end from the beginning,

And from ancient times things which have not been done,

Saying, 'My purpose will be established,

And I will accomplish all My good pleasure'. . .

[11] Truly I have spoken; truly I will bring it to pass.

I have planned *it, surely* I will do it.

Another example:

Isaiah 48:3, 11

[3] "I declared the former things long ago

And they went forth from My mouth, and I proclaimed them.

Suddenly I acted, and they came to pass. . . .

[11] For My own sake, for My own sake, I will act;

For how can *My name* be profaned?

And My glory I will not give to another."

The promises of a New Covenant to be ratified with national Israel[30] also find ground on the sovereignty of God's person and the efficacy of his forecasts:

Isaiah 55:10–11

[10] "For as the rain and the snow come down from heaven,

And do not return there without watering the earth

And making it bear and sprout,

---

[30] No text in Scripture, NT or OT, specifically says or necessarily implies that the New Covenant is ratified ("cut") with any other legal party besides national Israel. See R. E. Beacham, "The Church Has No Legal Relationship to or Participation in the New Covenant," in *Dispensational Understanding of the New Covenant*, ed. Mike Stallard (Schaumburg, IL: Regular Baptist Press, 2012).

And furnishing seed to the sower and bread to the eater;

[11] So will My word be which goes forth from My mouth;

It will not return to Me empty,

Without accomplishing what I desire,

And without succeeding *in the matter* for which I sent it."

Jeremiah states, as well, that national Israel's eschatological New Covenant stands grounded on God's immutable person and sovereign authority:

Jeremiah 31:35–37

[35] Thus says the LORD,

Who gives the sun for light by day

And the fixed order of the moon and the stars for light by night,

Who stirs up the sea so that its waves roar;

The LORD of hosts is His name:

[36] "If this fixed order departs

From before Me," declares the LORD,

"Then the offspring of Israel also will cease

From being a nation before Me forever."

[37] Thus says the LORD,

"If the heavens above can be measured

And the foundations of the earth searched out below,

Then I will also cast off all the offspring of Israel

For all that they have done," declares the LORD.

When the sovereign Creator God of heaven speaks, the sovereign Creator God of heaven acts—precisely as he has spoken. Asserting the nonliteral fulfillment of a divine forecast is comparable to alleging the nonliteral outcome of a creative pronouncement (e.g., "Let there be light." Gen 1: 3) or the nonliteral outcome of an enjoined miracle (e.g., "*Talitha kumi*" Mark 5:41). In each case (the performance of a creative act, the invoking of a divine miracle, and the foretelling of a future event) it is untenable to imagine that God would proclaim one thing as about to occur, while the outcome would consist of a different thing altogether.[31] To suggest, further, that the alternate outcome might be *better* than

---

[31] Gen 1:3 states, "Then God said, 'Let there be light,' *and there was light*" [emphasis added]. Mark 5:41–42 says, "Taking the child by the hand, He said to her, '*Talitha kumi!*' . . . and immediately *the girl got up*" [emphasis added]. In like manner with his creative and miraculous pronouncements, the prescient words of God can be nothing but efficacious in exact accord with their affirmations. One should neither expect nor suggest an alternate outcome.

the one originally proclaimed only exacerbates the anomaly.[32] All forms of partial nonliteral fulfillment (less-than-literal, other-than-literal, or more-than-literal) stand in stark contradiction to the very nature of God and his spoken word as described by God himself.

If God's purpose in predictive prophecy evidenced his singular deity and if the ground of his evidential foretelling rested on his divine perfections, then he most certainly intended his foretelling to find accomplishment in precise accord with its propositional claims. Any divergence or variation would both abrogate his purpose and repudiate his character. Deviant fulfillment would, in fact, *disprove* his singularity and *discount* his perfections. There is neither explicit nor implicit evidence anywhere in Scripture that necessarily induces, much less requires, the Bible interpreter to believe that God commissioned some of his predictions (or parts thereof) to find fulfillment exactly as he had spoken, while God commissioned others of his predictions (or parts thereof) later to be resignified, typified, or otherwise modified. As with his creative speech, his sustaining decrees, and his miracle-inducing words, so with his prophetic foretelling: he speaks, and it comes to pass ("I, Yahweh, have spoken, and I will do [it]," Ezek 17:24; 22:14; 24:14; 36:36; 37:14; et al.). Predictive prophecy, *all* predictive prophecy, was intended by God to be interpreted in precise accord with its original propositions and accomplished in exact fulfillment of its details. Both God's stated purpose and definitive ground for this revelatory genre affirm the hermeneutical rubric of consistent literal interpretation.

The Nature of Predictive Prophecy

If predictive prophecy served the *purpose* of proving the absolute exclusivity of God and if the *ground* of this genre rested decisively on the immutable perfections of God, what was the *nature* of God's revelatory foretelling? The Scriptures assert unambiguously that predictive prophecy was univocal in nature. The words and the meaning of true prophetic forecasts were exclusively the words and the meaning of God.

---

[32] The argument seems almost ubiquitous among partial nonliteralists and complementary hermeneuticians that people should be thankful and that God should be admired if he produces a "more expansive" fulfillment than those that he originally swore. According to this innovative hermeneutical theory, God can do more than he promised, he just can't do less. See, for example, S. H. Travis, *I Believe in the Second Coming of Jesus* (Grand Rapids: Eerdmans, 1982), 140, or Rod Decker, "The Church's Relationship to the New Covenant," *BSac* 152 (July 1995): 297, et al. For this author's specific response to Decker on the issue of expanded fulfillments, see R. E. Beacham, "The Church Has No Legal Relationship," 234n6. In any case, the outworking of expanded nonliteral fulfillment usually does not result, formulaically, in the equation "God promises to do x but instead he does $x+$," (something *more* than x). Rather, it results in the equation "God promises to do x but instead he does y, which, in their view, is $> x$," (something *greater* than x). In reality, however, y is not x at all. It seems more theologically sound to assert, in every case, that if God swears on his own person and nature to do x, then God will in fact do x, nothing more and nothing less. Any other outcome, expanded or diminished, would call into question the efficacy of his words, not to mention the integrity of his person. No outcome can be "better" than the exacting accomplishment of God's self-sworn pronouncements all the time.

Many interpreters argue that the dual nature of the authorship of Scripture generally, and of predictive prophecy specifically, allows for a divergence of meaning between the human authors and the divine author.[33] In this view, God might have meant something other than, less than, or more than what the human prophet meant.[34] Such a view, they argue, allows God in the New Testament to reinterpret, resignify, expand, typologically fulfill, or otherwise transmute the evident meaning of Old Testament foretelling.[35] The question could be framed as follows: did the prophets who communicated God's future works mean exactly what God meant when they prophesied, or could God have meant something other than, more than, or less than the human prophet's meaning? Debate on this question is complicated by the claims of complex hermeneutical theories and

---

[33] Numerous Bible interpreters advance this bold assertion in support of nonliteralism. Longman, for one, states it directly: "What do we really mean when we say that our goal is the author's intended meaning? . . . God's intention may surpass the conscious intention of the human author. The ultimate meaning of a passage resides in the intention of the ulti-mate Author," Tremper Longman III, *Making Sense of the Old Testament: Three Crucial Questions* (Grand Rapids: Baker, 1998), 28; cf. G. K. Beale, "Positive Answer to the Question Did Jesus and His Followers Preach the Right Doctrine from the Wrong Texts?" in *The Right Doctrine from the Wrong Texts? Essays on the Use of the Old Testament in the New,* ed. G. K. Beale (Grand Rapids: Baker, 1994), 393. Similarly, Gentry and Wellum write: "Since Scripture is God's Word through human authors, we discover *God's intent* [emphasis added] through the writing(s) of the human authors. . . . Ultimately, this point leads us to a canonical reading of Scripture in order to discover how to interpret the meaning of specific texts. It is not enough to read Scripture in a 'thin' manner, that is, as isolated texts apart from the whole. Instead we must read texts in a 'thick' way, that is, in light of the entire canon of Scripture. *We discover God's intent* [emphasis added] through the writing(s) of the biblical authors, but given the diversity of authors throughout time, we must interpret biblical authors in light of the entire canon. It is only by reading Scripture 'thickly' that we discover *its true meaning–that is, God's intent*. . . . [emphasis added]" *Kingdom through Covenant,* 111. Notice carefully the verbiage engaged in these citations with regard to "meaning" in Scripture: "the ultimate meaning" (Longman) and "the true meaning" (Gentry and Wellum). The idea that any one proposition, especially a proposition in Scripture, can have an "ultimate" meaning and a "true" meaning that differs from the *original* and *apparent* (untrue?) meaning becomes problematic at best. Beyond the issue of the intrinsic nature of language, the theological implications of such assertions should be troubling to anyone who ponders these ideas deeply.

[34] Gentry and Wellum state that a canonical reading as described above "is also another way of speaking about the 'fuller meaning' of Scripture or what has been labelled the *sensus plenior.*" *Kingdom through Covenant,* 111.

[35] As Gentry and Wellum express it, "It is for this reason that the New Testament's interpretation of the Old Testament becomes definitive. . . . In other words, we must carefully allow the New Testament to show us how the Old Testament is brought to fulfillment in Christ. In this way . . . the New Testament's interpretation of the Old Testament may expand the Old Testament author's meaning." *Kingdom through Covenant,* 112. Although Gentry and Wellum claim that their understanding of *sensus plenior* is limited only to the "implications and applications" of the meaning of earlier authors, and that it does not include an entirely different sense of an earlier text (112n14), ultimately they declare that the "literal" land promises and the future role of national Israel, along with the Abrahamic covenant, only "serve as a type of Eden's recovery and expansion in the new creation" (112–13). Despite their claims, the reality of their hermeneutic leads them to these conclusions: where the Old Testament author said (and meant) national Israel, that now means "the 'true Israel,' (the) Lord Jesus Christ" (155, cf. 150, 801); and where the Old Testament author said (and meant) the Levantine "land" of Israel's promise, that now means the "new creation," the "new heavens and new earth," the "entire world" (150, 154–55, 834–35). In the end, then, the expanded "fulfillments" of these Old Testament promises that originally referred specifically to national Israel and to Israel's land are not "implications" or "applications" of the words and the meaning of the original authors, but they are alterations and resignifications of their words and meaning. This "reinterpretive" view of Old Testament predictive prophecy is nothing new. The notion that the New Testament reinterprets Old Testament predictive prophecy is as old, if not older, than the popularization of inaugurated eschatology. See George Ladd's review of Alva J. McClain's *Greatness of the Kingdom* (1959) where Ladd says, "McClain achieves this structure [i.e., a literal, eschatological, reestablished Jewish kingdom] not from an inductive exegesis of the New Testament but from the Old Testament. . . . This brings us to the fundamental dispensational hermeneutic in contrast with that of classical theology [i.e., covenant theology]. Classical theology recognizes progressive revelation and insists that the *final meaning of the Old Testament* is to be discovered as it *is reinterpreted by the New Testament* [emphasis added]," George Eldon Ladd, "Books in Review, Dispensational Theology," *Christianity Today* (October 12, 1959), 38.

sophisticated literary methodologies,[36] but once again the answer to the question becomes far simpler to discover than innovative theories might suggest if not demand. The answer can be addressed by examining (1) explicit statements in Scripture regarding the unitary nature of predictive prophecy specifically, (2) biblical, theological truths regarding the unitary nature of inspiration generally, and (3) the singular nature of propositional speech universally.

The Unitary Nature of Predictive Prophecy

The question of the dual authorship of prophecy and its possible connection to dual meaning should drive the inquisitor, first, to the most definitive text in the Old Testament regarding the verbal nature of divine foretelling—Deuteronomy 18:15–22.[37] In this context, Moses delineates the legal requirements pursuant to the eventual office of kingship (Deut 17:14–20). He then addresses the qualifications and qualities of those serving in the office of the priest (18:1–8). Finally, Moses turns to the office of the prophet (18:9–22). He first raises the question of pagan worship and, specifically, the bogus arts of corrupt prognosticators. Moses's warning against divination, witchcraft, augury, sorcery, mediums, spiritism, and necromancy leads him to rehearse God's portrayal of the nature and content of true prophecy as exercised by those whom God selects to serve in that divine office:[38]

---

[36] The new "sophistication" of hermeneutical methodology in argument against consistent literalism was claimed early, even within progressive dispensationalism. Bock and Blaising, in their definitive work on that movement, asserted that "hermeneutics has become much more complex today than when Charles Ryrie affirmed literal interpretation as the 'clear, plain, normal' method of interpretation. . . . Even at the time [Ryrie] was published, evangelical biblical scholars were beginning to move toward a more consistent grammatical-historical interpretation, but it was a grammatical-historical interpretation which was developing in sophistication beyond that which was predicted by classical dispensationalists or even early revised dispensationalists. . . . Literary interpretation has developed so that some things which earlier interpreters thought they 'clearly' saw in Scripture, are not 'clearly' seen today at all." *Progressive Dispensationalism*, 36. Unfortunately, as an ever-increasing number of fashionable literary theories are devised, more and more nonliteralistic methodologies are applied to the text of Scripture, affecting not just the supposed resignification of predictive prophecy but the wholesale reinterpretation of historical narrative as well (e.g., the creation accounts). These kinds of urbane hermeneutical hypotheses raise troubling questions about the ability of the original recipients of God's revelation, their immediate progeny, and the ensuing students of Scripture to understand Scripture's "ultimate" and "true" meaning long before such sophisticated methods were contrived (see note 29). Gentry and Wellum assert that we can "only begin to read Scripture in the way God intended and thus 'biblically'" when Scripture is "ultimately interpreted in light of the culmination of God's plan in Christ." *Kingdom through Covenant*, 127. It seems almost arrogant to allege that no one could possibly process God's age-old truth-claims "biblically," rightly discern the divine author's "intent," or clearly understand what God's words really ("ultimately") meant until millennia after those revelatory words were spoken.

[37] This classic text remained the standard for defining and interpreting God's prophetic speech well after the death and resurrection of the Lord (see Acts 3:22, 23; 7:37, 52).

[38] Although the reference to "a prophet" in this text is singular, the context indicates a broader inclusion of the office in general and of any prophet who would claim to fill that office (see vv. 20, 22; see Eugene H. Merrill, *Deuteronomy*, NAC (Nashville: Broadman and Holman, 1994), 272. Of course, the singular use also allows for applicability to a penultimate prophet who would embody the office perfectly, as he would with the penultimate office of king and priest (see John 1:21, 25; 6:14; Acts 3:19–23). The fact that there would be a penultimate representative of these offices in no way dissolves or resignifies the original descriptions or representatives of these offices.

Deuteronomy 18:15–22

[15] "The LORD your God will raise up for you a prophet like me from among you, from your countrymen, you shall listen to him.[16] This is according to all that you asked of the LORD your God in Horeb on the day of the assembly, saying, 'Let me not hear again the voice of the LORD my God, let me not see this great fire anymore, lest I die.' [17] And the LORD said to me, 'They have spoken well. [18] 'I will raise up a prophet from among their countrymen like you, and I will put My words in his mouth, and he shall speak to them all that I command him.[19] 'And it shall come about that whoever will not listen to My words which he shall speak in My name, I Myself will require *it* of him.[20] 'But the prophet who shall speak a word presumptuously in My name which I have not commanded him to speak, or which he shall speak in the name of other gods, that prophet shall die.'[21] And you may say in your heart, 'How shall we know the word which the LORD has not spoken?' [22] When a prophet speaks in the name of the LORD, if the thing does not come about or come true, that is the thing which the LORD has not spoken. The prophet has spoken it presumptuously; you shall not be afraid of him.'"

In this defining speech, the verbal nature of the prophetic office and of predictive prophecy itself is quantified emphatically.[39] God says through Moses, "I will put My words in his mouth, and he shall speak to them all that I command him" (Deut 18:18). God then reaffirms that the pronouncements of a true prophet consist of "My words which he shall speak in My name" (18:19). The imposter, on the other hand, is said by God to speak "word[s] presumptuously in My name which I have not commanded him to speak" (18:20; see also Jer 14:14).

One can grant the general idea of more than one author, so to speak, of any given prophecy recorded in Scripture (i.e., a divine and a human author), given that all Scripture (*graphe*) was, of necessity, penned (*written*) by the hands of men as borne along by the Holy Spirit (2 Pet 1:20–21). But does this fact also suggest the reality or even the potential of more than one meaning? Clearly, according to God's description in Deuteronomy 18, true predictive prophecy fundamentally entailed the direct and unembellished word(s) of God, not at all the word(s) of the

---

[39] The triliteral root *dbr* ("to speak") with its derived noun ("word[s]") is engaged fifteen times in this nine-sentence description of a prophet and his prophecy (Deut 18:18-22; see Duane L. Christensen, *Deuteronomy 1–21:9*, rev. ed., WBC (Dallas: Thomas Nelson, 2001), 406

human prophet.[40] Every word of all true predictive prophecy consisted of *God's* words and *only* God's words, divinely communicated through human voices and, when recorded in Scripture, through human hands (1:18–19).[41] The words of genuine predictive prophecies from God admitted absolutely no admixture with the words of the human prophets themselves (1:20). That being the case, no need exists to wonder about the *prophet's* meaning in any genuine prophetic forecast.

This emphatic prescription for genuine prophecy in Deuteronomy 18 unquestionably affirms the univocality, over against the bivocality, of God's foretelling. The words of every true predictive prophecy, whether spoken or recorded in writing, were not human words at all; they were God's words exactly and God's words exclusively. The human prophet served as no more than a mouthpiece ("I will put My words in his mouth," Deut 18:18, compare the herald of Dan 3:4–6).[42] A prophet who determined to speak any of his own words, much less to convey his own meaning, through a prophetic speech in the name of the Lord stood guilty of a capital offense (Deut 18:18–21).

The modern interpreter's skepticism with regard to a biblical prophet's meaning, or even his prophetic cognizance or intent, creates a false dilemma. What the true prophet personally meant, intended, imagined, or understood by the words of his prophecy has no essential analytical warrant. The prophet may have fully understood the prediction that he announced on behalf of God (1 Kgs 22:17, see 22:28) or the prophet may have found the forecast utterly perplexing (Dan 7:15–16), but neither case affected the prophecy's meaning or intent whatever. If a true prophecy consisted of God's words alone, and it did, then that true prophecy bore God's meaning alone. The question of the human author's meaning is wholly irrelevant; it has no factual warrant.

By nature, then, no true predictive prophecy concerned any of the prophet's

---

[40] Consider as well the stock prophetic formula "Thus says the LORD . . ." and similar formulas, recorded over twelve hundred times in the writings of the prophets.

[41] This assertion in no way advances the idea of the dictation theory of inspiration. God certainly did not dictate every word of Scripture. On the other hand, he did, as it were, dictate some. Further, when a true prophet spoke and wrote a prophetic message from God in his official function as God's messenger (Deut 18:18–19), he spoke and wrote all of and only the words of God, according to this and many other texts that describe this particular process. See also the broader discussion of the nature of inspiration immediately below.

[42] Should we wonder about the meaning, understanding, or intent of Nebuchadnezzar's herald (Dan 3:4–6) as he announced the decree that originated with the king (3:10)? God clearly enlisted Jonah as a herald of God's words alone (Jonah 3:1–2: "Go to Nineveh . . . and proclaim to it the proclamation which I am going to tell you."). Should we concern ourselves with Jonah's meaning, understanding, or intent (3:4)? Note also Micaiah's reply when enjoined to speak "favorably to the king": "As the LORD lives, what the LORD says to me, that I shall speak" (1 Kgs 22:13–14). Balaam, when told to curse Israel multiple times, blessed them because, as he queried, "Must I not be careful to speak what the LORD puts in my mouth?" (Num 23:12, cf. 23:26 and 24:13). Indeed, the Balaam narrative is replete with affirmations that a genuine prophecy can only recount the words of God and none of the prophet's (see 22:20, 35, 38; 23:3, 5, 12, 16, 17, 20, 26; 24:13, 16). We need not concern ourselves with the prophet's surmised meaning, conjectured understanding, or possible interpretation of his announced message from God. The words were God's words alone. Deuteronomy 18:18–19 places all true prophets in the same category: heralds of the word(s) of God.

meaning. The words of the forecast, along with their intent, meaning, and significance, derived from God exclusively. Any modern interpreter who argues for partial nonliteralism of predictive prophecy on the basis of dual authorship and, thus, dual meaning, stands in error. That interpreter's argument rests, fundamentally, on a false premise according to God's own description of this revelatory genre. If, as some suppose, the meaning of any predictive forecast was modified over time, then, in reality, God must have modified *his own* meaning, not the prophet's, for no true predictive prophecy entailed any of the prophet's meaning at all. God was the sole propositional agent of all true prophecy, its words, its meaning, and its intent. To suggest, then, that God, at one time, intended one of his own propositions to mean *x*, and then, at some later time, intended that same proposition to mean *y* seems wholly untenable if not impertinent. The divinely stated nature of predictive prophecy as recorded in Deuteronomy 18 precludes even the possibility that God could mean something other than, more than, or less than what the human prophet meant, for both the prophetic words and their meaning were God's alone.

The Unitary Nature of Inspiration

Beyond the specific question of the dual authorship of God's foretelling stands the more general question of the dual authorship of Scripture as a whole. Is it possible that *any* Scripture, even those recorded words that were not directly announced by God, could have dual meaning as the result of dual authorship? The view that *any* Scripture could have dual meaning is itself dubious.

Rather than the notion of the "dual" nature of the authorship of Scripture, it seems more accurate to speak of the "unitary" nature of the authorship of Scripture.[43] The unitary nature of scriptural authorship can be illustrated by analogy with the doctrine of inspiration itself. In the *graphe* of an inspired document, the human authors *said* no more, no less, and nothing different than the divine author intended to say.[44] There is one unified body of *verba*. If the human authors said no more, no less, and nothing different than the divine author intended to say, it follows that the human authors *meant* no more, no less, and nothing different than that which the divine author intended to mean. In other words, if there is one unified body of *verba*, then there is one unified *vox*. As Geisler affirms,

God, inasmuch as He inspired the text (2 Timothy 3:16), knows infi-

---

[43] See Rolland D. McCune, "What Is Literal Interpretation?" *Sola Scriptura* 3 (2002).

[44] 2 Tim 3:16–17; 2 Pet 1:19–21

nitely more about the topic and sees more implications and applications in a biblical affirmation than does the human author (I Peter 1:10–12). *But He does not affirm any more meaning in the text than the human author does* [emphasis Geisler's], for whatever the Bible says, God says; whatever the Bible affirms is true, God affirms is true. *Both the divine and human authors of Scripture affirm one and the same meaning in one and the same text. There are not two texts, and there are not two meanings of the text.* [emphasis added][45]

It should be noted, again, that the unitary authorship of predictive prophecy specifically stands as unquestionable with regard to both *verba* and *vox*. Unlike inspiration in general, predictive prophecy consists, by nature, of the heralded words and thus the exact meaning of the divine author *alone*. On the other hand, it appears just as untenable to assert that *any* text of Scripture can have more than one meaning on the ground of having more than one author. Such a view calls into question the nature of inspiration itself by creating an artificial disjunction between the divine and human authors, if not in *verba*, then certainly in *vox*. If the human and divine authors were united in their *words*, as the Scriptures themselves attest, would they not also be united in their *meaning*? The doctrine of verbal, plenary inspiration implies if not demands as much.

The Nature of Propositional Speech

What about the nature of language itself, apart from the question of either prophecy specifically or Scripture generally? Does not the nature of propositional speech itself argue for singular meaning and, thus, exacting fulfillment of *all* God's foretelling, not just of some?[46] The purpose and nature of language find ground in the person and nature of God. Both the idea and the function of language proceed from the mind of God. Language is expressed chiefly by means of speech or texts spoken or written fundamentally as propositional statements. These statements communicate objective ideas or truth-claims by engaging words in basic syntactic constructions (sentences) which own fundamental linguistic correspondence between the infinite mind of God, the Creator of language, and the finite human mind.[47]

---

[45] Norman Geisler, *Systematic Theology* (Minneapolis: Bethany House, 2002), 1:106.

[46] This complex debate can be only introduced here.

[47] For an extended discussion of objectivity in meaning and a defense of the theory of linguistic realism over against essentialism or conventionalism, see chapters 6, "Language: The Semantical Precondition," 9, "Language: The Linguistic Precondition," and 10, "Interpretation: The Hermeneutical Precondition" in the first volume of Geisler, *Systematic Theology*.

This nexus of language with God's communicative nature and God's purpose in creating humans in his image leads, logically, to two conclusions: (1) the meaning of any proposition or sentence derives from the intent of the author/speaker as embedded in its original context, and (2) there is only one meaning in any standard proposition or sentence in any one context, specifically the meaning intended by the author or speaker in that context.[48] As a rule, conventional propositions cannot have relative, hidden, or fuller meanings unknown to the author.[49] No statement can later obtain some (or any) legitimate meaning which differs from that which the original author or speaker intended.[50] Any statement can only mean what it originally meant, no more or no less.

Humans, like the God in whose image they are made, speak in order to communicate meaning. God's special revelation through language (spoken and written) constitutes the most effective and essential form of divine self-disclosure. If people are to know God personally, they must know him through God's self-revelation. God's special revelation is chiefly invested in speechcraft. When humans and God speak, meaning is found in the words (or text) of their speech. Both the delimitation and the substantiation of meaning are bound by the intent of the speaker/author as found in the context of his or her propositions.

To the contrary, if meaning is subjective and not objective, and if statements are governed by semantic relativism and not semantic realism, then the very notion of meaning becomes meaningless. Even those who argue against the objectivity, reality, and univocality of rational speech must engage the objectivity, reality, and univocality of rational speech even to communicate their assertions against it. Their arguments are self-defeating. Further, since a philosophy of language with its associated hermeneutical rubrics logically precedes the exegesis of Scripture,[51] any philosophy of language or set of hermeneutical rules that deny the objectivity and univocality of meaning as grounded in authorial intent will greatly skew the interpreter's exegetical conclusions with regard to the biblical text. This reality is, perhaps, most apparent in the interpretation of predictive prophecy and the notion

---

[48] Geisler, *Systematic Theology*, 1:106.

[49] Even word play, figures of speech, puns, double entendres, codes, etc. find exceptional value and meaning only because of the rule of univocal language, not in defiance of the rule. See McCune, "What Is Literal Interpretation?" 158.

[50] "Words can have but one meaning, or one set of propositional, cognitive values, in any given place; they cannot have two or more meanings in the same usage. . . . Without this [rubric], language is incapable of communicating anything. . . . A passage of Scripture cannot have 'deeper' meaning, multiple meanings, or any other forms of interpretation that are essentially *sensus plenior*" (McCune, "What is Literal Interpretation?" 158).

[51] See the earlier discussion of this idea in the introduction of this study. Roy E. Beacham, "Exegesis: The Focal Point of Textually Based Theological Education: A Preliminary Study" (paper at Bible Faculty Leadership Summit, Summer, 2000).

of its alternate fulfillments. Any interpretive conclusions that argue for any form of other-than-literal, less-than-literal, or more-than-literal fulfillment must rely on some philosophy of language and derived hermeneutical presupposition(s) that controvert the idea of linguistic realism, semantic objectivity, and the principle of univocal meaning as grounded in authorial intent. Those arguments themselves, however, depend upon the very ideas that they deny.

It certainly is true, of course, that even though a proposition has only one meaning, every proposition has multiple (perhaps countless) implications and potential applications.[52] Implications and applications *derive* from univocal, propositional meaning, but implications and applications do not *constitute* meaning.[53] No human author or speaker knows all (or even most of) the implications or potential applications of his or her words. Of course, God can know all the implications and applications of his divine speech, but God did not communicate to the human authors of Scripture all the implications and potential applications of his revelation. God only communicated the specific words, and thus the inherent meaning, of the declarations and assertions of their writings.[54]

The predictive prophet stood in no less a relationship to God's predictions than did any other agents of divine revelation. In fact, the true prophet stood in an even greater relationship to God than most agents, for the predictive prophet in his official declarations and forecasts spoke only and all of God's words and none of his own. The implications and potential applications of the prophet's heralded announcements may have been no more apparent to the prophet than they were to anyone else other than God. Still, what was said constituted what was meant as grounded in God's words and intent because the predictive prophets spoke only God's words and, thus, only God's intent. Implications and applications were left, as always, to derive from God's spoken words and original meaning. The meaning of God, however, was objective, contextual, fixed, and univocal as grounded in his intentions as the sole speaker and in his intentions alone.

So, in consideration of the words and meaning of a genuine predictive prophecy, the interpreter cannot legitimately drive a wedge between the *prophet's words* and *God's words* because the words spoken and written by the prophet were

---

[52] See Geisler's affirmation above under "The Unitary Nature of Inspiration."

[53] Geisler, *Systematic Theology*, 1:106.

[54] Joel 2, for example, is *applied* argumentatively by Peter in his sermon recorded in Acts 2, much like James engages Amos 9 as applicable to his argument recorded in Acts 15. See R. E. Beacham, "Joel 2, Eschatology of," in *Dictionary of Premillennial Theology*, ed. Mal Couch (Grand Rapids: Kregel, 1996), 216–19. The *application* of these predictive prophecies in the logical arguments of Acts 2 and 15 in no way necessitates or even suggests their actual *fulfillment*, and certainly these argumentative applications do not resignify the inherent meaning of the prophecies and, thus, assign them to a different time, place, people, or outcome in contradistinction to those originally stated.

the very words of God, no more and no less. Likewise, the interpreter of Scripture cannot legitimately drive a wedge between the *prophet's words* and *God's meaning* since the prophet's words recounted exactly and only what God intended, and God's meaning inhered to God's words as precisely spoken by the prophet, no more and no less. Finally, the interpreter cannot legitimately drive a wedge between the *prophet's meaning* and *God's meaning* because the prophet's meaning could only consist of God's meaning since the prophet spoke only God's words, no more and no less. The singular nature of predictive prophecy, the unitary nature of divine inspiration, and the univocal nature of propositional speech all argue for the literal understanding, interpretation, and fulfillment of predictive prophecy: *all* predictive prophecy. All God's forecasts were intended to find realization in precise accord with his objective statements and their univocal meaning apart from any disjunction between God's words and intent in contradistinction to the prophets' words and intent. Any such disjunctive argument stands in fundamental error according to God's clear prescriptions for this genre. The unitary nature of the divine words of predictive prophecy argues for consistent literal interpretation.

The Function of Predictive Prophecy

Not only does Deuteronomy 18:15–22 describe the *nature* of predictive prophecy as God's words exclusively, but this primary text also describes the *function* of predictive prophecy as requisite truth-claims. God's warning is clear:

Deuteronomy 18:19

"It shall come about that whoever will not listen to My words which he [the prophet] shall speak in My name, I Myself will require *it* of him."

Implicit in this warning is the assumption that God's words through the prophet, *all* God's words, functioned both as discernable truth-claims and as requisite principles for the response of the audience, both the immediate audience and the succeeding audience. The recipients of God's growing body of prophetic revelation must not only hear and understand those prophecies but must also believe them and act upon them ("listen").[55] They were responsible to trust the pronouncements, forecasts, and promises, and obey the associated precepts and principles. Failing to heed this injunction would result in personal liability before God himself.

---

[55] The verb "to listen" in the OT "has the basic meaning 'to hear,'" which "is extended in various ways, generally involving an effective hearing or listening: 1) 'listen to,' 'pay attention,' 2) 'obey'. *TWOT*, s.v. "שָׁמַע."

vThe fact that God enjoined national Israel to understand, believe, and act upon his prophetic words, all his prophetic words, demands two assumptions. (1) God's warning assumes that his prophetic words were perspicuous. The echoed announcements of the Lord as heralded through the mouths of his true prophets were truth statements spoken by Yahweh God himself to his chosen nation Israel as revelatory data that they could (and must) both cognize and interpret. No complex hermeneutical schema was needed.[56] (2) God's stated warning in Deuteronomy 18 also assumes that God's prophetic words were both trustworthy and actionable. The people of Israel were not to live by faith in the prognostications of pagan charlatans (Deut 18:9–14). Instead, they were responsible to live on the basis of faith in the foretold plans and promises of Yahweh God, all those plans and promises precisely as God declared them through their prophets (18:15–19).

Stated simply, what the prophets foretold to the people of Israel, all that they foretold, was both comprehendible and practicable by the ordinary person. God intended this overt self-revelation to be both trusted and applied to the lives of his audience. The forecasts, images, and symbols represented one reality with one meaning and a singular, unified fulfillment. They did not represent multiple realities with variegated meanings and pliable fulfillments that were transferrable to other peoples at alternate times. Otherwise, how could the recipients of God's forecasts heed this warning? If the original hearers were responsible to understand and to believe God's forecasts and to live by constant and obedient faith in the words of those forecasts, then God's forecasts needed no intricate, sophisticated hermeneutical overlay. There could be no vast passing of time until the ultimate and true meaning of God's words to Israel could acquire their final significance through canonical reinterpretation and/or typological fulfillment. If God, in this warning, meant what he said, then the time for Israel to hear, understand, trust, and obey was immediate and perpetual.

It seems highly unreasonable to assert that some of God's preannounced plans and directives regarding Israel's wellbeing and destiny were to be believed and acted upon in absolute faith and in lifelong intergenerational complicity, while others of those same preannounced plans and directives could and should have been ignored because God never intended the nation to see the fulfillment of those

---

[56] Certainly, there were times when prophetic messages were obscured from the understanding of recalcitrant Israelites in judgment (Ezek 6:9–10). There were also times when God spoke through his prophets using striking imagery (apocalyptic prophecy, e.g., Dan 7–8) and symbolic acts (prophetic theater; e.g., Ezek 4–5). Often, in conjunction with these more opaque messages regarding the future, God also provided the overt meaning of those images and actions (see both Daniel and Ezekiel *in loco*). In any case, God fully intended his prophetic revelation to consist essentially of information that humans could cognize, both immediately and perpetually.

forecasts exactly as predicted.[57] It seems impossible to believe legitimately that God would tell Israel that their disbelief in his prophetic words would endanger their souls (Deut 18:19) without any hint that in some instances disbelief would not endanger their souls because God intended to fulfill many of those prophecies about Israel's future in some other way with some other people at some other time and in some other location, none of which pertained to national Israel in the final outcome.

In this view, the dire warning of Deuteronomy 18:19 becomes unintelligible and impractical. The Old Testament recipients of God's word had no New Testament revelation to suggest to them the priority-status of the ultimate canonical words of God that would resignify and, thus, negate most though not all of God's earlier prophetic revelation with regard to Israel as a nation.[58] How were the original recipients of Old Testament revelation to know which of God's predictive prophecies were demanding of their faith, hope, life-choices, and destiny, at peril of their wellbeing, and which were only typological, mystical, or spectral, intended by God to be accomplished in some reconstituted sense that would nullify that which was so precisely stated as theirs? Such a view wholly robs Old Testament Israel of knowable truth, not to mention their glorious, divinely sworn destiny as God's chosen nation.

Again, it seems evident that only presupposed theological tenets could force such an inconsistent and drastic hermeneutical stance with regard to the fulfillment

---

[57] How should the Bible interpreter suppose that Moses's original audience and the ensuing generations of national Israel were to respond to God's prophetic revelation and its dire warning given the hermeneutical construct of, for example, Klein, Blomberg, and Hubbard, *Introduction to Biblical Interpretation*, 485–86? They say, "Readers must interpret predictive prophecy tentatively rather than dogmatically. . . . Certainly, God's sovereign purposes do not change, and we may expect him to adhere to *much of* the prophetic design. . . . But as he has in the past, *he may delight to ad-lib some unexpected lines.* . . . Jesus Christ and the Christian Church *represent the fulfillment of Israel's God-given mission in history.* The NT writers regard Jesus as the new David and the Church as the new Israel. . . . They stand convinced that *Jesus and the Church . . . fulfill Israel's prophetic hopes* and, hence, constitute God's one, true elect people" (emphasis added). In the view of Klein, Blomberg, and Hubbard, the "prophetic hopes" of Moses's audience (Israel, and Israel's physical progeny) could find no genuine faith-basis in the words that the prophets actually spoke to them, for God never ultimately intended their "hopes" to be realized as actually spoken. Instead, Israel's "prophetic hopes" were to be "fulfilled" by "Jesus Christ and the Christian Church." Indeed, if this common hermeneutical stance is correct, many OT predictive prophecies stood without merit as originally announced. The hearers were left clueless as to what was "true" at the moment, and what was to be resignified centuries later; to which "prophetic design(s)" God would "adhere," and to which he would not; which lines God literally meant at the time, and which lines God "ad-lib[bed]." The warning recorded in Deut 18:19 is rendered wholly impracticable by such a hermeneutical theory. Even more disconcerting is the impact of this theory on theology proper.

[58] Gentry and Wellum, *Kingdom through Covenant*, 115, frame it this way, "The Old Testament is the predictive word that anticipates greater realities tied to the coming of Yahweh and his Messiah; the Gospels give the account of the redemptive-revelatory fact of the coming of God the Son incarnate; and the remainder of the New Testament unpacks the final interpretation. . . ." One nonliteralistic Old Testament scholar concedes the point: "Even as an OT professor, I can appreciate the attraction of the NT. After all, the New Testament is the fulfillment of the Old. Why spend an inordinate amount of time with the shadow when the reality has already come?" Longman, *Making Sense of the Old Testament*, 11. This view, unfortunately, leaves OT saints in revelatory limbo. These men and women in biblical history had no way of discerning which of God's prophetic words to trust implicitly in expectation of exacting fulfillment and which to ignore since those words were mere shadows and would never *actually* be fulfilled as stated.

of predictive prophecies directly sworn to national Israel by the God of heaven.[59] Any theological system that pre-assumes the possibility that the church can in some way fulfill predictive prophecies directed specifically to national Israel must, of necessity, deny the consistent literalness of God's prophetic words and ignore God's clear warning in Deuteronomy 18:19. Apart from systemic theological and hermeneutical preunderstandings, why would any interpreter suppose that some of God's forecasts should be heard and believed with exacting literalness, while others should never expect to find fulfillment precisely as God said? Would it not be better for the modern interpreter, like ancient Israel, to believe what the prophets say rather than to make the prophets say what they want to believe?

Clearly, the function of predictive prophecy both as perspicuous and as obligatory argues for consistent literal interpretation. God's warning in Deuteronomy 18:19 makes no allowance for limited literality or, thus, for partial liability. Certainly, Old Testament recipients of God's revelation were afforded no basis for determining which of two hermeneutical methods they should employ for interpreting and, thus, acting upon God's prophetic pronouncements. It appears most tenable, then, to believe that they were afforded no basis for dual interpretation because no alternate meaning was intended by God, then or ever. By its very nature, predictive prophecy was intended by God to be interpreted with consistent literalness.

The Test of Predictive Prophecy

The foundational text that defines prophecy in general and predictive prophecy specifically, Deuteronomy 18:15–22, not only describes the *nature* and *function* of this revelatory method but also its *test*. In fact, God himself introduces the question at hand. In reference to the presumptuous prophet who speaks falsely in Yahweh's name, God says:

> "You may say in your heart, 'How will we know the word which the LORD has not spoken?'" (Deut 18:21)

God's answer is clear and has significant bearing on how he intended predictive prophecy to be interpreted and fulfilled.

> "When a prophet speaks in the name of the LORD, if the thing does not come about or come true, that is the thing which the LORD has not spoken. The prophet has spoken it presumptuously; you shall not be afraid of him." (Deut 18:22)

---

[59] As stated earlier, theological tenets should *follow* hermeneutics in the logical order of biblical studies, not drive hermeneutics (see note 4).

This test of predictive prophecy would give evidence to the authenticity and veracity of any messenger of God who genuinely announced God's foretold events. Among other objective assessment criteria (e.g., Deut 13:1–5), the people of Israel could discern the validity of a prophet's claim to speak truth in the name of Yahweh by comparing the prophet's *forecasts* of the future with the actual *outcomes* of the future. In perfect correspondence with the evidential test of God's sole deity, a genuine prophet of God, over time, would be validated by precise correspondence between the spoken prediction and the fulfillment of its details. Any outcome that diverged from the clear descriptions of the predicted event not only marked the prophet as presumptuous (Deut 18:22), it rendered him worthy of death (18:20).

No caveat existed in God's declared test of genuine prophecy to allow for spiritualized, typified, multiple-intentioned, expanded, or canonically resignified fulfillments. No exceptions were made in this prescription, or in any other text of Scripture, that would exculpate a prophet or his prophecy, in whole or in part, from this objective standard. Any exception to God's rubric would, in fact, invalidate the test altogether. If, as many suggest, God planned to diverge from this exacting assessment of predictive prophecy and purposed, rather, to bring about other-than-literal fulfillments to vast segments of his Old Testament forecasts, there existed no hint of that possibility in Scripture. No criteria was given to aid the original hearers, or the ensuing readers for that matter, in distinguishing between those parts of God's forecasts that must "come about or come true" exactly as predicted (18:20, 22), and other parts of God's forecasts that were intended by God to "come about or come true(?)" in some other way, at some different time, in some other place, with some different peoples.[60] No alteration of this prophetic test was ever announced in Scripture. In fact, this test remained the standard in Israel even into the days of Jeremiah and Ezekiel:

Jeremiah 28:7–9
[7] "Yet hear now this word which I am about to speak in your hearing and in the hearing of all the people! [8] The prophets who were before me and

---

[60] Gentry and Wellum affirm that Scripture is "without error" and wholly trustworthy ("completely authoritative, sufficient, and reliable"). Yet, at the same time, they believe that Scripture is infused with a *sensus plenior* that could not be known for centuries if not millennia (*Kingdom Through Covenant*, 110–12). This otherwise apparent contradiction is explained, in their view, by segregating the meaning of the human and divine authors (111–12) and by stretching out meaning canonically until "redemptive-history" finally makes "God's intent" truly known "even though the New Testament does not seem to apply it in the same way that the Old Testament does" (113). Despite their herculean endeavor to reconcile divine authenticity, sufficiency, and reliability with time-suspended "truth" and semantically amended (final) "meaning" (109–12), if "Israel" in "truth" means "Jesus" (150, 801) and if "the land of Israel" "finally" means "the new creation" or "the entire world" (113, 834), then the test of Deut 18:22 is utterly ineffectual, not to mention specious. In that case, neither Moses's original audience nor their progeny had any hope of testing, and thus trusting, any predictive prophecy. In this view, the words of the prophets, both genuine and charlatan, could mean anything as far as they knew.

before you from ancient times prophesied against many lands and against great kingdoms, of war and of calamity and of pestilence. [9] The prophet who prophesies of peace, when the word of the prophet comes to pass, then that prophet will be known *as* one whom the LORD has truly sent."

Ezekiel 33:30–33

[30] But as for you, son of man, your fellow citizens who talk about you by the walls and in the doorways of the houses, speak to one another, each to his brother, saying, 'Come now and hear what the message is which comes forth from the LORD.' [31] They come to you as people come, and sit before you *as* My people and hear your words, but they do not do them, for they do the lustful desires *expressed* by their mouth, *and* their heart goes after their gain. [32] Behold, you are to them like a sensual song by one who has a beautiful voice and plays well on an instrument; for they hear your words but they do not practice them. [33] *So when it comes to pass—as surely it will— then they will know that a prophet has been in their midst."* [emphasis added]

In this extended prophecy (Ezek 33:21–33), God affirms through Ezekiel the divine *purpose* of prophetic foretelling. The literal fulfillment of God's foretelling will prove God's singular deity: "Then they will know that I am the LORD" (33:29). As to the *ground* of predictive prophecy, Ezekiel's record confirms that divine foretelling rested fully on the absolute efficacy of God's pronouncements: "So when it comes to pass—as surely it will . . ." (33:33). The *nature* of predictive prophecy also finds emphatic reiteration in this pericope since clearly the words of Ezekiel were nothing more or less than the words of God: "He opened my mouth. . . . so my mouth was opened." (33:22); "Then the word of the LORD came to me saying . . ." (33:23); "Therefore say to them, 'Thus says the Lord GOD . . .'" (33:25); "Thus you shall say to them, 'Thus says the Lord GOD . . .'" (33:27). Ezekiel's account further affirms the *function* of divine foretelling as both perspicuous and obligatory to the hearer: "They come to you as people come, and sit before you *as* My people and hear your words, but they do not do them" (33:31); "You are to them like a sensual song by one who has a beautiful voice and plays well on an instrument; for they hear your words but they do not practice them" (33:32). Finally, the *test* of true predictive prophecy, literal fulfillment, remains valid: "So when it comes to pass—as surely it will—then they will know that a [genuine] prophet has been in their midst" (33:33).[61]

Once again the syllogism stands as both unambiguous and evident, and the synthesis holds without doubt. In simplest terms, this test by outcome only succeeds if all true prophetic prediction finds fulfillment with consistent, self-evident, literalistic equivalence. Clearly, the passing of revelatory time in this test was intended by God to *affirm* his astounding exactitude in the fulfillment of his prophecies (see Isa 48:3–5 et al.); the passing of time was not intended by God to *bypass* exacting fulfillment by means of canonical resignification and typological alteration. How can one espouse any view of prophetic fulfillment that is other-than-literal, less-than-literal, or more-than-literal when any fulfillment besides literal fulfillment is said by God himself to evidence prophetic duplicity and presumption over against prophetic veracity and fidelity? Any supposed divine prophecy that finds fulfillment in nonequivalent, modified, expanded, or otherwise resignified ways is deemed false, and the prophet is death-worthy according to God's self-decreed test (Deut 18:20–22). To assert that any biblical prophecy can find any degree of divinely sponsored fulfillment that fails in any way to correspond in objective and exacting precision with the words of the original forecast negates the very assessment mechanism imposed by God himself in evidence of true predictive prophecy. In light of this test, the idea of partial nonliteral fulfillment is untenable, incongruous, and contradictory. God's test of true predictive prophecy demands the consistent, literalistic interpretation of predictive prophecy, *all* predictive prophecy.

Conclusion

The sovereign Creator God of this universe has chosen to reveal himself through spoken and written truth. His written word stands as our only source and authority today for knowing this singular God intimately. The multiple facets of his written revelation are worthy of a lifetime of study and learning. The direct predictive prophecies of Scripture are doubtless among the most astonishing of God's verbal revelatory methods and messages. In direct predictive prophecies, the sovereign Creator meticulously describes future events,[62] events that he himself has prearranged

---

[61] This extended prophecy clearly concerns the withholding of land promises from disobedient generations of those under the Mosaic covenant, precisely as the curses of the covenant stipulated (e.g., Deut 28:63–65; 29:22–29). This long removal from the land, however, was explicitly nonpermanent. God also foretold and swore by himself that in the end a faithful remnant of national Israel, a New Covenant people whose hearts *he* would circumcise, would be restored to their national land in righteousness and in perpetuity (Ezek 34, 36; see also Deut 30:1–10; Jer 31:27–40, et al.)

[62] God's predictive prophecies include, for example, the exact names of yet unborn individuals, specific time-referents with detailed chronological indicators (sometimes to the very moment), place names with exacting locational identifiers (regions, mountains, valleys, rivers, fields, cities, gates, streets, houses, etc.), the appellations of particular nations with reference to specific national leaders, the progression and digression of kingdoms, political aspirations and accomplishments, treaties, hostilities, battles, conquests, and losses, the make-up of people-groups, the future of ethnic descendants, exact geophysical

even millennia before they are to happen.

On what foundation, then, should Bible interpreters ground their hermeneutic for the proper interpretation of predictive prophecy? Certainly, the student of prophecy must examine the forecasts themselves along with the outcomes of those forecasts that have, beyond question, already found fulfillment. There also exist, however, criteria that rise above and, in fact, set precedent for the study of the prophecies themselves since God did not just foretell the future but also described precisely how he intended his foretelling to work. God himself established exacting and unambiguous prerequisites for understanding and interpreting predictive prophecy, and all God's descriptions and prescriptions argue for a unified hermeneutical method: consistent literalism over against partial nonliteralism.

1. The Purpose of Predictive Prophecy: God's Exclusive Deity. Partial nonliteralism contradicts God's intention to prove his exclusive deity by means of foretelling the future. Genuine irrefutable evidence of God's absolute uniqueness was only possible through the perfect accomplishment of all the details of every part of each foretold event. Transmogrified fulfillments were the industry of false gods, not acts of the sovereign God of heaven.

2. The Ground of Predictive Prophecy: God's Immutable Person and Word. Partial nonliteralism calls into question God's divine perfections, his integrity, and his veracity along with the efficacy of his spoken words. God swore to accomplish his foretold plans, all his foretold plans, in unyielding accord with his ineffable essence, his unchanging nature, and his inflexible truth-telling righteousness and faithfulness. He himself attested, repeatedly, that his prophetic oaths would be accomplished by the absolute proficiency of his speech. God speaks, and what he says happens, precisely as spoken in part and in whole, all on the ground of who he is as the one and only true God. To imagine that God would utter one thing and fulfill it with something different is, at best, a contradiction. In fact, the very idea derogates the essence of his person, the constitution of his perfections, and the veracity of his word.

3. The Nature of Predictive Prophecy: God's Words Exclusively. Partial nonliteralism overlooks exacting biblical statements and repeated generic formulas that affirm the singular origin and authorship of God's predictive words. According to God's own prerequisite, all true prophetic foretelling must consist only of the words of God, and, thus, only of the intent and meaning of God.

---

features, specific weather patterns and climatic events, celestial constancies and oddities, agricultural and pastoral phenomena, human dreams, thoughts, hope, fears, words, etc., many of which God foretells hundreds or thousands of years ahead of time. The list of the intricate and minute details that can be discovered in God's vast foretelling as recorded in Scripture is almost endless and is certainly staggering.

There could be no human voice and, thus, no human meaning in genuine predictive prophecy beyond a mere echo of the voice and meaning of God himself. No legitimate hermeneutical rubric can dichotomize the divine and human agents in this revelatory genre. There is one prophetic voice: the voice of God. There is one prophetic meaning: the meaning of God.

4. *The Function of Predictive Prophecy: Requisite Cognizance, Faith, and Obedience.* Partial nonliteralism robs Old Testament prophecy of perspicuity and divests Old Testament saints of their faith-base. Nonliteral fulfillment is not self-evident; absolute prophetic forecasts become impossible to distinguish from oblique shadows and eventual alternatives as canonically resignified and typologically reshaped. Any warrant for an ancient Israelite's unwavering faith and dutiful living based on each and every one of God's prophetic pronouncements and promises becomes forfeit. No multiplex, time-altering, urbane interpretational methodology existed to exculpate national Israel from hearing, understanding, and grounding their walk of faith and hope on every detail of all of God's sworn predictions and promises to them. On the contrary, they were bound by God himself to understand and to believe his predictive promises, and to live by faith in the actual accomplishment of their truth-claims, all of them, exactly as spoken.

5. *The Test of Predictive Prophecy: Consistent Literal Fulfillment.* Partial nonliteralism eviscerates God's decreed assessment mechanism for distinguishing true, God-generated foretelling from the artificial prognostication of frauds. Partial nonliteral fulfillment means that some parts of predictive prophecy would be verified, over time, as genuine by means of the exacting fulfillment of God's foretold events, while other parts of God's forecasts, over time, would be assigned new, ultimate, and true meanings, coming to pass in alternate ways at substitute times with different people in resignified locations. Such a construct renders God's self-affirmed test of true predictive prophecy to be wholly inept and without value.

In the end, the God-ordained *purpose, ground, nature, function,* and *test* of predictive prophecy all argue forcefully against any hermeneutical preunderstanding of partial nonliteralism including *sensus plenior,* spiritualization, canonical resignification, authorial distinction, meaning expansion, and/or typological or complementary fulfillment. All God's stipulations regarding predictive prophecy assume the consistent literalistic interpretation and fulfillment of his forecasts. None of God's affirmations remain as constants if select portions of his revelatory prophecies can be fulfilled in any other way than literally, exactly as stated. All the Old Testament passages that record a pre-announcement of God with regard to the future must be interpreted by the unambiguous standards that God himself established for this prophetic genre. All the New Testament passages that record a pre-announcement of God with regard to the future, or that cite an earlier pre-announcement of God with reference to the future, must be interpreted on the same basis: God's explicit prescriptions for this predictive genre.

Well-established and broadly accepted exegetical procedures have long been applied by traditional dispensational scholars to New Testament citations of Old Testament predictive prophecies with careful, rational, and defensible results that find perfect accord with the prescription of consistent literal fulfillment. Credentialed, consistent literalists have developed and published diachronically unified and biblically sound story lines for the outworking of God's plan throughout time. Hermeneutical foundationalists with terminal degrees from duly accredited educational institutions have written and published systematic and biblical theologies along with technical exegetical commentaries, fully vested in the idea and application of consistent literal interpretation.

It seems doubtful that God intended sophisticated literary theories, complex hermeneutical schemes, and/or classical theological preconditions to supersede both his clear instructions for this genre and its undeniable outworking in antiquity. There are no necessary or compelling reasons to question, much less to abandon, consistent literalism when it comes to interpreting and correlating all the prophetic words of the sovereign God of space and of time. There *are* compelling reasons, on the other hand, to embrace it. These reasons are grounded in God's own self-revealed prerequisites. If God's preconditions for predictive prophecy truly govern this important revelatory corpus, then all genuine prophetic forecasts in Scripture were intended by God to be *understood* literally, *fulfilled* literally, and therefore *interpreted* literally, only and always. The foundational hermeneutical rubric of historic dispensationalism, the consistent literal interpretation of predictive prophecy, stands in absolute accord with God's clear affirmations and his divine claims.

Ezekiel 12:23–25

[23] Thus says the Lord GOD . . .

"The days draw near as well as the fulfillment of every vision.
[24] For there will no longer be any false vision
   or flattering divination within the house of Israel.
[25] For I the LORD will speak,
   and whatever word I speak will be performed."

Israel and the Church:
Is There Really a Difference?

Kevin T. Bauder
Central Baptist Theological Seminary
Plymouth, Minnesota

In his famous discussion of the sine qua nons of dispensationalism, Charles Ryrie emphasized that a dispensationalist "keeps Israel and the Church distinct." In fact, Ryrie thought that this Israel-church distinction was the most basic way to recognize dispensationalism. Michael Vlach notes that some contemporary dispensationalists might wish to nuance this distinction. Nevertheless, all dispensationalists reject the notion that "the New Testament church is viewed as the replacement or fulfillment of the nation Israel as the people of God."[1]

If Israel and the church are distinct, then what is the nature of that distinction? Vlach hints at the answer with the expression *people of God*. Most dispensationalists say that Israel and the church are distinct because they are distinct peoples. Christians have understood the relationship between Israel and the church in various ways. Some suppose that the church either replaces or continues Israel as the people of God. Others see a faithful remnant of believing Israel continuing within the church, which has now become the people of God. Still others draw a contrast between Israel and the church, resulting in distinct peoples of God. Some see an analogous relationship between Israel and the church within the one people of God.[2]

Within contemporary evangelical theology, dispensationalists emphasize a distinction between Israel and the church. Other evangelical theologies assume that Israel and the church are somehow included in one and the same people of God, though they offer different explanations of how both are included. Many of these theologies teach that denying the unity of the people of God is a serious error. Consequently, their adherents may see

---

[1] Charles Ryrie, *Dispensationalism Today* (Chicago: Moody, 1965), 44–45; Michael J. Vlach, *Dispensationalism: Essential Beliefs and Common Myths* (Los Angeles: Theological Studies, 2008), 24.

[2] This typology is adapted from Markus Barth, *The People of God*, JSNTSup, 5 (Sheffield, England: JSOT Press, 1983), 22–26. I employ Barth's schema (modified slightly) because his classification reflects an ideal typology rather than a partisan evaluation of the debate between dispensationalism and its alternatives.

dispensationalism as a serious error.[3]

This judgment is unnecessarily harsh. At least part of the disagreement between dispensationalists and others may stem from a lack of clarity about the expression *people of God*, which, while often used, is seldom defined. This chapter will offer an understanding of this expression that will explain why many dispensationalists treat Israel and the church as distinguishable peoples of God. It will also demonstrate how dispensationalists can and do see important continuities between the church and Israel, perhaps mitigating elements of the disagreement between dispensationalism and other alternatives.

The Nations

Conversation about the people(s) of God is hindered by a peculiarity of the English language. Anglophones most often use the word *people* as a plural for *person*. In this sense, the word *people* usually refers to multiple individuals. If we talk about the *people of God* in this sense, we mean something like "the sum total of all saved individuals," whether from every era or at a particular time and place.[4] But English also has another use for the word *people*: it can refer to *people groups*, such as the Romanian, Han, or Mbunda peoples. Here, the word *people* is a singular; the correct plural is *peoples*. This distinction is important: discussions about the people of God are not about individuals but about people groups.

Nations and Peoples

In the Old Testament, especially in poetry, the terms *peoples* and *nations* are often used interchangeably. These terms stand for at least three Hebrew words: *goyim* (often translated as *nations* or *Gentiles*), *'amim* (usually translated *peoples*), and *l'umim* (also translated as *peoples* or *nations*). For example, the three terms are set side by side in the first five verses of Psalm 67:

> God be gracious to us and bless us,
> And cause His face to shine upon us—Selah.

---

[3] Clarence Bass states that this distinction "sets [dispensationalism] off from the historic faith of the church," *Backgrounds to Dispensationalism* (Grand Rapids: Eerdmans, 1960), 27. Keith A. Mathison adds that it is "biblically indefensible" *Dispensationalism: Rightly Dividing the People of God?* (Phillipsburg, NJ: P&R, 1995), 37. John Gerstner goes even further: "The dispensational distinction between Israel and the church implicitly repudiates the Christian way of salvation," *Wrongly Dividing the Word of Truth: A Critique of Dispensationalism* (Brentwood, TN: Wolgemuth and Hyatt, 1991), 206.

[4] Examples of this usage can be found in Robert W. Yarbrough, "The Kingdom of God in the New Testament: Matthew and Revelation," in *The Kingdom of God*, ed. Christopher W. Morgan and Robert A. Peterson, Theology in Community 6 (Wheaton: Crossway, 2012) 95, and in Greg R. Allison, "The Kingdom and the Church," in ibid., 180–81.

That Your way may be known on the earth,
Your salvation among all nations [goyim].
Let the peoples ['amim] praise You, O God;
Let all the peoples ['amim] praise You.
Let the nations [l'umim] be glad and sing for joy;
For You will judge the peoples ['amim] with uprightness
And guide the nations [l'umim] on the earth. Selah.
Let the peoples ['amim] praise You, O God;
Let all the peoples ['amim] praise You.

The psalm uses the three terms virtually synonymously; from its perspective, a *nation* and a *people* are the same thing or nearly so. What kind of thing? Not a modern nation-state with fixed territory and a stable government. The biblical understanding of a nation or people usually includes a significant ethnic component. In normal usage, a biblical nation was constituted mainly by its descent from a common ancestor. Whatever other considerations enter the biblical description of a people or nation, its solidarity rests in its union with a common forebear.[5]

This usage is illustrated by the pregnancy of Rebecca in Genesis 25:23, where the Lord told Rebecca,

Two nations [*goyyim*] are in your womb;
And two peoples [*l'umim*] will be separated from your body;
And one people [singular of *l'umim*] shall be stronger than the
other [people—singular of *l'umim*],
And the older shall serve the younger.

Here the two infants are viewed as two nations. The implication is that each child will become the progenitor of a people. Each people will find its solidarity in its ancestor. Thus, a biblical nation is an extended family. Whatever other factors enter into the definition, a nation is an ethnic unit.

Prior to the tower of Babel, no distinguishable nations existed. Rather, humanity functioned as a single people (Gen 11:6). Identifiable peoples

---

[5] For an extended discussion of ethnic and other components that enter into the definition of a people or nation, see Andrew H. Kim, *The Multinational Kingdom in Isaiah: A Study of the Eschatological Kingdom and the Nature of Its Consummation* (Eugene, OR: Wipf and Stock, 2020), passim. Craig Blaising, "A Critique of Gentry and Wellum's *Kingdom through Covenant*: A Hermeneutical-Theological Response," *MSJ* 26, no. 1 (Spring 2015): 120–21, notes that a "holistic anthropology" including the "national, tribal, ethnic dimensions" of humanity is necessary for a right understanding of both the biblical story line with its covenants and the holistic nature of the kingdom, which also includes "national, tribal features."

emerged as a consequence of the division of languages at Babel (indicating that language is another factor in the biblical understanding of a people). God used the division of languages to separate humanity into family groups that were distinguishable, not only linguistically and ethnically but also geographically (Acts 17:26).[6]

The same defining factors are mentioned in the genealogies of Genesis 10. This text shows how the descendants of Noah's sons separated into nations (goyim), distinguishing them by clans (another word for family connections), languages, and lands (Gen 10:4, 5, 20, 31, 32). In other words, besides common descent, a biblical nation would ordinarily share a common language and territory. To be deprived of land or language is to lose some element of national identity.[7]

Another factor in the biblical definition of a people is religion. Biblical nations were typically known as worshipers of particular gods, such as Baal and Asherah (the Canaanites), Dagon (the Philistines), or Milcom and Molech (the Ammonites). The Moabites are twice named the "people [singular of 'amim] of Chemosh" (Num 21:30; Jer. 48:46).

In the biblical notion of a nation or people, ethnic identity (common descent) is the central feature. Other factors also help distinguish one people from another. These include language, territory, and especially loyalty to a god or gods.[8]

God's Plan for the Nations

Humanity was not divided into nations from the fall of Adam until the tower of Babel. From Babel until the calling of Israel, all nations were in rebellion against the true and living God. While individuals believed in God and were justified, no nation *as a people* turned to God. False gods had their peoples, but the true and living God had no nation that called upon him or was called by his name.

---

[6] While it is beside the point of the present discussion, it needs to be said that these observations provide no biblical justification for modern racial prejudice or segregation, contra, e.g., Harry Lacey, *God and the Nations* (New York: Loizeaux, 1942).

[7] See the third chapter of Kim, *The Multinational Kingdom*.

[8] Further discussion of nations and peoples can be found in Daniel I. Block, "Nations/Nationality," *NIDOTTE* 5:966–72; Andreas J. Köstenberger, "Nations," *NDBT*, 676–78; J. G. Millar, "People of God," *NDBT*, 684–87; see also Peter J. Gentry and Stephen J. Wellum, *God's Kingdom through God's Covenants: A Concise Biblical Theology* (Wheaton: Crossway, 2015), 103–4, which emphasizes the distinction between the terms people and nation. Hendrikus Berkhof, *Christian Faith: An Introduction to the Study of the Faith* (Grand Rapids: Eerdmans, 1979), 340, gives reasons for not pressing any distinction too far. On the other hand, Wayne Grudem underplays the difference between a biblical nation and a modern nation state in his *Christian Ethics: An Introduction to Biblical Moral Reasoning* (Wheaton: Crossway, 2018), 465, though his definition is adequate for his argument.

God's plan did not focus exclusively upon calling and saving individual believers. It also included a role for nations, as seen in the section of Psalm 67 cited above. God has always wanted all the peoples of the earth to praise him. His purpose has always been to judge and guide the nations. The psalm even concludes with a prophecy that God will bless Israel and "all the ends of the earth will fear Him" (67:7).

Other psalms articulate the same vision. In Psalm 22:27, David foresaw a day when all the ends of the earth would remember and turn back to the Lord, a day when all the families of the nations would worship him. In Psalm 57:8 David determined to thank God among the peoples (*'amim*) and glorify him among the tribes (*'emmiym*—another term for an ethnic grouping). In Psalm 89:9, David prophesied that all nations (*goyim*) would worship before the Lord and glorify his name. Psalm 102 teaches the afflicted to anticipate a day when the nations (*goyim*) will fear Jehovah's name and the kings of the earth will fear his glory, also specifying that the peoples (*'amim*) and kingdoms will gather to serve Jehovah (Ps 102:15, 22). Psalm 105 exhorts its readers to make God's deeds known among the peoples (*'amim*, 105:1). Psalm 148 calls upon all peoples (*l'umim*) to praise the Lord.

Psalm 96 provides a particularly interesting glimpse into God's plan for the nations. The psalm calls for God's glory to be recounted among the nations (*goyim*, 96:3) and his marvelous works among all peoples (*'amim*, 96:3). It declares that Jehovah is to be praised and feared above all gods because the gods of the peoples (*'amim*) are worthless (96:4–5). Then in a climactic parallelism, it calls directly upon the earth's nations (96:7–9):

Give to Jehovah, clans of the peoples (*'amim*),
Give to Jehovah glory and strength,
Give to Jehovah the glory of His name,
Lift up an offering and come into His courts.
Bow down to Jehovah in holy adornment,
Tremble before Him, all the earth.

Here is a direct appeal to the world's nations to worship Jehovah, to sacrifice to him, and even to enter his courts—surely a reference to the temple. The psalm continues (96:10) with an exhortation to announce Jehovah's reign and justice among the nations (*goyim*). It concludes (96:13) by rejoicing that Jehovah is coming to judge the earth, at which time he will judge the world with righteousness and the nations (*'amim*) with faithfulness.

The prophet Isaiah also foresaw a day when foreigners will join themselves to Jehovah, serve him, and love his name (Isa 56:6–7). At that time Jehovah will bring them into his holy mountain and make them joyful in his house of prayer. They will offer burnt offerings and sacrifices upon his altar. Consequently, God's house will be called a house of prayer for all peoples (*'amim*). Jesus later reminded Israel of these very words (Matt 21:13; Mark 11:17).

Isaiah also articulated a rich vision of multiple peoples worshiping the true and living God. Early in his prophecy he foretold a time when the "mountain of the house of Jehovah" will be lifted up above all mountains (Isa 2:2). In that day, all nations (*goyim*) will stream into it, and many peoples (*'amim*) will go to the "house of the God of Jacob" (2:2–3). They will want God to teach them his ways so that they might walk in his paths (2:3). Furthermore, God will judge between the nations (*goyim*) and decide disputes between many peoples (*'amim*, 2:4). The result will be peace between nations (cf. Mic 4:1–3).

Isaiah 11 opens with a description of the reign of the Messiah leading to a golden age on the earth. The earth will be full of the knowledge of Jehovah as the waters cover the sea. At that time, Messiah will become like God's signal or banner for the peoples (*'amim*) and will attract all nations (*goyim*) to himself.

Isaiah 25 tells of a day when God will judge rebellious Gentiles (25:2). These previously ruthless nations will then serve and fear Him (25:3). Subsequently, Jehovah will prepare a banquet for all peoples (*'ammiym*) on his mountain (25:6—a reference to Zion). Furthermore, Jehovah will swallow up the "covering" which is over all peoples (*'ammiym*), i.e., the "veil" which is over all nations (*goyim*). This veil probably refers to the blindness of rebellion that has enveloped the nations of the earth, though it could symbolize their mourning in the presence of death (25:7).

Long before Isaiah, Solomon foresaw a time when foreigners from outside Israel would hear of God's name and power. They would come and gather in Jerusalem to pray "toward this house," the temple (2 Chr 6:32–33). Solomon invoked God to answer their prayers so that all the peoples (*'amim*) of the earth might know God's name and fear him along with the people of Israel.

Zechariah also saw a day when many nations (*goyim*) would join themselves to Jehovah and become his people (Zech 2:11). Here, the word *people* is the singular *'am* rather than the plural *'amim*, leading to a question: does this text imply that the nations will lose their distinctiveness and become a single people, or was Zechariah using the singular distributively, so that each nation becomes a people of God?

Other Scriptures speaking of the same event favor a multiplicity of peoples. Malachi foresaw of a time when many nations (*goyim*) will go to the house of God to learn his ways, and Jehovah will judge between many peoples (*'amim*, Mal 4:2–3). According to Micah, this event will occur "in the last days" (Mic 4:1–4). When God judges among many peoples, the result will be profound peace among the nations. Zephaniah 3:8–9 says that God will gather nations (*goyim*) to judgment, but then he will give to the peoples (*'amiym*) purified lips so that all of them will call upon the name of Jehovah. These and other passages indicate that the nations do not lose their individual identities, but that each nation becomes a people of God, submitting to Jehovah and following him.[9]

The multiplication of the peoples of God is vividly illustrated in Isaiah 19:18–25. The events in this passage occur after God judges Egypt by sending oppressors (19:20). Under distress, the Egyptians will cry out to Jehovah, and he will send them a savior and a mighty defender. Then there will be an altar to Jehovah in the middle of Egypt. A pillar at its border will mark Egypt as God's own. The Egyptians will present sacrifices and offerings to Jehovah. Furthermore, a highway will run between Egypt and Assyria (necessarily through Israel), so that Assyrians and Egyptians worship Jehovah together. At that time, Israel, Egypt, and Assyria will stand together as distinguishable peoples of God and channels of the Lord's blessing in the earth.[10]

Peoples of God

What is a people of God? A formal definition has been delayed to this point, mostly because the expression *people of God* is meaningless unless the term *people* is rightly defined. A people is a nation or people group, unified

---

[9] An unusual use occurs in Psalm 47:8–9, where *people* is used in both the plural and the singular. The text, which is eschatological, declares that God rules over the nations and that the princes of the peoples gather as the people of God. This context recognizes multiple nations and peoples, but the gathered princes are also called a people. Most likely the singular is being used distributively; each prince represents a people.

[10] Of course, nondispensationalists are not ignorant of the texts that I have cited here, but they apply the texts differently. For example, Geerhardus Vos, "The Eschatology of the Psalter," in the *Pauline Eschatology* (Princeton: Princeton University Press, 1930; repr. Phillipsburg, NJ: P&R Publishing, 1994), 347–48, views these texts as a missionary incentive for reaching individuals from many nations for inclusion in the church.

by its descent from a common ancestor and sharing a common language, culture, territory, and especially religion. A people normally devotes itself to the worship of a specific god or gods.

This definition of a people provides important clues for the meaning of *people of God*. A people of God is a nation that worships Jehovah, the true and living God. They are a people of God because he is their God and they are his people.

Isaiah's discussion of Egypt and Assyria highlights several features that distinguish peoples of God (Isa 19:18–25). After being judged, Egypt will erect an altar (which speaks of worship) to Jehovah in the middle of the land and a pillar (which speaks of identification) to Jehovah at its border. In other words, Egypt will turn *as a nation* to worship the true and living God. The Egyptians will cry out to God and God will send a savior and champion to deliver them. He will make himself known to Egypt, and Egypt will know him. Egypt will even make a vow to Jehovah, perhaps implying some covenant relationship. Because Egypt will respond rightly to the Lord's judgment, the Lord will heal them (19:20–22). These are the qualities that distinguish a people of God.

Amazingly, Assyria then enters the discussion (19:23–25). Egypt and Assyria were the two great powers that flanked Israel in the ancient world. When Israel broke God's covenant, he used both Egypt and Assyria as instruments of judgment. Nevertheless, someday the highway that runs from Egypt to Assyria (through Israel) will link these two ancient realms in the worship of the true and living God. They will forsake their idols and turn to him. In that day, Israel will be one of three on whom the Lord showers remarkable blessing. God himself will name them "Egypt My people, and Assyria the work of My hands, and Israel My inheritance" (19:25).

A people of God is distinguished by its worship of and sacrifice to the true and living God. It knows Jehovah because he makes himself known to it. It cries out to him, and he delivers it. It marks itself out as a nation under the name and rule of Jehovah. A people of God forsakes idols, turning toward other peoples of God and joining them in worshiping the one and selfsame God.

God wants the nations to worship him. He is not content with one people. He wants many, and he will have them. If God were to have only one people, then his temple could not be called a house of prayer for all nations

(Isa 56:7). Calling upon the nations to praise God makes no sense if those who praise God constitute only one people. The plurality of the peoples of God is implied by every Old Testament passage that exhorts the Gentiles (i.e., the nations or the peoples) to recognize Jehovah as the true and living God.[11]

Israel

From the time humanity divided into peoples after Babel, no nation devoted itself to the worship of the true and living God. That situation began to change with the calling of Abraham, whom God chose to be the father of many nations (Gen 17:4–8). God promised Abraham a blessing upon his offspring—a blessing that would extend to all the nations of the earth (22:15–18). When Abraham begat more than one son, God specified that the blessing would flow through Isaac (21:12). God later repeated the Abrahamic promise to Isaac (26:24) and then to Jacob (28:13–15). The nation that God would raise up through Abraham, Isaac, and Jacob would become his people.[12]

Seventy of Jacob's descendants accompanied him into Egypt—not yet a people. In Egypt, his offspring became numerous (Exod 1:7). Pharaoh was the first to recognize them as a people (1:9). Then, speaking to Moses, God called Israel as his own people (3:7). The events of the exodus transformed the children of Israel into a self-aware nation. These same events also turned the nation into a people of God. Rather than calling an existing nation to be his, God created an entirely new people to serve him.

Israel's identity as a nation was bound to its occupation of the Promised Land. This land was one part of God's original covenant with Abraham (Gen. 12:7; 15:18–21). For Israel, to be in the land was to be a people of God. To be out of the land was to lose identity as a people, especially as a people of God. Consequently, an obedient Israel would enjoy God's blessing *in the land* (Deut 28:8). A disobedient Israel would be driven from the land and reduced to servitude at the hands of foreign idolaters (28:36; 64–68). Scattered Israel

---

[11] Some interpreters (dispensational and otherwise) attempt to maintain national distinctions within a single people of God. One example is Robert L. Saucy, "Israel and the Church: A Case for Discontinuity," in *Continuity and Discontinuity: Perspectives on the Relationship Between the Old and New Testaments*, ed. John S. Feinberg (Westchester, IL: Crossway, 1988), 240

[12] Gentry and Wellum, *Kingdom through Covenant*, 243–44, contrast the goy that God promises to make of Abram with the mishpachoth that resulted from the division of Babel. In their view, the term *goy* suggests an organized political, social, and governmental kingdom of God in contrast to the "derogatorily termed" *mishpachoth* of Gen 10–11. This negative view of the division of people groups prior to Abraham, however, overlooks the importance of Acts 17:26, which declares God himself to be the determiner of all national identity and ascendency. While the division of nations was occasioned by sin, it is likely that God would have divided humanity into nations in any event.

would be called "not my people" (*lo-ammi*, Hos 1:9–11).

For Israel to be a people of God meant that God would make himself known to them. They would call out to him, and he would deliver them. He would be their God, and they would worship and sacrifice to him alone. They would bear his name and submit to his rule. The events surrounding the exodus, including the conquest of the land, brought Israel into this relationship to God.

The Marriage Metaphor

The biblical writers sometimes compared Israel's relationship with God to a marriage. For example, Ezekiel painted a word picture of Israel as an abandoned baby girl. In the analogy, God rescues the infant and saves her life. When the girl grows to maturity and is ready for marriage, God chooses her to become his own wife, and he swears the marriage oath to her (Ezek 16:1–8).

Where was this marriage oath sworn? The answer lies in Exodus 19–24, the most pivotal moment in Israel's history. With the newly delivered Israelites gathered at Sinai, God announced his intention to enter into covenant with them. If they kept his covenant, then they would be God's own possession among all the peoples, a kingdom of priests, and a holy nation (Exod 19:5–6). In response, the Israelites vowed to do all that the Lord said (19:8). Through Moses, God then stipulated the terms of his covenant, and the Israelites answered with one voice that they would obey (24:3). Finally, the Israelites repeated this vow while Moses sprinkled them with the blood of burnt offerings and peace offerings. Moses referred to this blood as the blood of the covenant which the Lord had made with them "according to these words" (24:5–8).

This event was the marriage ceremony of which Ezekiel would later remind Israel. It was the point at which Israel entered into God's covenant. It was the event that transformed a company of related individuals into a nation and into a people of God.

Later, when Israel was about to enter the Promised Land, Moses reminded a new generation of the events at Sinai: "The LORD our God made a covenant with us at Sinai." He insisted that the Lord had not made this covenant simply with their fathers, but with "all of us alive here today" (Deut 5:1–3). Moses then repeated the terms of the covenant, stating that Israel was "a people set apart" to God, a chosen people and treasured possession out of all the peoples of the earth (7:6).

After rehearsing these words with the children of Israel, Moses announced that they had become a people of God that very day (27:9–10). He arranged the tribes on the mountains of Gerizim and Ebal, pronouncing over them the blessings and curses that would follow obedience or disobedience. The covenant was reaffirmed with the generation that entered Canaan, just as it had been affirmed with the generation that left Sinai. The oath of Gerizim and Ebal represented a re-solemnization of the marriage vow that had been sworn at Sinai.

In the imagery, marriage depicts devotion. As a nation, Israel was to devote itself entirely to the Lord. To worship idols would violate the marriage vow and could consequently be seen as spiritual adultery. Later prophets pictured idolatrous Israel as an adulterous wife (e.g., Jer 3:1–10). Idolatry broke the marriage covenant between Israel and God (Jer 31:32). Consequently, God brought the nation under judgment, which was depicted as divorce (Hos 2:1–13). The effect of this divorce was to uncouple Israel from its status as a people of God (1:9).

God never intended this divorce to remain permanent. He promised that he would win Israel away from idols so that the nation would serve him alone. At that time he would betroth Israel to him forever so that Israel would once again become a people of God (2:14–23).

God's Purpose for Israel

From the first articulation of his promise to Abraham, God made two commitments. The first was that Abraham's descendants would become a great people. The second was that this great nation would become God's agent for blessing all the families of the earth (Gen 12:1–3). In other words, Israel was meant to function in a mediatorial role with other nations. This function was underlined by God's later promise that Israel would be "a kingdom of priests" (Exod 19:6). God wanted Gentile nations to see that Israel was called by his name (Deut 28:10). By devotion to Jehovah, Israel would draw other peoples to God and provide a model for them to emulate in their relationship with him.

The success of Israel's mediatorial role depended on obedience. If the Israelites obeyed God's voice, then they would be a kingdom of priests (Exod 19:5). God meant his laws to set Israel apart, to establish a difference between

Israel and the surrounding Gentile nations (Lev 20:26). By keeping God's laws, Israel would become an example to the Gentile nations. These nations would perceive Israel as a wise and understanding people. Jehovah would respond whenever Israel called on him, and the nations would marvel at God's availability to his people. The Gentiles would stand in awe before God's righteousness (Deut 4:5–8).

After Israel crossed the Jordan River into Canaan, Joshua erected a monument of twelve stones taken from the bed of the Jordan. This memorial served a double purpose. First, the memorial reminded the Israelites of the crossing of the Jordan, leading them to fear the Lord God forever. Second, the monument stood as a visible declaration to "all the peoples of the earth" of the strength of God's hand (Josh 4:20–24).

Centuries later, Solomon anticipated a time when Gentiles, hearing of God's great name and power, would travel to the temple in Jerusalem. They would pray toward the temple, and God would hear them. In this way the nations would come to fear God just as the Israelites did (1 Kgs 8:41–43).

This theme is repeated throughout the Old Testament. The children of Israel were to declare God's glory among the nations (Ps 96:3). They were to proclaim his mighty deeds (Ps 9:11). They were to declare his name and his wonders (Ps 105:1–2). The nations would see God's covenant faithfulness to the children of Israel. By perceiving the Lord's salvation and righteousness, all the nations would be moved to praise and worship the true and living God (Ps 98).

In all these ways, Israel was supposed to fulfill its mediatorial role among the nations. By drawing Gentile peoples into the worship of the true and living God, Israel would genuinely become a kingdom of priests. The nation would accomplish the purpose for which it had been called.

Israel's Future

Does the nation Israel have a future as a people of God? Dispensationalists are among those who affirm that it does, and other chapters in this book make that argument. The reasons need not be rehearsed here. Before this discussion is complete, however, it will need to return to the question of how Israel will be related to the church and other peoples during the eschaton.[13]

---

[13] Many nondispensationalists see a future for *ethnic* Israel (one might say *Israelites*) as saved Jews within the church. Millard Erickson, *Christian Theology*, 3rd ed. (Grand Rapids: Baker, 2013), 965, 970, asserts that believing OT Israelites have also been incorporated into the church. Dispensationalists, however, emphasize a future for *national* Israel as a people.

In the eschatological future, Israel will be restored to full blessing as a people of God. There will always be something special about Israel. Since Israel's mission was always to attract Gentile nations, however, Israel will someday be joined in the worship of Jehovah by many peoples. Egypt and Assyria are mentioned by name, but many others are implied. These nations will still be identifiable peoples with their own ethnicities. They will all stand with Israel as peoples of God.[14]

The Church

A people of God is first of all a people. A people is a nation. A people or nation is an ethnic unit, bound together by its solidarity with a common ancestor. These considerations seem beyond serious question.

They also present a problem. In the New Testament, the church is called a people of God. Furthermore, the church is often described by referencing Old Testament descriptions of Israel as a people of God (Rom 9:22–26; Titus 2:14; 1 Pet 2:9; cf. Exod 19:5–6; Hos 2:23). This phenomenon raises two questions. First, how can the church be called a people if a people is fundamentally an ethnic unit? Second, how is the church related to Israel, such that descriptions of the one can be applied to the other? These questions will be answered in order.

The Church as a People

The answer to the first question is that the church is constituted "in Christ." Romans 12:5 declares that church saints are one body "in Christ." Whether Jews, Greeks, slaves, free, male, or female, all church saints are one "in Christ Jesus" (Gal 3:28). They have now received every spiritual blessing in the heavenlies "in Christ" (Eph 1:3). They are accepted "in the beloved one," in whom they have redemption, namely the forgiveness of sins (Col 1:14). Positionally, they are now seated in the heavenlies "in Christ Jesus" (Eph 2:6).

The expression *in Christ* is used rather flexibly in the New Testament. It does not always function as a technical expression. Its referent does not always exclude believers during other dispensations. Nevertheless, when it references the church as in the citations above, the expression *in Christ* is

---

[14] Michael Vlach, "A Non-Typological Future-Mass-Conversion View," in *Three Views on Israel and the Church: Perspectives on Romans 9–11*, ed. Jared Compton and Andrew Naselli (Grand Rapids: Kregel, 2018), 21, 22n1; Michael Vlach, *He Will Reign Forever: A Biblical Theology of the Kingdom of God* (Silverton, OR: Lampion Press, 2017), 14–15 affirms the existence of these nations as "geo-political entities."

highly theologically significant. It implies that the church stands in some relationship to Christ that is not shared with any other people. Only the church has been so united to Christ as to constitute his body. This is the relationship that makes the church unique.[15]

This relationship is defined in 1 Corinthians 12:13, which informs Christians that "we all" have been baptized in or by one Spirit into one body. In context, the one body is clearly the body of Christ, of which every church saint is a member. The "we all" who compose this body includes at least Paul and the Corinthians but likely also Paul's co-author Sosthenes, as well as the other addressees of the book ("all who in every place call upon the name of our Lord Jesus Christ," 1 Cor 1:2). In other words, with reference to church-age believers, 1 Corinthians 12:13 is genuinely universal in scope.

Equally clearly, the word *Spirit* in 1 Corinthians 12:13 must refer to the Holy Spirit. In the immediately preceding context, the noun *pneuma* occurs in the singular no less than nine times. In every one of these occurrences, it refers to the Holy Spirit. Paul could hardly have shifted his usage of the term without giving his readers some clue as to what he was doing. The clear statement of this verse is that all church saints are baptized into one body in or by the Holy Spirit.

The question of whether this baptism is *in* or *by* the Spirit is really subordinate. Either way, this baptism is what unites church saints to Christ's body. During the present age, every believer becomes a member of the one body of which Christ is head (1 Cor 12:14–27; Eph 1:22–23; Col 1:18). The one body is even identified with Christ himself (1 Cor 12:12). Therefore, believers who have been united to the body of Christ are rightly said to be "in Christ." They are united to the Savior himself because the body is his.

All the other peoples of God are (or will be) constituted as peoples by their solidarity with a biological ancestor. The church is a people, not because of its natural genealogy but by virtue of its spiritual union with Christ. This union is what constitutes it both as a people and as a people of God.

In other words, the church is not merely a different people than every other people of God but actually a different kind of people. All peoples of God have a spiritual dimension because they all devote themselves to

---

[15] For a full discussion of "in Christ" language, as well as parallel expressions, see Constantine R. Campbell, *Paul and Union with Christ: An Exegetical and Theological Study* (Grand Rapids: Zondervan Academic, 2012). Campbell's meticulous work convincingly demonstrates that "in Christ" and related expressions can carry a variety of meanings.

worshiping the true and living God, who is spirit. Only the church, however, is spiritual in its very nature and constitution as a people. Only the church is united to Christ, and only the church is positionally seated with Christ in the heavenlies.

The spiritual constitution of the church carries significant implications. Since the church is a unique people with a unique nature, those who are incorporated into it become members of a new people. They receive a new identity that supersedes their old ethnic identifications.

The Church as the New Humanity

Given the foregoing, how is the church related to other peoples of God? Particularly, how is it affected by the distinction between Israel and the other peoples? This question is answered in at least two passages of Scripture. Both these passages make essentially the same point with respect to the church. One is Paul's discussion in Ephesians 2:11–22.

Paul was addressing Gentile believers (Eph 2:11). He reminded them that, before their conversion, they were ridiculed as *akrobustia* (literally, "foreskin," a coarse insult) by unsaved Jews (the self-identified "circumcision," whose only circumcision, however, was "performed in the flesh by human hands"). This derogatory attitude reflected the contempt with which many Jews viewed the Gentile world.

At that time, conceded Paul, Gentiles were in a sad plight. They were without Christ, aliens from the citizenship of Israel, foreigners to the covenants of promise, without hope, and without God in the world (Eph 2:12). In other words, they were in a position of distance from God and from his blessings.

During the Old Testament era, God viewed humanity under the rubric of two ethnicities. First were the Jews, who had many advantages. They were entrusted with the oracles of God (Rom 3:1–2). To them belonged the national adoption, the glory, and the covenants. To them was given the law, the temple rituals, and the promises. They were descended from the patriarchs. From them would come (humanly speaking) the Messiah (9:4–5). These privileges gave Israel a position of nearness to God.

The rest of humanity consisted of Gentile nations that enjoyed none of these privileges. God did not speak to them. He gave them no adoption, no covenants, no promises, no law. Lacking these and other advantages, the Gentiles were seen as "far off." Through His mediatorial work, however, Christ Jesus brought believing Gentiles into a position of nearness (Eph 2:13). Furthermore, he made peace where once only enmity existed. He broke down the barrier between Jew and Gentile and somehow made both into one (2:14).

God still reckons upon Jewish humanity and Gentile humanity—a Jewish race and a Gentile race (with all Gentile nations being viewed as an ethnic bloc). Indeed, Paul's argument in Romans 11 turns on a continuing difference between Israel and the Gentiles. Yet somehow both have been made into one. How? God has created out of Jewish humanity and Gentile humanity a new humanity (Eph 2:15). In other words, God has taken some who were Jewish and some who were Gentile, and out of these he has created a third category—so to speak, a third ethnicity. In this third ethnicity (this "one new humanity") some who were once Jews and some who were once Gentiles are united under a new identity and given a new solidarity. God has reconciled them in one body (2:17).[16]

That body is the body of Christ, which Paul has already identified in Ephesians 1:22–23. It is the very same body that is constituted of believers who are united to Christ by the baptizing work of the Spirit (1 Cor 12:13). Within this body, Christ is head and each believer becomes a member.

The implications are profound. When individuals are united to Christ by the Spirit, they become part of a new body and gain a new ethnicity. This ethnicity is defined by their union with Christ. Within the church their old ethnic identifications drop away. In Christ a Jew is no longer reckoned as Jewish, nor a Gentile as Greek, Barbarian, or Scythian (Col 3:11). When they believe on Christ, both Jews and Gentiles lose their old identities and become part of the new humanity. They are simply Christians.

Before Pentecost, God reckoned upon two categories: Jew and Gentile. Now God reckons upon three categories: Jews, Gentiles, and the church. The church *is* a people. It can be spoken of as a nation (1 Pet 2:9) in the biblical sense, but its solidarity comes from its spiritual identity in Christ rather than its genealogical identity in an ancestor. Consequently, the church stands as a

---

[16] *Pace* Gentry and Wellum, *God's Kingdom through God's Covenants*, 228, which suggests that when Paul speaks of one new man "he is obviously thinking of a new *Adam* and is saying that the *church*—by virtue of the new creation resulting from the resurrection of Jesus Christ, and by virtue of the union of head (Christ) and body (church)—constitutes this new Adam, a renewal of the Adamic role initiated with Abraham and his family." This inference is less obvious than Gentry and Wellum seem to think. The language about one new man or humanity is not a reference to Adam but to the two older humanities, Jewish and Gentile.

distinct people of God beside Israel. It will someday stand as a distinct people of God beside Gentile nations that will seek the Lord and will be called by his name.[17]

The Church, the Fold, and the Flock

Decades before Paul wrote Ephesians 2, Jesus foretold the union of Jews and Gentiles in the parable of John 10, where he illustrated the difference between Israel and the church by comparing them to a fold and a flock. The miracle story of John 9 is crucial to understanding this parable. In the earlier chapter, Jesus gave sight to a man who was born blind, selecting a method of healing that he knew would provoke the Pharisees. Eventually the Pharisees cast the man out of the synagogue (John 9:34), which was a highly significant act. The synagogue was more than a place of instruction and worship. It was the center of Jewish life, social interaction, and community activity. To be cast out of the synagogue was effectively to be put out of Israel. It was the most extreme measure that the Jewish authorities were authorized to take against a member of their community.

The formerly blind man was cast out because of his loyalty to Jesus. By the end of the narrative, he had clearly become Jesus's disciple. Once he was cast out, however, he was no longer reckoned as a member of the covenant community, no longer a recipient of the promises, and no longer an heir of the patriarchs. In terms of his standing as an Israelite, this was the worst thing that could have happened to him.

In the parable of John 10, Jesus reframed what had happened to the man, and he did it to make a point about his own intentions. Crucial to Jesus's parable is his reference to the sheepfold (10:1–6). As his listeners would have recognized, a fold (*aule*) was an enclosure in which sheep were kept. A fold is visible, tangible, and external. Sheep belonging to many flocks might share one fold. They were held together by external restraint; their unity was an external unity.

In Jesus's parable, the fold contains two kinds of sheep. Some belong to the shepherd (Jesus), while others do not. So what visible, external entity in

---

[17] A typical nondispensational interpretation of this text sees it moving, not from two peoples (Jews and Gentiles) to three peoples (Jews, Gentiles, and the church) but to only one people; Gentiles are now added to Israel within the one people of God. Thus, Riddlebarger states that, "in Christ, God takes the two peoples and makes them one." Further, Riddlebarger argues from Gal 3:28 that "Christ destroys all racial, gender, and socioeconomic distinctions in his kingdom." The last phrase in that sentence is illustrative. Dispensationalists believe that Paul applies these verses to the *church*, while at least some antidispensationalists apply them to God's *kingdom*. Kim Riddlebarger, *A Case for Amillennialism: Understanding the End Times* (Grand Rapids: Baker, 2003), 134–35.

the context of John 9–10 includes both some who follow Jesus and some who reject Jesus? The answer must be Israel. This answer is reinforced by Old Testament imagery presenting Israel as God's sheep (e.g., Isa 40:10–11). In the parable, Israel is the fold.

Jesus said that the shepherd calls his sheep by name, they hear his voice and follow him, and he leads them "out." Out of what? The answer again must be Israel. The healed man was only the first who, following Jesus, found himself outside of Israel. Jesus intended to sever his flock—those who truly believed on him—from the fold, which was national Israel. The parable implies that God was about to set Israel aside and to shift the focus of his work to some other people.

In the parable, those who follow Jesus constitute a flock (*poimne*). Unlike sheep in the fold (Israel), sheep in a flock are not unified by external and tangible things. They are kept together by something internal and organic. Each sheep hears the shepherd's voice and follows him. The source of their unity is invisible and internal. It is their following Jesus—at minimum, a metaphor for saving faith.

This parable had to be startling news for those who understood it, but Jesus went even further in John 10:16. He stated that he had other sheep that were never in the fold. These must be Gentile believers, and their presence raises an important question. What will be the relationship between Jesus's sheep that used to be in the fold and Jesus's sheep that were never in the fold? Jesus's answer was clear: his sheep will constitute one flock with one shepherd. Jesus did not intend to have separate Jewish and Gentile flocks. He intended to unite all of his followers in a single flock.

The one flock of John 10 is the same thing as the one body of 1 Corinthians 12:13 and the one new humanity of Ephesians 2:15. It is the church, which incorporates individuals who used to be reckoned as Jews and individuals who used to be reckoned as Gentiles. Within the church, those old identifiers drop away. Believers are simply one flock, Jesus's sheep without differentiation.

The church is a people of God. Because it is a people of God, it is like Israel in some respects, but it is also different. Israel was a visible nation with visible descent from a common ancestor. The church is a spiritual nation with invisible union created both by Spirit baptism and by following a common Shepherd. Israel and the church are both peoples of God, but they are not the same people. They are not even the same *kind* of people. The element that constitutes each as a nation is different.[18]

The Church and Israel

If Israel and the church are not the same people of God, then how can New Testament writers apply texts to the church that were meant for Israel? An example of this phenomenon occurs in 1 Peter 2:9–10, where Peter paraphrased multiple Old Testament passages and applied them to the church. One is Exodus 19:5–6, where God spoke to Israel at Sinai. Another is Hosea 2:23, in which God promised that he would restore blessing to Israel. Without any explanation or qualification, Peter applied these passages to the church. How could Peter make this application if Israel and the church are distinct peoples?

The answer to this question helps to guard against overplaying the distinction between Israel and the church. All forms of dispensationalism emphasize the discontinuity of these peoples, but some older dispensationalists saw virtually no connection or continuity between them. Some even assigned Israel to a permanent station as God's earthly people and the church to a permanent station as God's heavenly people. This difference was applied not merely in terms of their nature as peoples but in terms of their actual eternal destiny. Such a radical break, however, overlooks important elements of continuity between Israel and the church.[19]

Continuity and Discontinuity

What do Israel and the church have in common? First and most obviously, they share a common way of salvation. At all times and in all places, sinners have been justified by grace through faith. The ground of their justification has always been the finished work of Christ. Of course, later saints knew more than earlier saints about what God would have to do to secure their salvation. For this reason, the content of saving faith becomes more specific

---

[18] Bruce Ware sees the New Covenant as a critical component in constituting both Israel and the church as the people of God. In this sense he sees them as a united people of God. Nevertheless, he argues that in another sense they remain differing peoples of God. For Ware, the result is that "Israel and the church are in fact one people of God, who together share in the forgiveness of sins through Christ and partake in his indwelling Spirit with its power for covenant faithfulness, while they are nonetheless distinguishable participants comprising what is one unified people." See "The New Covenant and the People(s) of God," in *Dispensationalism, Israel and the Church: The Search for Definition*, ed. Craig A. Blaising and Darrell L. Bock (Grand Rapids: Zondervan, 1992), 96–97. It is not clear how Ware's definition improves on saying that Israel and the church are two peoples with certain common features, standing in an analogous relationship.

[19] Lewis Sperry Chafer, *Dispensationalism* (Dallas: Dallas Seminary Press, 1936), 107; Lewis Sperry Chafer, *Systematic Theology*, vol. 4 (Dallas: Dallas Seminary Press, 1948), 41, 47.

with the progress of revelation. Nevertheless, the exercise of faith in God and his gracious promises has always been the requirement for God to justify sinners.[20]

Israel and the church also share a common life of faith. All would agree that God prescribed different rules of life in different dispensations. For example, Israel had to observe dietary laws and to follow a sacrificial system that never applied to the church. Nevertheless, the underlying structure, enablement, and goal of godly living have remained substantially the same. The book of Hebrews—especially chapter 11—beautifully illustrates the commonality of the life of faith across the dispensations. Indeed, in some sense, apart from us (Christians), Old Testament believers will not be made perfect (Heb 11:40).[21]

Furthermore, both Israel and the church are branches from a common root (Rom 11:16–25). Interpreters disagree about the identity of the root, but dispensationalists normally hold that it cannot be Israel. Israel is represented by branches broken out of the tree. Gentiles are represented by branches grafted in. Whatever the root might represent, it is the common source that places both Israel and the church in a position of favor as peoples of God.

Another continuity between Israel and the church is suggested in Hebrews 3. The text states that Moses was faithful as a servant in God's entire household (3:2, 5). Then it says that Christ was faithful as a Son over the household, adding that "we are Christ's household if we hold fast to the glory and boasting of our hope to the end." This text appears to position both Moses and church saints within the same household of God even though they are distinct peoples.[22]

Finally and most obviously, Israel and the church both belong to the category of "people of God." Even though they are not the same people, they stand in an analogous relationship. The same will be true of other, future

---

[20] Amazingly, some contemporary covenant theologians continue to write as if the difference between their view and dispensationalism involved multiple plans of salvation. See, for example, Michael Horton, *Introducing Covenant Theology* (Grand Rapids: Baker, 2006), 111–12, 121–22.

[21] Robert H. Gundry, *The Church and the Tribulation: A Biblical Examination of Posttribulationism* (Grand Rapids: Zondervan, 1973), 22.

[22] Myron J. Houghton, *Law and Grace* (Schaumburg, IL: Regular Baptist Press, 2011), 84, states, "Whether Reformed or non-Reformed, conservative evangelical theologians agree that all believers, from the beginning of time until its end, are part of the family of God." Carl B. Hoch, Jr., *All Things New: The Significance of Newness for Biblical Theology* (Grand Rapids: Baker, 1995), 284, reasons that the one household of Hebrews 3 entails one people, which he separates "into different groups who lived during different eras of redemptive history." My response is that the "household of God" is essentially a trope, while "people of God" should be understood in a straightforward sense. Given this difference, it is quite reasonable to have distinguishable peoples or nations united in a single (metaphorical) household.

peoples of God. Israel and the church, however, have something in common that no others will share. The existence of both is tied to divine calling. God called both into existence explicitly in order to be his peoples. No other people of God will be able to make that claim. Other peoples will already have a long history as peoples *not* of God or even as peoples opposed to God. Only Israel and the church will never have existed as peoples before being called as peoples of God.[23]

Israel was not only constituted as a people of God but was also later reconstituted. After centuries of rebellion, God scattered Israel among the nations, essentially (though temporarily) rejecting the nation and dissolving its status as a people. That is the calamity behind Hosea's promises: the rejected people, the people-no-longer-a-people, will again be restored to its status both as a people and as a people of God.

These continuities explain why Peter could apply Exodus 19 and Hosea 2 to the church. The church is not Israel, but the church and Israel stand in analogous positions. Consequently, some of the things that God said about Israel in Exodus 19 he could also say about the church in 1 Peter 2. Some of the things that he said about Judah through Hosea were also true of the church once it began.

At one time, Israel was not a people. When God created Israel to be a people, he created the nation to be a possession of his own, a kingdom of priests, and a holy nation. After Israel was "unpeopled" by the captivity, God reconstituted the nation, declaring to those who were not his people, "You are My people" (Hos 2:23). In an analogous manner, God created the church on the day of Pentecost, calling it into being through the baptizing work of the Holy Spirit. Prior to that day, the church had never been a people, but now God was calling it to be his people. He was saying to those who had never been a people, "You are my people." Like Israel, the church was to be God's own possession, a royal priesthood, and a holy nation.

On a dispensationalist reading, Peter's use of Exodus and Hosea is entirely appropriate, not because the church is Israel but because the church and Israel are both peoples of God. Among all the nations, only they were

---

[23] Nondispensationalists understand this relationship differently. Stanley Grenz, *Theology for the Community of God* (Nashville: Broadman and Holman, 1994), 607, argued, "Just as Israel had been chosen to be the people of God—God's nation—so now the New Testament church enjoys this relationship. Despite the profound similarity between the two, there is also one important difference. No longer is status as God's nation based on membership within a specific ethnic group. Now people from the entire world are called together to belong to God; the church is an international fellowship comprising persons 'from every tribe and language and people and nation' (Rev. 5:9)."

created explicitly to be peoples of God. Their analogous positions represent a significant element of continuity that must not be ignored.[24]

God has dealt with both Israel and the church in distinct ways. Nevertheless, in terms of their standing *as peoples*, Israel and the church exhibit remarkable similarity. Because of this similarity, some things that can be predicated of Israel *as a people of God* can also be predicated of the church *as a people of God*. The analogy between them is the key.[25]

True Israel and Inward Jews

The continuity between Israel and the church is a continuity that comes from analogy. Both belong to the same class of things: peoples of God. Because they are both peoples of God, they exhibit similarities. Because they are not one and the same people, however, they also exhibit differences. Israel remains Israel, and the church remains the church.

Nevertheless, do not some Scriptures suggest a closer connection between Israel and the church? Can they not be read in ways that indicate actual identity between the two, as if the church has actually replaced Israel? To be complete, this discussion must examine at least some of the passages that appear to identify Israel and the church or even to make the church into a new Israel.

One side of the problem arises from Romans 2:23–29. Here, the apostle Paul was dealing with persons of Jewish descent (Israelites) who bore the mark of God's covenant with Israel (circumcision) and who boasted in the possession of God's law. Yet, by breaking the law, these Jewish people brought dishonor to God's name and caused it to be blasphemed among the Gentiles (2:23–24). For Paul, this was no new phenomenon, but was the very problem that had already been addressed by the prophets (Isa 52:5; Ezek 36:20).

---

[24] *Pace* Wayne Grudem, *Systematic Theology: An Introduction to Biblical Doctrine* (Grand Rapids: Zondervan, 1994), 863n1, "With all these evident New Testament examples of clear application of these promises to the church, there does not seem to be any strong reason to deny that this really is the only fulfillment that God is going to give for these promises." By way of contrast, Robert D. Culver, *Systematic Theology: Biblical and Historical* (Fearn, Ross-Shire, UK: Mentor, 2005), 822, observes that the continuity must not be pressed too hard: "If the church began at some point after the Ascension of Christ it is not specifically an extension of the people of God known as Israel, however many parallels may be drawn, or analogies, for our instruction. . . . Parallels drawn by New Testament passages between the Old Testament people and the New Testament people of God, the members of the church are then just that—parallels, analogies, types."

[25] Some of the more progressive dispensationalists take these continuities to indicate that Israel and the church, while distinct in some sense, are nevertheless the same people. See Glenn R. Kreider, "What Is Dispensationalism?" in D. Jeffrey Bingham and Glenn R. Kreider, *Dispensationalism and the History of Redemption: A Developing and Diverse Tradition* (Chicago: Moody, 2015), 18, 21, 24, 25; Craig Blaising, "God's Plan for History: The Consummation," in ibid., 210, 212, finds the mechanism for this union of many nations into one people of God in the indwelling Spirit who unites them to Christ and to one another.

To these individuals, Paul stated that circumcision is only useful for lawkeepers, not for lawbreakers (Rom 2:25). Indeed, he argued that lawbreaking had the effect of nullifying circumcision. Theologically, the reasons seem obvious. Circumcision was the sign of God's covenant with Israel. The law specified the terms of that covenant. To wear the badge that identified one with the covenant (circumcision) while violating the terms of the covenant (the law) was simply oxymoronic. Consequently, a lawbreaking Jew has no better standing before God than a Gentile. As Paul put it, "The one who is a Jew visibly is not [a Jew], and the one who is circumcised visibly in the flesh is not [circumcised]" (2:28).

Paul also addressed the opposite question. What about a Gentile (an uncircumcised person) who actually keeps the righteous demands of the law? What Paul probably had in mind was not a detailed observance of all 613 commands and prohibitions of the Sinai code but rather a life that was consistent with the righteousness that the law sought to foster. The apostle concluded that such a man uncircumcision "would be regarded as circumcision" (2:26).

In his summary statement (2:29), Paul brought together two ideas. First, being a true Jew is an inward matter. Second, true circumcision is a matter of the heart, a matter of what is praised by God and not by humans.

Did Paul mean to obliterate the distinction between Jews and Gentiles in general? Or to put it in other words, when Gentiles believe on Christ, in what sense are they reckoned as circumcised? Does their circumcision "of the heart by the Spirit and not the letter" mean that they are now reckoned as Jews and recipients of all the promises made to Israel as a people of God? These questions gain even greater force from other Scripture that speaks of church saints being circumcised in some sense.

Circumcision and the Church

Paul also discussed circumcision and church saints in Philippians 3. He was warning against false teachers, whom he labeled as dogs, evil workers, and the "mutilation" (Phil 3:2). The last term is a pun: *mutilation* (*katatomē*) plays on the word *circumcision* (*peritomē*). It is a slap at teachers who tried to persuade Christian Gentiles that circumcision was essential to their Christian lives. But Paul went even further; with ironic flair, he referred to these Judaistic teachers as *dogs*, a term that was typically applied to Gentiles by Jews. He certainly did not think much of these teachers or their message.

Paul insisted that if anyone could have confidence in the flesh, he could. He even recounted his qualifications: circumcised, an Israelite, a Benjamite, a Hebrew, a Pharisee, a persecutor of the church, and a blameless man as far as the law was concerned (3:3–6). These external qualifications, however, were exactly what Paul had to abandon for the sake of Christ (3:8). They constituted a righteousness of his own that derived from the law (3:9). In its place, he recognized his need for a righteousness that came from God on the basis of faith. Only in that way could he be found to be "in Christ" and know him, the power of his resurrection, and the fellowship of his sufferings, being conformed to his death. Paul saw a stark contrast between the righteousness that derives from the law and the righteousness that comes from God. This contrast corresponds to the earlier contrast between the *katatomē* (the mutilation or false circumcision; i.e., the purveyors of Judaizing theology) and the *peritomē* (the true circumcision).

According to Paul, true circumcision includes those who worship by the Spirit of God, who glory in Christ Jesus, and who place no confidence in the flesh. In other words, the true circumcision comprises people who have appropriated the righteousness that comes from God, rejecting their own righteousness that derives from the law. Paul specifically said that "we" are the circumcision, and in this context "we" can only mean church saints—Paul and the Philippians.

Church saints—those who believe on the Lord Jesus Christ—are the circumcision. Paul's words here (Phil 3:3) correspond closely with his insistence that true circumcision is inward rather than outward (Rom 2:29) and that even a Gentile who keeps the righteousness of the law will be reckoned as circumcised (2:26). No reasonable reading of Paul can avoid the affirmation that church saints are, in some meaningful sense, among the circumcised.

Many serious students of the Bible see these texts as major obstacles to recognizing Israel and the church as distinct peoples of God. They reason that if the church is the circumcision and if the circumcision necessarily means Israel, then the church has become Israel. This understanding leaves scant room for a two-peoples doctrine, let alone for a teaching that God will someday have many peoples.

At least one other understanding of the text is possible, however. The church might be the circumcision, and yet not be Israel. How can that be? In order to answer that question, a detour through the biblical notion of circumcision is necessary.

Circumcision Outer and Inner

God first commanded circumcision in Genesis 17:11 as a token of the covenant that he had made with Abraham. It was to be applied not only to Abraham and his descendants but also to servants who were born in his house and to slaves he had purchased from foreigners (17:12–13). Circumcision modified the body as a sign that God had chosen Abraham and his offspring. It was a mark of inclusion in the promised nation. In principle, to be circumcised was to claim a share in the promise and to wear the badge of participation as an heir. Paradoxically, however, the introduction of circumcision also implied that not everyone who received the sign would actually receive the promise. At the very time that Abraham was commanded to institute circumcision, he was clearly told that Ishmael would not receive the promise (17:18–21). Nevertheless, Ishmael received circumcision (17:26).

From Ishmael onward, it should have been clear that circumcision was neither an efficacious means of gaining nor an infallible sign of possessing the promise. All those who were heirs of the promise were required to receive circumcision, but not all those who received circumcision became heirs of the promise. Something more was always required.

The need for something more than outward identification was reinforced by the events that followed the exodus. God delivered the Israelites from Egypt and led them into the wilderness, where they were constituted as his people. They were under the cloud, they passed through the sea, they were baptized into identification with Moses in the cloud and the sea, and they all ate the same spiritual food and drank the same spiritual drink (1 Cor 10:1–4). By these events, the nation became devoted externally and visibly to God. Nevertheless, God was not pleased with most of them, and struck them down in the desert (10:5). Even though the nation was devoted externally and visibly to God, most of the individuals within the nation fell under God's judgment instead of his blessing. Only two of the men who left Egypt would enter the Promised Land.

God judged Israel because the inner dedication of the Israelites did not match their external position. Externally, they constituted a nation set apart to God. They all wore the mark of that devotion—circumcision. Internally, however, their hearts were often hardened toward God. Outwardly, they wore the sign of the covenant, but inwardly they were rebels.

Before the Israelites went in to take possession of the Promised Land, Moses warned them against their inward rebellion. He urged them to fear God, to obey him, and to serve and love him with all their heart and soul (Deut 10:12). To do this, they would need to change their minds toward God and to alter their attitudes from rebellion toward submission and devotion. In short, the Israelites would have to repent. The metaphor that Moses used for this repentance and devotion was to "circumcise the foreskin of [their] heart[s], and stop being stiff-necked."

The metaphorical use of the word *circumcision* was not new. When Moses wanted to express his inability to speak properly about divine things, he said that he had "uncircumcised lips" (Exod 6:12, 30). In other words, he believed that his speech was not sufficiently disciplined and developed in the area that he was supposed to address. To have "circumcised lips" would mean to devote oneself to the task of framing speech about divine things until one could discourse about them freely.

Similarly, to circumcise the heart is to devote oneself to the things of God, to learn to fear him, to study obedience and submission, and most of all to cultivate a genuine love for him with all one's heart and soul. A circumcised heart is the opposite of a stiff neck. The latter is resistance and rebellion, the former is repentance and devotion. Physical circumcision was a symbolic outward badge of devotion to God in a covenant relationship. Circumcision of the heart was a metaphor for real inward devotion to God for his own sake—the very thing that the New Testament calls *regeneration* or being *born again.*

Earlier in the Pentateuch, God spoke of a future time when he would bring judgment on rebellious Israel (Lev 26:14–39). He also promised that when the Israelites confessed their treachery and hostility, he would remember his covenant with the patriarchs and restore them (26:40–45). God described the condition of Israel as that of treacherous rebels by saying that they had "uncircumcised hearts" (26:41) that needed to be humbled.

Much later, the prophet Jeremiah foretold a time when God would judge both the circumcised and the uncircumcised. Amazingly, he listed Judah among the Gentile nations, observing that "all the nations are uncircumcised"

(Jer 9:25–26). But he immediately clarified this juxtaposition by declaring that "all the house of Israel are uncircumcised of heart." This language anticipates what the apostle Paul would say in Romans 2:25–29. Jeremiah also spoke of the "uncircumcised ears" of God's people (Jer 6:10). He equated uncircumcised ears with unwillingness to receive God's message because they "have no delight in it." Stephen echoed this language in his address to the Jewish leadership when he announced that they were "uncircumcised in heart and ears" (Acts 7:51), which he also identified as "resisting the Holy Spirit."

The solution for Judah was to "circumcise [them]selves to the Lord, and remove the foreskins of [their] hearts" (Jer 4:4). Again, the circumcised heart speaks of an inner change, of repentance, of a shift in disposition from rebellion against God to devotion toward him. This change was an individual responsibility for each Old Testament Israelite, but it was also a national duty. The thrust of the New Covenant was that God would someday work this inner change for the entire nation. Jeremiah referred to it as God writing his laws on their hearts (31:33). Ezekiel spoke of it as God taking away their heart of stone and giving them a new heart, a heart of flesh (Ezek 36:26). The earliest form of this promise occurs in Deuteronomy 30:6, in which God promised to circumcise their heart.

This new heart, this heart of flesh, this circumcised heart, was promised to the nation as a whole. Yet it was always available to the individual. Indeed, all individual Israelites had a duty to circumcise their hearts. To have a circumcised heart was simply to believe the Lord God for his promise. To have an uncircumcised heart was to rebel against him in unbelief.

From the Pentateuch onward, the Old Testament maintains a contrast between inner and outer circumcision. Outer circumcision is the external mark of a participant in the covenant or one who is devoted to God. Inner circumcision is a metaphor for repentance followed by genuine inner devotion to God. The Old Testament nowhere indicates that inner and outer circumcision can substitute for each other. A son of Israel who truly trusted and loved God could not imaginably have neglected outer circumcision. By the same token, outer circumcision without inner devotion could neither secure God's blessing nor deliver from God's judgment. These are the themes that lie behind New Testament references to Gentile believers as "the circumcision."

Heart Circumcision and the Gentiles

If indeed the circumcision of the heart is equivalent to regeneration, then every saved individual of every era has experienced it. Regeneration has never been restricted to a particular people or nation. Consequently, many who were not circumcised physically have experienced the circumcision of the heart. Every pre-Abrahamic believer would have been externally uncircumcised but internally circumcised. For some time Abraham himself would have been in this position. No Israelite female was circumcised physically, but any who were regenerated would have experienced the circumcision of the heart. Gentile believers such as Barzillai, Naaman, and Ebed-Melech were not outwardly circumcised, but their hearts were.

Circumcision of the heart conferred spiritual benefits, though it did not bring Gentile believers under the specific promises of God to Israel. It was also necessary for the children of Israel. According to Romans 2:25, people who were formally within Israel might as well be uncircumcised if they were unregenerate. The absence of inward circumcision would disqualify them from experiencing the blessings of the nation. On the other hand, Gentiles who experienced regeneration could properly be spoken of as circumcised since they really were circumcised inwardly.

When Paul wrote as if regeneration constitutes a kind of circumcision, he was saying nothing new. Both circumcisions were included in the message of the Old Testament from Moses onward. Since both were in play throughout the Old Testament, neither could be made to serve in the place of the other. This is the point that Paul was making at the end of Romans 2. He was not suggesting that believing Gentiles become Jews, but that they share the inward circumcision. By the same token, he was not arguing that external circumcision is a matter of indifference for Jews, but that it is not a sufficient condition for entering into the covenant blessings. As in the Old Testament, neither circumcision can substitute for the other.

Paul's point in Philippians 3 is identical. Without inward circumcision, the outward act is merely so much mutilation, certainly nothing in which to take pride. On the other hand, those who truly believe in God through Christ (worship God in the spirit and rejoice in Jesus Christ) enjoy a true inward circumcision. They are genuinely regenerated. This inward circumcision does not transform Gentiles into Jews, but it is something that both Israelites and Gentiles must experience if they are going to enjoy God's blessing.

God promised a circumcision of the heart to the entire nation of Israel, and someday he will keep that promise. What is promised to the nation *as a nation*, however, is presently available to any individual. It always has been. God wants individuals to be born again, and his Spirit performs this transformation in all who believe. All believers have been regenerated; they have experienced inner circumcision. In this sense, even Gentiles who believe may be reckoned among "the circumcision" (i.e., those who have experienced repentance and inner transformation).

Peoples of God in the New Earth

Israel was the first, and for many centuries the only, people of God. Nevertheless, even within the Old Testament, God revealed a purpose that extended to other peoples. The initial form of the Abrahamic Covenant included blessing for all the families of the earth (Gen 12:1–3), and Paul recognized that this promise included the salvation of the Gentiles. Passages such as Psalms 67 and 117 imply that God wants many nations to devote themselves to his worship. And why not? In individual salvation, God displays the abundance of his grace by extending salvation to many (Rom 5:15). Why, then, in national calling, should God's exhibition of grace be restricted to only one?

During the millennium, God will exhibit his pluriform grace by calling many peoples. Many nations will offer their worship to God through Israel's Messiah. While Israel will retain a unique position (Zech 8:20–23), many peoples and mighty nations will come to seek Jehovah Tsabaoth and to entreat His favor.[26]

What happens to these peoples after the end of the millennium? Even among dispensationalists, opinions vary. Originally, the human race was a single people with no division into separate nations (Gen 11:6). Only after Babel did humanity begin to fragment into distinct peoples. The existence of nations is a consequence of God's judgment on a disobedient humanity. Hypothetically, the lifting of the judgment could mean that the human race would once again become a single people, undivided into nations. All national distinctions would vanish, all of redeemed humanity would be one people, and this one people would be the people of God.

This is a glorious vision, and it includes several elements that resonate

---

[26] These nations will be reconstituted from saved survivors after the destruction of the nations at the end of the tribulation. See Matt Waymeyer, *Amillennialism and the Age to Come: A Premillennial Critique of the Two-Age Model* (The Woodlands, TX: Kress, 2016), 277–78.

with anyone who desires God's glory. Furthermore, it is not necessarily incompatible with dispensationalism. Yet God has not worked in a parallel way with respect to individual salvation. When believers stand in their glorified bodies, they will not be presented as if they had never sinned. On the contrary, God will get glory precisely from the fact that they were sinners who have been redeemed and sanctified and glorified. The fact of their previous sinful condition will serve to magnify God's grace and multiply the glory that redounds to God. If this pattern is appropriate for individual believers, might not something similar be appropriate for believing nations? Rather than restoring the human race to its original, seamless uniformity, might God not choose to highlight different aspects of his grace by receiving the adoration of many peoples and placing them on display forever?

The clearest hints about the glories of eternity future are found in the closing chapters of the book of Revelation. These chapters describe the everlasting home of all believers, the New Jerusalem. Revelation 21:3 speaks of this city as a place where God dwells among humans. Then the text becomes ambiguous: some manuscripts read that "they will be His people [singular]," while other manuscripts say that "they will be His peoples [plural]." The most likely reading is *peoples*, referring to multiple nations or peoples of God even in eternity future. Since the reading is disputed, however, other evidence would be helpful.[27]

That evidence can be found later in the passage. Revelation 21:24 says that the nations will walk by the light of the city, and the kings of the earth will bring their glory into it. Then Revelation 22:2 states that the leaves of the tree of life are for the wellbeing of the nations. These constitute clear indications that the new earth will include multiple nations offering worship to God. Throughout all the unending ages, God will have peoples and not merely a people.[28]

---

[27] The view that multiple nations will become one and that "all ethnic and racial distinctions will disappear" is advocated by (among others) Grant R. Osborne, *Revelation*, BECNT (Grand Rapids: Baker, 2002), 578; see also Osborne's *Revelation Verse by Verse* (Bellingham, WA: Lexham, 2016), 226–227, 230. The view that multiple peoples will enter eternity is represented by Robert L. Thomas, *Revelation 8–22: An Exegetical Commentary* (Chicago: Moody, 1995), 444, 476–78, 484–85. James Montgomery Boice put the view bluntly: "Nothing will abolish distinctions between nations. There will always be nations," *Foundations of the Christian Faith*, rev. ed. (Downers Grove: InterVarsity: 1986), 575. Robert Culver, *Systematic Theology*, 1098, also notes and favors the plural *peoples*.

[28] Similar views are expressed by Erich Sauer, *From Eternity to Eternity: An Outline of the Divine Purposes* (Grand Rapids: Eerdmans, 1954), 55; Houghton, *Law and Grace*, 86, 99; Vlach, *He Will Reign Forever*, 48–49; John MacArthur and Richard Mayhue, eds., *Biblical Doctrine: A Systematic Summary of Bible Truth* (Wheaton: Crossway, 2017), 831–32. On the other hand, Herman A. Hoyt, *The End Times: Biblical Eschatology* (Chicago: Moody, 1969), 230–31, complicates the picture unnecessarily. Hoyt believed that the new earth will be populated by both glorified saints (from both testaments) and unglorified tribulation saints, who keep their natural bodies. I see no reason to suppose

Every nation has its own culture, perspectives, and expressions. Each nation can see and say something about God better than any other nation. Each nation can learn something about God's glory from every other nation. The inhabitants of each nation should be listening to other nations for their unique understandings of God's grace.

God is using the nations to create a chandelier rather than a spotlight. If humanity were a single people, God could focus the light directly on a few aspects of his character, but other aspects might remain obscure. A multiplicity of peoples, however, will reflect the manifold glory of God, each highlighting some aspect that might otherwise remain unseen. For all the unending future, God's variegated glory will be reflected through the multiple perspectives of the many peoples of God.[29]

---

that tribulation saints will not be glorified in connection with the judgment at the end of the millennium. Nevertheless, Hoyt is quite correct to see a role for Israel, the church, and the nations in the new earth.

[29] Amillennialist Michael Horton captures the right sensibility when he writes that "all the nations stream not to Sinai but to Zion for their part in the new creation, in the great parade of the creature kingdoms before their Creator in the everlasting Sabbath day," *Introducing Covenant Theology*, 128. If we disagree about the details, we nevertheless yearn together for the day when God's glory will be on full display.

Biblical Covenants and Their Fulfillment

William D. Barrick
The Master's Seminary
Los Angeles, California

God's written revelation displays an amazing unity from Genesis through Revelation. An examination of that revelation reveals a grand vista in which Scripture focuses on the message concerning Jesus as Messiah of Israel and Savior of the world. As Messiah and Savior, Jesus fulfills the prophetic word of God. Another aspect of the full scope of Scripture is its theocentric message about knowing God—to know God is to know Christ, his Messiah, and to know Christ is to know God the Father (e.g., John 6:45; 14:7; 17:3). The early messianic elements of progressive revelation find their fulfillment when Jesus Christ, the second Adam, completes the created potential initially given to the sinless pre-fall Adam (see Ps 8; Heb 2:5–8). In the same fashion, Israel's covenanted potential also comes to completion in Jesus Christ. So where can Israel's covenanted potential be discovered? How can we understand its significance for God's theological program? The answer is that the covenants the Hebrew writers identified as such in the Old Testament provide us with knowledge concerning Israel's potential as part of God's kingdom program as well as his redemption program.

Readers of Scripture who desire to know more about the biblical covenants seek the meaning and purpose of the biblical covenants. Some questions to ask include the following: What is a covenant? Why did God enter into covenants with his people? How has God, does God, or will God fulfill his covenants? How do those covenants relate to the concept of dispensations in Scripture? Only biblically based answers will suffice; we must avoid basing our answers on white spaces in the Bible's text. This study purposes to illumine the believer's mind regarding the fulfillment of the covenants within the scope of their interrelationship with biblical dispensations.

Biblical Covenants

Some readers might wonder why dispensationalists focus on the concept of biblical covenants. Many students of the Bible tend to associate biblical covenants with covenant theology rather than with dispensational theology.

However, dispensationalists must emphasize the significance of the biblical covenants because Scripture itself speaks very precisely about those covenants. Also, the biblical covenants relate directly to biblical prophecy. Indeed, dispensationalists track redemptive history through the biblical covenants.[1] Likewise, biblical covenants provide us with the progressive development of God's kingdom program. Scripture uses the term *covenant* to identify stages in progressive revelation as the Bible unfolds God's plan for his people. Without the biblical covenants we cannot develop a biblical dispensationalism. In fact, the Scriptures are far more specific about the covenants than about the dispensations. Therefore, the topic demands our attention.

According to Scripture, God established six covenants with the nation of Israel: the Abrahamic Covenant, the Mosaic (or Sinaitic) Covenant, the Priestly (or Zadokite) Covenant, the Deuteronomic (or Palestinian) Covenant, the Davidic Covenant, and the New Covenant. The Noahic Covenant is the only other definitive covenant specifically identified in the Old Testament. God did not establish that covenant with Israel but with all humanity and all animal life (Gen 9:8–17). Through the Noahic Covenant, God obligated himself to preserve, provide for, and rule over all that he had created in the beginning.[2] The rainbow became not only a sign of the Noahic Covenant but also of the constancy of the divinely established environment that makes the planet hospitable to life in all its amazing forms.[3] The purpose and content of the Noahic Covenant set it apart as a different covenant than those which God later made with Israel. Certain covenant elements present in the Israelite covenants are absent in the Noahic Covenant, such as a seed (or offspring/descendants), a blessing, a land, a nation, and a kingdom.[4]

The apostle Paul wrote of these six Israelite covenants when he identified the Israelites as those "to whom belongs the adoption as sons and the glory

---

[1] T. Maurice Pugh, "Dispensationalism and Views of Redemption History," in *Dispensationalism and the History of Redemption: A Developing and Diverse Tradition*, ed. D. Jeffrey Bingham and Glenn R. Kreider (Chicago: Moody Publishers, 2015), 234–35, explains this focus involved in the dispensational viewpoint.

[2] Peter J. Gentry and Stephen J. Wellum, *Kingdom through Covenant: A Biblical-Theological Understanding of the Covenants* (Wheaton: Crossway, 2012), 161.

[3] For a fuller discussion of the Noahic Covenant as a theological covenant, see Irvin A. Busenitz, "Introduction to the Biblical Covenants: The Noahic Covenant and the Priestly Covenant," *TMSJ* 10, no. 2 (Fall 1999): 173–89 (esp. 183–86).

[4] The Noahic Covenant does manifest a relationship to God's kingdom program by means of its mandate, which, according to Gentry and Wellum, *Kingdom through Covenant*, 174, indicates that "the human community must express obedient sonship in faithful love to the creator God and rule over the creation with humble Servanthood and responsible stewardship." I have listed these elements in their logical and historical order although most appear in God's initial revelation to Abraham (Gen 12:1–3) and in the Abrahamic Covenant's subsequent restatements.

and the covenants and the giving of the Law and the *temple* service and the promises" (Rom 9:4). Table 1 (below) identifies the five previously mentioned covenant elements with regard to each of these six biblical covenants. The original covenant, the Abrahamic Covenant, reveals all five elements as God unilaterally and unconditionally announced the stipulations involved with each of the biblical covenants. But what is a covenant—how can we identify Genesis 15:1–21 as a statement of the Abrahamic Covenant? First, God himself said that he was making a covenant with Abraham (15:18). Secondly, that which God called a "covenant" consisted of his making a declaration regarding his relationship to and plan for his chosen people (15:5–7, 13, 18). Thirdly, God proclaimed certain stipulations either that he himself identified with the covenant (15:13–16, 18–19) or that he indicated should be obeyed by his people (as in the Mosaic Covenant). Fourthly, a sacrifice often accompanied the establishing of the covenant 15:9–10).

Table 1: The Elements of Biblical Covenants

	Seed	Blessing	Land	Nation	Kingdom
Abrahamic[5]	•	•	•	•	•
Mosaic[6]		•	•	•	•
Priestly[7]		•	•	•	•
Deuteronomic[8]		•	•	•	•
Davidic[9]	•	•	•	•	•
New[10]		•	•	•	•

The contents of the Israelite covenants reveal how God intends to fulfill both his kingdom and redemption programs on earth. His programs' purposes are fivefold: (1) to reveal himself, (2) to glorify himself, (3) to conform his people to his kingdom program, (4) to redeem humans from sin, and (5) to restore his fallen creation.[11]

---

[5] Gen 12:1–3; 15:1–21; 17:1–8; 22:15–18.

[6] Exod 19–24.

[7] Num 25:10–13; Jer 33:17–18; Ezek 48:11

[8] Deut 27–30; 29:1–9.

[9] 2 Sam 7:8–16.

[10] Jer 31:27–40.

[11] In regard to the conditionality of the biblical covenants, even the Abrahamic Covenant includes a condition— obedience. Abraham had to leave Ur of the Chaldeans. Such conditionality does not mean that God will not fulfill the covenant. He will never fail to fulfill his covenants—their ultimate fulfillment is never in jeopardy.

Theologically, each covenant may be associated with a particular attribute of God's character. Although some divine attributes might fit with more than one covenant, Table 2 presents a potential identification of divine attributes for each covenant. Theologians too often overlook the theocentric nature of the Israelite covenants. The divine attributes as a focus of biblical covenants arise out of the fact that God calls upon his people to reflect his character in how they live out the terms of each covenant. The covenant recipients display the Lord's communicable attributes in their behavior so that they declare to everyone that they are his people and he is their God ("I will also walk among you and be your God, and you shall be My people," Lev 26:12). We should consider this identification as a covenant obligation. According to Schreiner, "The substance of the covenant was a pledge to be faithful to covenant obligations."[12] Thus, both the covenant maker (God, the Sovereign Lord) and the covenant recipients (vassals) have obligations to fulfill. The first obligation of the recipients consists of identifying themselves with the Lord of the covenant by displaying attributes that demonstrate that they belong to him

Table 2: The Biblical Covenants and Divine Attributes

Covenant	Attribute	Scripture
Abrahamic	God is good and kind. He is the source of all blessing.	Exod 1:20; 18:9; cp. Gen 15:13–16
Mosaic	God is righteous. He is the source of all righteous laws, judgments, statutes, and decrees.	Deut 4:8; 32:4; Ps 119:137–138
Priestly	God is holy. He calls his people to holiness through the concepts of sacrifice and priesthood.	Num 25:10–13; Ezek 48:11
Deuteronomic Covenant	God is faithful to fulfill his promises. Among his promises that of land attains special prominence for Israel.	Jer 32:41; cp. 2 Cor 1:18–20
Davidic	God is sovereign. As Creator, he intends through the greater son of David to fulfill his original intent regarding man as vice-regent.	Pss 2:4–9; 8:6; 22:28; 72:8–11; 110:2
New	God is forgiving. His final covenant focuses on this necessary aspect of his redemption program.	Jer 31:34; Eph 4:32; cp. Ps 32:1–2; Matt 9:2–6; Luke 24:46–47

---

[12] Thomas R. Schreiner, *The King in His Beauty: A Biblical Theology of the Old and New Testaments* (Grand Rapids: Baker Academic, 2013), 217.

Announcing his covenants on behalf of his servants, the Lord God typically proclaimed them at times of crisis or change for his people. At such times their sovereign and benevolent God allowed circumstances for which they needed his mercy, forbearance, and goodness. The promulgation of a covenant instructed his people to focus on him rather than on their circumstances. Let's look at each of the Israelite covenants from this perspective of crisis and change.

1. Abrahamic Covenant

In Genesis 12:1–3, God commanded Abraham to leave his family and his homeland. Obedience to the divine mandate required Abraham to leave Ur and all its idolatry in order to serve the living God in a new and distant land. God promised that Abraham's descendants ("seed") would become a blessing to all the world. When God inaugurated his covenant with Abraham in Genesis 15:1–21, he chose the Hebrews as his possession and his official representatives on earth as vassals to the Abrahamic Covenant. The selection of Abraham and his descendants represented change. It required Abraham to separate from idolatry and to depart from Mesopotamia. Abraham's migration to Canaan testified to the fact that God had chosen a specific people for himself to serve him in a location of his choosing. In the initial (or, near) fulfillment, the Hebrew people were vassals of the covenant. The far fulfillment will take place following a continual narrowing of the covenant people's identity through the passing generations. From Abraham's descendants the Lord selected only the descendants of Isaac; from Isaac's descendants he chose only Jacob's descendants. Eventually the focus narrows to the tribe of Judah among the sons/tribes descended from Jacob; then, out of Judah's descendants God chose David. This narrowing line of descent leads to the Messiah, the greater son of David and the Lion of the Tribe of Judah. Of all Abraham's descendants (seed), the Messiah will bring the ultimate blessing on the world, and he will establish his Davidic throne over the future millennial kingdom.[13]

2. Mosaic Covenant

The covenant that God gave to Moses on Mount Sinai separated Israel from Egypt, removing the nation from slavery (Exod 19:1–6). Out of all Abraham's descendants, God selected the Israelites as his special possession and identified

---

[13] See Keith H. Essex, "The Abrahamic Covenant," *TMSJ* 10, no. 2 (Fall 1999): 191–212.

them as his covenant vassals. By his promulgation of the Mosaic Covenant, God demanded his people's obedience to his law (Torah). The covenant's stipulations (or, obligations) consisted of the statutes, ordinances, and commandments of the law. The near fulfillment applied to the nation of Israel and to its citizens individually and corporately. The covenant's distant fulfillment, however, awaits the future messianic kingdom during which time the Lord will repeat his former instructions to Israel, so that they might finally learn the significance of the sacrificial system that he had commanded them to observe (cf. Ezek 40–48).[14]

3. Priestly Covenant

How did the Priestly Covenant gain a place among God's other covenants with Israel? It focused on a specific line of Levi's descendants, the Zadokites (Ezek 40:46; 48:11; Zech 6:13). The selection and separation of the Zadokites from among the Levites heralded a discontinuation of the high priesthood at some point in God's future program with Israel. In fact, Jesus eventually became high priest at God's appointment even though he descended from Judah, not Levi (Heb 5:4–10). An inherent relationship existed between the Mosaic and the Priestly Covenants because the obedience required of the priests involved obeying the law of Moses. Phinehas (Num 25:10–13) had proven zealous for God's holiness, so God rewarded him by choosing his descendants to serve alongside the future Messiah in his kingdom (Jer 33:17–18).[15]

4. Deuteronomic Covenant

Major mileposts in Israel's history included the miraculous crossing of the Red Sea (Exod 14–15) and the miraculous crossing of the Jordan River (Josh 5). The latter event separated Israel from the wilderness just like the earlier event separated Israel from Egypt. The similarities speak to their historical and theological significance. God promulgated the Mosaic Covenant at Mount Sinai, and thirty-eight years later Moses announced the Deuteronomic Covenant on the Plains of Moab. As the Scriptures explain, this covenant was not the same covenant as the one proclaimed at Sinai. Therefore, it was more than just a renewal of the older covenant (Deut 29:1–9).[16] There is a degree of continuity since both covenants

---

[14] See my fuller discussion of the Mosaic Covenant as a theological covenant in William D. Barrick, "The Mosaic Covenant," *TMSJ* 10, no. 2 (Fall 1999): 213–32.

[15] For a fuller discussion of the Priestly Covenant as a theological covenant, see Busenitz, "Introduction to the Biblical Covenants," 186–89.

[16] Other scholars also identify this covenant as separate from the Mosaic: "Deut also adds to the Horeb covenant another, made in the land of Moab, prior to the entry into the land, a covenant that seems to be a renewal of the former

required Israel's obedience to the law as God's people. The Deuteronomic Covenant, however, focused specifically on a new era, a new beginning, within the land of promise itself, Canaan. Referring to this covenant as the "Palestinian" Covenant results in an anachronistic misnomer because Moses proclaimed this covenant at a time when that region's identification was Canaan, not Palestine. Palestine does not exist as a historical title for that geographical location until the Persian period, although the Persians refused to officially recognize the region by that name. Subsequent to the Israelite conquest of Canaan, the territory was known primarily as Israel until the Persian era.[17]

5. Davidic Covenant

When Israel rejected God as their only King (theocratic rulership), they reached a key point in their history catapulting them into yet another major crisis (1 Sam 8). They wanted to crown one of their own as their king (human monarchy). Saul's kingship had failed to live up to high expectations because he did not submit his will and desires to the nation's true King, Yahweh (1 Sam 16). Back in Genesis 49:10, God had announced through Jacob that King Messiah would descend through the tribe of Judah. Indeed, the prophetic record narrowed the expectation to a specific clan within the tribe of Judah according to Micah 5:2. The ever-narrowing focus concentrated on the line of David. Obedience to the Torah still stood as the standard of conduct since the Davidic Messiah must be obedient in fulfilling the law.[18]

6. New Covenant

Last among the six biblical covenants with Israel, the New Covenant revealed the ultimate spiritual blessing: forgiveness of sins. Jeremiah 31:27–40 identified the ultimate separation as the separation from sin. In actuality, God already had provided a preview of the New Covenant at the time he told Moses that

---

and similar in character"; Gordon J. McConville, "תּירֹב," in *NIDOTTE*, ed. Willem A. Van Gemeren (Grand Rapids: Zondervan, 1997), 1:750. The Deuteronomic Covenant is sometimes given the title of Palestinian Covenant. See also Renald E. Showers, *There Really Is a Difference: A Comparison of Covenant and Dispensational Theology* (Bellmawr, NJ: Friends of Israel Gospel Ministry, Inc., 1990), 77–83; Charles Caldwell Ryrie, *The Basis of the Premillennial Faith* (Neptune, NJ: Loizeaux Brothers, 1953), 58–59; Otto Eissfeldt, *The Old Testament: An Introduction*, trans. Peter R. Ackroyd (New York: Harper & Row, 1965), 214–17, 226, 230.

[17] On the issue of the name *Palestine*, see H. G. M. Williamson, "Palestine, Administration of: Persian Administration," in *Anchor Bible Dictionary*, 6 vols., ed. David Noel Freedman et al. (New York: Doubleday, 1992), 5:82. "Gk. *Palaistinē* occurs first in the writings of Herodotus, who uses it imprecisely for the Philistine coast from Syria to Egypt (Herodotus *Hist* vii.89)"; "Palestine," in *Eerdmans Bible Dictionary*, ed. Allen C. Myers (Grand Rapids: Eerdmans, 1987), 790; see also J. M. Houston, "Palestine," in *New Bible Dictionary*, 3rd ed., ed. D. R. W. Wood and I. Howard Marshall (Downers Grove, IL: InterVarsity Press, 1996), 855.

[18] For a fuller discussion of the Davidic Covenant, see Michael A. Grisanti, "The Davidic Covenant," *TMSJ* 10, no. 2 (Fall 1999): 233–50.

there must be a covenant differing from the Mosaic Covenant. In Deuteronomy 30, God revealed to Moses that the circumcision of the heart supersedes the circumcision of the flesh. Whereas physical circumcision operated as the symbol (or sign) of the Abrahamic Covenant, spiritual circumcision served as the New Covenant's sign. Israel still remained as God's people; God established the New Covenant with *them* (see Jer 31:31, 38–40). This tying of the New Covenant with Israel does not indicate that New Testament Christians have no relationship to or benefit from the New Covenant. Hebrews 8:6–10:39 speaks about the high priestly ministry of Christ (including his offering himself as the ultimate sacrifice to initiate a covenant) and the salvation of New Testament believers in terms familiar to the New Covenant in Jeremiah 31 (cp. Luke 22:20). All New Covenant blessings experienced by the church are routed through Israel via the Messiah, Israel's covenant Lord and King. Israel still owes covenant obedience to the Mosaic law, but they will obey from a new heart recognizing the spirit of the law, not just the letter of the law (cp. Rom 2:25–29; 7:6; 2 Cor 3:6).[19]

The preceding summary of the six biblical covenants with Israel progressively and chronologically unfolds divine revelation for God's covenant people. God has revealed his program step by step in successive periods of time. Each covenant adds to the previous covenant to expand its purview. However, throughout the succession of progressively revealed covenants in Scripture no covenant supersedes or nullifies any previous covenant. None of the covenants accomplish or provide salvation from sin. Instead, God's people only inherit the covenant blessings after their salvation spiritually. In addition to the historical crises noted above with regard to the establishment of each covenant, the individual covenant proclamations lead to a subsequent event of significance:[20] (1) following the Abrahamic Covenant, Israel's sojourn in Egypt, the house of slavery; (2) following the Mosaic Covenant, Israel's wandering in the wilderness for violating the first commandment even as God was giving the two tablets of the law to Moses on Mount Sinai; (3) following the Priestly Covenant, the corruption of the Levitical priesthood; (4) following the Deuteronomic Covenant, Israel's failure to completely conquer and inherit the land of Canaan; (5) following the Davidic Covenant, the Davidic dynasty's disobedience to the law of God and their apostasy,

---

[19] For a greater discussion of the New Covenant and its relationship to both Israel and to the church, see Larry D. Pettegrew, "The New Covenant," *TMSJ* 10, no. 2 (Fall 1999): 251–70.

[20] Biblical references for each covenant appear in the footnotes to Table 1.

leading to exile in Babylon; and, (6) following the church's participation in the New Covenant, the great tribulation or "time of Jacob's distress" (cf. Jer 30:7; Dan 12:1; Rev 7:14) that will occur before Israel finally turns to God in true faith.

The Lord God of Israel has always revealed to his people his goodness and kindness, righteousness, holiness, faithfulness, sovereignty, and grace-filled forgiveness. These divine attributes encompass the theological heritage of the biblical covenants with Israel. Repeatedly, the Lord tests his people with regard to the degree to which their goodness, kindness, righteousness, holiness, faithfulness, rulership, and forgiveness reflect his attributes. Historically, their failure to consistently live godly lives in obedience to covenant stipulations has led to harsh circumstances brought about through divine judgment.

Biblical Dispensations

Turning now to the topic of biblical dispensations, we will briefly examine their relationship to and comparison with the six biblical covenants. A detailed identification and description of the individual dispensations would require a much longer study than the current one. A biblical term *dispensation* (equivalent to the NT Greek word *oikonomia*, "administration of a household"; 1 Cor 9:17; Eph 1:10; 3:2, 9; Col 1:25; 1 Tim 1:4) identifies God's "household rules" governing his people in different eras throughout the history of the human race. In other words, instructions concerning how someone ought to behave as a member of God's household change over time. Today a father might use the same concept to explain how his twenty-something son must live under "house rules" as long as he chooses to live in his parents' home. However, those house rules will be altered somewhat in recognition that the son is no longer the fifteen-year-old he had been just a few years prior. God reveals his will (either through oral or written revelation) to his people, so that they might know how to live for him as they change, the times change, and the geographical location or setting might also change. Each era brings new or added revelation built progressively on prior revelation to explain the changing requirements for the subsequent period of time (and sometimes the new geographical setting) God's people are entering.

We can take God's household rules involving his people's diet as an example of progressive revelation providing a series of changes in what God expects of his people or allows for his people. Table 3 presents those changes in diet as revealed in the Scriptures.

Table 3: God's People and Their Divinely Changed Diets

Era	Diet	Scripture
At creation	Vegetation	Gen 1:29
After the fall	Vegetation and possibly meat[21]	Gen 3:21; 4:4, 20
After the flood	Addition of meat from wild game	Gen 9:2–4
Post-Sinai (under Mosaic law)	Meat from clean animals only	Lev 11; Deut 14
Church age	All previous dietary restrictions removed	Acts 10:9–15; 1 Tim 4:3–5
Future messianic kingdom	A possible return to Edenic conditions, or to the restrictions of Mosaic law[22]	Isa 11:6–9; Ezek 40:38–43; 43:18–27; 44:28–31; 45:13–25

Thus, since God has changed the diet of his people from one era to the next, perhaps we should be searching the Scriptures for similar time-limited changes in other areas of his people's daily lives. The matter relates to Scripture-sanctioned lifestyle, not to salvation from sin.

We cannot emphasize too strongly that, though God's instructions for how his people live out their lives have changed from time to time, the message of the gospel for salvation has not changed. Throughout all periods of human history, the message of salvation from sin preserves the same essential elements. Consider the historical continuity of the following theological elements related to the message of salvation:

- *The need for salvation:* humanity's fallen, disobedient, sinful condition
- *The instrumentality:* by faith, not by works
- *The object of faith:* always the Messiah alone
- *The work of the Messiah:* his substitutionary sacrifice in his death and his resurrection from the dead
- *The recipients:* both Jew and Gentile—people from throughout the whole world
- *The result:* forgiveness of sins and a right relationship to God

---

[21] In the post-fall era, the use of animals for clothing (Gen 3:21) might imply the use of the meat as food, as well as Abel's offering of the fat of slaughtered animals from his livestock (4:4, 20). The Scriptures, however, make no specific mention of a change in humanity's diet.

[22] Space does not permit a discussion of the issue concerning the millennial sacrifices. For a succinct statement of the problem through a covenant theologian's eyes, see Robert L. Reymond, "The Traditional Covenantal View," in *Perspectives on Israel and the Church: Four Views*, ed. Chad G. Brand (Nashville: B&H Publishing Group, 2015), 33. For a dispensationalist's response, see Charles H. Dyer, "Ezekiel," in *Bible Knowledge Commentary: Old Testament*, ed. John F. Walvoord and Roy B. Zuck (Wheaton: Victor Books, 1985), 1305, and John C. Whitcomb, "Christ's Atonement and Animal Sacrifices in Israel," *Grace Theological Journal* 6, no. 2 (Fall 1985): 211–17.

What elements have changed? Only the time perspective changes: the time prior to the work of Messiah in his death and resurrection and the time following his accomplished work. The people prior to Messiah's work looked *forward* to the fulfillment of the messianic prophecies; the people living after Messiah's work look *back* on the past fulfillment of the same messianic prophecies. Therefore, Peter revealed that the ancient prophets never asked "Why?" "How?" "Who?" "What?" "For whom?" or "With what result?" They only asked "When?" and "In what kind of time?" (1 Pet 1:9–12).[23] God gave progressively clearer revelation regarding the details of salvation from sin, but that message of salvation was sufficient throughout every era, and many believed and were saved by it.

Readers of Scripture can identify eight potential dispensations by identifying (1) the content of progressive stages in divine revelation, (2) the changes in the household rules, and (3) the divine judgments responding to continued and endemic disobedience to divine revelation. Careful identification of the extent of biblical texts potentially associated with each possible dispensational era will depend on (1) the general purpose and content tied to a specific period of time, (2) the initial revelation marking commencement of the period, and (3) the judgment marking the closing of the period. In the Scriptures, God has revealed past, present, and future dispensations. An example of a future dispensational period of time involves the revelation concerning the messianic kingdom occurring in many of the prophetic books in the Old Testament. Therefore, the following outline of possible dispensational eras may depend on a variety of texts outside the general framework of texts utilized here.

1. The Dispensation of Innocence (Gen 1:1–3:21)
2. The Dispensation of Conscience (Gen 3:22–8:12)
3. The Dispensation of Human Government (Gen 8:13–11:32)
4. The Dispensation of Promise (Gen 12:1–Exod 18:27)
5. The Dispensation of Law (Exod 19:1–Acts 1:26)
6. The Dispensation of Grace/the Church (Acts 2:1–Rev 19:21)
7. The Dispensation of the Messianic Kingdom (Rev 20:1–15)
8. The Dispensation of the Eternal Kingdom (Rev 21:1–27; 22:1–5)[24]

---

[23] The NASB's translation ("what person or time") of τίνα ἢ ποῖον καιρὸν in 1 Pet 1:11 represents but one interpretation of the four Greek words. An alternate interpretation, equally supported lexically and grammatically, consists of "which or what kind of time." This second view seems more in keeping with the near context and the remoter context of all prophetic revelation. See Thomas R. Schreiner, *1, 2 Peter, Jude*, NAC, vol. 37 (Nashville: Broadman & Holman Publishers, 2003), 73–74.

[24] See the following works for the development of these different dispensations: Charles Caldwell Ryrie, *Dispensationalism Today* (Chicago: Moody Press, 1965) and Charles C. Ryrie, *Dispensationalism*, rev. ed. (Chicago: Moody, 2007).

An Intricate Interrelationship

With these things in mind, let's attempt to track the interrelationship between the biblical covenants and divine dispensations. In order to understand the dispensations, we must first grasp the significance of dominion and the role of fruitfulness and multiplication. God's mandate in Genesis 1:28 was to "be fruitful and multiply, and fill the earth, and subdue it; and rule over the fish of the sea and over the birds of the sky, and over every living thing that moves on the earth." The phrase "rule over" ought to turn the mind to the topic of God's kingdom program. His kingdom ought not to be limited to the millennial kingdom of Christ. The millennial kingdom represents the final outworking of God's kingdom program over a world marred by the fall. However, the Lord's universal kingdom exists through all time (Ps 10:16). The universal kingdom's realm includes all the created universe, not just humans, not just planet Earth (Ps 103:19; Isa 24:23). High King and Sovereign over the kingdom is God himself. Nevertheless, he chose to rule his kingdom mediately through the human beings he created (Ps 59:13; cf. Ps 8). Thus, the unfallen Adam served as God's first mediatorial ruler—vice-regent to the Creator himself, as he intended (cp. Ps 8:4–8; Heb 2:5–9; 2 Tim 2:12).

Humans are not God, so no human being could rule over the earth alone. Even with Eve's help as his God-appointed co-regent, the unfallen Adam could not fulfill all that God planned. Therefore, to fulfill their kingdom role, Adam and Eve had to "be fruitful and multiply." God thus determined to exercise his kingship over planet Earth by multiplying co-regents. An increase of fruitfulness and population growth (cf. Isa 60:22) in the future messianic kingdom will also accompany the reign of joint heirs and rulers with Christ in his messianic kingdom (Rev 20:6). Yes, God intended all of this at creation, but Adam's disobedience interrupted the program until the one "born of a woman" (Gal 4:4; cp. Gen 3:15) could become the second Adam. Messiah, as the "Son of Man," will fulfill humanity's originally intended role as the human race's only perfect representative.[25]

Hebrews 2:8 states, "But now we do not yet see all things subjected to [Christ]" because his mediatorial kingdom has not begun. When Christ does take the Davidic throne, even the current "ruler of this world," Satan (John 12:31; cp. Eph 2:2, "the prince of the power of the air"), will be subject to the Messiah and his kingdom. As long as Satan continues to reign as "ruler of

---

[25] See a fuller discussion of God's kingdom in William D. Barrick, "The Kingdom of God in the Old Testament," *TMSJ* 23, no. 2 (Fall 2012): 173–92.

this world," the Messiah's kingdom has not yet commenced. That is exactly why Jesus taught his disciples to pray with accuracy, "Your kingdom come" (Matt 6:10).

The dispensational eras began with three that involve the whole of the human race in regard to their created potential in God's programs of kingdom and redemption. God revealed his kingdom program and what he planned regarding the participation of humanity (Gen 1:26–28) at the outset of the *Dispensation of Innocence* (Gen 1:17–3:21). Following Adam's disobedience, the Creator revealed that his program of redemption would involve the woman's "seed" (3:15). Next, in the *Dispensation of Conscience* (Gen 3:22–8:12), Scripture records how God set about to provide for humans, especially regarding the problem of sin. God began by providing Adam and Eve with clothing made from animal skins (3:21). Immediately thereafter, Scripture tells of the sacrifices brought by Cain and Abel. Evidently, God had provided instructions about sacrifices, perhaps through their father, Adam. Soon after, humans started calling on Yahweh (4:26), perhaps expecting God to respond by sending the victorious "seed" (offspring) of the woman promised in 3:15. Such a hope certainly seems to have been in Lamech's thinking when he named his son Noah ("comfort"; 5:29). The conscience of fallen humanity could not deal adequately with the sinful behavior erupting throughout the human population, so God brought this era to a close with a catastrophic global flood as his judgment (6:1–8:12).

The *Dispensation of Human Government* (Gen 8:13–11:32) may be adopted as a title for the third dispensation. During this period of time, God allowed human beings to organize themselves for fulfilling their mandate to rule over the earth. In so doing, they continued to make use of earth's resources (as they had already done in the pre-flood world according to 4:17–22) for sustaining human life, worship, and cultural development. However, instead of combining their resources and efforts to accomplish something good, humans chose, once again, to rebel against their Creator. In an outright abuse of their God-given mandate to rule over the earth, they tried to add heaven itself to their self-appointed kingdom. Again, as with Eve (3:1–5), Satan appears to have enticed them to follow the pattern of his own rebellion to fulfill his desire to rise above the throne of God (Isa 14:13–14). The result was another global judgment at Babel to divide humans into separate language groups and spread them across the world (11:5–9).

Because these three dispensations precede the history of Abraham and the ultimate selection of Israel from among his descendants, they do not possess any connection with the biblical covenants God made with Abraham's descendants. However, this brief introduction to biblical dispensations provides a foundation for suggesting a preliminary outline for developing this trajectory in future studies to explore the interrelationship between the six biblical covenants with Israel and the next five dispensations.

The following proposal outlines the potential overlapping progress of these dispensations and their parallel biblical covenants. An analysis of the relationships will uncover Israel's historical, theological, and spiritual potential with regard to God's programs of kingdom and redemption.[26]

Table 4: Overlapping Relationships between Biblical Covenants and Dispensations

Covenants	Dispensations
Abrahamic Covenant Gen 12:1–3; 15:1–21; 17:1–8; 22:15–18	*Dispensation of Promise* Gen 12:1–Exod 18:27
Mosaic Covenant Exod 19–24 *Priestly Covenant* Num 25:10–13; Jer 33:17–18; Ezek 48:11 *Deuteronomic Covenant* Deut 27–30; 29:1–9 *Davidic Covenant* 2 Sam 7:8–16 *New Covenant* Jer 31:27–40	*Dispensation of Law* Exod 19:1–Acts 1:26
New Covenant Jer 31:27–40	*Dispensation of Grace/the Church* Acts 2:1–Rev 19:21
	Dispensation of the Mediatorial Kingdom Rev 20:1–15
	Dispensation of the Eternal Kingdom Rev 21:1–27; 22:1–5

---

[26] My earlier foray into this extended topic can be found published online in eight parts in 2016 by Dispensational Publishing House in a blog series: https://dispensationalpublishing.com/tag/william-d-barrick/; accessed May 9, 2022. See especially Parts 5–8. Parts 1–4 of that series include topics covered by this chapter.

Conclusion

A brief study can provide only an introduction to this topic (or perhaps, series of topics), transporting the biblical student into an ever-expanding field of study. Biblical dispensations and covenants involve not only an analysis of human history (dispensations) and Israel's history (covenants) but also an analysis of prophetic revelation concerning the Messiah from Genesis through Revelation. Both of God's programs (kingdom and redemption) require development along the lines of progressive revelation, relating the programs to each covenant and each dispensation. Recurrent threads of continuity and discontinuity help to draw appropriate distinctions and to identify true similarities (or even identical entities). The entire interaction between covenants and dispensations demands more study to demonstrate how they fit into the overarching metanarrative of Scripture.

In addition to history and prophecy, the study of covenants and dispensations leads to an examination of how God expected his people to live in each particular era under its respective covenant(s) or corpus of revelation. Such an analysis will undoubtedly reveal additional continuities and discontinuities. For example, how did God's expectations for Israel under Mosaic law differ from his expectation for Christians under the New Testament? How might Matthew 22:34–40 be included in the answer? If the gospel for salvation is the same in all eras, do other theological subjects exhibit a kernel of unchanging truth(s)? Another topic involves the relationship between pre-Israelite humanity, Israel, and the church. It might be pointed out that we must also talk about the peoples populating a post-church planet following the rapture. Can the church fulfill the Old Testament prophecies identified with Israel? Replacement theology argues for the church replacing Israel and the elimination of any future for Israel.[27]

In other words, there is much yet to pursue in studying God's written revelation. As we do so, we must avoid inverting the respective roles of theology and hermeneutics. Dispensationalism is not a hermeneutic, and neither is covenantalism. A biblical theology of both covenants and dispensations must arise out of the consistent application of a proper and consistent method of hermeneutics. Dispensationalism should be the result of a consistent application of literal-grammatical-historical hermeneutics. In this postmodern age the development of a proper hermeneutic must battle the influence of a prevailing hermeneutic of doubt and the denial of absolute truth.

---

[27] For an outstanding reply to replacement theology, see Michael J. Vlach, *Has the Church Replaced Israel? A Theological Evaluation* (Nashville: B&H Academic, 2010).

In our efforts to expand this study, may our prayer ever be,

> Lead me in Your truth and teach me,
> For You are the God of my salvation. (Ps 25:5)

The "Kingdom of Heaven/God" and the Church: A Case Study in Hermeneutics and Theology

R. Bruce Compton
Detroit Baptist Theological Seminary
Allen Park, Michigan

Among the issues that continue to divide evangelicals, two are addressed in this essay. The first issue is the meaning of the New Testament expressions *kingdom of heaven* and *kingdom of God*. The second issue is the relationship of this kingdom to the church.[1] The debate over these issues raises three related questions. The first question concerns the nature of the kingdom. Do these expressions refer metaphorically to a spiritual kingdom, literally to a physical kingdom, or to both? The second question is linked to the first: is this kingdom already in existence or is it yet to come? The third question is about the relationship between the kingdom and the church. Are the kingdom and the church identical entities in God's unfolding plan of redemption, or are they distinct?

I will address these questions in the following steps. First, I seek to determine whether the expressions *kingdom of heaven* and *kingdom of God* are synonymous or refer to distinct kingdoms. Next, I present the major evangelical views on the meaning of the two expressions, along with the theological systems represented by each. Third, I examine the key texts in the debate. My approach to these texts is intentionally deductive. I begin with the assumption that these expressions refer to a still-future kingdom over which Jesus will reign and then seek to determine whether the evidence from the key texts supports this assumption. Finally, the discussion concludes by exploring the relationship between the kingdom of heaven/God and the church.

Synonymous or Distinct Kingdoms?

The first step in answering the above questions is to determine whether *the kingdom of heaven* and *the kingdom of God* are synonymous phrases or refer to two distinct kingdoms. Looking at their use throughout the New Testament,

---

[1] For a broader theological perspective, see the discussion in Nicholas Perrin, *The Kingdom of God: A Biblical Theology* (Grand Rapids: Zondervan, 2019), 23–36.

the two expressions are not distributed equally. The expression *kingdom of heaven* is found only in Matthew's Gospel, where it is used thirty-four times.[2] In contrast, the expression *kingdom of God* is used four times in Matthew,[3] fourteen times in Mark, thirty-two times in Luke, twice in John, six times in Acts, eight times in Paul's letters, and once in Revelation.[4]

Although most interpreters treat the two expressions as synonymous, older dispensationalists often distinguished the kingdom of heaven from the kingdom of God. These older dispensationalists understood *kingdom of heaven* to refer to Jesus's future messianic kingdom and defined it as a worldwide kingdom that includes both saved and unsaved. They understood *kingdom of God* to refer to God's universal, spiritual rule over the redeemed. These two kingdoms are related in that all who are members of the kingdom of God are also participants in the kingdom of heaven.[5]

The problem with this distinction is that it runs counter to the evidence. Particularly in view is the evidence from the Synoptic Gospels, where most uses occur and where comparisons can be made. For example, whenever Matthew records a statement by Jesus referring to the kingdom of heaven, parallel passages in Mark and/or Luke invariably use *kingdom of God* instead of Matthew's *kingdom of heaven*.

Thus, in Matthew 19:23, Matthew records Jesus declaring, "It is hard for a rich man to enter the kingdom of heaven." In the next verse, Matthew records Jesus essentially repeating the declaration, except that he uses *kingdom of God* instead of *kingdom of heaven*: "It is easier for a camel to go through the eye of a needle than for a rich man to enter the kingdom of God" (19:24).

The parallel account in Mark 10:23–25 records the same two declarations. The difference is that Mark uses *kingdom of God* in both declarations. In 10:23, Mark records Jesus declaring, "How hard it will be for those who are wealthy to enter the kingdom of God." Then, in 10:25, Mark records Jesus declaring, "It is easier for a camel to go through the eye of a needle than for a rich man to

---

[2] *Kingdom of heaven* occurs as a secondary reading in John 3:5.

[3] *Kingdom of God* is one of several variants in Matt 6:33. The genitive "of God" is placed in the text in brackets and given a {C} rating in Barbara Aland, Kurt Aland, Johannes Karavidopoulos, Carlo M. Martini, and Bruce Metzger, eds., *The Greek New Testament*, 5th ed., rev. (New York: United Bible Societies, 2014), 21.

[4] I. Howard Marshall, ed. *Moulton and Geden Concordance to the Greek New Testament*, 6th ed., rev. (London: T & T Clark, 2002), 144–46.

[5] John F. Walvoord, *Matthew, Thy Kingdom Come: A Commentary on the First Gospel* (Grand Rapids: Kregel, 1974), 30–31.

enter the kingdom of God."

Both Matthew's account and Mark's account record these declarations of Jesus in connection with the story about the rich young ruler. As such, the two accounts cite Jesus's words in the same historical context. Consequently, what Matthew records Jesus declaring about the rich and the kingdom of heaven, Mark records Jesus declaring about the rich and the kingdom of God. Moreover, in Matthew's account, the initial declaration about the rich uses *kingdom of heaven*, while the subsequent statement, essentially repeating the first, switches to *kingdom of God*.

Such parallel references imply that the two expressions *kingdom of heaven* and *kingdom of God* are virtually synonymous and are used interchangeably.[6] Such parallels occur both between Matthew's and Mark's Gospels, and within Matthew's Gospel itself. For that reason, most dispensationalists agree with interpreters in general that there is no distinction between the two expressions.[7]

Why does Matthew prefer *kingdom of heaven*, while Mark and Luke always use *kingdom of God*? Perhaps because Jews treated the names of God with the greatest reverence and often would use a euphemism such as *heaven* in place of the divine name so as not to violate the sanctity of God's name.[8] Writing primarily to Jews, Matthew reflects this practice and uses *kingdom of heaven* as a euphemism for *kingdom of God* to protect the religious sensitivities of his readers. Furthermore, Matthew can do this without violating Jesus's authorial intent in that the two expressions are synonymous and refer to the same kingdom.

This is not to say that Matthew avoids using God's name altogether. In fact, the name *God* appears over fifty times in his Gospel. When Jesus linked God's name with the expression *kingdom*, however, Matthew felt constrained to use a euphemism to guard God's transcendent holiness and to

---

[6] While agreeing that the two expressions have the same referent and denotation, Pennington demurs regarding the two having the same nuance or connotation. He argues that the expression *kingdom of heaven* highlights certain nuances not necessarily found in the expression "kingdom of God." Specifically, the expression *heaven* in Matthew's Gospel highlights "the tension that currently exists between heaven and earth, between God's realm and ways and humanity's, especially as it relates to God's kingdom ('the kingdom of heaven') versus humanity's kingdoms." See Jonathan T. Pennington, *Heaven and Earth in the Gospel of Matthew*, vol. 26 in Supplements to Novum Testamentum (Leiden: Brill, 2007), 7, 279–330.

[7] Herbert W. Bateman IV, "Dispensationalism Yesterday and Today," in *Three Central Issues in Contemporary Dispensationalism: A Comparison of Traditional and Progressive Views*, ed. Herbert W. Bateman IV (Grand Rapids: Kregel, 1999), 23–31.

[8] See, for example, Dan 4:26; Matt 21:25; Luke 15:18, 21.

avoid offending his Jewish readers.[9] The four times Matthew uses *kingdom of God* are all in citations where, apparently for contextual reasons, he records the actual expression Jesus used.[10]

Major Views

While most today agree the two expressions are synonymous, there is continuing debate over the identification of this kingdom. At the risk of oversimplification, there are roughly three views. The first is that the expressions *kingdom of heaven* and *kingdom of God* refer principally to Christ's present spiritual rule over the church. This view is generally embraced by those who hold to either amillennialism or postmillennialism, including both traditional covenant theologians and some progressive covenantalists.[11]

The second view is that the expressions *kingdom of heaven* and *kingdom of God* refer essentially to Christ's future earthly rule in the millennial kingdom. While allowing for exceptions, traditional dispensationalists generally champion this view.[12]

The third view represents a combination of the first two. Depending on the context, the expressions *kingdom of heaven* and *kingdom of God* may refer either to the present spiritual rule of Christ over the church or to the future earthly rule of Christ in the millennial kingdom. This is the view often supported by covenant premillennialists, progressive dispensationalists, and some progressive covenantalists.[13]

As mentioned earlier, this study assumes that the expressions *kingdom of heaven* and *kingdom of God* in the New Testament refer primarily to Christ's

---

[9] So Leon Morris, *The Gospel According to Matthew*, PNTC (Grand Rapids: Eerdmans, 1992), 52–53; David L. Turner, *Matthew*, BECNT (Grand Rapids: Baker, 2008), 39, 41–42, 107. Contra, among others, R. T. France, *The Gospel of Matthew*, NICNT (Grand Rapids: Zondervan, 2007), 101.

[10] Matt 12:28; 19:24; 21:31, 43. Similarly, Pennington, *Heaven and Earth in the Gospel of Matthew*, 303–10.

[11] For those representing amillennialism, see Anthony A. Hoekema, "Amillennialism," in *The Meaning of the Millennium: Four Views*, ed. Robert G. Clouse (Downers Grove, IL: InterVarsity Press, 1977), 155–87; Robert B. Strimple, "Amillennialism," in *Three Views on the Millennium and Beyond*, ed. Darrell L. Bock (Grand Rapids: Zondervan, 1999), 83–129. For those representing postmillennialism, see Loraine Boettner, "Postmillennialism," in Clouse, *The Meaning of the Millennium*, 117–41; Kenneth L. Gentry, Jr., "Postmillennialism," in Bock, *Three Views on the Millennium*, 13–57. Gentry's discussion represents theonomic postmillennialism.

[12] Herman A. Hoyt, "Dispensational Premillennialism," in Clouse, *The Meaning of the Millennium*, 63–92.

[13] Representing covenant premillennialists, see George Eldon Ladd, "Historic Premillennialism," in Clouse, *The Meaning of the Millennium*, 17–40; representing progressive dispensationalists, see Craig A. Blaising, "Premillennialism," in Bock, *Three Views on the Millennium*, 157–227; representing progressive covenantalists, see Chad O. Brand and Tom Pratt, Jr., "The Progressive Covenantal View," in *Perspectives on Israel and the Church: Four Views*, ed. Chad O. Brand (Nashville: B & H, 2015), 248, 250–51, 258, 275–79; Fred G. Zaspel and James M. Hamilton, Jr., "A Typological Future-Mass-Conversion View," in *Three Views on Israel and the Church: Perspectives on Romans 9–11*, ed. Jared M. Compton and Andrew David Naselli (Grand Rapids: Kregel, 2018), 97–140.

future millennial kingdom. This assumption identifies the study with the second view. The key texts must now be examined to determine whether this assumption—and the second view—can be sustained. My strategy will be to discuss the Old Testament references to a future kingdom, then to examine the arguments against the second view, and finally to respond to those arguments.

The Old Testament Antecedents

Although the expression *kingdom of God* is not found in the Old Testament, the concept of a future kingdom established by God over which the Messiah will rule is present throughout the Old Testament canon.[14] Furthermore, the corresponding concepts of the Messiah and the messianic kingdom frequently occur in extrabiblical Jewish literature from the intertestamental period onward.[15] Consequently, Jesus's proclamation of a coming kingdom in first century Palestine would naturally have been associated by his Jewish audience with the kingdom promised in the Old Testament. Specifically, Jesus's announcement of an impending kingdom would have called attention to the prior prophecies in the Old Testament involving the Messiah and his kingdom.[16]

In addition, while recognizing a measure of diversity in Judaism on the nature of the messianic kingdom, nevertheless the description of this kingdom in intertestamental literature is essentially consistent with what is found in the Old Testament.[17] In other words, the Old Testament presents something of a unified picture in its predictions of the messianic kingdom, and this unified picture is picked up and repeated in the intertestamental literature. Taken at face value, the Old Testament texts consistently depict an earthly kingdom with national Israel restored to its land as the head of the nations and with the Messiah ruling from Jerusalem and exercising worldwide dominion.[18]

Using Daniel's prophecies as an example (beginning in Dan 2 with the

---

[14] C. C. Caragounis, "Kingdom of God/Kingdom of Heaven," in *Dictionary of Jesus and the Gospels*, ed. Joel Green, Jeannine Brown, and Nicolas Perrin (Downers Grove: IL: IVP Academic, 2013), 417–20.

[15] Ibid., 418–20. Commenting on the concept in Judaism as evidenced by the intertestamental literature, Caragounis notes, "Although the term 'kingdom of God' is rare in Judaism, the idea is almost ubiquitous, either explicitly as the kingdom of the Messiah or implicitly in descriptions of the messianic age" (ibid, 418).

[16] G. R. Beasley-Murray, *Jesus and the Kingdom of God* (Grand Rapids: Eerdmans, 1986), 3–68.

[17] Caragounis, 418–20, sees two basic concepts in Judaism's expectations concerning the messianic kingdom: a temporary Davidic kingdom, sometimes thought of as encompassing the whole world, and a transcendental, everlasting kingdom encompassing the universe.

[18] See, among others, Alva J. McClain, *The Greatness of the Kingdom: An Inductive Study of the Kingdom of God* (Winona Lake, IN: BMH Books, 1974), 274–303.

interpretation of Nebuchadnezzar's dream), Daniel describes five successive kingdoms or world empires that arise in sequence. That these are earthly kingdoms is made clear in that Daniel identifies the first kingdom as the neo-Babylonian empire under Nebuchadnezzar (2:38). Following the fourth world empire, Daniel declares "the God of heaven will set up a kingdom which will never be destroyed . . . ; it will crush and put an end to all these kingdoms" (2:44). Since the first four kingdoms are all earthly kingdoms, this final kingdom should also be understood as an earthly kingdom.

This interpretation is further supported by Daniel's dream-vision of the four beasts recorded in Daniel 7. Like Nebuchadnezzar's dream (2:41–45), Daniel's vision is of four beasts arising in succession, each beast representing a king and his respective kingdom (7:17). Following the activity of the fourth beast, Daniel sees an individual he describes "like a Son of Man" coming with the clouds of heaven and being presented to one called "the Ancient of Days" (7:13).

Daniel notes that this "Son of Man" was given dominion, glory, and a kingdom in order that all mankind might serve him (7:14). This future kingdom is further said to belong to the "Highest One" and includes the sovereignty and dominion of all the kingdoms under heaven that have come before it (7:27). Again, this future kingdom of the Highest One is described in the same terms as the kingdoms that have preceded it. That is, it will be an earthly worldwide kingdom, having dominion over the inhabitants of the earth.

Finally, Daniel receives a revelation from the angel Gabriel regarding the destiny of Daniel's people, the Jews, and their capital city, Jerusalem. Gabriel gives Daniel a chronological timetable that includes the coming of Messiah the Prince, his being cut off, the razing of Jerusalem, and the making and breaking of a covenant in the end times, accompanied by warfare (9:25–27). All this, according to Gabriel, is a prelude to the bringing in of "everlasting righteousness" and the "anointing of the most holy place" (9:24). Based on Daniel's previous prophecies depicting this future kingdom, Gabriel's references to bringing in "everlasting righteousness" and the "anointing of the most holy place" must refer to Messiah's kingdom with Jerusalem as its capital.

Taken together, the evidence from Daniel defines the kingdom promised in the Old Testament as a worldwide kingdom with the Messiah ruling from Jerusalem and exercising dominion over the nations of the earth.

Furthermore, in that the New Testament identifies Jesus as the Messiah, his proclamation of the kingdom of heaven/God in the Gospels refers to this kingdom promised in the Old Testament.[19]

This conclusion is consistent with the fact that Jesus, like John the Baptist before him, uses the expressions *kingdom of heaven* and *kingdom of God* throughout his ministry without ever defining it. In other words, he uses the expression without defining it precisely because the Jews already understood from their Old Testament the nature of this kingdom. Had a different kingdom been intended, Jesus would need to provide a definition for this kingdom to distinguish it from that which was promised in the Old Testament.[20]

An Examination of the Key Texts

Synoptic References to the Nearness/Presence of the Kingdom of Heaven/God

Arguments for a present spiritual kingdom. Those taking *kingdom of heaven* and *kingdom of God* as referring to a present spiritual kingdom interpret the announcement by Jesus that "the kingdom of heaven is at hand" (Matt 4:17) to mean that this kingdom has, in some sense at least, presently arrived. They support this interpretation with Jesus's declaration in Matthew 12:28 that "the kingdom of God has come upon you" (Matt 12:28). In other words, Jesus's statement in 4:17 that the kingdom is "at hand" and his statement in 12:28 that the kingdom "has come" are taken as synonymous, both referring to a present kingdom.[21] That being the case, this kingdom must be different from the kingdom promised in the Old Testament: specifically, unlike the Old Testament promise, Jesus did not sit on David's throne and exercise worldwide dominion at any point during his first advent.[22]

This view finds additional support in Jesus's response to the question about the timing of the kingdom (Luke 17:20–21). Jesus declares that the kingdom of God is not coming with signs to be observed. Rather, Jesus states, "The kingdom of God is within you" (17:21 NIV). Taking the words *within*

---

[19] See, for example, Stephen R. Miller, *Daniel*, NAC (Nashville: Broadman & Holman, 1994), 99–102, 207–10, 216–17, 252–73.

[20] *TDNT*, s.v. "Βασιλεία," by K. Schmidt, 1:584. See also McClain, *The Greatness of the Kingdom*, 276–77.

[21] For example, R. T. France, *The Gospel of Matthew*, 103–4, 480.

[22] Cf. 2 Sam 7:8–29; 1 Chr 17:7–27; Ps 89:20–37; 132:10–18. See the discussion in George Eldon Ladd, *A Theology of the New Testament*, rev., ed. Donald A. Hagner (Grand Rapids: Eerdmans, 1993), 372–73. Ladd argues that in Acts 2:29–36 and elsewhere, the NT redefines the Davidic throne, locating the throne as presently in heaven at the Father's right hand, and, consequently, redefines the Davidic kingdom to include a present, spiritual form of the kingdom where Christ rules from heaven over the lives of his followers (ibid.).V

you to describe the internal nature of the kingdom, proponents conclude that the kingdom Jesus announced must be an internal spiritual kingdom, not a physical kingdom.[23]

Arguments for a future earthly kingdom. Several problems surface with the above reading of these texts. The expression Jesus uses in Matthew 4:17, that the kingdom is "at hand," has a temporal force and uses the perfect tense. The same expression is frequently found in the New Testament to describe events that have drawn near in time and are impending or imminent.[24] As such, this expression is regularly used of events surrounding Christ's second advent that, though future, are spoken of as having drawn near.

For example, this same expression with the perfect tense is used to describe the second coming in James 5:8, the final salvation of Christians in Romans 13:12, and the end of the present age in 1 Peter 4:7. In all these instances, the expression describes something that is approaching or coming near in terms of time but still in the future. Thus, consistent with the use of this expression to describe future events, Jesus in Matthew 4:17 can simply mean that the earthly kingdom promised in the Old Testament has drawn near in time, not that it is already present. In fact, a case can be made that when used in a temporal sense in the New Testament, the expression with the perfect tense never refers to an event that is present, only to one that is approaching or drawing near.[25]

Turning to Jesus's declaration in Matthew 12:28 that "the kingdom of God has come upon you," we observe that this declaration can also be interpreted consistently with the concept of a future kingdom. Since Jesus's declaration is made in connection with his casting out demons by the Spirit of God, the thought can be that the kingdom has come in the sense that the king himself is present. This interpretation sees Jesus using a metonymy of association, where one thing (a kingdom) is substituted for something associated with it (a king).[26] Or the expression can be taken as proleptic, describing

---

[23] Supporters generally take the plural *you* in Luke 17:21 as generic to avoid the implication that Jesus was addressing his unbelieving opponents with this statement (e.g., William Hendriksen, *Exposition of the Gospel According to Luke*, New Testament Commentary [Grand Rapids: Baker, 1978], 805, 809–10).

[24] BDAG, s.v. "ἐγγίζω;" Verlyn D. Verbrugge, ed., *The NIV Theological Dictionary of New Testament Words* (Grand Rapids: Zondervan, 2000), 363–64.

[25] The temporal use of the expression with a perfect tense is found in Matt 3:2; 4:17; 10:7; 26:45; Mark 1:15; Luke 10:9, 11; 21:8, 20; Rom 13:12; Jas 5:8; 1 Pet 4:7.

something that is so certain that it is stated as if it were already a present reality.[27] With either interpretation, Jesus's statement in Matthew 12:28 can be harmonized with Matthew 4:17, with both expressions referring to a future earthly kingdom consistent with the Old Testament promises.

The same can be said about Jesus's declaration in Luke 17:21, "The kingdom of God is within you." The context effectively argues against taking this statement as a reference to a spiritual kingdom that resides within. Jesus is responding to the Pharisees, who have rejected Jesus's messianic claims and are asking Jesus why they are not seeing the prophetic signs that serve as a precursor to the kingdom. Jesus's response cannot mean that the kingdom is a spiritual kingdom that resides within these unbelieving Pharisees.[28] Furthermore, the expression Jesus uses is better translated "among you" or "in your midst" rather than "within you."[29]

What Jesus is saying is that the signs of the kingdom will not be observed (i.e., will not be recognized) by unbelievers like the Pharisees. For the Pharisees, the real question is not about the signs of the coming kingdom, which they have already seen and rejected. Rather, the real question is about who Jesus is—the King of the coming kingdom standing in their midst. The kingdom of God is in their midst in the sense that Jesus the King is standing before them. Access to this kingdom can only be gained through repentant faith in him.[30]

In sum, the expression "is at hand" is used in a temporal sense with the perfect tense throughout the New Testament to describe an event in the future that has drawn near in time. The expression is never clearly used of an event that is present. This usage argues for taking "the kingdom of heaven is at hand" (Matt 4:17) to refer to a future kingdom, not a present kingdom.

Furthermore, the expression "the kingdom of heaven is at hand" is used

---

[26] Stanley D. Toussaint, "The Kingdom and Matthew's Gospel," in *Essays in Honor of J. Dwight Pentecost*, ed. Stanley D. Toussaint and Charles H. Dyer (Chicago: Moody Press, 1986), 28. Cf. Luke 11:20, "The kingdom of God has come to you."

[27] For an example of the proleptic use of the aorist tense elsewhere, see Paul's statement in Rom 8:30 that all those whom God has justified he has also "glorified." Similarly, *DJG*, s.v. "Kingdom of God/Heaven," 423.

[28] A generic *you* in Luke 17:21 is unlikely in that, according to 17:20, Jesus is directly addressing the unbelieving Pharisees. See note 25.

[29] BDAG, s.v. "ἐντός." See the discussion in Darrell L. Bock, *Luke*, 2 vols., BECNT (Grand Rapids: Baker, 1994–96), 2:1415–17.

[30] This view is similar to Bock's, though he still interprets the statement about the Lord being present or among them as supporting an initial or inaugurated form of the kingdom (*Luke*, 2:1417–18).

several times in the Gospels, while the parallel expression "the kingdom of God has come" (12:28) is used only once. Thus, it makes better sense to interpret the one use of the expression "has come" based on the several uses of the expression "is at hand" rather than the reverse. In addition, consistent with single meaning and authorial intent, Jesus cannot be saying that the kingdom of heaven is both future ("is at hand") and present ("has come") at the same time and still be referring to the same kingdom. For that reason, Jesus's several uses of "is at hand" to describe his coming kingdom must interpret his single use of "has come."

Lastly, it seems difficult, if not impossible, to take Jesus's statement in Luke 17:21 ("the kingdom of God is in you") to refer to a present spiritual kingdom in the life of the unbelieving Pharisees. Thus, that statement is best translated as "the kingdom of God is in your midst," referring to the presence of the King in a metonymy of association in which *kingdom* stands for *king*.

The Parables of Matthew 13 and the Mysteries of the Kingdom

Arguments for a present spiritual kingdom. Proponents of a present spiritual kingdom offer three lines of evidence from the parables in Matthew 13 and the parallel accounts of these parables elsewhere. (1) The first relies on Jesus's explanation in 13:11 that these parables represent the "mysteries of the kingdom of heaven,"[31] arguing that Jesus uses the term *mysteries* to describe new revelation about the kingdom.

Specifically, the "mysteries of the kingdom" are thought to provide new revelation about the *nature* of the kingdom. As such, Jesus uses these parables to redefine the kingdom. The "mysteries of the kingdom" reveal a "mystery form" of the kingdom that exists during the period between Jesus's first and second advents. In short, Jesus redefines the kingdom in these parables to refer to his present spiritual reign in the life of his disciples.[32]

In support of this interpretation, proponents assert that the formulas used to introduce the individual parables in Matthew 13 identify the kingdom as presently existing. The first such formula ("the kingdom of heaven *may be compared to* . . ." (Matt 13:24) uses the aorist tense. Based on the tense, the expression is translated with the sense that the kingdom of heaven "has now become like." The following parable describes some truth about

---

[31] The parallel passage in Mark 4:11 uses the singular, "the *mystery* of the kingdom of God."

[32] See, among others, Ladd, *A Theology of the New Testament*, 91–102.

the kingdom in its present or inaugurated form.[33] The remaining parables in Matthew 13 use a similar formula but with the present tense. Since the first formula ("may be compared to") uses the aorist tense to describe something that is now in existence, the formulas with the present tense are interpreted in harmony with the first. Each introduces a parable that reveals something about the present form of the kingdom.[34]

(2) The second line of evidence is that Jesus's description of the kingdom in these parables demands a present form of the kingdom. For example, in both the parable of the mustard seed (13: 31–32) and the parable of leaven (13:33), the kingdom is depicted in terms of it starting out small and gradually growing or spreading until it fills the entire earth. While this is consistent with a present form of the kingdom—the gradual increase in the number of believers submitting to the kingship of Jesus in the present age—it is not consistent with what Daniel and others in the Old and New Testaments say about the sudden establishment of the messianic kingdom at the Lord's return.[35]

(3) The third line of evidence is found in Matthew 13:41, where Jesus states that individuals will be removed from his kingdom when he returns. The thought is that there must be some form of the kingdom already in existence when the Lord returns if he needs to remove individuals from his kingdom at that time. The conclusion proponents draw from this statement is that a present inaugurated form of the kingdom must already exist. Furthermore, this present form is a spiritual kingdom where Jesus rules in the lives of his followers.[36]

Arguments for a future earthly kingdom. It must be granted that the evidence for a present "spiritual" form of the kingdom in Matthew 13 appears weighty. However, the evidence can also be interpreted such that Jesus does not redefine the kingdom and, therefore, does not teach a present form of the kingdom. Each of the above issues must be examined in sequence.

First, the expression in Matthew 13:11, "the mysteries of the kingdom

---

[33] D. A. Carson, "Matthew," in *The Expositor's Bible Commentary*, ed. Tremper Longman III and David E. Garland (Grand Rapids: Zondervan, 2010), 9:363–64.

[34] Ibid. Carson appears to view the formula with the present active ("is like") and the aorist passive ("has become like") as synonymous, both referring to what the kingdom has become like in its inaugurated form. Only when the formula is future passive ("will become like") does the parable focus on the future consummation of the kingdom (e.g., Matt 7:24, 26; 25:1).

[35] Donald A. Hagner, *Matthew*, 2 vols., WBC (Dallas: Word, 1993–95), 1:385–91.

[36] So apparently Carson, "Matthew," 371–74.

of heaven," refers to truths about the kingdom which were previously hidden but are now being disclosed.[37] The specific truths that are being revealed must be determined from the parables themselves. The concept of a mystery "form" of the kingdom reads something into the text that is not required by the context.

Second, in Matthew 13, the first parable is that of the sower. What it reveals is an ongoing proclamation of the gospel during the period between the Lord's first and second advents. In effect, the first parable and its interpretation set the pattern by which the subsequent parables in this chapter are to be understood. With that in mind, the "mysteries" of the kingdom of heaven introduce the revelation that there will be an interval between Christ's first and second advents, with his kingdom being established at his second advent.

To restate the point, nothing in the parable of the sower suggests a present form of the kingdom but only a present proclamation of the gospel. That being the case, the subsequent parables in Matthew 13 must also address the events and activities during the present interval between the first and second advents in preparation for the coming kingdom, while the kingdom itself remains future.[38]

Applying the above pattern to the parables of the mustard seed and the leaven indicates that these parables point to the interval between the advents and the ongoing proclamation of the gospel during this interval. As the gospel continues to be proclaimed, the number of those saved, like the mustard seed and the leaven, continues to grow. The result is that at the end of the age there is a great host of believers qualified to participate in the kingdom the Lord establishes at his return.

Some will enter the kingdom in their natural bodies, having survived the tribulation judgments and the Lord's subsequent removal of unbelievers from the earth (Matt 25:31–46). Many others will have been resurrected and will enter in glorified bodies. The point is that when the Lord returns to establish his kingdom, the number of believers will be great, like the mature mustard seed, and the earth will be filled by the redeemed, like the leavened lump.[39] As such, nothing in these parables requires interpreting the "mysteries of the

---

[37] BDAG, s.v. "μυστήριον;" cf. Rom 16:25–26; Eph 3:2–5, 8–10; Col 1:26.

[38] Similarly, Toussaint, "The Kingdom and Matthew's Gospel," 29–30.

[39] McClain, *The Greatness of the Kingdom*, 440–41.

kingdom" as introducing a hidden spiritual form of the kingdom. Both parables address the spread of the gospel and the growth of the numbers of believers qualified to participate in the Lord's future kingdom.

The same may be said of the formulas introducing the parables. To argue that the aorist tense in Matthew 13:24 ("the kingdom of heaven may be compared") means that the parable describes a present form of the kingdom ignores the evidence. The Synoptics show considerable variation in the formulas used to introduce these parables, from the aorist subjunctive to the present and future indicative. Furthermore, the authors appear to use them interchangeably. The parable of the mustard seed is introduced with the present indicative in Matthew 13:31, with the aorist subjunctive in Mark 4:30, and with both the present and future indicative in Luke 13:18, all three Gospels introducing the same parable.

According to those arguing for a present form of the kingdom, the aorist and present tense in these formulas introduce parables about the present form of the kingdom, and the future tense introduces parables about the future form of the kingdom. Yet, as can be seen with the parable of the mustard seed, where all three tenses are used, such distinctions simply cannot be maintained.

Furthermore, parables using the future tense appear to be teaching the same point as others where the aorist or present tense is used. For example, the parable of the wedding feast is introduced in Matthew 22:2 with an aorist tense while the similar parable of the ten virgins is introduced in Matthew 25:1 with a future tense. Both parables describe similar events and activities associated with the kingdom of heaven. Thus, it is better to view all three tenses in these introductory formulas as gnomic (i.e., introducing general or proverbial truths) and explain the use of one tense versus another as simply a matter of stylistic variation.[40]

The evidence from the parables themselves further supports viewing the kingdom as strictly future. If the parables in Matthew 13 are describing a present form of the kingdom, defined as the Lord ruling in the hearts of believers, a problem arises. Two of these parables, the parable of the wheat and tares (13:24–30) and the parable of the dragnet (13:47–50), describe that which is good existing side by side with that which is bad or evil. If that which is

---

[40] On the gnomic use of the present, aorist, and future tenses, see Daniel B. Wallace, *Greek Grammar Beyond the Basics: An Exegetical Syntax of the New Testament* (Grand Rapids: Zondervan, 1996), 523–25, 562, 571.

good represents believers and that which is bad unbelievers, in what sense can both be part of this kingdom? In other words, how can both believers and unbelievers be a part of this kingdom if this kingdom represents the Lord's spiritual rule in the life of believers?

Proponents of a present form of the kingdom attempt to counter the above criticism by arguing that the field in which the good and bad are found growing together in the parable of the wheat and tares does not represent the kingdom. Rather, the field in this parable is specifically identified as the world (13:38). As such, the good wheat and the bad tares are located together in the world, not in the kingdom itself.[41]

However, this explanation fails to address the Lord's statement in 13:41 at the conclusion of this parable. The Lord declares that he will send forth his angels to gather the evil ones "out of his kingdom" at the end of the age. If the kingdom in view is the Lord's spiritual reign in the lives of believers, as proponents of a present form of the kingdom have argued, in what sense must the Lord remove evil ones from this kingdom when he returns?

Furthermore, in the parable of the dragnet, the Lord directly links the kingdom with the dragnet. He says, "The kingdom of heaven is like a dragnet cast into the sea" (13:47). He then describes this net as containing both good fish and bad (13:48). Thus, the tension remains. How can this kingdom, depicted by the dragnet, include both the good and the bad, if this kingdom represents the Lord's present spiritual rule in the lives of believers?

A related question is, if these parables introduce a mystery form of the kingdom, defined as Jesus Christ's present spiritual rule in the lives of believers, is this rule something that Christ did not exercise in the lives of Old Testament believers? Or if Christ rules in the lives of all true believers, whether in the Old Testament or the New, in what sense is Jesus introducing a present spiritual form of the kingdom? Jesus cannot both rule in the lives of all true believers (both Old Testament and New Testament believers) and at the same time introduce a mystery form of the kingdom involving his present spiritual rule in the lives of believers.

Perhaps the key passage in these parables that seemingly describes a present form of the kingdom is Matthew 13:41, in which individuals are said to be removed from the kingdom when Jesus returns, suggesting that a kingdom exists when Jesus returns. However, when this passage is compared with simi-

---

[41] Ladd, *Theology of the New Testament*, 94–95.

lar passages in Matthew, no present form of the kingdom is seen.

According to Matthew 25:31–33, when Christ returns, he will sit on his throne and judge the nations, separating the sheep (believers) from the goats (unbelievers). The goats are removed from the earth (25:46), and Jesus says to the sheep, "Come, you who are blessed of My Father, inherit the kingdom prepared for you from the foundation of the world" (25:34). The sequence is clear. The Lord returns, sits on his throne, judges the nations, removes unbelievers, and invites believers to receive their inheritance, that is, to enter his kingdom. Thus, based on Matthew 25:31–33, what the Lord describes by the expression "gather out of his kingdom" in Matthew 13:41 is his removing unbelievers from the earth just prior to the inauguration of his kingdom.[42] These unbelievers are being removed from his kingdom in the sense that they are not allowed to enter his kingdom.

Relating Those in the Church to the Kingdom

Arguments for a present spiritual kingdom. There are three passages in Paul's letters where Paul mentions the kingdom of God or God's Son that proponents use to support a present spiritual form of the kingdom. (1) The first is Romans 14:17. In the surrounding verses, Paul discusses how the strong in the faith, those who have greater freedom in things no longer prohibited by Scripture, are to relate to those weak in the faith. In the context of eating meat that was once prohibited, Paul cautions the strong not to eat if the weaker brother is encouraged to do what his conscience prohibits. Were the weaker brother to eat, that would mean he would be sinning against his own conscience and, consequently, against God.

Paul's support for prohibiting the strong from eating meat if it causes the weaker to stumble is that "the kingdom of God is not eating and drinking, but righteousness and peace and joy in the Holy Spirit." Proponents of a present spiritual kingdom argue that Paul's reference to the kingdom of God locates this kingdom in the present age—those strong in the faith are to heed Paul's warning as members of this kingdom—and describes it as spiritual rather than physical—the kingdom is not eating and drinking.[43]

---

[42] For example, McClain, *The Greatness of the Kingdom*, 441. Interestingly, Ladd concurs. He takes the reference to the "kingdom of heaven" in 13:41, the only time the expression is used in Matthew 13, to refer to the future consummation of the kingdom, not to its inaugurated form. He is forced to do this because he cannot have unbelievers being taken out of this kingdom if this kingdom represents the present spiritual reign of Christ in the lives of believers (*A Theology of the New Testament*, 94–95).

[43] Douglas J. Moo, *The Epistle to the Romans*, 2nd ed., NICNT (Grand Rapids: Eerdmans, 1996), 865–80.

A similar statement is found in 1 Corinthians 4:20. In this context, Paul warns his opponents that he intends to come to Corinth to confront them. When he does come, he will expose their false claims of power with a display of his own power. Paul expresses his confidence in the outcome of this confrontation by saying, "The kingdom of God does not consist in words but in power." Again, proponents of a present spiritual kingdom interpret Paul's declaration to mean that there is a present form of the kingdom where Christ rules in the lives of believers and where apostolic power is on display.[44]

Perhaps the strongest Pauline evidence for a present form of the kingdom is found in Colossians 1:13. In the preceding context (1:9–12), Paul records his prayer for the readers. In his prayer, Paul mentions the readers giving thanks to the Father. Part of the reason the readers are to give thanks, Paul says, is that the Father "has rescued us from the domain of darkness and transferred us to the kingdom of His beloved Son." Using the aorist tense, Paul appears to describe a present form of the kingdom. This kingdom is one in which Christ as God's Son rules and in which the readers have already been established or "transferred."[45]

Arguments for a future earthly kingdom. Outside the Gospels, the expression "the kingdom of God" is not often found, and that is true of Paul's writings. On those occasions where Paul speaks of the kingdom of God, he generally locates this kingdom in connection with Christ's second advent, as even those who hold to a present form of the kingdom acknowledge.[46] The question is whether the passages mentioned above are an exception to the overall rule. That is, do they refer to a present kingdom or, consistent with Paul's common use, to a future kingdom?

Paul's reference to the kingdom of God in Romans 14:17 ("the kingdom of God is not eating and drinking, but righteousness and peace and joy in the Holy Spirit") is somewhat enigmatic. Paul does not further define the nature of this kingdom, and his statement can be taken to refer to a present form of the kingdom, but it can also be interpreted to refer to a future kingdom. In short, Paul may simply be contrasting the characteristics of the present world with the characteristics of the future kingdom.

---

[44] Gordon D. Fee, *The First Epistle to the Corinthians*, 2nd ed., NICNT (Grand Rapids: Eerdmans, 2014), 198–209.

[45] James D. G. Dunn, *The Epistles to the Colossians and to Philemon*, NIGTC (Grand Rapids: Eerdmans, 1996), 67–80.

[46] Thomas R. Schreiner, *Romans*, 2nd ed., BECNT (Grand Rapids: Baker, 2018), 716–17.

Specifically, Paul could be saying the present world is characterized by eating and drinking and the pursuit of temporal pleasures. The future kingdom is characterized by righteousness, peace, and joy in the Holy Spirit. In their relationship with each other, the Roman believers should not be driven by that which characterizes this present world. Rather, they should be driven by that which characterizes the world to come. Thus, Paul is calling on his readers to measure their present conduct in a fallen world by the conduct that will characterize God's future kingdom.[47] That being the case, there is nothing in this passage that requires a reference to a present kingdom.

A similar case can be made for Paul's remarks about the kingdom in 1 Corinthians 4:20 ("The kingdom of God does not consist in words but in power"). The future kingdom will be characterized not only by righteousness but also by the overt display of divine power as Jesus, the messianic King, rules with absolute authority. As an apostle, Paul is an official emissary of the Messiah and his kingdom. Just as Jesus displayed his credentials during his first advent as the messianic King, so Paul can display his credentials as Jesus's apostolic emissary.

What Paul asserts in this verse is that, as an official representative of the future kingdom, he has true apostolic power and authority. Those opposing him in Corinth should beware. He will not allow anyone who opposes the work of God to go unchallenged. And when he does challenge those who oppose him, it will not be with words only but with the display of divine power.[48] Again, there is nothing in this passage that demands Paul to have a present form of the kingdom in view.

The same may be said of Paul's reference to the kingdom in Colossians 1:13, "He rescued us from the domain of darkness and transferred us to the kingdom of His beloved Son." The debate over this passage focuses on the meaning of the two phrases "rescued from the domain of darkness" and "transferred to the kingdom of His Son." According to the tense of the verbs—aorist indicatives—these statements describe something that the Father has accomplished for the readers. With that in mind, do Paul's statements refer to what the readers presently experience,

---

[47] James D. G. Dunn, *Romans*, 2 vols., WBC (Dallas: Word, 1988), 2:823. Dunn holds to a present spiritual form of the kingdom; nevertheless, his comment offers support for the above interpretation: "For both Jesus and Paul the character and power of the still future rule of God can provide inspiration and enabling for the present." Cf. 1 Cor 6:9–10; Gal 5:21.

[48] Hans Conzelmann, *1 Corinthians*, trans. James W. Leitch, Hermeneia (Philadelphia: Fortress, 1975), 93. Conzelmann appears to support this reading of Paul's words, "The eschatological character of the 'kingdom of God' is not abrogated by the fact that it provides a criterion in the present."

in which case Paul has in view a present kingdom? Or do Paul's statements refer to the readers' present position rather than to their present experience, in which case Paul has in view a future kingdom?

The second option is viable because Paul employs the aorist indicative elsewhere in similar ways. For example, Paul describes God as having "seated" the Ephesian believers "in the heavenly *places* in Christ" (Eph 2:7). Clearly, Paul describes the position believers enjoy "in Christ," not their present experience. Believers are not now actually sitting in the heavens.[49] The same may be said of Paul's two statements in Colossians 1:13. In fact, the evidence from the immediate context argues that Paul describes the readers' present position, not their present experience. And, if that is the case, then the kingdom in view is the future millennial kingdom of the Son, not a present spiritual kingdom.

Paul's statement in Colossians 1:13 clarifies and supports his previous statement in 1:12 about what the Father has done that should provoke the readers' thanksgiving. They should thank the Father, Paul writes, because the Father has qualified them "to share in the inheritance of the saints." Paul explains that the Father has done this by transferring the readers "to the kingdom" of his Son. Thus, the inheritance Paul's readers share is further defined as God's having transferred them to the kingdom of his Son. An inheritance can refer to something one already has (e.g., Acts 1:17) or to something one expects to receive in the future (e.g., Titus 3:7). Assuming for the moment it is the latter, Paul can be describing the kingdom as a future inheritance, which the readers now have as their right but not yet as their experience (cf. Eph 5:5).

The counterpart to the Father's transferring the readers to the Son's kingdom is his removing or rescuing them "from the domain of darkness." From the larger context, the expression "the domain of darkness" refers to the present world system, over which Satan rules and which is characterized by the darkness of sin and unbelief. Again, Paul can refer to the actual experience of the readers. They are no longer enslaved to sin and under Satan's reign but are under the authority of the Son in his kingdom. Or Paul can refer to the position of the readers. They are true citizens of the coming kingdom, though still living in the present fallen world.

---

[49] Harold W. Hoehner, *Ephesians: An Exegetical Commentary* (Grand Rapids: Baker, 2002), 334–35. Hoehner's comments reflect this understanding of the text: "Although we are in the heavenlies positionally, we remain on the earth to live a resurrected life in connection with the resurrected Christ."

Elsewhere, Paul exhorts believers to put on the whole armor of God to guard against Satan's strategies (e.g., Eph 6:11). While believers are no longer enslaved to sin and under Satan's sway, they must guard themselves against his influences because they are still residents of Satan's domain. As such, Colossians 1:12 describes believers' present position—they are no longer in the "domain of darkness" in the sense that they are no longer under Satan's control. Yet, their deliverance from Satan's domain is still future. Thus, their present position is not yet their present experience.

Assuming Paul is discussing his readers' present position, Paul's subsequent statement in 1:13 about the readers being transferred into the kingdom of God's Son can also describe the readers' position instead of their present experience. They have been "transferred" into this kingdom in the sense that they have been made its citizens. Their actual participation in this kingdom, however, is in the future.[50] In sum, the kingdom in view in Colossians 1:13 is future not present, and this future kingdom harmonizes well with Paul's references to this kingdom elsewhere.

Conclusion

Scripture teaches that the triune God exercises absolute control over creation and, as such, is the eternal King and Sovereign of the universe and all that it contains (e.g., Dan 4:25–26). Scripture also teaches that the triune God rules in the lives of believers, and this has always been the case (e.g., Rom 10:6–13). This essay argues that the expressions *kingdom of heaven* and *kingdom of God* as used in the New Testament refer exclusively to the future millennial kingdom promised in the Old Testament and fulfilled by Christ at his second advent.

This conclusion contributes to two larger theological discussions that are simply mentioned here and not developed. The first discussion involves the question of continuity versus discontinuity in the relationship between the testaments and between Israel and the church. Those championing greater continuity between the Old and New Testaments and between Israel and the church argue that in some sense, at least, the church is presently fulfilling the kingdom promises given to national Israel in the Old Testament. A key argument in defending this continuity is the interpretation of the expressions *kingdom of heaven* and *kingdom of God* in the New Testament to point to a present spiritual form of the kingdom.

---

[50] Similarly, Homer, A. Kent, Jr., *Treasures of Wisdom: Studies in Colossians & Philemon*, New Testament Studies (Grand Rapids: Baker, 1978), 43–44.

Yet if the expressions *kingdom of heaven* and *kingdom of God* are not used in the New Testament to describe a present form of the kingdom, then a key argument for greater continuity between the testaments and between Israel and the church is negated. As was argued above, the expressions are used in the New Testament to refer to the future messianic kingdom promised to national Israel in the Old Testament and established by Christ at his second advent. At the same time, the Scriptures teach that the church fully participates in the promised kingdom during the eschaton as co-regents with Christ (e.g., Rev 2:26–27; 3:21). In sum, there is no compelling evidence for a present form of this kingdom or for the church to be presently fulfilling the Old Testament promises.

The second discussion involves the relationship between the social responsibilities described as part of the promised kingdom in the Old Testament and in the Gospels versus the application of these responsibilities to the church. Those holding to a greater continuity between the Old and New Testaments and between Israel and the church argue that these social responsibilities are a part of the church's mandate and must be implemented by local churches. The justification for placing these kingdom responsibilities on the church is the understanding that the church represents, in at least some sense, a present form of the promised kingdom.[51]

However, if the expressions *kingdom of God* and *kingdom of heaven* are not used in the New Testament to describe a present form of the kingdom, then the justification for applying a kingdom social ethic to the church is significantly undermined. This is not to say that church saints are free from social responsibilities. The New Testament is filled with commands directing church saints to be fully engaged in helping fellow believers and in helping those outside the church. This is all part and parcel of Christ's command to love one's neighbor (e.g., Rom 13:8; Gal 6:10; Jas 2:8; cf. Matt 22:39). Nevertheless, the church itself does not have a social mandate. Local churches are not tasked with implementing the social responsibilities that are a part of the future kingdom. The primary mandate for the church is the Great Commission, the making and maturing disciples who are progressively being conformed to the image of Christ (Matt 28:19–20). And it is these disciples *as disciples* who are to pursue loving one's neighbor and helping those in need.

---

[51] See, for example, the discussions in Russell D. Moore, *The Kingdom of Christ: The New Evangelical Perspective* (Wheaton: Crossway, 2004); Christopher W. Morgan and Robert A. Peterson, *The Kingdom of God* (Wheaton: Crossway, 2012).

Israel in the Church Fathers

Larry D. Pettegrew
Shepherds Theological Seminary
Cary, North Carolina

As a committed dispensationalist, Charles Hauser held firmly to the doctrines of the pretribulational rapture and the premillennial second coming of Christ.[1] So it might come as a mild surprise to read in his doctoral dissertation that "the Church Fathers believed that the Church would be on earth during the tribulation period. This is seen in the earliest writers and there is nothing in the other writers to contradict this."[2] Of course, Hauser makes it clear in the introduction to his dissertation that in his understanding of the New Testament, these Fathers were wrong on this point.

Chapters in Hauser's dissertation are devoted to key eschatological topics: "The Great Tribulation," "The Antichrist," "The Second Advent of Christ," "The Resurrection," and "The Kingdom." Each chapter is divided chronologically into three epochs: "The Fathers from A.D. 96 to A.D. 150," "The Fathers from A.D. 150 to A.D. 200," and "The Fathers from A.D. 200 to A.D. 250." Seventeen of the early Church Fathers show up in the study. Hauser concludes his study as follows:

> Down through the Church Fathers considered in this paper runs a central core of teaching. Although it may vary slightly from one writer to another, it remains essentially the same. This is true until the time of Origen. These men believed that what they taught had come to them from the New Testament times through the disciples of Apostles. . . . The core of this teaching . . . was the following: a future time of tribulation with the rise of the Antichrist followed by the second advent of Christ; at the same time the resurrection of the righteous took place which prepared them for entrance into the kingdom; the kingdom of Christ on earth then was established which would last for a thousand years; this would be followed by the universal resurrection

---

[1] This chapter is adapted by permission from Larry D. Pettegrew, "The Curious Case of the Church Fathers and Israel," chapter 1 in *Forsaking Israel* (The Woodlands, TX: Kress, 2020).

[2] Charles August Hauser, Jr., "The Eschatology of the Early Church Fathers" (ThD diss., Grace Theological Seminary, 1961), 234.

and judgment. The different writers elaborated on various aspects of these points as their inclinations led them. However, these remain the basic points of the eschatology of the early Church Fathers.[3]

The eschatological system held by these early Fathers, according to Hauser, was therefore premillennialism but not necessarily the kind of premillennialism that goes hand in hand with pretribulationism.

The Church Fathers and Eschatology

The study of the Church Fathers is called "patristics." The Fathers were pastors, bishops, and theologians who lived from the time of the completion of the canon of the Scriptures up to about AD 600, or some would say a little longer. They gave testimony of being holy and generally orthodox though their theologies were certainly not consistent with one another on many points.

Some church historians divide this period into the Ante-Nicene Fathers (before the Council of Nicaea in 325) and Post-Nicene Fathers. Others have classified the Fathers as Apostolic Fathers, who theoretically could have been alive when one or more of the apostles were living, Apologetical Fathers, who wrote defenses of Christianity against pagans and state officials, and Polemical Fathers, who attacked the heretical groups such as the Gnostics. Some of them were Greek-speaking from the Eastern part of the Roman Empire, and some spoke Latin from the Western part. Most of this chapter concerns the Ante-Nicene Fathers from both the East and the West.

The Ordinariness of the Church Fathers

However much we may respect the Church Fathers, especially those who suffered horrendous persecution and martyrdom, they were not on the same level as the apostles of Christ. They were not borne along by the Holy Spirit in the way the apostles were, as is obvious from the Fathers' many disagreements with each other. Most of them changed their minds about various aspects of theology—even as we do sometimes. Augustine, for example, was a premillennialist in his early career but later became an amillennialist.[4] Abelard, a twelfth-century philosopher, even wrote the book *Sic et Non* to demonstrate

---

[3] Ibid., 251.

[4] Augustine, *The City of God*, 20.7, NPNF 2/2:426.

the biblical and theological inconsistencies of the Church Fathers.[5]

From the perspective of an evangelical Protestant, the Church Fathers also brought many errors into Christian theology. Always, when I teach the first semester historical theology course, the students are stunned at how soon major doctrinal errors were accepted into the belief system of many Christian leaders. Within one hundred years of the death of the last apostle, some were teaching false doctrines such as baptismal regeneration, the ransom theory of the atonement, salvation only through the church, asceticism and celibacy as a means of sanctification, and legalism.[6]

Moreover, there are research problems for modern-day scholars who study the Church Fathers. In the words of one patristic scholar, "Reading the church fathers is difficult. Simply to pick up Irenaeus' treatise *Against the Heresies* and read invites confusion and boredom if one does not know the point of the many digressions."[7] Some patristic literature is still not translated out of the Greek or Latin. In many cases, the ancient manuscripts are fragmentary, and some copies disagree with other copies. Some scholars, in fact, do textual criticism on the extant copies trying to determine the correct reading of a passage in a Father's sermon or book.[8]

Beyond all these problems, the historical and cultural context of the Fathers is so different from ours that we can easily err by trying to find a short, snapshot statement from them about any one specific topic. One paragraph in the *Shepherd of Hermas*, for example, could easily persuade us, if we were not observant of the context, that Hermas believed in the pretribulational rapture of the church. Hermas writes,

> You have escaped from great tribulation on account of your faith, and because you did not doubt in the presence of such a beast. Go, therefore, and tell the elect of the Lord His mighty deeds, and say to them that this beast is a type of the great tribulation that is coming. If then ye prepare yourselves, and repent with all your heart, and

---

[5] Peter Abelard, *Yes and No*, trans. Priscilla Throop (Charlotte, VT: Medieval MS, 2007).

[6] For a discussion of the doctrinal deviations in the Church Fathers, see Ken Guindon, *History Is Not Enough!* (n.p.: Xulon, 2007).

[7] John J. O'Keefe and R. R. Reno, *Sanctified Vision* (Baltimore: Johns Hopkins, 2005), 1.

[8] See, for example, Kenneth B. Steinhauser and Scott Dermer, eds., *The Use of Textual Criticism for the Interpretation of Patristic Texts* (Lewiston, NY: Edwin Mellen, 2013). This book contains seventeen case studies. Chapter 16 as a specific example is written by Scott Dermer and entitled, "*Vellet* or *Vellent*? A Textual Variant in Augustine's *Enchiridion*," 479–510.

turn to the Lord, it will be possible for you to escape it.[9]

The Shepherd of Hermas is a sort of allegorical novel, so it is even more difficult to derive distinct doctrinal ideas from it than it is from other more formal patristic documents. But the speaker in this section is actually the church herself, who is encouraging Hermas for going through a personal trial, symbolized by the beast. What "the church" means by the "great tribulation" is not clear.

The Millennial Theology of the Early Church Fathers

No one doubts that many (but certainly not all) of the later Fathers, beginning with Origen (d. 254), were amillennialists—or maybe incipient postmillennialists if they were especially optimistic in their eschatology. But the question is whether the Fathers who lived before the time of Origen were premillennialists as Hauser concluded. Some do, in fact, doubt that they were.

The Early Fathers Were Not Premillennialists

Charles Hill, for example, argues mainly from silence that some of the early Fathers were amillennialists, believing "in an eschatological return of Christ and his kingdom to earth for a final judgment of the quick and the dead, ushering in the ultimate and eternal state of salvation or ruin for humanity, with no intervening, earthly, golden age. This alternative to chiliasm may be distinguished as 'orthodox' non-chiliasm or amillennialism."[10] Others have presented the view that the early Fathers were preterists who saw the tribulation as entirely past.[11] And still others have argued that premillennialism was dominant in only one part of the empire.[12] These views have been shown to be without merit by Hauser's study and other scholars such as Donald Fairbairn.[13]

---

[9] *Shepherd of Hermas*, V.4.2, AF 180.

[10] Charles Hill, *Rednum Caelorum*, 2nd ed. (Grand Rapids: Eerdmans, 2001), 6.

[11] Gary DeMar and Francis X. Gumerlock, *The Early Church and the End of the World* (Powder Springs, GA: American Vision, 2006).

[12] George Lyons, "Eschatology in the Early Church," in *The Second Coming: A Wesleyan Approach to the Doctrine of Last Things*, ed. H. Ray Dunning (Kansas City, MO: Beacon Hill, 1995).

[13] Donald Fairbairn, "Contemporary Millennial/Tribulational Debates: Whose Side Was the Early Church On?" in *A Case for Historic Premillennialism*, ed. Craig L. Blomberg and Sung Wook Chung (Grand Rapids: Baker Academic, 2009), 107–13. Although Fairbairn's defense of premillennialism in the early church is excellent, his critique of pretribulationism in his next section is curious. In this section of his chapter, Fairbairn presents a three-point polemic against pretribulationism in the early Church Fathers. I have no problem agreeing with his first and third arguments. First, he argues, they did not have the same hermeneutic as do modern-day pretribulationists, an argument that pretribulationists today would happily grant. In fact, one of the main reasons that the New Testament teaching on pretribulationism was lost in the Fathers was their disappointing hermeneutical system. His third argu-

The Early Fathers Were Premillennialists

The purpose of this chapter is not to give all the evidences for premillennialism among the early Fathers since Hauser and many others have done that. According to some scholars, at least fifteen of the better-known early Fathers were premillennialists.[14] For the sake of illustration and to make the point, the following are some of the generally known passages from the writings of a few early Fathers.

Papias (d. 150?) was apparently a pastor in Hierapolis, a city located in modern day Turkey. He was a friend of the martyred Polycarp, who in turn was a disciple of the apostle John. Papias was the author of *Exposition of the Lord's Oracles*, which may have been five volumes and contained stories and teachings about Christ that he had gathered over the years from first-generation Christians. Only fragments of his work have been preserved, and these are found in *Ecclesiastical History*, written by Eusebius of Caesarea, the "father of church history" (d. 339). Eusebius, although an opponent of premillennialism, cites Papias as writing "that there will be a period of some thousand years after the resurrection of the dead, and that the kingdom of Christ will be set up in material form on this very earth."[15] Eusebius comments, "I suppose he got these ideas through a misunderstanding of the apostolic accounts, not perceiving that the things said by them were spoken mystically in figures. . . . But it was due to him that so many of the Church Fathers after him adopted a like opinion, urging in their own support the antiquity of the man; as for instance Irenæus and anyone else that may have proclaimed similar views."[16]

Irenaeus (d. 200) was born in Asia Minor, possibly Smyrna, and is

---

ment is that the early Fathers did not show any awareness of a two-part return of Christ. This can also be granted, though Fairbairn's posttribulationism also has a two-part return. For posttribulationists, the two-stage return happens at about the same time rather than being separated by seven (or more) years as pretribulationists teach. But his second argument is problematic. Fairbairn says, "Modern dispensationalism shies away from asserting that God would allow his people to suffer severely, and this attitude is part of the reason for affirming a pretribulational rapture of the church" (122). Fairbairn admits that this is not the view of every dispensationalist but says, "It is fair to argue that dispensationalism as a whole is undergirded by the assumption that God will protect his people from excessive suffering" (123). I personally don't know any pretribulationists who would argue this as a top-ten reason for pretribulationism, and *undergirded* is way too strong a term. Impugning motives—we are pretribulationists because we don't want to suffer—is not a good argument. If Fairbairn had said that one of the main reasons for the pretribulational belief is the doctrine of imminency—that pretribulationists believe that they might see Jesus Christ today—he would have been far more accurate.

[14] H. Wayne House, "Premillennialism in the Ante-Nicene Church," *BSac* 169 (July–September 2012): 273.

[15] Eusebius Pamphilus, *The Church History of Eusebius* 3.39.12, NPNF 2/1:172.

[16] Ibid., 3.39.12–13, NPNF 2/1:172.

therefore a representative of the theology of Asia Minor, which is known as being based generally on a more literal method of hermeneutics. Irenaeus was later sent to France as a missionary and was appointed the bishop of Lyons. He devoted his life to the study and refutation of false doctrine—more from the perspective of a pastor than a philosopher. Toward the end of his life, he wrote his major five books *Against Heresy*. Book 5 in particular contains several passages teaching premillennialism. Irenaeus outlines the end events as follows:

> But when the Antichrist shall have devastated all things in this world, he will reign for three years and six months, and sit in the temple at Jerusalem; and then the Lord will come from heaven in the clouds, in the glory of the Father, sending this man and those who follow him into the lake of fire; but bringing in for the righteous the times of the kingdom, that is, the rest, the hallowed seventh day; and restoring to Abraham the promised inheritance, in which kingdom the Lord declared, that "many coming from the east and from the west should sit down with Abraham, Isaac, and Jacob."[17]

Irenaeus also argues that if we "shall endeavor to allegorize prophecies. . . , they shall not be found consistent with themselves in all points."[18] Quoting Isaiah 65:21, Irenaeus writes, "For all these and other words were unquestionably spoken in reference to the resurrection of the just, which takes place after the coming of Antichrist, and the destruction of all nations under his rule; in the times of which resurrection the righteous shall reign in the earth.[19] Moreover, "all these things being such as they are, cannot be understood in reference to super-celestial matters; 'for God,' it is said, 'will sow to the whole earth that is under heaven thy glory.' But in the times of the kingdom, the earth has been called again by Christ to its pristine condition, and Jerusalem rebuilt after the pattern of the Jerusalem above."[20] Irenaeus goes on to quote other Old

---

[17] Irenaeus, *Against Heresies*, 5.30.4, ANF 1:560.

[18] Ibid., 5.35.1, ANF 1:565.

[19] Ibid.

[20] Ibid. When we read these confident defenses of premillennialism in Irenaeus, as well as his meticulous apologetics against heresies, we may be tempted to look to him as a representative of evangelical orthodoxy. But, in spite of many areas in which we can respect him, there are serious problems in his theology. Irenaeus may be the earliest of the Fathers to promote Mariology as well as apostolic succession as an unbroken chain in the Roman Church. He is designated a saint in both the Roman Catholic and Eastern Orthodox Churches.

Testament prophecies in this section in support of his premillennial doctrine.

Justin Martyr (d. 162) in his early life was a wandering philosopher in search of truth. He tried out Stoicism, Platonism, and Pythagorean numerical philosophy before he was converted to Christianity. In his *Dialogue with Trypho*, Justin writes: "Moreover, a man among us named John, one of Christ's Apostles, received a revelation and foretold that the followers of Christ would dwell in Jerusalem for a thousand years, and that afterwards the universal and, in short, everlasting resurrection and judgment would take place."[21] Justin admits there may be other Christians who do not believe in a millennial kingdom here on earth but states, "I and every other completely orthodox Christian feel certain that there will be a resurrection of the flesh, followed by a thousand years in the rebuilt, embellished and enlarged city of Jerusalem, as was announced by the Prophets Ezekiel, Isaias and others."[22]

Tertullian (d. ca. 225), born in Carthage, North Africa, is a representative of the Western branch of the church. He practiced law but after his conversion in about 180 turned his rhetorical abilities to the defense of Christianity. He apparently became a presbyter in the Carthage church but converted to Montanism after he decided that the Carthage church was too lax in Christian living. Tertullian also was a premillennialist. In his apologetic work *Against Marcion*, he writes,

> But we do confess that a kingdom is promised to us upon the earth, although before heaven, only in another state of existence, inasmuch as it will be after the resurrection for a thousand years in the divinely built city of Jerusalem 'let down from heaven.' . . . After its thousand years are over, within which period is completed the resurrection of the saints, who rise sooner or later according to their deserts there will ensue the destruction of the world and the conflagration of all things at the judgment.[23]

Even though Tertullian sees the city of Jerusalem as let down from heaven, he is clearly a premillennialist like Papias, Irenaeus, Justin, and others.

---

[21] Justin, *Dialogue with Trypho*, 81, ANF 1:240.

[22] Ibid., 80, ANF 1:239

[23] Tertullian, *Against Marcion*, 3.25, ANF 3:343.

The Fathers Were Posttribulationists

But were the Fathers also pretribulationists? There were elements of pretribulationism in their teaching, such as the doctrine of imminency. But Hauser straightforwardly admits, in his typical honest, no-nonsense approach to life and ministry, that these sixteen early Church Fathers before Origen did not teach a pretribulational rapture as far as we can know.

Clement of Rome could have been pretribulational, perhaps, but he says nothing that would prove it.[24] Irenaeus could have believed in pretribulationism because in all of his discussions about the tribulation he does not say that the church will be there.[25] Moreover, in Irenaeus's understanding, one of the results of the tribulation will be the salvation of Israel.[26] But we really cannot argue from silence that Irenaeus accepted a pretribulational rapture, and many of the early Church Fathers did teach or imply that the church would be in the tribulation. For example, Hippolytus (a student of Irenaeus and one of the most important theologians of the third century) interprets the woman persecuted by the Antichrist in Revelation 12 as being the church rather than Israel.[27] Moreover, almost all the Fathers, including the early Fathers who were premillennialists, were inconsistent in their hermeneutics, engaging in some doubtful typological interpretations. Though there are some differences of detail between the posttribulationism of the Church Fathers and that of twenty-first-century adherents, they are essentially the same.[28]

The Role of Israel in Premillennial Systems

One of the key questions in unraveling the debate between premillennial posttribulationists and premillennial pretribulationists is, How does the nation of Israel fit into their eschatological system? Many churches and Christian academic institutions that teach a pretribulational rapture have a

---

[24] Clement does say that the apostles in their post-resurrection ministries "went forth with the glad tidings that the kingdom of God should come." Clement, *First Epistle to the Corinthians*, 42, AF 31.

[25] Some of the earliest Church Fathers such as Polycarp, Ignatius, and Clement of Rome, except for their commitment to the resurrection of the body and a coming kingdom, wrote almost nothing about the specific eschatological topics that Hauser examines, so it is impossible to know their precise views.

[26] Irenaeus, *Against Heresies*, 5.25.2, ANF 1:553.

[27] Hippolytus, *Christ and Antichrist*, 61, ANF 5:217.

[28] Posttribulationist Timothy Weber does recognize that though current posttribulationists like to call themselves "historic premillennialists," the term *historic* "must be qualified since futurism in its present form is in fact a post-Reformation perspective or at best a late medieval one." Timothy Weber, "Dispensational and Historic Premillennialism as Popular Millennialist Movements," in *A Case for Historic Premillennialism*, ed. Craig L. Blomberg and Sung Wook Chung, 14. At least one of the Fathers was an intra-tribulationist, believing that the church was already in the middle of the tribulation.

statement in their confession of faith about Israel like the following:

> We believe that God sovereignly selected Israel as His eternal covenant people. Israel is now dispersed because of disobedience and rejection of their Messiah, Jesus Christ, but will be regathered in Israel during the Tribulation. According to God's grace and His eternal covenant with the Jewish nation, God will prepare their hearts in repentance for the second coming of Christ (Genesis 13:14–17; Ezekiel 37; Romans 11:1–32).[29]

The role of Israel in eschatology is a foundational issue. The truth of the matter is that unless the Scriptures teach that Israel as a nation will have the central place in the future tribulation and the millennial kingdom while living in the land of Israel, pretribulationism is wrong and posttribulationism is right.

According to Contemporary Pretribulationism

Pretribulationists believe that the tribulation is a seven year period after the rapture of the church to heaven for which God has two purposes. First, it is a time of devastation on the world in judgment for the centuries of anti-God wickedness that has been committed during earth's history. In the Old Testament, the tribulation period is described as the coming Day of the Lord. Not necessarily a single twenty-four-hour day, the Day of the Lord generally pictures God's special interventions into the space-time continuum of the earth, often in some terrible judgment. Sometimes the warnings about the Day of the Lord deal with Old Testament Israel, which was about to be judged because of its apostasy.

Frequently, however, the warnings about the Day of the Lord look toward a distant future time when "all the earth will be devoured in the fire of His jealousy" and God "will make a complete end, indeed a terrifying one, of all the inhabitants of the earth" (Zeph 1:18). In the New Testament we learn that "the day of the Lord will come just like a thief in the night. While they are saying, 'Peace and safety!' then destruction will come upon them suddenly like labor pains upon a woman with child, and they will not escape" (1 Thess 5:2–3). After the three series of worsening judgments described in the book of Revelation, about three-fourths of the world's population will have died.

---

[29] Seminary Catalog (Cary, NC: Shepherds Theological Seminary, 2022–2023), 21.

The second main purpose of the tribulation is to separate out from the nation of Israel a remnant who will welcome their Messiah at his second coming. The tribulation is described in Daniel 9 as the seventieth week of Daniel's prophecy about the future of Israel. The seventy "weeks" are seventy periods of seven years (490 years), and the seventieth period of seven years is described as a time when the Antichrist rises to power and rules the earth with special sufferings for the nation of Israel. The entire 490 years, including the last period of seven years, is specifically focused on the nation of Israel. Daniel writes, "Seventy weeks have been decreed for *your people and your holy city*, to finish the transgression, to make an end of sin, to make atonement for iniquity, to bring in everlasting righteousness, to seal up vision and prophecy and to anoint the most holy place" (Dan 9:24, emphasis added). The seven-year tribulation clearly does not deal with the church. This seven-year period serves as a judgment on Israel with the result that by the end of that time, all the "rebels" are purged out. Ezekiel records Yahweh saying,

> "And I will bring you into the wilderness of the peoples, and there I will enter into judgment with you face to face. As I entered into judgment with your fathers in the wilderness of the land of Egypt, so I will enter into judgment with you," declares the Lord GOD. "I will make you pass under the rod, and I will bring you into the bond of the covenant; and I will purge from you the rebels and those who transgress against Me; I will bring them out of the land where they sojourn, but they will not enter the land of Israel. Thus you will know that I am the LORD." (Ezek 20:35–38)

Specifically, during the seven years of tribulation, and according to the old covenant prophets, two-thirds of the people in Israel will "be cut off and perish; but the third will be left in it, and I [the Lord] will bring the third part through the fire, refine them as silver is refined, and test them as gold is tested. They will call on My name, And I will answer them; I will say, 'They are My people,' And they will say, 'The LORD is my God,'" (Zech 13:8–9).

In short, the tribulation is a future seven-year time of horrifying judgment on the world, during which time the Lord will "pour out on the house of David and on the inhabitants of Jerusalem, the Spirit of grace and of supplication, so that they will look on [him] whom they have pierced; and they will mourn for Him, as one mourns for an only son, and they will weep bitterly over Him like the bitter weeping over a firstborn" (Zech 12:10). Those who do not turn to the Lord will be "cut off and perish." The tribulation thus serves as a preparation for the millennial kingdom when Israel's Messiah rules the world from the earthly city of Jerusalem (Zech 14:9–11). The prophet Jeremiah recorded Yahweh's words:

> "Alas! for that day is great, there is none like it; and it is the time of Jacob's distress, but he will be saved from it. It shall come about on that day," declares the LORD of hosts, "that I will break his yoke from off their neck and will tear off their bonds; and strangers will no longer make them their slaves. But they shall serve the LORD their God and David their king, whom I will raise up for them." (Jer 30:79)

A multitude of Gentiles are also saved in the tribulation period, many of whom are martyred (Rev 7:9–10). But recognizing that Gentiles are saved in the tribulation is not the same thing as saying that the true church is on earth during the tribulation. The Bible gives a specific definition of the church as Jews and Gentiles together in one body on equal footing (Eph 3:1–7), and there is nothing that fits that description in the tribulation. In fact, neither the word *church* nor any of the New Testament metaphors for the church (e.g., body) are found in Revelation 4–18—the section that describes the tribulation period in detail.

Interestingly, to be a little more specific, there is one description of the church that shows up in this section of Revelation. On my view, the term *twenty-four elders* is a metaphorical description of the church, and these elders are spoken about several times in Revelation 4–18. But in each case, John is careful to show us that these are resurrected, already-judged believers in heaven during the tribulation (Rev 4:1–4; cp. 4:4 with 3:5, 11, 21). In other words, the church is already in heaven while the tribulation is transpiring on earth.

The point, without going into other evidences for the pretribulationist view, is that pretribulationism is based to a significant degree on the teaching in Scripture (which we have only skimmed) regarding a future judgment and conversion of Israel that will occur during the tribulation. As a result, Israel will be the center of the millennial kingdom. Israel will live joyfully with the Messiah, who will rule over the nations of the world from earthly Jerusalem. In other words, if there is no future for the nation of Israel as a separate entity from the church, there is no future for pretribulationism.

According to Contemporary Posttribulationism

Posttribulational premillennialists, on the other hand, are replacement theologians to some degree. They, along with covenant theologians, believe that beginning on the Day of Pentecost, the church replaced Israel and assumed Israel's promises and place in God's plan for the ages. Though there is a future millennial kingdom, it will not be centered on the nation of Israel in their land. Posttribulational premillennialists assert the following:

(1) The nation of Israel refused to accept Jesus as its Messiah at his first coming.

(2) Therefore, God replaced Israel with the church.

(3) The church is the focus of God's program here on earth during the church age, the tribulation, and the millennial kingdom.

(4) God's agenda for Israel as a nation has been completed.

(5) Gentiles and Jews who convert to Christ in the church age, tribulation, and millennial kingdom become a part of the church, not some sort of revived national Israel.

(6) Because there are both believing Gentiles and Jews in the tribulation, the church must be in the tribulation.

(7) The rapture of the church must therefore occur after the tribulation at the second coming of Christ to earth.[30]

As we noted above, it would seem that most of the early Church Fathers generally understood eschatology in this way. They were premillennialists, but they had concluded that Israel as a nation had lost its central place in God's plan permanently.

The Early Church Fathers and Israel

The question of this chapter is, why didn't the Church Fathers, including the early Fathers who believed in premillennialism, teach the pretribulational rapture of the church when, in the view of Hauser (and of the authors of this book), the New Testament writers taught pretribulational premillennialism? The answer to this question is found in several intertwining issues, most of which focus in some way on the Gentile-Jew relationship.

---

[30] For a development of posttribulational premillennialism, see Blomberg and Chung, *A Case for Historic Premillennialism*; George Eldon Ladd, *The Blessed Hope* (Grand Rapids: Eerdmans, 1956), esp. 89–104.

Social Background of the Jew-Gentile Problem

Besides the biblical and theological issues, which we will be able only to survey here, certain social issues ought to be mentioned to round out the picture of early Jew-Gentile perspectives within Christianity. For example, Israel encountered three military disasters in the first and second centuries. The first was the Jewish revolt in AD 70, when the Romans destroyed Jerusalem and the temple and killed thousands of Jews. Most twenty-first-century historians of this period do not believe that this was a decisive point of division between Jews and Gentiles. James Dunn writes that "talk of a clear-cut or final parting of the ways at 70 C.E. is distinctly premature."[31]

The second Jewish rebellion, the Kitos War (AD 115–117) was a disorganized rebellion that spread throughout the empire to Egypt, Cyprus, Mesopotamia, and Judea itself. The Jewish rebels were able at first to defeat the depleted Roman forces in some of these territories, but eventually they were overrun by the Roman armies.

The third rebellion was the Bar Kokhba revolt that began in AD 132. Simon Bar Kokhba, the commander of the revolt, was a messianic figure who took the title "Prince" and promised to restore national independence to Israel. The Jews thus had a choice between two messianic figures: Jesus and Simon.[32] When this revolt was crushed, almost 600,000 Jews were killed in battle and thousands more died of hunger and disease. The emperor made plans to build a new Roman city, *Aelia Capitolina*, on the site of the rubble of the city, and he forbade any Jews to enter Jerusalem. According to some historians, the failure of Gentile Christians to aid the Jews in this last revolt was a significant development in the Jew-Gentile problem. A few years after this war, the Fathers began to argue that the church is Israel.

The Centrality of the Jew-Gentile Problem

In contemporary theology, the Jew-Gentile problem affects more than just eschatology. It is also central to contemporary soteriological debates between traditional Reformed theologians and the New Perspective on Paul theologians. This fact is beyond the scope of our study, but it is important to point out how it intertwines with eschatological issues. The traditional interpretation of many of the Church Fathers as well as the Protestant leaders

---

[31] James D. G. Dunn, *The Parting of the Ways*, 2nd ed. (London: SCM, 2005), 311.

[32] Ibid., 317–19.

of the Reformation is replacement theology, also known as supersessionism. According to this view, the Jews rejected Christ, and thus Judaism became a useless religion so that the church has forever superseded national Israel as the people of God. Historians such as Adolf von Harnack and other nineteenth-century historians promoted this view.

The Contemporary "Parting of the Ways" Solution

After the Holocaust and World War II, a much milder and more ecumenical approach to the "parting of the ways" between the Jews and early Christians gained popularity among some scholars. In fact, the term "parting of the ways" has become a common description for this view, which emphasizes good in both religions. Andrew Jacobs explains, "The 'parting of the ways' is a clear yet benign metaphor that allows each religion to maintain a robust history and a common genealogy, just connected enough to justify ongoing, friendly relations, but not so connected that the distinctive tradition of each religion becomes too blurred. This amicable model, however, rests on several contestable presuppositions."[33]

The "parting of the ways" interpretation requires a "new perspective on Paul," and tries to soften the Church Fathers' clash with the Jews. In some more extreme forms, it even suggests that the writings of the Church Fathers against the Jews were basically symbolical and not necessarily based on historical events. So Justin, for example, created Trypho the Jew in his work, *Dialogue with Trypho*, in order to dramatize through dialogue the superiority of Christianity over Judaism. The hope of this softened parting of the ways is that it will lead to a better ecumenical relationship between Christians and Jews. Many modern-day historians, however, argue that the Fathers' writings tell the truth about the bad relationship of Jews and Christians. [34]

The Biblical Source of the Jew-Gentile Problem

It is easy to forget that the mission of Jesus the Messiah was restricted, in his early ministry, to Jews. Jesus was a Jew, his followers were Jews, and the earliest mission of the apostles after the death and resurrection of Christ focused on the Jews. Moreover, much of Christ's teaching "would have been

---

[33] Andrew S. Jacobs, "Jews and Christians," in *The Oxford Handbook of Early Christian Studies*, ed. Susan Ashbrook Harvey and David G. Hunter (New York: Oxford, 2008), 170.

[34] Ibid., 270–72. See Dunn, *The Parting of the Ways*, for further development of this approach to the Jewish problem.

unintelligible if addressed to Gentiles. . . . The men to whom Jesus spoke knew the Law, the Prophets, and the Psalms, and followed the Tradition."[35]

When the Jewish religious leaders steered the nation to reject Christ and his kingdom, Jesus promised that he would build his church (Matt 16:18). The church was consequently formed on the day of Pentecost with "Jews living in Jerusalem, devout men from every nation under heaven" (Acts 2:5) and Jewish proselytes (2:10) being the nucleus of this new body. But the Jewish-Gentile problem is highlighted in the following chapters of Acts when other groups were added to the church. In Acts 8, believing Samaritans were brought into the church by the Holy Spirit through Peter and John. In Acts 10, Gentiles were added in.

The Gentile problem. At first, the problem was more of a Gentile problem. The entrance of the Gentiles into the church was a puzzle to the Christian Jews in Jerusalem, who had formed the nucleus of the church on the day of Pentecost. They were not upset about the Gentiles being saved. They were confused over the fact that the Gentiles were added into the body of Christ in the same way that they, as believing Jews, had been brought into the church. It didn't seem to match up with what they expected from the Old Testament's teaching about a coming kingdom. The Jewish Christians no doubt thought that the Gentiles who wanted to participate in the New Covenant program should go to Jerusalem and participate in some sort of proselyte ceremony as was required in the past. But Peter explained when questioned about his ministry with Cornelius,

> I remembered the word of the Lord, how He used to say, 'John baptized with water, but you will be baptized with the Holy Spirit.' Therefore if God gave to them the same gift as *He gave* to us also after believing in the Lord Jesus Christ, who was I that I could stand in God's way? When they heard this, they quieted down and glorified God, saying, "Well then, God has granted to the Gentiles also the repentance *that leads* to life" (Acts 16–18)

The Jewish-Gentile problem is not answered once and for all here in Acts 11, however. The first major church council was held to deal with the details of having Jews and Gentiles together on equal footing in the body of Christ

---

[35] F. J. Foakes-Jackson, *The Rise of Gentile Christianity* (New York: George H. Doran Co., 1927), 38.

(Acts 15). The specific controversy centered on whether "those converted to Christianity from outside of Judaism needed also to become Jews as well."[36] But before too many years had passed in the Christian era, a vast majority of Christians were Gentiles; then the issue became less of a Gentile problem and more of a Jewish problem.[37]

The Jewish problem. Understanding the Jewish problem in the apostolic and patristic era is made more complicated by the fact that there were different kinds of Jews and eventually different kinds of "Christians." Even basic terms such as *Jews* and *Judaism* "were also in some state of flux." [38] Some scholars have also pointed out that in second temple Judaism, the term *Jew* was a designation by which Jews were distinguished from other ethnic and religious groups, but *Israel* or *Israelite* denoted a self-understanding in terms of election and covenant promise."[39] Moreover, there were different kinds of Jews, culturally speaking: Palestinian Jews who spoke Aramaic, Greek-speaking Jews or Hellenists, Jewish proselytes, and apostate Jews such as the Samaritans. In addition, there were the Jews at Qumran, and, of course, Christian Jews. These Jewish groups debated each other, especially over the question of observing the law. "The least weakening on this point aroused a storm of indignation as it had done during the ministry of Jesus."[40]

Jews against Jews. Indeed, both the Old and New Testaments are filled with strong denunciation of Jews by Jews—and for good reasons. The ancient kings of Israel and Judah neglected their godly responsibilities and often led the nation to worship other gods. The priests failed to perform their religious duties, and the people often disregarded Yahweh and his law. From the beginning of the nation, Moses, Joshua, Samuel, and all the other prophets condemned God's people for their sin, calling them to repent. If it were not for the fact that God had made an irrevocable covenant with the nation, Israel would no doubt have been destroyed as were many other ancient nations.

If anything, the condemnation of Israel—especially of its religious

---

[36] Stanley E. Porter and Brook W. R. Pearson, "Ancient Understandings of the Christian-Jewish Split," in *Christian-Jewish Relations Through the Centuries*, ed. Stanley E. Porter and Brook W. R. Pearson (New York: T & T Clark, 2004), 41.

[37] Origen, writing in the middle of the third century, says that there were fewer than 144,000 (cf. Rev 7:4) Jewish Christians at that time. Origen, *Commentary on John*, 1.2 in ANF 9:298.

[38] Dunn, *The Parting of the Ways*, 189.

[39] Ibid., 192.

[40] Foakes-Jackson, *The Rise of Gentile Christianity*, 83.

leaders—became even more severe in the New Testament. The religious leaders of Israel led the nation to reject the kingdom of God that Christ presented. The climax of the struggle between Christ and these leaders is described in Matthew 12. When Jesus healed a man with a withered hand on the Sabbath, the Pharisees "conspired" how they could "destroy" Christ (12:14). Christ continued healing, and when he healed a demon-oppressed man who was blind and mute, the people were "amazed," and wondered if he was indeed the Son of David, the Messiah (12:23). The Pharisees, to head off any kind of a groundswell, gave their interpretation of the miracle: "This man casts out demons only by Beelzebul the ruler of the demons" (12:24). The Pharisees had proposed this defense before, and now it became in effect their official evaluation of Jesus. He was not the Messiah. He was a demon-inspired magician.

Jesus responded with several reasons why this could not be true and concluded with a curse on that "brood of vipers" (12:34). "Whoever speaks a word against the Son of Man, it shall be forgiven him," he said, "but whoever speaks against the Holy Spirit, it shall not be forgiven him, either in this age or in the *age* to come" (12:32). The Pharisees had committed the so-called "unpardonable sin" in not only blaspheming against Christ but also blaspheming against the Holy Spirit who empowered him in his incarnational ministry.

The pathos of this struggle between Jesus and the leaders of Israel is vividly portrayed in Matthew 23 when Christ pronounces eight devastating "woes" on the scribes and Pharisees for their hypocrisy but concludes with a lament and prophecy:

> Jerusalem, Jerusalem, who kills the prophets and stones those who are sent to her! How often I wanted to gather your children together, the way a hen gathers her chicks under her wings, and you were unwilling. Behold, your house is being left to you desolate! For I say to you, from now on you will not see Me until you say, "BLESSED IS HE WHO COMES IN THE NAME OF THE LORD!" (Matt 23:37–39)

Christ had withdrawn his offer of his kingdom to that generation of Jews and promised to give it to a later generation of Jews "producing the fruit of it" (21:43).[41]

After Pentecost and the beginning of the church, there is some fluctuation in the apostles' references to the Jews. Christian Jews struggled with "the Jews," as Luke calls them in his early history of the church. Some of Luke's references to the Jews—those that became Christian Jews—are positive, and a few of his descriptions are both positive and negative: "Now these [Jews] were more noble-minded than those in Thessalonica, for they received the word with great eagerness, examining the Scriptures daily *to see* whether these things were so" (Acts 17:11). Many of Luke's references to the Jews, however, are critical (9:22, 23; 12:3; 13:45, 50; 14:2, 4, 19; 16:3; 17:5, et al.). The Jews killed Stephen (Acts 6–7), and a Jew named Saul (later Paul) "was in hearty agreement with putting him to death" and began "ravaging the church, entering house after house, and dragging off men and women, he would put them in prison" (8:1, 3). After Paul's conversion, the Jews from Antioch and Iconium, "having won over the crowds . . . stoned Paul and dragged him out of the city [of Lystra], supposing him to be dead" (14:19).

The apostle Paul, a Jew who is sometimes "credited with being the chiefest factor in bringing about the final rupture between the Church and the synagogue,"[42] also wrote discourses against those Jews who tried to maintain Jewish lawkeeping in Christianity. His belief was that "no one is a Jew who is merely one outwardly, nor is circumcision outward and physical. But a Jew is one inwardly, and circumcision is a matter of the heart, by the Spirit, not by the letter. His praise is not from man but from God" (Rom 2:28–29; cf. Gal. 6:16). Throughout these discourses, "Paul may have been disowning the Judaism in which he had been brought up (Gal. 1:13–14), but he did so self-consciously as an Israelite—that is, as one who sought to maintain and promote the true character of Israel's election."[43]

Paul also made it clear that he saw a future for the nation of Israel (Rom 9–11). In fact, Paul's "heart's desire and prayer to God" for the people of Israel was "that they may be saved" (10:1). In one of the most passionate

---

[41] Matthew 21:43 is regularly misinterpreted as Jesus assigning the kingdom to the church. But there is nothing in the context that would imply this. Christ's teaching is all about the wickedness of that generation of Jews. He is specifically condemning the "chief priests and Pharisees" who "perceived that he was speaking about them" (21:45). As I noted in a preceding section, the OT prophets show that there will be a later generation of Jews that respond to their Messiah's outpoured grace during the tribulation. They will be the "people producing the fruit of it."

[42] Foukes-Jackson, *The Rise of Gentile Christianity*, 84.

[43] Dunn, *The Parting of the Ways*, 196.

expressions in Scripture, Paul states,

> I am speaking the truth in Christ—I am not lying; my conscience
> bears me witness in the Holy Spirit—that I have great sorrow and
> unceasing anguish in my heart. For I could wish that I myself were
> accursed and cut off from Christ for the sake of my brothers, my
> kinsmen according to the flesh. They are Israelites, and to them
> belong the adoption, the glory, the covenants, the giving of the law,
> the worship, and the promises. To them belong the patriarchs, and
> from their race, according to the flesh, is the Christ, who is God over
> all, blessed forever. Amen. (Rom 9:1–5)

Moreover, in the conclusion of his diatribe against the Jewish legalists in
Galatia, he praises the believing Gentiles and "the Israel of God" (Gal 6:16),
a title not for the church but for true godly Israelites whom he differentiated
from the "Judaizers." There were true Jews and false Jews, according to Paul's
theology.

But most of the Jews continued to despise Paul. One of the most striking
events in the early history of the church is found in Acts 21–22 when Paul
went to the temple in Jerusalem. The "Jews from Asia . . . began to stir up
all the crowd and laid hands on him, crying out, 'Men of Israel, come to our
aid! This is the man who preaches to all men everywhere against our people
and the Law and this place; and besides he has even brought Greeks into
the temple and has defiled this holy place'" (21:27–28). When Paul gave
his defense and told the story of his conversion, the Jewish crowd was quiet
until Paul mentioned the Lord's commission to him to take the gospel to the
Gentiles. Luke records, "They listened to him up to this statement, and *then*
they raised their voices and said, 'Away with such a fellow from the earth, for
he should not be allowed to live!'" (22:22). Seemingly even the mention of
the word *Gentile* nearly brought on a riot.

Finally, the letter to the Hebrews makes a significant contribution to
dealing with the Jewish problem. It is written to warn Christian Jews, in
particular, about the dangers of relapsing into Judaism. The writer builds the
case that New Covenant Christianity is better than Old Covenant Judaism.
Jesus is far superior to the Old Testament prophets, who spoke for God many
times and in many ways (Heb 1:1). The New Covenant is better than the Old
Covenant, which was passing away. If we forsake the Christian faith, there is

nothing left for us, and we will be judged. In the Old Testament, those who set aside the Mosaic law were subject to capital punishment. "How much severer punishment," the writer asks, "do you think he will deserve who has trampled underfoot the Son of God, and has regarded as unclean the blood of the covenant by which he was sanctified, and has insulted the Spirit of grace?" (10:29).

Gentiles against Jews. Perhaps we should not be surprised, in light of both the Old and New Testament Jewish authors' often negative evaluation of unbelieving Israel, to discover that the Church Fathers were also critical of "the Jews." Occasionally there is a word of kindness from the Fathers that accompanies a harsh reproach. Justin Martyr writes, "Even when your city is captured and your land ravaged, you do not repent. Rather, you dare to utter curses on Him and all who believe in Him. Nevertheless, we do not hate you."[44] And again, "You curse in your synagogues all those who are called from Him Christians. . . . And in addition to all this, we pray for you that Christ may have mercy upon you."[45] But these kind statements are few and far between and seem to be couched in the midst of negative evaluation, so they hardly soften the debate. "It is rare," writes Andrew Jacobs, "to find an early Christian text that does not speak about Jews and Judaism, and usually in a highly charged (though multifaceted) manner."[46]

From the Jewish perspective, there were good reasons for not becoming Christians, of course. The Jews did not appreciate the easy entrance requirements into the church, in contrast to the rather involved Jewish proselyte procedure. Then there were the conclusions of the Jerusalem Council that allowed the Christians not to follow the Sabbath, dietary laws, and circumcision. The Christians' preference for the Septuagint Old Testament was a problem. And more foundationally, the Christians' claim that Jesus was not only the Messiah but also God was a roadblock. It was also difficult for the Jews to believe that Jesus was in fact the Messiah since he was crucified on a cross, his kingdom did not come into existence, and his second coming did not happen.[47] Jesus's resurrection claim "would do little in a Jewish context to

---

[44] Justin Martyr, *Dialogue with Trypho*, 108, ANF 1:253.

[45] Ibid., 96, ANF 1:247.

[46] Jacobs, "Jews and Christians," 172.

[47] See further, Craig A. Evans, "Root Causes of the Jewish-Christian Rift from Jesus to Justin," in Porter and Pearson, *Christian-Jewish Relations Through the Centuries*, 21.

mitigate the evident failure of Jesus's bid to be Israel's Messiah."[48]

From the Fathers' perspective, some of the Christian Jews apparently had kept too much of their Judaism. Ignatius, in his letter to the Magnesians (ca. 110), echoes the New Testament author of the letter to the Hebrews in admonishing the Magnesians, "Be not seduced by strange doctrines nor by antiquated fables which are profitless. For if even unto this day we live after the manner of Judaism, we avow that we have not received grace."[49] But we do not really know how Christian Jews reacted during the early patristic era. Marcel Simon writes, "As far as Jewish Christians are concerned, we are hampered by the total lack of documentary evidence. We possess no document that may with certainty be ascribed to this party and giving information about their reactions."[50] So, when we begin to study the Church Fathers, the Gentile-Jewish problem, with a couple of exceptions noted above, almost entirely focuses on Jews who had not become Christians.

The Fathers Were Gentiles

The Church Fathers continued the New Testament authors' arguments against the Jews in at least a couple of areas: the superiority of the New Covenant over the Old and Jewish guilt in the rejection and crucifixion of Christ. But in several ways the debate had become more complex.

In the first place, instead of Jews debating Jews, these were now Gentiles debating the Jews. To some degree at least, the Fathers seem to have forgotten the context of the New Testament anti-Jewish talk, interpreting it as an attack on Jews *per se* rather than a response to particular Jewish opposition. Interpreting the New Testament debates as anti-Judaism, writes House, "should be seen as preposterous in view of the fact that all of the authors (except Luke) were Jews and that our *Lord* was a Jew."[51] The Jews' debates among themselves in the New Testament, though often highly theological, were in some ways intramural. But because most of the Church Fathers were Gentiles, their reproach of the Jews became not only theological but also an

---

[48] Ibid, 33.

[49] Ignatius, "Epistle to the Magnesians," 8.1, AF 70. Ignatius makes a similar comment in his "Letter to the Philadelphians."

[50] Marcel Simon, *Versus Israel*, trans. H. McKeating (Portland, OR: Litman Library of Jewish Civilization), 65.

[51] House, "Premillennialism in the Ante-Nicene Church," 89. See also David L. Allen, "The Identity of Luke and the Jewish Background of Luke-Acts," in *Lucan Authorship of Hebrews*, NAC Studies in Bible and Theology, vol. 8, ed. E. Ray Clendenen (Nashville: B & H Academic, 2010), 261–323. Allen argues that Luke was a Jew.

ethnic issue.[52]

In some passages, at least, the Church Fathers argued not so much as Christian against non-Christian Jew but as Gentiles against the Jews. True enough, Jesus, near the end of his ministry, talked about the "times of the Gentiles" (Luke 21:24). And the apostle Paul says that "a partial hardening has happened to Israel until the fullness of the Gentiles has come in" (Rom 11:25). But the emotional atmosphere surrounding Jesus and the apostles is different from what we find in some of the Church Fathers. Jesus mourned over Jerusalem before he gave his prophecy about the "times of the Gentiles" (Matt 23:37), and Paul's point in Romans 9–11 is that there is a future for Israel. When Paul asks, "God has not rejected His people, has He?" he answers his own question, "May it never be!" (Rom 11:1).

Whether intended or not, some of the Fathers' statements gave the impression of being anti-Jewish. Irenaeus (d. 202), a premillennialist, wrote that because the Jews "have rejected the Son of God, and cast Him out of the vineyard when they slew Him, God has justly rejected them. He has *given to the Gentiles* (outside the vineyard) the fruits of its cultivation."[53] It seems to me that Irenaeus would have been more in line with the New Testament if he had added "temporarily" or had written "given to the Christians" or perhaps even "given to the church." As previously mentioned, the church is composed of Jews and Gentiles in one body on equal footing.

Hippolytus (d. 235), a premillennialist disciple of Irenaeus, wrote *The Expository Treatise Against Jews,* most of which is lost to us. His view of the church being essentially Gentile is evidenced when he argues that when Christ on the cross said, "Father forgive them," it was "namely the Gentiles, because it is the time for favor with Gentiles.[54] Tertullian (d. 220) writes that, in contrast to Abraham's willingness to sacrifice his son Isaac, it behooved Christ "to be made a sacrifice *on behalf of all Gentiles.*"[55] Even though Irenaeus, Hippolytus, and Tertullian were premillennialists, the replacement of the nation of Israel by a Gentile church is certainly implied in these kinds of statements. The

---

[52] One possible exception may be Melito of Sardis (d. ca. 190) who probably was a Jew. There may have been other lesser known Jewish bishops who qualify as Church Fathers. Melito was apparently a premillennialist, but he was very critical of the Jews who rejected Christ. See Alistair Stewart-Sykes, in his introduction to Melito of Sardis, *On Pascha* (Crestwood, NY: St. Vladimir's Seminary Press, 2000), 3. See pp. 56–65 for Melito's poetic attack on unbelieving Israel.

[53] Irenaeus, *Against Heresies*, 4.36.2, ANF 1:515, emphasis mine.

[54] Hippolytus, *The Expository Treatise Against Jews*, 3, ANF 5:220.

[55] Tertullian, *An Answer to the Jews*, 13, ANF 3:171, emphasis mine.

later Fathers, either historic premillennialists or amillennialists, repeat and emphasize these same sentiments.[56]

God Had Disowned Israel

As pointed out above, it would seem that what the Fathers were teaching about God's replacement of Israel with the Gentile Church ran counter to what the New Testament taught. In the theology of the New Testament writers, "The Jews have not entirely forfeited their election."[57] Paul strongly warned the Gentiles that though they, as wild branches, had been grafted into God's covenant program with Israel, they were not to be arrogant. The "gifts and the calling of God" with Israel are "irrevocable" (Rom. 11:29). Paul writes,

> But I am speaking to you who are Gentiles. Inasmuch then as I am an apostle of Gentiles, I magnify my ministry, if somehow I might move to jealousy my fellow countrymen and save some of them. For if their rejection is the reconciliation of the world, what will their acceptance be but life from the dead? If the first piece of dough is holy, the lump is also; and if the root is holy, the branches are too. But if some of the branches were broken off, and you, being a wild olive, were grafted in among them and became partaker with them of the rich root of the olive tree, do not be arrogant toward the branches; but if you are arrogant, remember that it is not you who supports the root, but the root supports you. You will say then, "Branches were broken off so that I might be grafted in." Quite right, they were broken off for their unbelief, but you stand by your faith. Do not be conceited, but fear; for if God did not spare the natural branches, He will not spare you, either. (Rom. 11: 13–21)

But a future conversion of the nation of Israel was not the message of the Fathers. They believed that Israel had been removed from God's covenant program. The Epistle of Barnabas (AD 120), which was not written by the Jewish Barnabas of the New Testament and is somewhat over-the-top in

---

[56] Origen, an amillennialist, writes, "We will go so far as to say that [the Jews] will not be restored again. For they committed the most impious crimes of all when they conspired against the Savior of mankind." Origen, *Contra Celsum*, 4.22, ANF 4:506. Simon comments, "This was henceforth to be the unshakable opinion of the whole of the early church." Simon, *Versus Israel*, 68.

[57] Jeremy Cohen, *Living Letters of the Law* (Los Angeles: University of California, 1999) 8. At the time of the writing of this essay, Cohen was the professor of medieval Jewish history at Tel Aviv University.

comparison to some of the other Fathers, vigorously emphasizes that Israel has been left behind with the formation of the church. After demonstrating that God has voided sacrifices, the Mosaic law, circumcision, the Sabbath, the temple (all of which agrees with the book of Hebrews), he urges the readers of his epistle "not to liken yourselves to certain persons who pile up sin upon sin, saying that our covenant remains to them also. Ours it is; but they lost it in this way for ever, when Moses had just received it."[58]

Clearly, Barnabas reflects a change from the New Testament authors. The thesis of the book of Hebrews is that Jesus Christ and the New Covenant are far "better" than Moses and the Old Covenant. The thesis of Barnabas is that the Old Testament was always intended to be taken allegorically, but the Jew, led astray by an "evil angel," had erroneously understood it literally, actually trying to follow an absurd system of laws and sacrifices.[59] No New Testament author teaches anything like this replacement theology.

A clear signal that the Fathers are thinking as replacement theologians occurs in Justin Martyr's *Dialogue with Trypho*, written about 160. Justin, a premillennialist, takes up the question whether Israel is Israel or the church is Israel. Justin quotes Isaiah 19:24ff and applies it to the church. "'What, then?' says Trypho; 'are you Israel? and speaks He such things of you?'"[60] Justin's extended reply is essentially "yes, the Church is Israel."

Justin's claim is the first time in church history that a Father argues that the church is a new Israel. It is obviously "a symptom of the developing take-over by Christians of the prerogatives and privileges of Jews," writes Peter Richardson. "Initially there is hesitancy about this transposition: but a growing recognition of the necessity to appropriate titles and attributes ensures a complete transfer."[61] Richardson observes that for Justin, "Christians are a *genos* which has superseded the Jewish race, and this demands a complete taking over of the name 'Israel.' . . . By the middle of the second century the Church in its apologetic has effected a total transposition."[62]

---

[58] *The Epistle of Barnabas*, 4, AF 139. See his premillennialism in ibid., 15, AF 182.

[59] Ibid., 9, AF 145

[60] Justin Martyr, *Dialogue with Trypho*, 123, ANF, 1:261.

[61] Peter Richardson, *Israel in the Apostolic Church*, Society for New Testament Studies Monograph Series 10 (New York: Cambridge, 1969), 1. Richardson's book, the result of his doctoral dissertation, is a major contribution to unfolding the Jewish problem in the early church.

[62] Ibid., 11–12 .

The Puzzle of the Old Testament

A major part of the Jewish problem for the early church was to understand the role of the Old Testament in Christianity. The heretic Marcion denied that there was any value at all in the Old Testament. He also claimed that the God of the Old Testament was not the true God. Marcion was wrong, said the Fathers. On the other hand, the Jews denied that the New Testament was a revelation from God, and the Fathers knew that they were wrong. So the orthodox Fathers were more or less in the middle of this debate in that they firmly believed that both the Old Testament and the New Testament were inspired and authoritative documents. "But having taken this stand," writes Simon, "the Church found that formidable difficulties were involved in maintaining it."[63] The New Testament documents were quickly becoming more available, and the Fathers knew how to use them. But the real problem was, how should Christians make use of the Old Testament?

An Apologetical Solution

One of the criticisms of early Christianity was that it was the new kid on the block. Greek philosophy stretched back into previous centuries as did Judaism. So both Greek philosophers and Jews asked why, if Christianity was such a good religion and philosophy, did it just now show up? As Simon writes, "The problem for Christians was that they believed the Church had superseded Israel. But Israel was still there, employing the OT. How could the Church claim that the OT belonged to them?"[64]

Moreover, it would appear that if the Old Testament were still a valid revelation of God, it would prove that Israel was more ancient than the newcomer, Christianity. So, in order to convince either the philosophers or the Jews of the legitimacy of Christianity, the Fathers had to insist that the church had existed from all eternity. To prove this, the Fathers taught that the Old Testament was really not a Jewish document but a Christian one. The author of Second Clement writes,

> Wherefore, brethren, if we do the will of God our Father, we shall be of the first Church, which is spiritual, which was created before the sun and the moon. . . . And I do not suppose that you are ignorant

---

[63] Simon, *Versus Israel*, 71.

[64] Ibid., 72.

that the living Church is "the body of Christ"; for the Scripture says, "God made man male and female." The male is Christ, the female is the Church. And the Books [Old Testament] and the Apostles plainly declare that the Church exists not now for the first time, but has been from the beginning.[65]

In the apocalyptic novel *The Shepherd of Hermas*, Hermas receives a vision of an aged woman who interacts with him and gives him a document to copy. In a later vision, a young person appears to explain his previous vision of the old woman. He explains that the old woman is the church. Hermas responds, "Why then is she aged?" The messenger replies, "Because . . . she was created before all things; therefore is she aged; and for her sake the world was framed."[66] The antiquity of the church is a common apologetic of the Church Fathers, and an important tool in their apologetical tool bag was the Old Testament. The Old Testament relates the history of the preexistent church, and Israel was only a "coarse outer shell for the spiritual reality within.[67]

A Hermeneutical Solution

It would take some hermeneutical gymnastics, however, to show that the Old Testament was in reality a Christian document. But this did not seem to deter the Fathers. The aforementioned Barnabas was the first and most daring of the Fathers to try. According to Barnabas, Abraham circumcised "eighteen males and three hundred" of his household. He goes on to try to show that in these numbers "Jesus" and "the cross" are hidden.[68] In another section Barnabas claims that the Old Testament prohibition against eating pork really means that we are to separate ourselves from people who are like pigs.[69] Others of the early Fathers, though not employing gross allegorical interpretation, employed extensive typological interpretation to find the church in the Old Testament. Justin, for example, taught that the twelve bells on the robe of the high priest were "a symbol of the twelve apostles who depend on the power of

---

[65] *Second Clement*, 14, AF 91. Second Clement is probably the earliest post-apostolic Christian sermon still extant. It was preached perhaps around 130. Although it goes by the name of Clement, it has no relationship to the letter that Clement of Rome wrote to Corinth in about AD 95.

[66] *Shepherd of Hermas*, V.2.4.1, AF 409.

[67] Simon, *Versus Israel*, 79.

[68] *Epistle of Barnabas*, 9, ANF 143.

[69] Ibid., 10, ANF 143.

Christ, the eternal Priest."[70] The two goats in the day of atonement "prefigure the two natures of Christ," according to Tertullian.[71]

Melito of Sardis, in his meditation *On Pascha*, explained how typological interpretation was supposed to work. Typology begins with a "first draft," he wrote, or a "preliminary sketch" (meaning Israel). But when the finished copy or the thing that was sketched actually comes into existence, and "then the type is destroyed." Melito explains,

> But when the church arose and the Gospel came to be, the type, depleted, gave up meaning to the truth: and the law, fulfilled, gave up meaning to the Gospel. In the same way that the type is depleted, conceding the image to what is intrinsically real, and the analogy is brought to completion through the elucidation of interpretation, so the law is fulfilled by the elucidation of the Gospel, and the people is depleted by the arising of the church, and the model is dissolved by the appearance of the Lord. And today those things of value are worthless, since the things of true worth have been revealed.[72]

In other words, Israel was just a type of the real—the church. And the type has been eliminated once and for all.

In the prophetic sections of the Old Testament, the Church Fathers regularly interpreted the great blessing sections of a future Israel as referring to the church. At the same time, they refused to apply the judgment sections of the prophecies to the church. These sections still referred to Israel. Tertullian, for example, quotes a series of verses on judgment from Isaiah and comments, "The Jews were predicated as destined to suffer these calamities on Christ's account, and we see they have suffered them, and see them sent into dispersion."[73] When he comments on a blessing passage such as Isaiah 2:2–3, which describes nations flowing into the house of the God of Jacob, Tertullian explains, "not of *Esau*, the former Son, but of *Jacob*, the second that is, of our 'people' whose 'mount' is Christ."[74]

---

[70] Justin Martyr, *Dialogue with Trypho*, 42, ANF 1:215.

[71] Tertullian, *Against Marcion*, 3.7–8, ANF, 3:327.

[72] Melito of Sardis, *On Pascha*, 42–43.

[73] Tertullian, *An Answer to the Jews*, 13, ANF 3:171.

[74] Ibid., 3, ANF 3:154.

Tertullian is a premillennialist, to be sure. He writes, "We do confess that a kingdom is promised to us upon the earth, although before heaven, only in another state of existence; inasmuch as it will be after the resurrection for a thousand years in the divinely built city of Jerusalem."[75] But the millennial kingdom is not about the Jews. Tertullian adds, "As for the restoration of Judea, however, which even the Jews themselves, induced by the names of places and countries, hope for just as it is described, it would be tedious to state at length how the figurative interpretation is spiritually applicable to Christ and His Church, and to the character and fruits thereof."[76]

For Tertullian, therefore, there will be a thousand-year period on earth, with the resurrection of the just happening before it begins and the resurrection of the unjust afterwards. But this kingdom is for the church, not for Israel.[77] He supports his opinion by a "spiritual" interpretation of the Old Testament prophecies.[78] Cohen concludes, "God had therefore disowned the Jews, annulled their ritual law, and transferred their inheritance to the Church, which now constituted the only true Israel, not a recently arrived impostor."[79]

A Philosophical Solution

Another cause for the use of "spiritual interpretation" of the Old Testament was the influence of Platonism and Neoplatonism. Platonism in one form or another elevated the spiritual realm to the point at which a physical material kingdom on this earth became unbelievable. According to specialists in the history of philosophy, the form of Platonism that was dominant between 80 BC and AD 220 was Middle Platonism. Middle Platonism was then gradually

---

[75] Tertullian, *Against Marcion*, 3.24, ANF 3:342.

[76] Ibid.

[77] An additional factor for further investigation is the role of the LXX in the Jewish question. Origen seems to be the first major Father to understand Hebrew. But the fact that Christians used the LXX was another evidence to the Jews that Gentile Christians had taken over the Jewish OT.

[78] The Fathers in the Alexandrian school followed Origen's hermeneutical approach in employing typological interpretation for the book of Revelation—if they interpreted it at all. Eusebius tells how Dionysius of Alexandria (d. 264) convinced some church leaders in Egypt to give up their belief in premillennialism even though he "rejoiced over the constancy, sincerity, docility, and intelligence of the brethren" (Eusebius, *Church History*, 7.24.8, NPNF 2/1:308). Eusebius references Dionysius's *On Promises*, where Dionysius writes about the book of Revelation, "But I could not venture to reject the book, as many brethren hold it in high esteem. But I suppose that it is beyond my comprehension, and that there is a certain concealed and more wonderful meaning in every part. For if I do not understand it I suspect that a deeper sense lies beneath the words. I do not measure and judge them by my own reason, but leaving the more to faith I regard them as too high for me to grasp. And I do not reject what I cannot comprehend, but rather wonder because I do not understand it" (Eusebius, *Church History* 7.25.4, NPNF 2/1:309). See further Augustine's tortured interpretation of Revelation 20 in *The City of God*, 20.7–17, NPNF 2/2:426–37.

[79] Cohen, *Living Letters of the Law*, 11.

replaced in the third century by Neoplatonism.[80] Both of these forms of Platonism were based on metaphysical dualism. Cowan and Spiegel explain,

> For Plato there were two worlds or levels of reality. There is the imperfect, changing world of particular things. . . . This world for Plato, could not be ultimately real nor could it provide any basis for the unity of things. . . . This led Plato to conclude that there must be another realm, a non-physical or spiritual reality that grounded the unity of things in the material world. Things in this spiritual realm are perfect, immutable, and eternal.[81]

This explanation of Platonism sounds strangely similar to Melito's explanation of how to interpret the Bible. The physical or material world is superseded by the spiritual realm.

Denis Minns, a Dominican friar who at one time was a member of the theology faculty of Oxford University, agrees that there was a "surprisingly large [body of Christians] at the end of the second century, who continued to believe in the imminent coming of the Kingdom of God in a quite literal sense."[82] But he continues:

> Half a century later, partly in consequence of the growing influence of Platonism within Christian theology, the "spiritual interpretation" of the coming of the Kingdom had triumphed, and the views on the Kingdom of Irenaeus and other like-minded theologians were derided as naïve or outlandish. . . . For these theologians, in the starkest contrast to Irenaeus, what really mattered was the spiritual dimension in the human being: the spirit or the soul. . . . But as God is spiritual, it is only the spiritual dimension that can be concerned in this salvation.[83]

So, Neoplatonism impacted hermeneutics by giving the Fathers a philosophical foundation for spiritualizing Scripture. Spiritualization of the Old Testament led naturally to the rejection of a future for Israel and eventually to the repudiation of premillennialism.

---

[80] Colin Brown, *Christianity and Western Thought* (Downers Grove, IL: Intervarsity Press, 1990), 1:84.

[81] Steven B. Cowan and James S. Spiegel, *The Love of Wisdom* (Nashville: B&H Academic, 2009), 154.

[82] Denis Minns, *Irenaeus* (New York: T & T Clark International, 2010), 140.

[83] Ibid., 14–141.

Conclusion

We have surveyed several intertwining issues that led to the dismissal of pretribulationism by the early Church Fathers. These individuals, though bearing witness to the saving power of the gospel of Christ even to their martyrdom in some cases, were ordinary men who often disagreed with each other. But on the topic of eschatology, the Church Fathers who lived and wrote up until the middle of the third century accepted a premillennial return of Christ. Still, as far as we can tell, they were not pretribulationists. I have argued that a major reason for the loss of pretribulationism among the early Fathers was their belief that Israel, as a nation, had permanently lost its place in God's agenda. According to their view, at no time in the eschaton would Israel have a national revival, repent of its sins, and accept Jesus as Messiah. Consequently, the Old Testament prophecies about Israel living in its Promised Land, with its Messiah ruling the world from Jerusalem, would go unfulfilled.

We who believe that the Bible teaches a pretribulational rapture of the church have often said that inadequate hermeneutics is the main reason for a rejection of this great doctrine. So the interesting question for us is whether the root problem is to be found in the misinterpretation of Scripture, especially of the Old Testament, or in the Jewish problem. I conclude that the place of Israel in the eschatology of the Church Fathers was fundamental in causing their departure from pretribulationism. Peter Richardson, in his analysis of the Fathers' interpretation of the Old Testament, casts a cautious vote for the Jewish problem being the main reason. He writes, "There is insufficient evidence for certainty, but it is likely that the formative factor is the author's attitude to Judaism, and then (consciously or subconsciously) his hermeneutical principle would follow."[84]

---

[84] Richardson, *Israel in the Apostolic Church*, 30.

Acts, the Church, and the Use of the Old Testament in the New Testament

Andrew Hudson
Pastor, Westside Baptist Church
Janesville, Wisconsin

The book of Acts is the only canonical document that records the beginning of the church in Jerusalem and its expansion to the ends of the earth. Thematically, Acts opens with a focus on national Israel and ends with a focus on the Gentile world. Its main character is Peter in the initial chapters and Paul in its later chapters. Acts records both the early history and the early preaching of the church.

This essay presupposes that, even though Acts is a unique book, it should be interpreted according to a literal or normal historical-grammatical hermeneutic. This method of interpretation will yield both the proper understanding of its content and the proper application of its teachings to the contemporary church. To arrive at a proper interpretation of the book of Acts, this essay examines four issues. First, it considers the historical setting of Acts. Second, it reviews the argument of Acts. Third, it addresses the use of the Old Testament in Acts. Fourth, it explains the transitional nature of Acts.[1]

Historical Setting of Acts

Interpreting the book of Acts requires us to understand its historical setting and literary genre. We need to know who wrote the book, to whom, and why. We also need to know what kind of book it is.

Relationship to the Gospel of Luke

The book of Acts was written by Luke.[2] The introductions to Luke and Acts identify Theophilus as the recipient of both books. The Gospel of Luke was written to assure Theophilus that what he had been taught about Jesus was true (Luke 1:1), and it records all that Jesus "began to do and teach" during his earthly ministry (Acts 1:1). Acts records all that Jesus continued to

---

[1] Dr. Charles Hauser was my teacher, mentor, and example of godly living. I thank the Lord for the opportunity to sit under Dr. Hauser. His detailed presentations of Scripture and his high expectations for students were both a blessing and a goal for which to strive. His sharing his Minnesota Golden Gopher football season tickets with me made a lasting impact on my life in so many ways.

[2] D. A. Carson and Douglas Moo, *An Introduction to the New Testament*, 2nd ed. (Grand Rapids: Zondervan, 2005), 290–96.

do and teach through the Spirit-filled apostles. The Gospel of Luke employs travel narratives that take Jesus to Jerusalem. Acts begins in Jerusalem and records the travels of the apostles to the uttermost parts of the earth (Acts 1:8). The Gospel of Luke culminates with the death, burial, resurrection, and ascension of Christ. Acts begins where the Gospel of Luke leaves off, culminating with a multiethnic church that has spread throughout the world.

Should we see Acts as the second volume of a two-volume work (i.e., Luke-Acts)? Or should we view Acts as a separate book that is mostly independent from the Gospel of Luke (i.e., Luke and Acts)? How we answer this question will affect how we interpret Acts. For example, when Acts speaks of the kingdom and the coming of the Holy Spirit (Acts 1:3–5), are the kingdom and Spirit defined by the Gospel of Luke or are they defined independently? The two documents are obviously and closely connected. Nevertheless, the early church placed the Gospel of Luke with the other Gospels but kept Acts separate from the Gospels. The Gospel of Luke and the book of Acts have remained separated in the canon. Bock concludes,

> So we read Luke-Acts as Luke-Acts on the basis of literary and theological unity, not on the basis of its being issued as two volumes from one author. We also keep an eye on the early church's use of the two volumes as distinctly treating Jesus on the one hand and the new community in the new era of the indwelt Spirit on the other. In this way we read it as Luke and Acts. We regard the former status as a unified work as most important for doing biblical theology, but regard the later canonical division as a recognition that the church's use of the material perceived that with the coming of the Spirit, what Jesus had promised and started came with a renewed vigor that took the new community some time to sort out as Acts shows us.[3]

In other words, when we interpret the book of Acts, we should consider both the theological connections to the Gospel of Luke and the unique content of the book of Acts.

Literary Genre

We normally read a newspaper differently from a written sermon. The type of literature influences the interpretation of the material. This principle

---

[3] Darrell Bock, *A Theology of Luke and Acts* (Grand Rapids: Zondervan, 2012), 60.

applies to the book of Acts—but what kind of literature is it? Answers to this question vary.

Couch suggests that Acts is a historical document: "The key element to remember is that the main purpose of the book of Acts is to record history and not develop doctrine; and doctrine must not be developed from historical events alone."[4] According to Couch, we should not look for any theology in the book of Acts because it is primarily a historical document.

Keener, on the other hand, describes Acts as historiography.[5] *Historiography* (as Keener uses the term) refers to history with a specific interpretive viewpoint. In this sense Acts is like the Gospel genre. Gospels tell the story of Jesus (history) to make a theological point (four Gospels, four theological emphases). The history of Acts is broader than the history of a single person, and this history is written to make a theological point. Therefore, Acts does teach theology. Keener says, "The expectation of models for imitation in ancient biography and historiography more generally would prime Luke's first century, ancient Mediterranean audiences to look for models also."[6] In other words, even the narrative sections of the book of Acts provide examples that believers should follow. Just as believers follow the example of Christ, they should also follow some examples of characters in Acts. Paul says as much in his epistles (e.g., 1 Cor 11:1; Phil 3:17–21).

Bock agrees with Keener that Acts is historiography, but he does not look for models of behavior to imitate. He identifies the theological focus as the new community (i.e., the church). Bock concludes, "Acts is a piece of Hellenist and Jewish historiography that treats the theme of how the new community is rooted in God's old promises, the Lord Jesus's current activity, and the Spirit's effective presence."[7]

Most likely, Acts is some form of historiography. Like the history in the Gospels, the history in Acts is very selective. The events are chosen to make a theological point. Also like the Gospels, Acts contains both historical narrative and historical sermons or speeches. Few would question that the

---

[4] Mal Couch, *A Bible Handbook to the Acts of the Apostles* (Grand Rapids: Kregel, 1999), 18. Couch does admit that the history in Acts is a "theological historical narrative." He says it is a "historical account of the shift from the dispensation of the law to the dispensation of grace."

[5] Craig S. Keener, *Acts: An Exegetical Commentary*, vol. 1 (Grand Rapids: Baker Academic, 2012), 90ff.

[6] Ibid., 440.

[7] Darrell L. Bock, *Acts*, BECNT (Grand Rapids: Baker Academic, 2007), 12.

Gospels make a theological point. The same should be said for the book of Acts.

Purpose of the Book

Several suggestions have been offered for why Luke wrote the book of Acts. In looking for a reason, the fact that Acts makes a theological point is critical. Interpreters should look for this theological point to determine Luke's purpose in writing. Consequently, explanations of Acts that do not see a specific theological point can be eliminated from consideration. Even so, several possibilities remain.

Mal Couch argues that the purpose of Acts is to describe the transition from the dispensation of law to the dispensation of grace.[8] In his view, however, the book of Acts is merely a historical description of this transition. He does not believe that Acts is the source for any theology; instead, theology must be verified in the epistles. Couch seems to overstate his case; while he is correct that Acts describes a transition, this transition is precisely theological in nature.

William Neil suggests that the primary purpose of Acts is evangelism: "Whatever other motives our author may have had in mind in writing this literary masterpiece, his fundamental object was to proclaim the Good News." It is true that the gospel is clear in the book of Acts, but the selection of narratives and speeches involves far more than evangelizing. Furthermore, Luke wrote the book to a believer who did not need to be evangelized.[9]

F. F. Bruce claims that Luke is presenting an apologetic: "Luke is, in fact, the pioneer among Christian apologists, especially in that form of apologetic which is addressed to the civil authorities to establish the law-abiding character of Christianity." Bruce rejects the suggestion that Acts was an apologetic for Paul's defense in front of Roman authorities since the book includes too much content that is unrelated to that purpose. Bruce also observes that the speeches in Acts reveal other apologetic aims, such as showing that the church is the true fulfillment of the Old Testament promises. While Luke does make a case for his theological point, he is writing to believers, not to civil authorities. It is unlikely that Acts is meant as an apologetic to convince civil authorities. [10]

---

[8] Couch, *Bible Handbook to the Acts of the Apostles*, 18ff.

[9] William Neil, *The Acts of the Apostles*, NCB (Grand Rapids: Eerdmans, 1973), 25.

[10] F. F. Bruce, *The Book of the Acts*, NICNT (Grand Rapids: Eerdmans, 1988), 12–13.

D. A. Carson and Douglas Moo argue that Acts is written to edify saints: "We agree with a growing number of scholars who think that Luke wrote with a variety of purposes and that these purposes are part of a larger, general purpose—the edification of Christians." Given that the recipient of the letter is a believer, this suggestion makes sense, but it may be too vague to be helpful. In what way does Luke intend to edify his readers? What specific themes accomplish this goal? Carson and Moo believe that only this broad theme can account for the "richness of Luke-Acts" while at the same time allowing for subsidiary purposes. [11]

J. B. Pohill is somewhat agnostic toward the purpose of Acts:

> In speaking of an author's "purpose," two problems arise. One is that this assumes we can pick the author's brain. I am not sure that we can. We only know him through his works and can ultimately only speak of the emphases that seem to stand out in his writings. The second problem is that attempts to delineate a single purpose of a writing tend to become overly focused and to omit other significant motifs. It seems better to speak of themes and to acknowledge a multiplicity of them in Acts. None of them is distinct. They all interweave and overlap with one another to furnish together the rich tapestry that is the story of Acts. [12]

There may be wisdom in Pohill's approach. A diversity of themes does run through the book of Acts. Nevertheless, this diversity may still rest upon one or two identifiable major themes.

Two interrelated primary themes in Acts can account for all the material in the book. First, Israel continues to reject the Messiah, preventing the arrival of the kingdom and placing the nation under the curses of the Mosaic Covenant. Israel will remain under the Mosaic curses without the kingdom until the nation repents at some future time. Second, the church begins and develops into a global, multiethnic body proclaiming God's glory and salvation. Rich spiritual blessings are given to the church through the blood of Christ. These two themes allow for a framework in which to interpret the book of Acts.

---

[11] Carson and Moo, *Introduction to the New Testament*, 305–06.

[12] J. B. Pohill, *Acts*, NAC (Nashville: Broadman & Holman, 1992), 57.

Argument of Acts

The primary focus of Luke's book to Theophilus is on the church. Acts is the story of Christ's work through his apostles and disciples to build the New Testament church. Luke's argument can be divided into three sections. First, Luke addresses the events surrounding the beginning of a Jewish church at Pentecost. Second, Luke explains the ethnic expansion of the church. Samaritans and Gentiles are added to Jews in the church, resulting in a multiethnic body. Third, Luke describes the explosion of the new multiethnic church to the "ends of the earth" geographically. Thus, Luke records the early history of the global church.

Foundation of the Church

Acts 1. Prior to discussing the birth of the church, Luke deals with several preliminary issues. In 1:1–12, Luke surveys the post-resurrection ministry of Jesus. During this time Jesus gave his final instructions to his disciples and ascended to heaven, both of which were necessary for the church to begin. Jesus announced that his disciples would be given power to live as witnesses for him starting in Jerusalem and reaching the ends of the earth (1:8), indicating that the church would become worldwide and multiethnic. In 1:13–26, Luke records the selection of Matthias as the twelfth apostle to replace Judas. The church could not begin until there were twelve apostles for the Jews (Matt 19:28). The events in Acts 1 complete the Mosaic dispensation.

Acts 2. Luke discusses the beginning of the church in Acts 2. The new ministry of the Holy Spirit that began on Pentecost provided the means by which the church was born and could move forward. In Acts 2:1–13, Luke records the arrival of this new ministry, and he shows how people reacted to it. Because it caused some confusion, Peter explained the arrival of the Spirit's ministry and related it to Christ's death, burial, and resurrection. Peter also explained how the Jews' rejection of their Messiah resulted in the establishment of the church (Acts 2:14–41). Luke concludes the chapter by summarizing the practice of the early church (2:42–47) and its results (2:41, 47), which were twofold. The church added about three thousand souls in one day (2:41), following which the Lord added to the church daily those who were saved.

Acts 3. Once Luke has presented the preliminary issues and detailed the birth and early growth of the church, he moves on to the preaching of the young church. The church is now somewhere over 3,120 members strong—each one presenting the gospel of Christ. In Acts 3, Luke addresses the message that they were preaching. First, he records the authentication of the message by means of a healing miracle (3:1–10). Second, he presents the message of the early church by recording one of Peter's sermons (3:11–16). This sermon shows that the early church was preaching salvation by faith in Christ, whom the Jews crucified but whom God raised from the dead. Third, Luke shows how Peter applied this gospel message to contemporary Jews (3:17–26). Peter appeals to these Jews to repent for rejecting and killing Christ and to place faith in Christ for forgiveness and restoration of all things as God promised in the Old Testament.

Acts 4:1–6:8. Luke next reveals that the early church also experienced problems. These problems came from both inside and outside the church, but the church continued to grow through the work of the Holy Spirit. Luke records four specific problems that threatened to halt the advance of the early church.

First, the church faced persecution. The Jewish leadership observed that the church was growing (4:4), now including some five thousand men, plus women and children. The Jewish leaders arrested Peter and John and threatened them to prevent them from preaching in the name of Jesus. They did not stop this preaching, however; instead, the apostles spoke the Word of God with boldness (4:31).

Second, Luke records an internal problem of dishonesty within the church (Acts 5:1–16). The deceptiveness of Ananias and Saphira threatened the purity of the early church. God addressed this threat by taking the lives of Ananias and Sapphira. Luke notes that more people were added to the church, multitudes of men and women (5:14).

Third, the Jewish leadership grew incensed at the continued growth of the church (5:17–42). They expanded their persecution by arresting all the apostles, whom they eventually beat and threatened. In response, the apostles filled Jerusalem with the doctrine of Christ (5:28) and did not stop preaching Jesus Christ (5:42).

Fourth, Luke records a problem of financial distribution (6:1–8). A disagreement arose over whether some widows were being treated fairly. This dispute threatened the unity of the church and kept the apostles from preaching and prayer. Under their leadership, the church selected men (perhaps proto-deacons) to ensure the fairness of the distribution, preserving the unity of the church and allowing the apostles to keep their focus on prayer and preaching.

Acts 6:9–7:60. This section records the events that culminated in the stoning of Stephen. It is also the bridge to the next major section of the book of Acts. The stoning of Stephen shows the extent to which the Sanhedrin (and Israel as a whole) rejected the message of the resurrected Christ. This rejection is what validates the expansion of the church to include both Samaritans and Gentiles. This passage can be divided into three major sections. Acts 6:9–15 records the events that resulted in Stephen's trial before the Sanhedrin. He was accused of blaspheming God, Moses, the law, and the temple. Acts 7:1–53 details Stephen's response to the Sanhedrin, showing that the accusations against him were false. In this response, Stephen turns the tables and accuses the Sanhedrin of killing Jesus, whom they should have accepted as their Messiah. Acts 7:54–60 records the actual stoning of Stephen, which stands as proof of Israel's rejection of Jesus. This is the point at which Saul (Paul) is introduced into the narrative.

Expansion of the Church

Having shown how Israel rejected the Messiah a second time, Luke provides an account of the church's expansion to include both Samaritans and Gentiles. He first notes the inclusion of the Samaritans in the church (Acts 8). Then, in Acts 9, Luke narrates the conversion of Saul, who would become the apostle to the Gentiles. In Acts 10–11, he records the inclusion of Gentiles in the church, also showing the initial reaction of the Jewish believers. Finally, Luke tells how Herod persecuted the expanding church (Acts 12) and how God stopped him.

Acts 8. Luke continues his narrative by showing how Philip took the gospel to the Samaritans. Several sections in chapter 8 introduce or involve ushering Samaritans into the church on an equal footing with the Jewish believers. Verses 1–4 show how Jewish persecution forced the Jerusalem believers to scatter throughout Samaritan territory. Verses 5–13 rehearse Philip's ministry in a Samaritan town, as the result of which many Samaritans believed the gospel message and were baptized in water. After hearing of these Samaritan conversions, the church in Jerusalem sent Peter and John to assess the situation. God used these apostles to bring the Samaritans into the church through Spirit baptism (8:14–17). This is the only time that there was a delay in Spirit baptism for Samaritans.

The narrative continues with 8:18–25 recording Simon's unsuccessful attempt to pervert the gospel. The apostles returned to Jerusalem, preaching the gospel to the Samaritans along the way. Acts 8:26–40 rehearses Philip's ministry to an Ethiopian eunuch who placed his faith in Christ and was water baptized. The chapter ends with Philip at Caesarea.

Acts 9. Having described the inclusion of the Samaritans in the New Testament church, Luke details the addition of Gentiles. First, he introduces a key figure in the Gentile inclusion by recording the salvation and call of Saul, who (under his Roman name, Paul) would become the apostle to the Gentiles. Acts 9:1–31 records a brief history of the conversion, call, and early Christian life of Paul. One consequence of Paul's conversion was that the church had rest, was edified, and multiplied (9:31). Acts 9:32–43 reintroduces Peter and provides a transition into the story of Cornelius. These verses place Peter at Joppa.

Acts 10. In this chapter Luke narrates the inclusion of Gentiles in the church. Cornelius and his household believed and entered the church as the result of Peter's preaching. God verified their admission into the church by pouring out on them the same Holy Spirit that he had poured out on Jews at Pentecost. The story develops in stages. Acts 10:1–8 introduces Cornelius and the vision God gave him to send for Peter. Then God gave Peter a vision (10:9–16), leading him to understand that Gentiles were not unclean. Acts 10:17–23 describes Peter's meeting with messengers from Cornelius. After accompanying them to Caesarea, Peter asked why Cornelius had sent for him (10:24–33). Peter then preached directly to Cornelius and his household (10:34–43). The result was that the Holy Spirit fell on the Gentiles just he had on the Jews at Pentecost (10:44–48), signifying that God was adding Gentiles to the church on equal footing with the Jews and Samaritans.

Acts 11. The continuing narrative shows how the Jerusalem congregation reacted to the addition of Gentiles to the church. This chapter can be divided into two sections. First, the Jews in Jerusalem questioned the legitimacy of Peter's ministry to the Gentiles (11:1–18). Apostolic authority centered in Jerusalem, and if the apostles had not supported Gentile inclusion, the church would have remained divided. Peter demonstrated that it was God's work that had brought Gentiles into the church. As a result, the Jews withdrew their objections to Gentile inclusion. Second, the Jewish Christians who had been scattered from Jerusalem created a headquarters for Gentile evangelism in Antioch (11:19–30). Here, Luke reaches back to the death of Stephen and the dispersion of Jewish believers from Jerusalem (8:4; 11:19). He aims to show the progress of the gospel as it spread from Jerusalem. Luke has already begun to describe the spread of the gospel by recording the evangelization of Samaria and the salvation of the Ethiopian eunuch, but he interrupts the narrative with two crucial events: the conversion of Saul and the expansion of the church to include the Gentiles. Now he resumes the description of the spread of the gospel to the ends of the earth, with Antioch as the center of activity.

Acts 12. Luke has demonstrated how God set the stage for the explosion of the church into the Gentile world. All the elements have been established. The Spirit has begun his ministry of baptizing believers into the church (the body of Christ). Samaritans have been added to the church. Gentiles have been added to the church. The apostle to the Gentiles has been called and commissioned. Luke now deals with one further issue before recording Paul's missionary endeavors to the Gentile world. In Acts 12, Luke records the severe persecution that the church faced under Herod's rule, demonstrating that the church faced opposition not only from Jews but also from Gentiles. Acts 12 has four sections: Herod's persecution (12:1–4), God's protection of imprisoned Peter (12:5–10), the various reactions to Peter's release from prison (12:11–23), and God's protection of the church through the supernatural death of Herod as God continued to expand the church (12:24–25). The point of this chapter is also its climax in these last two verses, where Luke shows that not even governmental persecution could slow the growth of the church.

Explosion of the Church

Acts 13–14. In these chapters Luke begins to record the explosion of the church to the "uttermost parts of the earth." The church in Antioch was led by the Spirit to send Paul and Barnabas to the Gentile world to preach the gospel. Each of Paul's missionary journeys took the gospel a little farther into Gentile territory. Paul's first missionary journey (Acts 13–14) resulted in the establishment and strengthening of many Gentile churches. Paul planted the churches on his outbound journey and then appointed elders and warned the churches of persecution on his return trip (14:21–23). Upon his return to the Antioch church, he reported how God had worked among the Gentiles.

Acts 15:1–35. With increasing numbers of Gentile converts, a new issue began to surface. Some Jewish Christians thought that the Gentiles needed to be circumcised to be saved. This issue first appeared in Antioch, and that church decided to send messengers (including Paul and Barnabas) to Jerusalem to discuss the problem with the apostles there. Luke records this meeting (15:1–21). The decisions that came from this meeting established policy for Paul's future ministry to the Gentiles (15:22–35). The Jerusalem congregation denied that Gentiles needed to be circumcised or to follow Jewish law to be part of the church. At the same time, Gentiles were responsible to avoid pagan worship practices (e.g., drinking blood).

Acts 15:36–18:22. After the Jerusalem meeting, Paul continued his ministry of taking the gospel to the Gentiles. Luke opens the account of Paul's second missionary journey (15:36–18:22) by showing a disagreement between Paul and Barnabas over including John Mark on the missionary team. Paul and Barnabas separated to form two missionary teams (15:36–40). Luke only records the activities of Paul's team. Paul began by revisiting some of the churches established on his first journey. He encouraged them by sharing the results of the Jerusalem meeting. Luke next records Paul's "Macedonian call," through which God sent the team farther west to take the gospel into Europe (16:6–11). During this journey Paul ministered in Philippi (16:12–40), Thessalonica (17:1–9), Berea (17:10–14), Athens (17:15–34), and Corinth (18:1–18). On his return trip to Antioch, he briefly visited Ephesus (18:19–22). This review of Paul's second missionary journey shows the advance of the church farther west, approaching the ends of the earth.

Acts 18:23–21:16. After a short period of reporting to the believers in Antioch, Paul set out for a third journey. His purpose was to strengthen the churches that he had already started (18:23). At this point Luke introduces Apollos into the narrative. Apollos was a disciple of John the Baptist who had never heard of Christ (18:24–28). Then, at Ephesus, Paul met a group of John the Baptist's disciples who had never heard of Christ (19:1–7). When Paul preached Christ and the kingdom to them, they believed on Christ. Paul laid hands on them, and the Holy Spirit was poured out on them just as on the Jews, Samaritans, and Gentiles. The significance of this event is that God was bringing these disciples of John into the church. Luke records further details of Paul's ministry in Ephesus (19:8–41) and of his ministry in

Macedonia, Achaia, and Troas (20:1–16). Against the advice of friends, Paul started for Jerusalem, greeting elders from Ephesus at Miletus along the way (20:17–21:16).

Acts 21:17–28:31. In the final section of Acts, Luke records the severe persecution that Paul faced when he reached Jerusalem. He was first arrested, tried, and held in Jerusalem (21:17–23:10). Then he was sent to Caesarea and kept in prison there (23:31–26:32). While in Caesarea, Paul appealed to have his case heard before Caesar. As a result, Paul was sent to Rome at the expense of the Roman government (27:1–28:31). Paul gained the opportunity to present the gospel to the most influential and powerful human leader on earth. Paul also preached the gospel to many others who came to him in Rome. The book of Acts concludes with Paul under house arrest in Rome. The gospel and the church had reached the ends of the earth.

The Use of the Old Testament in Acts

Luke often uses the Old Testament in Acts. These uses take different forms, from direct quotations to repeating Old Testament language.[13] Sometimes Luke shows Old Testament prophecies as fulfilled in Acts, but many times he is doing something else. His repeated appeal to the Old Testament is not surprising because the early church preached the gospel from the Old Testament (Acts 8:35; 18:28; 26:22–23; 26; 28:23). Christ also explained his death and resurrection from Old Testament texts (Luke 24:25–27). While the Old Testament does not mention the New Testament church, it has much to say about national Israel, Christ, and Gentile salvation. Since Acts teaches about these themes, Luke naturally refers to Old Testament teachings that deal with them. A few references to the Old Testament in Acts are more generic, simply explaining some contemporary situation by alluding to Old Testament truth.

Uses That Identify Jesus

Luke uses several Old Testament passages to clarify truths about the identity and ministry of Jesus Christ. His point is that Jesus truly is both Lord and Christ who, through his crucifixion and resurrection, offers salvation to both Jews and Gentiles. Luke depicts episodes in which Peter, Paul, and

---

[13] I. Howard Marshall lists nine different uses of the OT in the book of Acts. He suggests summary references, citations with formulas, citations without formulas, paraphrases, allusions, echoes, scriptural terminology, language, and motifs/structures. I. Howard Marshall, "Acts," in *Commentary on the New Testament Use of the Old Testament,* ed. G. K. Beale and D. A. Carson (Grand Rapids: Baker Academic, 2007), 519.

others use the Old Testament to substantiate four specific claims about Jesus.

First, Luke shows Peter appealing to the Old Testament to explain the crucifixion of Jesus. After healing the lame man on the way to the temple, Peter claimed that all the prophets foretold the sufferings Jesus would face (Acts 3:18). He then concluded that the Old Testament prophecies about a suffering Messiah were fulfilled in Jesus.

In view of this claim, the Jewish leadership arrested Peter and John for preaching salvation in the name of Jesus, partly because the apostles were implicating these leaders in the crucifixion. After threatening Peter and John, the Jewish leaders forbade these two disciples from preaching in the name of Jesus. Peter and John reported these threats to the rest of the disciples, who responded by praising God for the prediction and accomplishment of the crucifixion. The disciples recognized that Jesus was crucified at the hands of Herod, Pontius Pilate, the Jews, and the Gentiles (Acts 4:27) just as God had planned beforehand (Acts 4:28; cf. Acts 2:23). The disciples saw Psalm 2:1–2 as evidence that God knew exactly how the crucifixion would occur (Acts 4:25–26).

Second, Luke shows how the Old Testament was used to explain the resurrection of Jesus. He records Peter's sermon on Pentecost, which claimed that Jesus was raised from the dead because death could not possibly hold or keep him (Acts 2:24). In support of this claim, Peter quoted Psalm 16:8–11, explaining that this psalm must be speaking of Jesus because King David was still dead and in his grave. Luke later shows how Paul used this same line of reasoning, appealing to Psalm 16 to show that the resurrection of Jesus was prophesied (Acts 13:35). Paul also appealed to Psalm 2:7 and Isaiah 55:3 as additional Old Testament prophecies of Jesus's resurrection. "With this psalm citation, Paul teaches that God raised Jesus from the dead for His messianic task. We assume that when Paul in his sermon first related the facts concerning the resurrection of Christ, the audience wanted proof from the Old Testament. The people desired to know whether the Scriptures predict that God would raise Jesus from the dead."[14]

Third, Luke reports episodes in which Peter uses the Old Testament to identify Jesus as both Lord and Christ. In Acts 2:36, Peter cited Psalm 16:8–11 to demonstrate that Jesus was raised from the dead (David was not). He alluded to Psalm 132:11 and 2 Samuel 7:12–13 to identify the resurrected

---

[14] Simon J. Kistemaker, *Acts*, New Testament Commentary (Grand Rapids: Baker, 1990), 484.

Jesus as the one who would sit on the Davidic throne forever (Acts 2:29–30). Peter then appealed to Psalm 110:1, claiming that the risen Christ had ascended to the right hand of God in heaven, received the promise of the Spirit, and poured out the Spirit at Pentecost (Acts 2:33–34).[15]

Fourth, Luke shows that the Old Testament was used to establish how Jesus, in his role as Christ or Messiah, would deliver his people from their sins. To explain this deliverance, Peter quoted Deuteronomy 18:15, 18–19 and identified Jesus as the Moses-like prophet who would save his people (Acts 3:22–23). In view of this truth, Peter appealed to the Jews to repent of their sins and trust in Jesus (Acts 3:19). Peter also argued that Jesus was the seed of Abraham through whom all nations of the earth would be blessed (Gen 12:3; Acts 3:25) when he turns them away from their iniquities.

Uses That Show God's Plan for Israel

Writing in Acts, Luke uses the Old Testament to show the place of Israel in God's plan. The entire scope of Israel's existence is reviewed in Acts. Starting with the origin of the nation, Luke goes on to point out how Israel rejected the Messiah and was subsequently placed under God's curse. Luke also affirms a future for national Israel. Specifically, Luke employs Old Testament citations in the book of Acts to illustrate the following points.

First, Luke uses the Old Testament to identify Israel as God's chosen people. He shows that Stephen, while refuting the accusation of blasphemy (Acts 6:11–14), rehearsed the history of Israel (Acts 7). The heart of this discourse is a quotation from Exodus 3:6, 15, cited in Acts 7:32, which is meant to reassure Stephen's accusers of his belief that Israel was God's chosen people. Stephen identified the God who spoke from the burning bush as the "God of Abraham, the God of Isaac, and the God of Jacob." This God who called Abraham and made a covenant with him (Acts 7:3) also told Moses to go to Egypt to lead Israel out of slavery. Stephen quoted Exodus 3:7, which has God describing Israel as "My people" (Acts 7:34). God heard and delivered the children of Israel because of his covenant with Abraham, Isaac, and Jacob (Exod 2:24–25). Nothing in the teaching of Stephen (or the apostolic church) negates God's commitment to Israel.

Second, Luke cites the Old Testament to demonstrate precedent for Israel's rejection of Jesus, the Messiah. In Acts 7:51, the rejection of Jesus

---

[15] Dispensationalists debate whether Jesus is sitting on the Davidic throne from the moment of his resurrection or whether he will take that throne in the future, after all his enemies are made his footstool.

mirrors earlier Jewish rejection of the prophets. After mentioning Israel's rejection of Moses (Exod 2:10; Acts 7:27, 35) and turning aside to worship of Egyptian gods (Acts 7:39–43; Exod 32:1; Amos 5:25–27), Stephen calls the Jews "stiff-necked and uncircumcised in heart and ears." Because of their hard-heartedness, contemporary Jews resisted the Holy Spirit "as [their] fathers did."

Israel's rejection of the Messiah is also evident in Luke's record of Pauline citations from the Old Testament. While preaching in the synagogue in Pisidian Antioch, Paul warned Jews who rejected the gospel that they would perish. He quoted Habakkuk 1:5 to show that the current Jewish rejection of Jesus was parallel to the disobedience of Jews in Habakkuk's day (Acts 13:40–41). As Marshall rightly notes, "Luke regards the present situation as a repetition of what happened in Habakkuk's time, in which God again does a 'work,' and this is perhaps to be understood in the light of the use of *ergon* to refer to the apostolic mission referred to in the broader context (13:2; 14:26), which provokes unbelief among the Jews and renders them liable to God's judgment."[16]

Third, Luke uses the Old Testament to confirm that Israel is under God's judgment. In Acts 28:26–27, Paul quoted Isaiah 6:9–10 to show that Israel stood under curses from the Mosaic Covenant. Isaiah 6:9–10 alludes to a similar statement in Deuteronomy 29:2–4 that lists curses for disobedience. As a result, quoting Isaiah 6:9–10 became shorthand for saying that Israel was disobedient and, thus, liable to these curses.[17] Jesus had quoted this passage several times to explain Israel's rejection of him (Matt 13:14–15; Mark 4:12; 8:18; Luke 8:10; John 12:40). In Acts 28, Paul was presenting the gospel and the kingdom to the Jewish leadership in Rome. Some believed but most did not. When the Jews could not agree among themselves Paul quoted Isaiah 6:9–10 to expose their unbelief. Bock says, "[Isaiah] presents the passage as describing something that has occurred instead of a strict prediction, because this is how the matter has in fact turned out."[18] The Jewish leaders in Rome were displaying the same unbelief as the Jews during Jesus's day and in Isaiah's time. Their rejection of their Messiah was both cause and result of God's judgment on the nation (i.e., the curses of the Mosaic Covenant).

---

[16] I. Howard Marshall, "Acts," 587.

[17] Andrew Hudson, "Whosoever Won't," *Frontline* 27.3 (May-June 2017), 19, 25, 36.

[18] Darrell L. Bock, *Acts,* 755.

Fourth, Luke also shows Paul using the Old Testament to intimate that the Gentiles will hear and accept the salvation of God (Acts 28:28). In other words, the rejection of Christ by the Jews opened the door for a multiethnic church that included both Jews and Gentiles. Preaching the gospel in the synagogue at Pisidian Antioch, Paul quoted Habakkuk 1:5 (Acts 13:41). He warned these Jews that rejecting Jesus would result in judgment, just as disobedience to God had brought judgment in the Old Testament. After warning the Jews with this message, Paul preached the gospel to Gentiles on the following Sabbath. He justified this turn toward the Gentiles by quoting Isaiah 49:6 (Acts 13:47). Marshall observes, "The refusal of the Jews to believe serves as permission for the apostles to go to the Gentiles, who are equally included in God's purpose of salvation. The apostles have fulfilled the obligation to go first to the Jews, and now they can take up the other part of the commission that has been laid down for them in Scripture."[19]

A similar account is given in Acts 15:16–17, a passage that addresses the question of Gentile salvation. Did Gentiles need to become Jewish proselytes? Peter rehearsed how God saved Cornelius as a Gentile. Paul and Barnabas explained how God saved Gentiles during their first missionary journey. In response to these reports, James (an elder in Jerusalem) stated that God was taking from the Gentiles a people for his name. He went on to observe that the Old Testament anticipated the inclusion of Gentiles, citing Amos 9:11–12 (with influence from Jer 12:15 and Isa 45:21). In the Old Testament context, Amos prophesied about a rebuilt tabernacle, a remnant who would seek the Lord, and God saving Gentiles whom He would call. One can debate whether James is saying that Gentile salvation in the early church is a fulfillment of Amos's prophecy or that Gentile salvation in the early church is simply parallel to Amos's prophecy.[20] What is clear is that James believed that Gentiles being saved without becoming Jews was consistent with Old Testament teaching. The fact that God was saving Gentiles in no way dismissed promises of a future restoration of Israel.

Fifth, Luke shows that the Old Testament guarantees a future for

[19] I. Howard Marshall, "Acts," 587.

[20] For the former alternative, see Bock, *Acts*, 503–5, "Thus James argues that this Gentile inclusion is part of the plan of Davidic restoration that God through the prophets said he would do. The prophets affirm what is taking place now." For the latter alternative, see Homer Kent, *Jerusalem to Rome: Studies in Acts* (Grand Rapids: Baker, 1972), 125–27, "Amos has shown what will occur in the future for Israel. Peter explained what God was doing in the meantime regarding salvation for the Gentiles."

national Israel. In Acts 1:6, the Jewish disciples asked Jesus whether he would restore the kingdom to Israel at that time. Though Jesus refused to answer their question, he also did not deny that there would be a restoration of the kingdom to Israel. The disciples understood this. In Acts 3:19–26, Peter preached about a restored kingdom that would follow a time when Jesus is in heaven. He claimed that all the prophets since the world began spoke of the restoration of all things (Acts 3:21). This restoration, Peter observed, will occur when Jesus returns to earth. He supported this claim by quoting Moses's prophecy of a greater prophet who would deliver Israel (Deut 18:15, 18–19).

Other Uses of the Old Testament

In the text of Acts, Luke uses the Old Testament in a variety of other ways besides those mentioned above. For example, he sometimes uses the Old Testament to support the point that he is making or to further explain a passage. One such use occurs near the opening of the book in Acts 1. The apostles and believers were tasked with finding a new apostle to replace Judas. Peter had to explain the rationale for replacing Judas since none of the other apostles would be replaced when he died. In Acts 1:20, Peter justified this action by appealing to two Old Testament passages. He quoted Psalm 69:25 to show that Judas's office was indeed empty. He then quoted Psalm 109:8 to argue that someone else should fill the office of apostle. The point seems to be that the apostleship of Judas was left empty not by his death but by his defection. Placing Matthias in Judas's apostleship restored the number of apostles to twelve. It was necessary to have twelve apostles so they could sit on the twelve thrones in the future kingdom as Jesus had promised (Matt 19:28).

How do Psalms 69 and 109 apply to Judas's situation? Neither passage is speaking about the office of apostle or the need for twelve Jewish apostles. F. F. Bruce suggests, "The former, from Ps. 69:25, is a prayer that the dwelling place of the psalmist's enemies may be deserted; the latter, from Ps. 109:8, prays that a certain enemy may die before his time and be replaced in his responsible position by someone else."[21] Even though the psalms do not speak of apostles, Bruce points out that they do speak of replacing someone "in his responsible position." Since Christ specified that the number of apostles would be twelve (Luke 22:30; Matt 19:28) to correspond to the number of the twelve tribes, Peter could use these Old Testament passages as warrant

---

[21] Bruce, *The Book of Acts*, 46.

for replacing Judas.[22] In this passage, a principle drawn from Old Testament passages finds a parallel to events in Peter's day.

Another example of Old Testament usage comes in Acts 23:5. The apostle Paul was under Roman arrest because of the stir that the Jews caused in Jerusalem. After the Romans realized that Paul was a Roman citizen, the soldiers stopped their plan to whip him and instead unbound him. On the following day, the Romans demanded that the Jewish chief priest and council come to examine Paul. After Paul stated that his conscience was clear before God, the high priest ordered that a soldier strike Paul on the mouth. Paul responded by questioning the legitimacy of the blow and by calling the high priest a whitewashed wall. Paul's response was met with a stern question about reviling the high priest. Paul then stated that he had not known the one who ordered the striking was the high priest. Paul next quoted Exodus 22:28 to imply that he would not have responded the way he did if he had recognized the high priest. Paul applied an Old Testament principle (not cursing the ruler of the people) to his own situation.

One of the most debated uses of the Old Testament in Acts is Peter's citation of Joel 2 in Acts 2. The coming of the Holy Spirit in Acts 2:1–4 marks the beginning of the church. The Spirit's ministry at Pentecost was later specifically identified as his baptizing work (Acts 11:15–17), which Paul elsewhere defines as the constituting element for the body of Christ (1 Cor 12:13). The speaking in foreign languages (Acts 2:6–11) authenticated this new ministry of the Spirit. Some mockers sarcastically attributed this phenomenon to drunkenness. Peter responded by pointing out that the hour was too early for anybody to be drunk. He offered an alternative explanation of the Spirit's activity by quoting Joel 2.

How does Joel 2 come to bear on the situation at Pentecost? This question has been answered in several ways. Each answer proposes a different relationship between the events in Acts 2 and the prophesied events in Joel 2. The three primary answers will be summarized here.

The first answer is that events in Acts 2 are a direct and complete fulfillment of the prophecy in Joel 2.[23] No future fulfillment of the Joel 2

---

[22] Ibid. Of course, whether the replacement of Judas with Matthias was warranted is not a settled question.

[23] Peter J. Gentry and Stepen J. Wellum, *Kingdom through Covenant* (Wheaton: Crossway, 2018), 761–62. Bruce, *The Book of Acts*, 61. Richard Longenecker, "Acts," in *The Expositor's Bible Commentary*, vol. 9, ed. Frank E. Gaebelein (Grand Rapids: Zondervan, 1981), 275–76.

prophesy is expected. In this view, the promises that God made in Joel 2 are fulfilled entirely in the church. Gentry and Wellum state, "The way that the Old Testament restoration promises for Israel are applied to the Church *in Christ* provides further evidence that the members of the Church, composed of believing Jews and Gentiles in Christ, equally and fully receive *all* God's promises."[24] Gentry and Wellum go on to say that Israel's end-time restoration begins in Acts 2 and extends to Samaritans and Gentiles, thus, creating a *"new humanity"* in Christ.[25]

The second answer is that the events in Acts 2 are a partial (initial, continuous) fulfillment of the prophecy of Joel 2.[26] The complete fulfillment of the prophecy to Israel awaits the future kingdom age. In the present-day church age, saints have the continuous ministry of the Holy Spirit as the down payment of the future complete fulfillment (2 Cor 1:22; 5:5; Eph 1:14; Rom 8:23). Believers presently enjoy the spiritual aspects of Joel's prophecy; the material aspects will arrive in the future for national Israel. The prophecy has been partly but not entirely fulfilled. Toussaint summarizes this view. "This does not mean, 'This is *like* that'; it means Pentecost fulfilled what Joel had described. However, the prophecies of Joel quoted in Acts 2:19–20 were not fulfilled. The implication is that the remainder would be fulfilled if Israel would repent."[27]

The third answer is that the events in Acts 2 do not actually fulfill the prophecy of Joel 2 at all.[28] Instead, the prophecy of Joel 2 provides a way for Peter to explain the new ministry of the Spirit that began at Pentecost. Gunn says, "Peter is drawing a comparison between the Spirit's activity in Joel's prophecy and the Spirit's activity on the day of Pentecost, without actually establishing a one to one fulfillment."[29] Beacham elaborates on this comparison: "Knowing that none of these qualifying events had yet occurred,

[24] Gentry and Wellum, *Kingdom through Covenant*, 761.

[25] Ibid., 762.

[26] Stanley D. Toussaint, "Acts," in *The Bible Knowledge Commentary*, ed. John F. Walvoord and Roy B. Zuck (Colorado Springs: David C. Cook, 1983), 358. Michael J. Vlach, *He Will Reign Forever: A Biblical Theology of the Kingdom of God* (Silverton, OR: Lampion, 2017), 408–9. Larry D. Pettegrew, *The New Covenant Ministry of the Holy Spirit* (Grand Rapids: Kregel, 2001), 101, 104. Bock, *Acts*, 112.

[27] Stanley D. Toussaint, "Acts," 358.

[28] David Gunn, "An Overview of New Covenant Passages," in *An Introduction to the New Covenant*, ed. Christopher Cone (Hurst, TX: Tyndale Seminary Press, 2013), 66–69. Roy E. Beacham, "Eschatology of Joel 2," *Dictionary of Premillennial Theology*, ed. Mal Couch (Grand Rapids: Kregel, 1996), 218.

[29] Gunn, "An Overview of New Covenant Passages," 67.

it seems most likely that Peter was citing Joel's prophecy as analogous to the events the Jews had witnessed on the day of Pentecost. By this means, Peter was arguing that extraordinary revelatory activity (Joel 2:28; Acts 2:4–11) was objective evidence of work of God's Spirit (Joel 2:28; Acts 2:4), not evidence of drunkenness (Acts 2:13–15)."[30]

A detailed review of the support for these answers is beyond the scope of this chapter. Nevertheless, several factors lead me to conclude that the third view is best. First, not all the prophecy was fulfilled at Pentecost in any obvious way (e.g., the cosmic signs). These unfulfilled portions pose difficulties for the first view. Second, New Testament authors frequently find analogies between Old Testament situations and New Testament situations. Third, the word *is* (in "this is that") often signifies that one person or thing represents another. For example, in John 10:7 Jesus says, "I am the door." Jesus here employs a metaphor, meaning that something about him is analogous to a door. Fourth, Joel says that the "pouring out of the Spirit" would come to pass "afterward." While the chronology in Joel is complex, it seems that the "pouring out of the Spirit" would be after the events of the Day of the Lord mentioned in Joel 2. Since these events are still future, it is likely that the literal fulfillment of Joel 2:28 is still future as well. Beacham summarizes this thought: "It seems likely that Peter was fully aware of the chronology that is specified in Joel chapter 2, a chronology consistent with other Old Testament prophets. These prophets invariably taught that the outpouring of God's Spirit would follow unprecedented national judgment and the ensuing repentance of Israel (Isa 32:9–18; 43:26–44:3; 59:1–21; Ezek 39:25–29; Zech 12:1–14)."[31]

Peter used the Joel 2 prophecy to explain why their speaking in foreign languages did not result from drunkenness. He knew that the foreign languages were a result of a new ministry of the Holy Spirit. How best to explain the Spirit's activity to Jews? Peter knew that they would value the testimony of the Old Testament, so he selected the Joel 2 prophecy to explain what was happening at Pentecost. The coming of the Holy Spirit was like the prophesied coming of the Holy Spirit in the last days. By drawing this comparison, Peter meant to help Jews understand that the foreign languages were from God. He repeated the entire quotation from Joel so that he could include the reference to

---

[30] Beacham, "Eschatology of Joel 2," 219.

[31] Ibid.

salvation at the end. Once Peter had explained that the foreign languages from God were authentic, he pleaded with his audience to repent and accept Christ.

The quotation of Joel 2 in Acts 2 takes the concept of the arrival of the Spirit in the last days and uses that concept to explain the events that occurred at Pentecost. Unger concludes, "Careful comparison will show that Peter employed the Joel reference merely as an illustration that such a spiritual outpouring as had taken place at Pentecost was not fanaticism or drunkenness, as some Jewish taunters alleged, but found a parallel in their own Hebrew prophecies to be fulfilled in connection with the future establishment of their kingdom."[32]

In summary, we see that Luke uses the Old Testament in several ways in the book of Acts. He uses the Old Testament to identify and clarify truths about Jesus and his ministry. He uses the Old Testament to explain the relationship between Israel and the church. He also uses the Old Testament as an analogy to events happening in the early church. Sometimes he does this to support his argument and other times to clarify his point. Most, if not all, quotations and allusions to the Old Testament in Acts fit into these categories.

The Transitional Nature of Acts

Many commentators refer to Acts as a transitional book, but they do not agree about the nature of the transition. The claim that Acts is transitional has been used in several different ways to support several different theological positions. This diversity has created a challenge for a proper interpretation. From what and to what does the transition in Acts take place? At what point in the book does the transition begin? Is there a single point of transition, or is this transition a gradual change? Are the dispensation of law and the dispensation of grace active at the same time? In what ways can any interpretation legitimately claim this transition as support?

In addition to the foregoing interpretive challenges, readers also face the problem of applying Acts to the present church. If the book of Acts is describing a time during which the church is in transition, then is the content of Acts relevant to the New Testament church once the transition is complete? In other words, what in Acts is binding on the New Testament church today, and what was temporary (i.e., intended for the "transitional church" only)?

---

[32] Merrill F. Unger, *Zechariah: Prophet of Messiah's Glory* (Grand Rapids: Zondervan, 1963), 215.

To answer these questions, I will first cite several examples of commentators claiming the transitional nature of Acts in support of their interpretations. Second, I will suggest several principles that may help to identify which verses in Acts are binding on the New Testament church and which are merely descriptive of events during the transition.

Examples of Transitional Interpretation in Acts

A transition implies a change from one thing to another over a period of time. In Acts, the church changes in some way(s) over the time period recorded in the book. The nature of those changes is significant for both the church's doctrine and its practice.

Proclaimers of the gospel. In the covenant system of the Old Testament, special revelation about God was communicated to the world through the nation of Israel. In the church age, special revelation about God is communicated to the world by the church. Thomas Ice sees this change taking place in the book of Acts: "Virtually all students of the Bible would acknowledge that the Book of Acts is a transition from Israel to the Church, as God's instrument through whom He uses to spread His message."[33] In other words, at the beginning of Acts, Israel was responsible for publishing news of God. By the end of Acts, the church was responsible for publishing news of God.

Church polity. Some suggest the polity of the church developed as the church progressed through the book of Acts. For example, McCune states, "The first local Church did not spring up with a complete organizational structure because the new *ekklesia* was in the early stages of the transition from the dispensation of Law to Grace."[34] McCune, while identifying a basic structure for early church polity, suggests that the early church focused more on preaching than organization.[35] As the church addressed problems and needs, the polity of the church also developed. It eventually became "fixed" and "permanent" when the canonical books of the New Testament became available.[36]

McCune identified four factors that contributed to the transition in

---

[33] Thomas Ice, "Transitions in the Book of Acts," *Bible Prophecy Blog*, April 13, 2012, accessed October 18, 2022, https://www.pre-trib.org/tom-s-perspectives/message/transitions-in-the-book-of-acts/read.

[34] Rolland McCune, *A Systematic Theology of Biblical Christianity*, vol. 3 (Allen Park, MI: Detroit Baptist Theological Seminary, 2010), 225.

[35] Ibid.

[36] Ibid., 226.

church polity from flexible, incomplete organizational structure to fixed, definite, and permanent organizational structures.[37] First, the early Jewish church still mediated a valid offer of the kingdom. Complex organization for the church would not be necessary if Israel repented and the kingdom arrived. Today, however, the church does not mediate an offer of an imminent kingdom. Second, the early church was led by apostles. Apostles were always meant to be temporary. While they were ministering, however, the organization of the church would include them. Third, the church developed organizational structures to meet new situations that it faced. An example of this organizational development is the choice of seven men in Acts 6. Pentecost states, "An expanding Church brought expanding needs, which were to [be] met by expanding overseers. This expansion will go on during the Transition Period."[38] Fourth, the apostles produced inspired writings that codified apostolic doctrine for the church. This apostolic doctrine included teaching on church organization.

Church practice. Writing from an ultra-dispensational perspective, Richard Church argues that baptism should not be practiced by churches today.[39] His dismissal of baptism is related to his view of the transitional nature of the book of Acts. He identifies his hermeneutic as follows:

> The general rule to follow with regard to the Acts period is that all practices of the previous dispensation which were carried over into the body of Christ cease by the end of the book of Acts. This applies to baptism, spiritual gifts, miraculous demonstrations, healings, etc. A reading of Acts will show that, while all of these were prevalent at the beginning of the book, they are scarcely mentioned at the end.[40]

Church's argument is based on his belief that a new dispensation began in Acts 9.[41] In other words, the church, which he calls the "body of Christ," did not exist until Acts 9. Even then, it began with some practices that were

---

[37] Ibid., 225–26.

[38] J. Dwight Pentecost, *New Wine: A Study of Transition in the Book of Acts* (Grand Rapids: Kregel Academic, 2010), 85. Whether the seven men were overseers, deacons, or something else is not the point of this discussion.

[39] Richard C. Church, "The Transitional Nature of the Acts Period," *Friendship Congregational Bible Church Website*, July 27, 2015, accessed October 18, 2022, http://www.friendshipbibleChurch.com/articles/transition.html.

[40] Ibid.

[41] Ibid.

carried over from the previous dispensation. As the church transitioned to become more governed by Paul's epistles, the "carryover practices" vanished. Church follows both Cornelius Stam and Charles Baker in seeing the book of Acts not as the birth and development of the church but as the account of the fall of Israel. [42]

Stam says that the book of Acts is not a pattern for churches today because it reflects a time prior to the "body of Christ" era.[43] Baker concludes, "It is both difficult and dangerous to try to establish permanent doctrines on the practices of a period of transition, when everything was in a state of flux."[44] This limitation on the applicability of Acts is also held by some who reject the ultra-dispensational position. For example, John Phillips, while not arguing for a mid-Acts change in dispensation, also diminishes the value of Acts for determining church practice. "This book is largely historical and transitional. It bridges the gap between the Gospels and the Epistles. Much that is in the Epistles would be unintelligible apart from this book. But, because it is a transitional book rather than a doctrinal book, we go to Acts for information rather than doctrine. We obtain doctrine from the Epistles."[45]

Similarly, Bobby Wood points out that today's churches do not practice communion every day, they do not select seven deacons when only two are needed, and they do not speak in other dialects when they are saved. The reason today's churches do not follow these practices, in his logic, is because Acts is a transitional book. [46]

Church experience. Certainly, the book of Acts mentions four instances of the "coming" of the Holy Spirit on believers after they were saved. In three instances, the believers on whom the Spirit came spoke in tongues. These episodes occurred with Jewish believers in Acts 2, Samaritan believers in Acts 8 (which does not record speaking in tongues), Gentile believers in Acts 10, and disciples of John the Baptist in Acts 19. These examples have led some interpreters to propose that a second work of the Spirit is normative for all

---

[42] Cornelius R. Stam, *Acts Dispensationally Considered* (Chicago: Berean Bible Society), xiv–xx; Charles F. Baker, *A Dispensational Theology* (Grand Rapids: Grace Bible College Publications, 1971), 506ff. Baker argued for a new dispensation beginning in Acts 13.

[43] Stam, *Acts Dispensationally Considered*, xxiii.

[44] Baker, *A Dispensational Theology*, 509.

[45] John Phillips, *Exploring the New Testament Book by Book: An Expository Survey* (Grand Rapids: Kregel Academic, 2009), 21.

[46] Bobby R. Wood, *A Passion for His Passion: A Devotional Commentary on the Book of Acts* (Bloomington, IN: Crossbooks, 2012), xi–xii.

believers. In refuting this "second blessing" teaching, other interpreters appeal to the transitional nature of the book of Acts. Kenneth Gangel says, "We also do not find some kind of 'second blessing' here in which the Holy Spirit comes to believers sometime subsequent to their salvation. Yes, that happens here, but Acts is a transitional book."[47] MacArthur argues that these events are one-time events that were intended as exceptional signs not normative expectations.[48] To support his argument, he quotes Joseph Dillow:

> We must not make the tragic mistake of teaching the experience of the apostles, but we must experience the teaching of the apostles. The experience of the apostles is found in the transitional book of Acts, while the teaching of the apostles is set forth clearly in the epistles, which are our guide for our Christian experience today.[49]

The argument against a "second blessing" of the Holy Spirit is based on the transitional nature of the book of Acts.

Jack Deere, while not denying the transitional nature of Acts, argues in favor of a continuation of speaking in tongues in the experience of believers today.[50] He says, "Some try to dismiss the testimony of Acts by calling it a transitional book. But transition to what?"[51] Deere goes on to answer his question, concluding that the "transition Jesus predicted was to an age of revelation by an omniscient Spirit who would surprise God's people by teaching, reminding, testifying, guiding, and showing."[52] Even though MacArthur and Deere come to different conclusions, both seem to accept and argue from the transitional nature of the book of Acts.

Most interpreters of the Bible would agree that there is some amount of transition in the book of Acts. A variety of theological positions is supported in some way by an appeal to the transitional nature of the book of Acts. Even opposing views on some issues are supported by appeals to the transitional nature of Acts.

---

[47] Kenneth O. Gangel, *Acts*, Holman New Testament Commentary (Nashville: Broadman & Holman, 1988), 123.

[48] John MacArthur, *Charismatic Chaos* (Grand Rapids: Zondervan, 1992), 226–27.

[49] Joseph Dillow, *Speaking in Tongues* (Grand Rapids: Zondervan, 1975), 66.

[50] Jack Deere, *Surprised by the Voice of God: How God Speaks Today through Prophecies, Dreams, and Visions* (Grand Rapids: Zondervan, 1988), 61.

[51] Ibid.

[52] Ibid

Guidelines for Transitional Interpretation in Acts

Two conclusions are apparent from the foregoing discussion. First, some transition does occur in the book of Acts. Few interpreters would dispute this conclusion. Second, few agree about what is transitional and how the transition affects one's application of Acts. Many claim transitions in Acts; few suggest criteria for determining what is transitional. How does one determine whether something in the book of Acts belongs to the transition? I suggest several guidelines to provide a structure for answering this question.

Apostolic teaching is normative. The teaching and preaching of the apostles and other leaders in the book of Acts is normative for the church. Jesus taught the apostles some church truth during his earthly ministry. Then Jesus told the apostles to teach that truth to the church (Matt 28:18–20). Christ continued to teach the apostles until his ascension (Acts 1:1–2). The apostles obeyed Christ and taught this new revelation Christ gave them to church saints (Heb 1:1–3; 2:1–4). Therefore, the teaching and preaching of the apostles (and those who were taught by them) is the revelation that Christ intended for the church to believe and to live. What the apostles taught or preached to the early church is normative for the entire church. Continuing in the apostles' doctrine (Acts 2:42) is normative.

Unchanging elements are normative. God's character, human nature, and the means of salvation never change. Therefore, any element in Acts that speaks of these unchanging truths is normative for the church. For example, the fact that God had a predetermined plan (Acts 2:23) is normative. Salvation by means of repentance and faith is normative because this is the means of salvation in all dispensations. For humans to display the image of God is normative since the divine image is sourced in God's creative purpose. Consequently, when the behavior of believers in Acts reflects God's image, it is normative. Keener concludes, "Acts, like Luke, is intended to edify Christians both by placing them in a broader historical perspective and by providing teaching and moral examples."[53] The moral examples of which Keener speaks are found in the behavior of church saints. For example, the apostles chose to obey God rather than man (Acts 4:19–20). The behavior of the apostles serves as a moral example or model of believing behavior that is normative for the New Testament church.

Actions that are clarified or repeated in the epistles are normative.

---

[53] Craig S. Keener, *Acts: An Exegetical Commentary,* 436.

The narrative sections of Acts are full of actions. The actions that are repeated or clarified in the epistles are normative for the church. For example, the Bereans searched the Scriptures to verify the truth of what Paul preached (Acts 17:11). The epistles make frequent reference to the authority and value of Scripture (Rom 4:3; 9:11; 10:11; 11:2; 1 Tim 5:18; 2 Tim 3:16; Jas 4:5; 1 Pet 2:6). In addition, Peter teaches that believers should long for the sincere milk of the Word (1 Pet 2:2). Therefore, the example of the Bereans should be taken as normative.

Another example of a normative action is found when the churches met the physical needs of those believers who were unable to provide for themselves. In Acts 4:32–35, believers were voluntarily selling their property and giving the money to the church to meet the material needs of other believers (see also Acts 2:44–45; 6:1ff). In the epistles, James teaches that genuinely mature believers will do what they can to provide for the needs of those who lack (Jas 1:27; 2:15–16).

Actions practiced by multiple churches are usually normative. Acts describes the Jerusalem church as having elders or pastors (Acts 11:30; 15:6; 16:4). Elders were appointed for each of the churches started on Paul's first missionary journey (Acts 14:23). Paul indicates that the Ephesian church had elders (Acts 20:17). Given the mention of many pastors in multiple churches in Acts, it seems likely that the ministry of pastors in churches is normative. This is also confirmed by teaching in the epistles.

One-time, foundational events are not normative. Events that occur only once at the beginning of the church are not normative. For example, when Ananias and Sapphira lied to the Holy Spirit, they were stricken dead immediately (Acts 5:1–11), but this is not a normative event. It never happens again in Acts or in the epistles. It was an event that occurred during the establishment of the church. Once God expressed his desire for purity in the church and "great fear came over the whole church" (Acts 5:11), there was no more need for God to express his desire for a pure church in this way.

Another one-time foundational event was the calling and commissioning of Paul as the apostle to the Gentiles (Acts 9:15, 16; Rom 11:13). Nowhere else does God call anyone to be an apostle to the Gentiles. Arguably, God replaced Judas with Matthias (Acts 1:15–26) as an apostle to the Jews. This replacement was necessary to have twelve apostles to the twelve tribes of Israel (Matt 19:28). But Paul was the apostle to the Gentiles, not to the Jews. Calling an apostle to the Gentiles is a non-normative event.

Recurring foundational events are not normative. There are some recurring foundational events that are not normative. They occur several times at the beginning of the church, but they cease as some point. For example, the early Jewish church met daily in the temple in Jerusalem (Acts 2:46). This was the continual practice of the church in Jerusalem. Boice suggests that Acts 2:42–47 "is intended as an example for us and our assemblies."[54] While Boice is correct, not every element in this passage is normative. Obviously, none of the churches outside of Jerusalem met in the temple daily. This was just the pragmatic practice of the Jerusalem church. It was not even normative for all the church in the first century.

One of the more debated foundational events is the delay in the coming of the Holy Spirit on believers (i.e., baptism of the Holy Spirit). This delay in the coming or falling of the Spirit on believers occurred four times in the book of Acts (Jews–Acts 2; Samaritans–Acts 8; Gentiles–Acts 10; and disciples of John the Baptist–Acts 19). Other than these four instances, there is no mention of a delay in this ministry of the Holy Spirit. Neither Acts nor the epistles present this delay as normative. Apparently, God had a foundational purpose for a delay in these four instances. The day of Pentecost in Acts 2 marked the beginning of the church (the body of Christ). Acts 8 and 10 mark the entry of Samaritans and Gentiles into the church on equal footing with the Jews. Acts 19 emphasizes that disciples of John the Baptist who had not accepted Christ were not part of the church. God made his desire for a multiethnic church clear by intentionally delaying Spirit baptism one time for each group. Once a multiethnic body of Christ was established, there was no longer a need to delay Spirit baptism.

Conclusion

The book of Acts is a unique book that describes the birth and growth of the early church. It records the expansion of the church both geographically and ethnically. It provides the historical context for the New Testament epistles. It states apostolic doctrine. It explains the relation of the church to ethnic Israel. It presents Jesus as the Messiah. It describes early church practices. It includes both normative and non-normative elements. A proper interpretation and application of the book of Acts is important for placing church saints in the position where God wants them.

---

[54] James Montgomery Boice, *Acts: An Expositional Commentary* (Grand Rapids: Baker, 1997), 55.

The Church, Israel, and Supersessionism

Ryan Martin
Pastor, Columbiaville Baptist Church
Columbiaville, Michigan

Since the decades after the apostles, Christian teachers have wrestled with the relationship of Israel and the church. What does the New Testament church have to do with Israel? Is the church identical to Old Testament Israel? Are Old Testament prophecies to Israel fulfilled in the church? Does Israel have any further relationship to God's plan to bring himself glory? Even dispensationalist teachers have variously articulated the relationship between Israel and the church.[1] As the body of Christ enters its twenty-first century, the distinction between Israel and the church remains an important theological question.

Romans 9–11 is essential for understanding the relationship between Israel and the church. These chapters are Paul's great apology for the faithfulness of God. Do God's promises stand in light of the Jewish rejection of Jesus Christ? No other New Testament passage says as much about the church and Israel with respect to God's Old Testament promises.

I intend to present an exegetical argument from Romans 9–11 that ethnic Israel has a distinct future in God's plan. In these three chapters, Paul shows how he understands Israel and its future. The apostle did not believe that the church had replaced Israel or that God had folded the church into Israel such that ethnic Israel had no distinct future. Paul teaches that God will fulfill his promises to Israel in his plan for history.

What is ethnic Israel? By this expression I mean what Paul means in Romans 9:3 and 11:1. Ethnic Israel comprises Paul's "kinsmen according to the flesh," the "descendant[s] of Abraham." Ethnic Israel is the physical seed

---

[1] For a brief history of dispensationalist interpretations of the future of Israel and the church, see Stanley D. Toussaint, "Israel and the Church of a Traditional Dispensationalist," in *Three Central Issues in Contemporary Dispensationalism: A Comparison of Traditional and Progressive Views,* ed. Herbert W. Bateman IV (Grand Rapids: Kregel, 1999), 228–30. For evidence of the continuing relevance of these questions within dispensationalism, see, for example, Charles Ryrie, *Dispensationalism,* rev. ed. (Chicago: Moody, 1995), 39–40; Robert L. Saucy, *The Case for Progressive Dispensationalism: The Interface Between Dispensational and Non-Dispensational Theology* (Grand Rapids: Zondervan, 1993), 187–218; Bateman, *Three Central Issues,* 227–303; and Michael Vlach, "What about Israel?" in *Christ's Prophetic Plans: A Futuristic Premillennial Primer,* ed. John MacArthur and Richard Mayhue (Chicago: Moody, 2012) 103–22.

of Abraham.[2]

The Church and Israel according to Nondispensationalists

Many nondispensationalists believe that the church has replaced Israel. Others prefer to say that Christ, who fulfills Israel as its antitype, has grafted Gentile believers into himself. Most nondispensationalists concede some discontinuity between the Old and New Testaments. Still, they find continuity between the remnant of Israel in the Old Testament and the body of Christ in the New. Should we interpret the Old Testament prophecies about Israel's future glories as referring to Israel or to the church? Should we follow a historical-grammatical interpretation (as do dispensationalists generally) or a typological or spiritual interpretation? The view that the church has, directly or indirectly, replaced Israel is often called *supersessionism*. [3]

According to nondispensationalists, God may choose to bless his people with fulfillments greater than the Old Testament literally promised. Those who hold this view believe that dispensationalism drags the future back into the realm of such types and shadows as dominated the Old Testament. Further, Christ is the New Israel in whom God's promises to Israel are fulfilled. Any remaining Old Testament promises for Israel will be fulfilled through Christ in the body of Christ, the church.[4]

Such a view is untenable in light of Romans 9–11. As I shall argue, Paul believed that ethnic Israel was a distinct entity from the church. Furthermore, the assumption that Israel had a real future in which God's promises would be fulfilled undergirds Paul's argument in Romans 9–11. Until Paul resolves the apparent failure of God's promises to Israel, he does not close his apology for God's justice and faithfulness.

---

[2] J. Lanier Burns, "The Future of Ethnic Israel in Romans 11," in *Dispensationalism, Israel and the Church*, ed. Craig A. Blaising and Darrell L. Bock (Grand Rapids: Zondervan, 1992), 189–90.

[3] For an example of a nondispensationalist who denies that the church has replaced Israel, see Benjamin L. Merkle, "A Typological Non-Future-Mass-Conversion View," in *Three Views on Israel and the Church: Perspectives on Romans 9–11*, ed. Jared Compton and Andrew David Naselli (Grand Rapids: Kregel, 2019) 161–208.

[4] *Catechism of the Catholic Church,* 2nd ed. (Washington, DC: Libreria Editrice Vaticana, 2000), 197–98 §751; 200 §§761–62; Francis Turretin, *Institutes of Elenctic Theology,* trans. George Musgrave Giger, ed. James T. Dennison, Jr. (Phillipsburg, N.J.: P&R, 1994), 2:486–90 (§14.16). Louis Berkhof, *Systematic Theology* (Grand Rapids: Eerdmans 1996), 570–72, 698–700. Michael Horton, *The Christian Faith: A Systematic Theology for Pilgrims on the Way* (Grand Rapids: Zondervan, 2011), 945–50.

Paul's Theology of Jews and Gentiles
in Romans 1–8

Paul's argument in Romans 9–11 hinges on the flow of his thought in the preceding chapters. These chapters are born out of the theological issues raised in Romans 1–8.[5] Paul's words about the plight and salvation of Jew and Gentile are particularly pivotal.[6]

The contrast between Jew and Gentile shows up almost immediately in Romans. The letter opens with the declaration of good news that God offers the grace of Christ to all, both Jews and Gentiles. In the first chapter, Paul says, "For I am not ashamed of the gospel, for it is the power of God for salvation to everyone who believes, to the Jew first and also to the Greek" (Rom 1:16). He then explains that the "righteousness of God is revealed" in the gospel (1:17).

Jews, Gentiles, and God's Wrath (Rom 1–2)

Having spoken of God's righteousness in the gospel, Paul pivots to speak of "the wrath of God," which has been "revealed" against all humanity for its sin (Rom 1:18). First, he describes the sinfulness of Gentiles, who lacked God's revelation (1:19–29). Then he turns toward Jewish people, who—despite their condemnation of the Gentiles (2:1–5)—are themselves hardened against God. God will thus judge all humans for their sin. Echoing Romans 1:16–17, Paul states that "there will be tribulation and distress for every soul of man who does evil, of the Jew first and also of the Greek, but glory and honor and peace to everyone who does good, to the Jew first and also to the Greek. For there is no partiality with God" (2:9–11). The wrath of God does not play favorites; all humanity, whether Jew and Greek, comes beneath its scrutiny. A mere knowledge of God's law does not justify (2:12–16), and neither does Jewish birth (2:17–19). Paul explains, "For he is not a Jew who is one outwardly, nor is circumcision that which is outward in the flesh. But he is a Jew who is one inwardly; and circumcision is that which is of the heart, by the Spirit, not by the letter; and his praise is not from men, but from God" (2:28–29). Being a true Jew—a Jew whose "praise is not from men, but from God" (2:29)—is not a matter of birth or even of circumcision but of the Spirit. A true Jew is one who believes in Christ.

---

[5] Leon Morris, *The Epistle to the Romans*, PNTC (Grand Rapids: Eerdmans, 1988), 34345.

[6] For an argument that Paul addresses both Jewish and Gentile believers in Romans, see David R. Wallace, *Election of the Lesser Son: Paul's Lament-Midrash in Romans 9–11* (Minneapolis: Fortress, 2014), 24–28.

Many interpreters read Romans 2:28–29 as a reference to all believers in Jesus Christ. Four considerations, however, indicate that Paul is referring to ethnic Jews who believe in Jesus Christ and are part of the church of God.[7] First, Paul's argument in Romans 3 continues to focus on Jews, their advantages, and their unfaithfulness. Second, later in his argument (4:11–12; 9:6–8; 11:5–7) Paul makes the same point he is making here, namely that *biological ancestry alone neither qualifies nor disqualifies one from receiving God's promises.* Third, if these verses are about Jews who believe, then they set up a relevant contrast to Paul's subsequent observations, which focus on the Jews who relied on their physical ancestry and circumcision to put them right before God. Finally, the interplay between *Jew* and *praise* (the name *Judah* means *praise*) confirms that 2:28–29 is a reference to Jews who have believed in Jesus Christ.[8]

Jews, Gentiles, and Justification in Christ (Rom 3–4)

The beginning of Romans 3 anticipates the questions that Paul will address in Romans 9–11. Jews do have advantages over Gentiles: "First of all, that they were entrusted with the oracles of God" (3:2). Moreover, a Jew who forfeits divine promises does not negate God's faithfulness: "Let God be found true, though every man be found a liar" (3:4). Even so, both Jews and Gentiles are under sin (3:9). This last point is crucial. Paul will underscore it when he declares the universality of humanity's death in Adam (5:12–21).

The apostle's argument in these chapters culminates in Romans 3:21–26. If all humans, both Jews and Gentiles, are condemned by sin, then all need the grace of Christ. Paul introduced God's righteousness in Romans 1:16–17. He then stated that God reveals his wrath against the unrighteousness of men (1:18). Now he returns to God's righteousness "But now . . . the righteousness of God has been manifested" (3:21). This righteousness comes apart from the law that condemns even though it is "witnessed by the Law and the Prophets." God's righteousness comes "through faith in Jesus Christ," and it is "for all those who believe" (3:22). "There is no distinction" between Jew or Gentile.

The main verbs in Romans 3:23–24 are *have sinned* (*hamarton*) and *fall*

---

[7] For the interpretation that Paul equates Jews and redeemed Gentiles in 2:28–29, see Thomas R. Schreiner, *Romans,* BECNT (Grand Rapids: Baker, 1998), 141–45; Douglas Moo, *The Epistle to the Romans,* NICNT (Grand Rapids: Eerdmans, 1996), 174–75.

[8] This seems to be the reading of Morris, *Romans,* 141–42.

short (*husterountai*). The word behind *are justified* in (3:24) is a participle (*dikaioumenoi*), which probably modifies the finite verbs in Romans 3:23. In other words, Paul is saying that justification can be applied to all because all have sinned. Furthermore, all can be justified only by Christ's propitiatory blood, and this justification can only be received "by faith" (2:24–25). God justifies only those who believe because both Jews and Gentiles have ruined themselves by their sin. The only way either can be saved is by the grace of Jesus Christ.

Salvation is for "all who believe" because neither Jews nor Greeks can save themselves (3:22). Paul draws an inference that would have surprised some Jews: "Or is God the God of the Jews only? Is he not the God of the Gentiles also?" (3:29). Since only one God exists, then both Jews and Greeks are reconciled to him through the work of Christ. [9]

The discussion of Jews and Gentiles continues into Romans 4, where Paul argues that works did not justify even the holy patriarch Abraham. Paul describes Abraham as "our forefather according to the flesh" (4:1). With the pronoun *our*, Paul is speaking as a Jew, and by the phrase *according to the flesh*, he identifies the physical descent from Abraham that he and the whole Jewish nation shared. In contrast to this physical lineage, God appointed Abraham as "the father of all who believe without being circumcised" because of his faith (4:11). The word *all* here once again underlines the unity of believers in Christ. Justification comes to all who believe. All believers become the spiritual descendants of Abraham and will together inherit the kingdom originally promised to Abraham (4:16–25; Gal. 3:29). [10]

None of this means that the church replaces Israel or that God's promises to Abraham's fleshly descendants can be completely fulfilled spiritually by and to the church. The *true* physical descendants of Abraham are those Jews who believe God as Abraham himself believed. Abraham's faith made him "the father of circumcision to those who not only are of the circumcision, but who also follow in the steps of the faith of our father Abraham which he had while

---

[9] *Pace* John Murray, *The Epistle to the Romans: The English Text with Introduction, Exposition and Notes* (Grand Rapids: Eerdmans, 1968), 113–14. For another example of this use of the participle, see John 5:18. Also see Daniel Wallace, *Greek Grammar Beyond the Basics: An Exegetical Syntax of the New Testament* (Grand Rapids: Zondervan, 1996), 637–39.

[10] Robert L. Saucy, "The Church as the Mystery of God," in *Dispensationalism, Israel and the Church*, ed. Craig A. Blaising and Darrell L. Bock (Grand Rapids: Zondervan, 1992), 134–35. Robert B. Chisholm, Jr., "Evidence from Genesis," in *A Case for Premillennialism: A New Consensus*, ed. Donald K. Campbell and Jeffrey L. Townsend (Chicago: Moody, 1992), 53; *pace* Robert L. Reymond, "The Traditional Covenant View," in *Perspectives on Israel and the Church: Four Views*, ed. Chad O. Brand (Nashville: B&H Academic, 2015), 39–40.

uncircumcised" (Rom 4:12). While Abraham is the father of all who believe, he remains the true physical *and* spiritual father of Jews justified by faith. Paul does not say that circumcision is necessary to be a true heir of Abraham, which would undermine his argument (cf. 2:28–29). Rather, circumcision functioned only as a sign and seal of Abraham's righteousness (4:11), which had already been credited to him by faith. Faith is more fundamental than ethnicity or circumcision.[11]

Beginning with chapter 5, Paul focuses on the riches of Christ's grace that extend to all who believe. For this reason, the Jew-Gentile motif, so prominent in Romans 1–4, moves to the background. Before moving on, certain points are worth summarizing. First, with the possible exception of Romans 2:28–29 (disputed above), nowhere in the first eight chapters does Paul speak as if the church has replaced Israel or as if *Israel* and *church* were interchangeable terms. Second, even though Paul does acknowledge true Jews at present to be those who believe the gospel and are part of the church, he does not identify the church with Jewish people or equate these Jews with the church. To all appearances, every reference to a Jew in Romans 1–8 is a reference to an *ethnic* Jew.

A Defense of the Present Hardening of Jews
(Rom 9:1–11:24)

Paul's argument in Romans 1-8 raises an urgent question. All humanity is condemned under sin. The Jewish people continue to pursue God through works of the law. Righteousness is credited through faith in the death and resurrection of Jesus, the son of David, who is the Christ (whom many Jews reject). What does this portrayal say about the Jewish people's standing before God? Worse, if Jewish people are dead in their sin and opposition to the Messiah, then what does this imply about God's faithfulness to his word? This key problem, which Harold Hoehner described as "the Jewish dilemma," would have been very much in the forefront of Jewish believers' minds as they considered their people and the promises of the Old Testament. This is the question that Paul must answer in Romans 9–11.[12]

---

[11] See Colin G. Kruse, *Paul's Letter to the Romans,* PNTC (Grand Rapids: Eerdmans, 2012), 208–11; Morris, *Romans,* 204.

[12] Harold Hoehner, "Israel in Romans 9–11," in *Israel: The Land and the People: An Evangelical Affirmation of God's Promises* (Grand Rapids: Kregel, 1998), 146; cf. F. F. Bruce, *Romans: An Introduction and Commentary,* TNTC 6 (Downers Grove: InterVarsity, 2008), 182–83.

Paul's Kinsmen According to the Flesh
(Rom 9:1–3)

Paul opens Romans 9 by expressing his wish that his "kinsmen according to the flesh" would be saved. His yearning is so strong that he, like Moses (Exod 32:32), would accept eternal damnation to secure their restoration.[13] He clearly refers to ethnic Israelites. The Greek word translated *kinsmen* is used to speak of those "belonging to the same people group."[14] At times Paul may use the term *kinsmen* analogically to refer to close associates or fellow believers (cf. Rom 16:7, 11, 21). Here the phrase *according to the flesh* and the accompanying description of his *kinsmen* makes it clear that Paul refers to ethnic Jews (cf. Mark 6:4; Luke 2:44; 14:12; 21:16).

Paul adds that they are "Israelites, to whom belongs the adoption as sons, and the glory and the covenants and the giving of the Law and the *temple* service and the promises, whose are the fathers, and from whom is the Christ according to the flesh, who is over all, God blessed forever. Amen." (Rom 9:4–5). In other words, God has proven his steadfast love for the people of Israel by blessing them abundantly. Indeed, Jesus Christ himself (whom Paul calls "God blessed forever" in 9:5) is "from them." Thus, Romans 9–11 begins with a reference to ethnic Jews. Indeed, in 11:13, Paul implies that these chapters are primarily written for the sake of Jews rather than Gentiles.[15]

Have God's Promises Failed? (Rom 9:4–13)

God granted tremendous privileges to ethnic Israel through the patriarchs and prophets—the adoption, the glory, the covenants and the promises (9:4) as well as "the Christ" (9:5). Yet Paul's kinsmen, the Jews, have not received the gospel of Christ (9:1–3). Should this deficiency lead us to question God's fidelity to his people?[16] This is the next problem that Paul addresses (9:6–13). Paul responds that the word of God has not failed in accomplishing its purpose.

---

[13] See Kruse, *Romans*, 368–69; and C. E. B. Cranfield, *A Critical and Exegetical Commentary on the Epistle to the Romans*, International Critical Commentary (Edinburgh: T. & T. Clark, 1982), 2:454–76.

[14] BDAG, s.v. "συγγενής."

[15] On the doxology in Rom 9:5 referring to Jesus Christ, see R. C. H. Lenski, *The Interpretation of St. Paul's Epistle to the Romans* (Minneapolis: Augsburg, 1961), 585–89; Murray, *Romans*, 1:245–48. For a contrary view, see Kruse, *Romans*, 372–74.

[16] The list of blessings given to ethnic Israel in Rom 9:34 implies an answer to Storms's objection: "We must . . . ask whether it is compatible with what we read in the New Testament to suggest that God will in the future obligate himself to save all (or at least most) of a particular group of people based on an external, which is to say, non-spiritual characteristic." Sam Storms, *Kingdom Come: The Amillennial Alternative* (Ross-shire, Scotland: Mentor, 2015), 330.

Just because children are born of Abraham does not mean that they are part of true Israel—the Israel to whom these promises were ultimately made (9:7). Paul offers a scriptural basis for this assertion: even among Abraham's many children, only Isaac was the appointed heir. The "children of the flesh" and the "children of God" are not coterminous (9:8; cf. 4:11–12). God promised to Abraham that the child of promise would come through Sarah. Moreover, God chose Jacob over Esau "so that God's purpose according to His choice would stand" (9:11). As Hoehner explained, "Only those who are related to Abraham physically *and* spiritually are the true Israel."[17]

Some interpreters understand Romans 9:6 ("For they are not all Israel who are descended from Israel") to show that by "Israel," Paul means more than merely ethnic Israel. Sam Storms says, "[God's] purpose has always been to save a remnant within, but not entirely of, ethnic Israel. Paul is telling us that there is an 'Israel' within 'Israel,' a spiritually elect remnant within the physically ethnic nation."[18] This interpretation takes "Israel" to include Gentile believers as well as Jews. The salvation of the Gentiles proves that God's "word" has *not* "failed."

The greater context, however, will not permit this interpretation. Paul is not distinguishing believers from unbelievers but saved Jews from unsaved Jews (cf. 2:28–29; 11:5–8). The two groups are subsets within the Jewish people. Unbelieving Jews fail to be true Jews; believing Jews truly "belong to Israel." As S. Lewis Johnson observed, "To the total body of ethnic Israel the apostle denies the term 'Israel' in its most meaningful sense of the believing ethnic seed. Gentiles are not in view at all." [19] As shown above, this is the sense in which Paul speaks of Israel throughout Romans, leading up to these pivotal chapters.[20]

The Sovereign Freedom of God (Rom 9:15–29)

That God has not chosen every ethnic Israelite to be among the "children of God" does not make God unjust or nullify his promises. God is free, as Paul shows from Exodus 33:19: "I will have mercy on whom I have mercy, and I will have compassion on whom I have compassion" (Rom 9:15). Human merit has no bearing on God's election, which depends solely on God's mercy

---

[17] Hoehner, "Israel in Romans 9–11," 147.

[18] Storms, *Kingdom Come*, 305.

[20] Ibid., 200–203.

(11:14–18).[21] God is absolutely sovereign in electing grace.

Some object to God's sovereignty in salvation. Paul addresses one such objection: how can God justly condemn those who remain in sin if his will determines who will receive mercy? Paul throws this question out of court: "Who are you, O man, to answer back to God?" (9:20). Sinful humans must not malign God's justice. Paul also offers a second response: "The thing molded will not say to the molder, 'Why did you make me like this,' will it?" (9:20). God created humanity according to his will, so it is unfitting for his creatures to respond to divine election by questioning his justice.

Using the analogy of a potter over the clay, Paul points out that God is the maker of every human being. As creator, he has the right to make his creatures as he sees fit, some for "honorable use" and others for "common use" (9:21). Paul then asks a question which, though hypothetical, constitutes a forceful argument:

> What if God, although willing to demonstrate His wrath and to make His power known, endured with much patience vessels of wrath prepared for destruction? And *He did so* to make known the riches of His glory upon vessels of mercy, which He prepared beforehand for glory, *even* us, whom He also called, not from among Jews only, but also from among Gentiles. (9:22–24)

God's sovereign rule over salvation demonstrates God's "wrath and power" (9:22). Paul's concern here expands from hardened Jews to all humanity. God is over all. He has patiently endured those who had rebelled against him— "the vessels of wrath"—so that he could "make known the riches of his glory" to those "vessels of mercy." The reference to *vessels* recalls the potter analogy and underscores the sovereignty of God over both groups. More importantly, the "vessels of mercy" (9:23) are identical with "even us whom he has called" (9:24). Note that God has called both Jews and Gentiles to be vessels of mercy. Paul still maintains the ethnic distinctions with which he began the chapter even though Jews and Gentiles together make the one body of Christ. Moreover, with the phrase *even us whom he has called*, Paul includes himself among the vessels of mercy (9:24).

As scriptural support, Paul quotes Hosea 2:23 and 1:10. Up to Romans

---

[21] See Mark A. Seifrid, "Romans," in *Commentary on the New Testament Use of the Old Testament,* ed. G. K. Beale and D. A. Carson (Grand Rapids: Baker, 2007), 641–44.

9:24, Paul's point has not been about the inclusion of the Gentiles in the church. Rather, he has been arguing that many Jews are now "vessels of wrath" although God gave wonderful promises to their forefathers. This situation finds a parallel in the context of Hosea's prophecy. Hosea is talking about the people of Israel, as does Paul's subsequent quotation from Isaiah (Rom 9:27–28). Hosea illustrates Paul's key point, namely, that although God has made promises to the patriarchs, he has not abandoned those promises when he chooses only some Jews to be vessels of mercy. Even though God rejected Israel in Hosea's day, he also intended to restore Israel in the future. Thus, they who were not God's people would be God's people.

What is the significance of this point? Simply that it makes little sense for Paul, at this stage of his argument, to introduce the idea that God now calls Gentiles "my people."[22] That does not seem to be Paul's point in citing Hosea. Instead, he seems to be quoting the prophet to prove that, even in the Old Testament, some children of Abraham were not God's people. Yet God remains faithful, and he will save the seed of Abraham as he promised.

Quoting Isaiah 10:22–23; 1:9, Paul further demonstrates God's sovereign authority to elect whom he will. Paul's appeal to the citations from Hosea and Isaiah shows that God has always chosen a remnant by grace and freely called them. To be faithful to his promises God does not have to call all of Abraham's children. Paul clearly limits the focus of these quotations to Israel: "Isaiah cries out *concerning Israel*" (Rom 9:27).

Mark Seifrid wants to apply this passage to both Jews and Gentiles, arguing that Paul's use of Isaiah's prophecy both "faintly suggests the restoration of Israel itself" and "primarily . . . the call of a new people from Jews and Gentiles."[23] Yet Paul's words are plain enough as they stand. He intends to vindicate God's sovereign freedom to elect only a small number of *Jews* at any given point of history, according to the mystery of the divine will. This very point is made in Isaiah 10:22–23, which shows from the Old Testament that only a remnant will be saved.[24] Indeed, as Isaiah 1:9 says, if the Lord had not acted to call out a remnant, all Israel might have perished: "We would be like

---

[22] This is not to deny that God considers all believers in all dispensations to be his people in truth. See 1 Pet 2:10.

[23] Mark Seifrid, "Romans," in *New Testament Use*, 648; a similar approach can be found in Bruce, *Romans*, 194–96.

[24] Cranfield, *Romans*, 2:501.

Sodom, we would be like Gomorrah."[25] The chosen remnant of saved Jews has always demonstrated God's free and sovereign grace.

Paul's Lament for the Jews (Rom 9:30–10:4)

The closing verses of Romans 9 introduce Paul's lament in 10:1–4. Paul explains the sad irony of the present circumstances in the history of redemption. Gentiles, who were uninterested in righteousness, have by faith achieved righteousness through Christ's finished work. Meanwhile, the children of Abraham, while pursuing righteousness through the law, have fallen short of righteousness because the law could never provide it (cf. Rom 2:12–24; 7:7–12; Gal 3:10–14). In this way Israel misused the law (Rom 9:31), seeking God's righteousness by works and not by faith: "They did not pursue it by faith, but as though it were by works" (Rom 9:32). Jesus thus fulfilled the prophecies of Isaiah 28:16 and 8:14—he is "a stone of stumbling," the "rock of offense."[26]

As Romans 10 opens, Paul laments that his fellow Jews have stumbled over the chief cornerstone. "Brethren, my heart's desire and my prayer to God for them is for their salvation." Paul is once again referring to his kinsmen. As Harold Hoehner observed, Paul's prayer is "another indication that Israel is not the church."[27] Israelites have zeal without knowledge. They have worked for their own righteousness by the law rather than turning to Christ. Israel neither kept the law nor established its own righteousness. Jesus is the end of the law for everyone who believes (Rom 10:4), which shows that God justifies anyone—whether Jew or Gentile—who receives the gospel. God's grace blocks every attempt in every dispensation to keep the law as a way of gaining righteousness before God. Christ is the stumbling stone specifically in Zion, but he universally saves all who believe in him.[28]

---

[25] J. Lanier Burns, "Israel and the Church of a Progressive Dispensationalist," in *Three Central Issues in Contemporary Dispensationalism: A Comparison of Traditional and Progressive Views,* ed. Herbert W. Bateman IV (Grand Rapids: Kregel, 1999), 268; Johnson, "Evidence from Romans 9–11," 203–11.

[26] On how the merging of two distinct passages is compatible with the doctrine of inerrancy, see Vern Sheridan Poythress, *Inerrancy and the Gospels: A God-Centered Approach to the Challenges of Harmonization* (Wheaton: Crossway, 2012), 172–73.

[27] Hoehner, "Israel in Romans 9–11," 148.

[28] Douglas J. Moo, "Israel and the Law in Romans 5–11: Interaction with the New Perspective," in *The Paradoxes of Paul,* in *Justification and Variegated Nomism: A Fresh Appraisal of Paul and Second Temple Judaism,* ed. D. A. Carson, Peter T. O'Brien, and Mark A. Seifrid (Grand Rapids: Baker, 2004), 2:185–216; Murray, *Romans,* 2:49–51; John Piper, *Counted Righteous in Christ: Should We Abandon the Imputation of Christ's Righteousness?* (Wheaton: Crossway, 2002), 87–90; Seifrid, "Romans," 653; Stephen Westerholm, *Perspectives Old and New on Paul: The "Lutheran" Paul and His Critics* (Grand Rapids: Eerdmans, 2004), 398–401.

Christ Is Righteousness for All (Rom 10:5–13)

In Romans 10:5–13, Paul contrasts the way of righteousness through the law with the way of righteousness through faith in Christ. He also explains God's current dealings with Jews and Gentiles. According to Paul, Moses addressed law-righteousness when he said (in Lev 18:5) that the person who keeps the law will live before God (Rom 10:5). The problem is that the "righteousness which is based on law" requires absolute obedience (cf. Gal 3:10, 12). Paul assumes that this pursuit of righteousness will fail (Rom 10:3–4; 2:13). Furthermore, Moses also claimed that salvation is by faith not by works. Paraphrasing Deuteronomy 30:11–14, Paul says "the righteousness based on faith" is a gift from God received by the heart's faith and the mouth's confession (Rom 10:6; see Deut 30:6).

Each of Paul's citations from Deuteronomy is introduced by the formula, "that is." Each shows God's grace supplying what Israel lacked. Paul explains, "If you confess with your mouth Jesus as Lord, and believe in your heart that God raised Him from the dead, you will be saved" (Rom 10:9). Paul further substantiates this claim by appealing to Isaiah 28:16, showing that salvation is by faith alone. With the word *everyone* (implicit in the Hebrew and inserted by Paul), Isaiah reveals that the call to believe is universal. The connection is confirmed in Romans 10:12–13, "For there is no distinction between Jew and Greek; for the same Lord is Lord of all, abounding in riches for all who call on Him; for 'WHOEVER WILL CALL ON THE NAME OF THE LORD WILL BE SAVED.'"

The citation of Joel 2:32 in Romans 10:13 represents the climax of Paul's argument. Joel's words seal three crucial teachings in the paragraph: (1) sinners are saved by faith in Christ (i.e., calling on the name of the Lord; cf. Rom 10:10); (2) *all* sinners may call on the name of the Lord, whether they are Jew or Greek; (3) and Jesus Christ is Lord Jehovah (cf. Rom 9:5, 9).[29]

The Problem of Jewish Unbelief (Rom 10:14–21)

The gospel applies to all without distinction, yet the Jews did not believe it. Why did Israel not believe? Was it because the Israelites did not hear the gospel? Hearing is indeed necessary for saving faith (10:14). God sent Israel preachers of the good news (thus the citation from Isaiah 52:7 in 10:15), but "they did not all heed the good news." An allusion to Isaiah 53:1 confirms the

---

[29] See Seifrid, "Romans," 653–60; Morris, *Romans*, 382–88; cf. Kruse, *Romans,* 413–14.

necessity of hearing for faith. "So faith comes from hearing, and hearing by the word of Christ" (Rom 10:17).

So then is the problem with Israel that they have not heard the gospel? "But I say, surely they have never heard, have they?" (10:18). Paul's answer is emphatic and again supported by Scripture: "Indeed they have." The scriptural proof comes from Psalm 19:4 (LXX 18:5): "Their voice has gone out into all the earth, and their words to the ends of the world." Paul's point is not that the gospel had already reached the whole world (cf. Rom 15:23–24). He cites Psalm 19 to recall the doctrine he already mentioned in Romans 1:19–20, that the display of God's "invisible attributes" in the created world makes Jews without excuse, just as this natural revelation renders the Gentiles without excuse.[30] Nor is Israel's problem a lack of understanding since the hardening that has come to Israel is part of God's plan, as evidenced by Moses's words in Deuteronomy 32:21: "I will make you jealous by that which is not a nation" (Rom 10:19).

In the closing verses of Romans 10, Paul shows Israel's general unbelief is not due to any deficiency in God's goodness. He appeals to Isaiah 65:1–2. First, the Lord says that he will reveal himself to those who were not seeking him (Rom 10:20). Then the Lord claims that Israel has rebuffed the patient mercy that he has shown (10:21). Although God in his sovereign wisdom permitted those who had no interest in him to find him, he had hardly been unkind to Israel. "All day long" God had "stretched out" his hands to them. Isaiah's prophecy—that "disobedient and obstinate" Israel would turn away from God, even while God showed them extraordinary mercy—is a staggering indictment of the present state of Paul's kinsmen. At the same time, and even more importantly, Isaiah 65:2 "looks forward to what is going to be said of hope for Israel, depicting vividly the steadfast patience of that divine grace against which Israel has so continually sinned."[31] The end of Romans 10 justifies God in the present hardening of Israel but adds a ray of hope that gleams from God's character.

The Present Jewish Remnant (Rom 11:1–6)

As Paul opens Romans 11, he continues to address the question of the ultimate status of Israel. Paul has just cited prophecies about Israel's hardening. This leads to the question he poses: "God has not rejected His

---

[30] Seifrid, "Romans," 663–64; *pace* Bruce, *Romans*, 206–7; Kruse, *Romans*, 418–19; Schreiner, *Romans*, 571–72.

[31] Cranfield, *Romans*, 2:541.

people, has He?" (11:1). Does the influx of Gentile believers and hardening of Israel mean that God is done with the Jewish people? Paul's answer is a resounding "May it never be!"[32]

Paul offers himself, an ethnic Israelite, as one proof of this answer: "For I too am an Israelite, a descendant of Abraham, of the tribe of Benjamin."[33] As a physical son of Abraham, he and all the other Israelites who believe in the Messiah presently constitute "a remnant according to God's gracious choice." This remnant is analogous to the remnant during the age of Elijah (11:2–5).[34] In Romans 11:7, Paul echoes the opening of chapter 10 where Jews misdirected their zeal when they pursued righteousness by the law. Here, too, any remnant must be chosen by God apart from works (11:2, 6). So Paul and the present saved remnant constitute evidence for the key assertion of Romans 11: "God has not rejected his people whom he foreknew."[35]

Perhaps a word should be said about "his people" and "the people he foreknew" in Romans 11:1–2. Who is "this people"? The immediate context demands that it be ethnic Israel. Not only does ethnic Israel occupy the attention of Romans 9–11 as a whole, but between the two references to "his people" Paul names himself as Abraham's descendant and an Israelite. Furthermore, in Romans 10:21 Paul speaks specifically of *Israel's* rebellion. In the argument that follows, he gives examples from *Israel's* history. Consequently, in Romans 11:1–2, God's people must be ethnic Israel. Paul affirms that God has foreknown and not rejected the remnant of ethnic Israel.[36]

Romans 11:1–6 provides a further reason that God has not rejected his people. Paul explains, "God has not rejected his people whom he foreknew"

---

[32] See Jim R. Sibley, "Has the Church Put Israel on the Shelf? The Evidence from Romans 11:15," *JETS* 58 (2015): 577–78.

[33] Paul's presentation of himself as exhibit A that God has not rejected his people is an important *part* of his defense of God's justice, but it is not the *end* of his argument; *pace* Storms, *Kingdom Come*, 308–9.

[34] J. Dwight Pentecost argues, however, that during the church age "there is no continuing remnant of Israel with whom God is particularly dealing," *Things to Come: A Study in Biblical Eschatology* (Grand Rapids: Zondervan, 1958), 294. Pentecost takes Paul's remark in Rom 11:5 to be prophetic of Israel at the end of the age. But this fails to account for the fact that Paul identifies himself with the remnant in 11:2. Furthermore, Paul says, "*at the present time* there is a remnant." The existence of a "remnant" of Israel during the church age does not necessarily damage the distinction between Israel and the church. The nation of Israel remains under judgment. Paul simply refers to God's (limited) salvation of ethnic Israelites in the body of Christ during the present age.

[35] Cranfield, *Romans*, 2:542.

[36] *Pace* Sam Storms, *Kingdom Come*, 306–7. Storms tries to argue Romans 9:6 back into Rom 11:12, claiming that the "people" of 11:1–2 are identical with the "remnant," which, as noted above, he takes to be elect Jews and Gentiles. See Hoehner, "Israel in Romans 9–11," 150.

(11:2). This statement recalls God's Old Testament promises to Israel, especially the promise of election (cf. 8:29–30). In Genesis 18:19, the Lord says of Abraham, "For I have chosen him, so that he may command his children and his household after him to keep the way of the LORD by doing righteousness and justice, so that the LORD may bring upon Abraham what He has spoken about him." Deuteronomy 7:6 expresses the same idea: "For you are a holy people to the LORD your God; the LORD your God has chosen you to be a people for His own possession out of all the peoples who are on the face of the earth." God did choose Israel, but God had not (yet) made all Israel the treasured possession he had promised. Seifrid is correct on this point: "As in 8:29, then, 'foreknowledge' here is prospective in nature: in speaking of Israel as 'those whom God foreknew,' Paul has in view the coming salvation of his people."[37]

The opening paragraph of Romans 11 is pivotal. It asks the very question at the heart of this study: "Has God rejected his people?" If the church actually has replaced Israel in God's program—if God's promises to Israel are now fulfilled in the body of Christ (cf. Rom. 9:4)—then rather than denying that God has rejected Israel, Paul should try to explain how the church is spiritually fulfilling all the promises that God made to Israel. Instead, Paul advances his own election as evidence that God has not utterly forsaken his people. Yet he knows that this is not the end of the problem. God's promises to Israel are more extensive than Paul has yet accounted for.[38]

The Present Hardening and Future Glorious Acceptance of the Jews (Rom 11:7–15)

Israel may have sought God after a certain fashion, but they sought him the wrong way, on the basis of works instead of faith. Throughout Israel's history, elect Jews obtained God's righteousness, but the rest were hardened (11:7). The Old Testament described this hardening as well. Citing Isaiah 29:10, Paul notes the "spirit of stupor" given by God to Israel (Rom 11:8), a stupor foretold in Deuteronomy 29:4. Israel also had blind eyes and deaf ears to God's ways. David employed this language when he prayed against the infidels of his own age, "May their eyes grow dim so that they cannot see" (Ps

---

[37] Seifrid, "Romans," in *New Testament Use*, 668.

[38] Barry E. Horner, *Future Israel: Why Christian Anti-Judaism Must Be Challenged,* New American Commentary Series in Bible and Theology (Nashville: B&H, 2007) 223

69:22–23; Rom 11:9–10).[39] The word translated *forever* in the NASB could better be translated *continually*, indicating that Israel's hardness will remain until faith comes (as is clear both from the context of Ps 69 and the flow of thought in Rom 9–11).[40]

The theme of Israel's hardening, first introduced in Romans 9, will resurface in Romans 11:25. The New Testament elsewhere teaches the current general blindness of the Jewish people. One such place is 1 Thessalonians 2:14–16, where Paul lauds the believers who received his message amidst Jewish persecution, such persecution as the Judean churches had already endured. Why would these Jews oppose the proclamation of the gospel to the Gentiles? Paul's explanation sounds much like the language of hardening: "with the result that they always fill up the measure of their sins. But wrath has come upon them to the utmost" (1 Thess 2:16b). During the present age the majority of Jews are hardened by God "to fill up the measure of their sins." Their opposition to the gospel is evidence of God's wrath; God's giving people up to complete their iniquities has Old Testament precedent (Gen 15:16; cf. Dan 8:23).[41]

Did God ordain this hardening so as to be done with the Jewish people? Paul asks, "Did they stumble in order that they might fall?" (Rom 11:11). His answer is the same as in Romans 11:1, "May it never be!" God intends the hardening of Israel to work toward Israel's salvation. Since Israel's salvation is brought about through the present hardening, that salvation is limited at the moment. Simultaneously, Israel's hardening is bringing salvation to the Gentiles, which in turn works to "make [Israel] jealous" (11:11). This jealousy operates right now to "save some of them" (11:14).[42] Lanier Burns observes,

---

[39] Cranfield offers helpful comments on Psalm 69 and its messianic interpretation in the early church. *Romans,* 2:551

[40] Cranfield, *Romans,* 2:552. For a helpful discussion of the OT texts used here, see Burns, "Future of Ethnic Israel," 196–200.

[41] Gene L. Green, *The Letters to the Thessalonians,* PNTC (Grand Rapids: Eerdmans, 2002), 146–50; Jeffrey A. D. Weima, "1–2 Thessalonians," in *New Testament Use,* 873–74; *pace* F. F. Bruce, *1 & 2 Thessalonians,* WBC 45 (Waco, TX: Word 1982), 48. The gift of tongues was also a sign of Jewish hardening. Paul cites Isa 28 in 1 Cor 14:21–22 as he does Isa 29 in Rom 11:8. In Acts, Luke chooses episodes of tongues-speaking that show (among other things) God sending the gospel to the Gentiles while hardening his own people (Acts 2:8–13; 10:44–47; 19:1–7). Thus, tongues were a sign of God's judgment especially upon Israel. Richard B Gaffin, Jr., *Perspectives on Pentecost: New Testament Teaching on the Gifts of the Holy Spirit* (Phillipsburg, NJ: Presbyterian and Reformed, 1979), 102–9; O. Palmer Robertson, *The Final Word: A Biblical Response to the Case for Tongues & Prophecy Today* (Carlisle, PA: Banner of Truth, 1993), 41–50; *pace* Roy E. Ciampa and Brian S. Rosner, *The First Letter to the Corinthians,* PNTC (Grand Rapids: Eerdmans, 2010), 701n140.

[42] On the use of τινὰς here, see Schreiner, *Romans,* 595–96.

"The church had not taken Israel's place in God's program. . . . There is a present continuum between past promised and future fulfillments, and there is ethnic identity in the coequality of the church."[43] Even within the one body of Christ, Paul admits some distinction between redeemed Jews and redeemed Gentiles (cf. Gal 6:16).

Paul further shows (Rom 11:12) that Israel's future is also tied to this present hardening and to God's gracious redemption of the church. God is still holding out his hands in mercy to his people (10:21). The hardening of Israel, though currently bringing "riches for the Gentiles," will, when God reverses it in the regeneration of the Jews, redound with even greater riches for humanity.

Paul refers to the future salvation of Jews as their *fulfillment*. Does this fulfillment refer to the full number of Jews saved (which may or may not be equal to *all Israel* in Rom 11:25) or of the fulfillment of the prophecy concerning Israel? In this verse the word *fulfillment* contrasts with Israel's "transgression" and "failure." Paul will later use the same word to speak of the "fullness" or "full number" of elect Gentiles: "A partial hardening has happened to Israel until the fullness of the Gentiles has come in" (11:25). Given this parallel, it is preferable to take the word to speak of the "full number" of the Jews, which includes the eschatological event where *all Israel* is saved (11:26). For the present, riches have come to the Gentiles through the hardening of Israel, but in the future riches will redound to the whole world when God saves all Israel.[44]

Down to Romans 11:12, Paul has been speaking of the Jews. Now he turns to address the Gentiles in Romans 11:13–14. Even though he was the apostle to the Gentiles (cf. Rom 15:16; Eph 3:1; 1 Tim 2:7), he continues to work to evangelize Jews. He magnifies his ministry (meaning his ministry to the Gentiles) so that he might evoke jealousy among the Jews, entice them towards the gospel "and thus save some of them" (Rom 11:14). As Storms notes, this statement is about the "present era."[45]

However, when the apostle resumes his explanation ("For if their rejection is the reconciliation of the world, what will *their* acceptance be but life from the dead?" (11:15), he largely repeats the argument of 11:12.[46]

---

[43] "Israel and the Church," 274–75.

[44] BDAG, s.v. "πλήρωμα;" Burns, "Future of Ethnic Israel," 200–201; Schreiner, *Romans*, 597–98.

[45] Storms, *Kingdom Come*, 312–13.

Still, the expressions "their rejection" and "their acceptance" are ambiguous.[47] Is the possessive pronoun objective, as if God rejects and accepts Israel, or subjective, as if Israel rejects and accepts the gospel? The evidence indicates the latter. First, Paul has already denied that God has rejected Israel (11:1).[48] Second, the argument in Romans 11:15–16 parallels the argument in 11:12, where Paul speaks of *their trespass.*[49] Most likely, then, Paul is speaking of Israel's rejection of its Messiah. This interpretation differs with Burns, who takes "the reconciliation of the world" to indicate that Paul is referencing the Jewish hardening that led to the crucifixion of Jesus Christ.[50] Throughout this chapter, however, Paul has been speaking of an actual reconciliation of (or application of Christ's reconciliatory work to) the world as Gentiles receive Christ's propitiatory death by faith. Moreover, the "reconciliation of the world" by God in Christ contrasts with God's rejection of Israel.[51]

Israel's rejection of Christ is not permanent, however. Paul anticipates Israel's coming acceptance. These two ideas of *rejection* and *acceptance* stand in contrast. Rejection will give way to acceptance. The effects of Israel's hardening were good ("the reconciliation of the world"), but the effects of Jewish acceptance of the gospel will be far more glorious. By "life from the dead," Paul could mean that the salvation of the Jews will precede the resurrection and establishment of Christ's earthly millennial reign. Alternatively, he could simply mean that when the Jewish people are saved, eschatological glory will result.[52] Given the proximity to Romans 8:18–30, the second option is preferable.[53] Ultimately, God's plan is not thwarted by Jewish unbelief. Indeed, his sovereign will is to accept Israel, which will bring about the glories of the eschaton.

---

[46] Schreiner, *Romans,* 596.

[47] The noun ἡ ἀποβολὴ connotes an act from the outside upon the object rejected, BDAG, s.v. "ἀποβολή.".

[48] See Sibley, "Has the Church Put Israel on the Shelf?" 577–78; Hoehner, "Israel in Romans 9–11," 152.

[49] Sibley, "Has the Church Put Israel on the Shelf?" 579–80.

[50] Burns, "Future of Ethnic Israel," 201–2.

[51] See Kruse, *Romans*, 430–31.

[52] Burns, "Future of Ethnic Israel," 202; Kruse, *Romans,* 431; Saucy, *Progressive Dispensationalism*, 260; Moo, *Romans*, 724; Schreiner, *Romans,* 598–99. Sibley argues, "The phrase, 'life from the dead' in Rom 11:15 . . . refers, in all likelihood, to the rebirth of the nation. See, for example, Rom 11:26; Zech 12:10; and Ezek 36–37," "Has the Church Put Israel on the Shelf?" 581n39.

[53] Hoehner similarly argues that "life from the dead" speaks to messianic blessing of the last days, "Israel in Romans 9–11," 152.

Storms argues that Paul's efforts to save the Jewish people (described in Rom 11:14) prove that "their acceptance" will happen during the times where the fullness of the Gentiles are coming in (see 11:25). He puts the matter pointedly: "My question for advocates of the [future restoration] view, therefore, is this: *"How can Paul's ministry in the first century contribute to Israel's 'fulfillment' (v. 12) and 'acceptance'* [sic] *(v. 15) if the latter pertains to only one generation of Jewish people living at the time of Christ's second coming at the close of human history?"*[54] Storms's point rests on the observation that Paul's labor to save Jews during the first century seems linked to the "acceptance" that brings about "life from the dead" (11:15).

By way of response, "fulfillment" and "acceptance" (11:12, 15) refer to the full number of the Jews accepting the gospel *after* the fullness of the Gentiles comes in at the end of the present age. Paul ties this full number to monumental future events: "reconciliation" and "life from the dead."[55] Such events cannot occur while the Gentiles are coming in. Paul does not see his ministry as contributing to either the future "fulfillment" or the "acceptance." It has much more modest goals. He hopes that God might save only "some of them" by his ministry (11:14). Why then does he draw attention to his ministry and to his effort to "move to jealousy" other Jews by preaching to the Gentiles? He does not want Gentiles to conclude that God is currently uninterested in Jewish salvation. He addresses the Gentiles directly, "Now I am speaking to you who are Gentiles" (11:13). The great future glory that comes from Israel's "fulfillment" and "acceptance," namely "reconciliation" and "life from the dead," show the high privilege of bringing Jews to Christ now, during the time of Gentile riches (11:12).

Metaphors of God's Dealings with Jews and Gentiles (Rom 11:16–24)

In Romans 11:16, Paul introduces two metaphors in which he compares the saved remnant to a meal offering ("lump" and "dough") and an olive tree ("root" and "branches"). Burns rightly insists that both the dough and the root picture God's covenant promises to the patriarchs.[56] Since the branches (11:17–24) depict both believing Jews (who remain) and unbelieving

---

[54] Storms, *Kingdom Come,* 313

[55] Storms, *Kingdom Come,* 317–8, recognizing this inconsistency, is forced to interpret "life from the dead" as a metaphor for Jewish salvation in the present.

[56] See Burns, "Israel and the Church," 277–78, and Burns, "Future of Ethnic Israel," 205–10.

Jews (who are removed), neither the dough nor the root can picture saved Israelites.[57] Now Gentiles have been grafted in among them and have become "partaker with them of the rich root of the olive tree" (11:17). Significantly, Paul's observation about the holiness of the dough and root directly follows Paul's statement of future life coming with the future conversion of the Jews.

In sum, Paul appears to be making a point about God's future acceptance of the Jews. If the dough and root are holy, then the whole lump and all the branches are holy. This means that the Jewish patriarchs, as graciously elected by God and as recipients of God's promises to them, are the ground of this future glorious turning. Schreiner observes, "The election of the patriarchs sanctifies Israel as a whole."[58] Burns (following Cranfield) reminds readers that this "holy" dough and root does not refer to the actual holiness of the patriarchs (or any other human merit), but the sovereign election of God.[59] Their election proves eternally beneficial to future Jews when they are finally converted. Romans 11:16 again foreshadows the certainty that God will save all of Israel, and that certainty is grounded in God's holy election of the Jewish patriarchs. God's promises to the patriarchs lie at the heart of Paul's apologetic.

Nevertheless, the election of the Gentiles still leads to a serious warning. The Gentiles' gracious calling should be no cause for arrogance on their part. The root supports the Gentiles, not the other way around. Jews have been removed from the olive tree because of their unbelief, but Gentiles are connected by grace through faith. Consequently, Paul warns, "Do not become proud, but fear" (11:20). God is both severe and kind. He is kind to those who believe and persevere in the faith. He is severe to those who disbelieve. Gentiles who reject Christ can no more be joined to the root than can unbelieving Jews. Meanwhile, the Jews who believe will be grafted back in since "God has the power to graft them in again" (11:23). The Jews are the natural branches—it is fitting for them to be grafted back in (11:24).

Given all of Paul's talk about Jews and Gentiles in these verses, Burns offers an observation that is worth repeating. Paul does not confuse his imagery—the wild branches remain Gentiles and the natural branches

---

[57] See Saucy, *Progressive Dispensationalism*, 251. Cp. Kruse, *Romans*, 432–34.

[58] Schreiner, *Romans*, 601.

[59] Burns, "Future of Ethnic Israel," 205; cp. Cranfield, *Romans*, 2:565; Moo, *Romans*, 700–701.

remain Jews. Burns adds, "For an apostle who proclaims the church as an indivisible unity (Eph 4), the careful ethnic distinctions of Romans 11 are extraordinary."[60] The identity of the Gentiles as wild branches grafted into the Jewish promises informs the further development of Paul's argument.[61] Moreover, God may already be grafting in "natural branches" or Jews during the present era. Such an act does not invalidate the glorious future restoration of Israel (Rom 11:26).[62]

All Israel Will Be Saved (Rom 11:25–32)

Romans 11:25–32 represents the climax of Paul's argument in Romans 9–11.[63] Paul himself emphasizes the importance of these verses. He wants believers to recognize that their standing before God is due solely to gracious divine sovereignty in the unfolding of salvation history ("so that you will not be wise in your own estimation" 11:25a; cf. 11:19–20). Therefore, he appeals for his readers' attention: "I do not want you, brethren, to be uninformed" (11:25). They had better listen to what Paul is about to reveal.[64]

What Paul describes in 11:25–32 is a "mystery"—a matter heretofore hidden from humans but now disclosed through the apostle. It could not be discovered naturally but had to be divinely revealed.[65] Paul mentions a trio of actions constituting the mystery of God's sovereign plan in this age: (1) Israel's hardening, (2) the fullness of Gentile conversions, and (3) the salvation of all Israel. While the Spirit had already revealed the salvation of all Israel in the Old Testament, the accompanying plan of God and the manner in which Israel would be saved constitute the mystery. God has now revealed the hardening of Israel until the elect Gentiles come in, which leads to the salvation of Israel as his people.[66]

---

[60] Burns, "The Future of Ethnic Israel," 210; cp. Ronald E. Diprose, *Israel and the Church: The Origin and Effects of Replacement Theology* (Waynesboro, GA: Authentic Media, 2004), 57.

[61] For more on the olive tree analogy, see Moo, *Romans*, 702–3; Kruse, *Romans*, 439–41; *pace* Roderick Campbell, *Israel and the New Covenant* (Philadelphia: Presbyterian and Reformed, 1954), 122–23.

[62] Burns, "Israel and the Church," 279–80.

[63] Moo, *Romans*, 712–13.

[64] Cranfield, *Romans*, 2:573, observes, that Οὐ . . . θέλω ὑμᾶς ἀγνοεῖν ("I do not want you to be ignorant") is "a formula which Paul uses when he wishes to bring home to his readers with emphasis something which he regards as of special importance;" cf. Schreiner, *Romans*, 613.

[65] Burns, "The Future of Ethnic Israel," 210–11; Lenski, *Romans*, 717–18; Murray, *Romans*, 2:91–93; Moo, *Romans*, 712–13.

[66] Cranfield, *Romans*, 2:575; Moo, *Romans*, 716–17; Schreiner, *Romans*, 621; cp. Lenski, *Romans*, 717–18.

A Hardening Has Come Upon Israel

God in his sovereign grace has ordained Israel's hardening to save the Gentiles. God's ultimate purpose is to keep his promises to the Jews and save them. Though Paul preached the gospel to bring salvation to "the Jew first and also to the Greek" (1:16), the Gentiles' salvation now will, in the mystery of God's foreordained grace, lead to the salvation of the Jews at the close of the age.[67] Up to this point Paul has been assiduously defending God's faithfulness to his people despite Jewish opposition to the Christ during the present age. He now begins to break through into the warm light of future hope in the fulfillment of God's promises to his people, Israel.

As Paul taught in the previous chapters, the "hardening" of Israel means that God, in his eternal plan, has chosen relatively few Jews to be saved at the present time. This hardening has "happened to Israel" (11:25). Paul is not specific on the mechanics of this hardening, but clearly God is actively involved (cf. 9:19–26) even though Jews have pursued God through their own works-righteousness and merit (cf. 10:3; 11:7). Paul further describes this hardening as "partial" (11:25) because some Jews *have* believed on the Messiah. Indeed, as Paul already made clear, he himself is one of the remnant who has received grace (11:1).

The Fullness of the Gentiles

The hardening has a God-ordained end. This hardening remains "until (*achris ou*) the fullness of the Gentiles has come in." The phrase underlying *until* is almost always used in the New Testament temporally to signal what brings about the end of the preceding circumstances (see Luke 21:24; Acts 7:17–17; 1 Cor 11:26; 15:25; Gal 3:19; Rev 2:25). Some scholars argue that Paul uses *achris ou* to refer to the final end of Israel's hardening. For example, O. Palmer Robertson asserts,

> Romans 11:25 speaks of eschatological termination. Throughout the present age, until the final return of Christ, hardening will continue among part of Israel. Too often "until" has been understood as marking the beginning of a new state of things with regard to Israel. It has hardly been considered that "until" more naturally should be interpreted as reaching an eschatological termination point. The

---

[67] Burns, "The Future of Ethnic Israel," 211; Kruse, *Romans*, 442.

phrase implies not a new beginning after a termination, but the continuation of a circumstance until the end of time.[68]

Robertson's proposed rendering of Romans 11:25 would be somewhat like this: "A partial hardening has come upon Israel that will last until the fullness of the Gentiles comes in, which is at the end of time." This interpretation requires that 11:26 be taken, not as the next development in the future ordained by God, but as what is happening parallel to the fullness of the Gentiles coming in.[69] This interpretation must equate the "partial hardening" of Israel and the salvation of all Israel. Such theological gymnastics—where two radically opposing notions are treated as complementary—strains credulity. If the hardening of Israel is actually a good thing, and if it is the same thing as the salvation of all Israel, then why did Paul need to begin this defense of God's dealings with Israel at all? Those circumstances would present no problem to explain.

A better approach is to take Romans 11:25ff as the culmination and resolution of Paul's apologetic. He has defended the way God has *presently* dealt with his people Israel by appealing both to the character of God and to the actual ways in which God historically handled the hardening. Now he resolves the question of the *future* with respect to God's promises to them and gives the *terminus ad quem* of the present tragic state of Jewish hardening. God's promises to them are true and binding. Israel will still be saved.[70]

The "fullness of the Gentiles" is virtually identical to the "full inclusion" of the Israelites in Romans 11:12. This verse is the clearer of the two because Paul here says that the "fullness . . . comes in." This language implies that some of the Gentiles have not yet "come in." Paul does not mean that all Gentiles will be saved but that the full number of Gentile elect "come in" by confessing that Jesus is Lord. Thus, in Romans 11, Paul describes God's current dealings with the Gentiles as bringing salvation to them (11:11), their being "grafted in" (11:19), and of God's kindness to them (11:22). The Gentiles are coming into the olive tree; they are coming into salvation through the sovereign election of God and justifying grace of Christ, the Deliverer (cf. 11:26–27). So the point at which the hardening ends must be the completion of God's

---

[68] O. Palmer Robertson, *The Israel of God: Yesterday, Today, and Tomorrow* (Phillipsburg, NJ: P&R, 2000), 180.

[69] Ibid., 181–82.

[70] Cranfield, *Romans*, 2:575; Schreiner, *Romans*, 618–19.

saving work among the nations during the present dispensation.[71]

The Old Testament taught in many places that Gentiles would be saved into the glorious kingdom of the coming Messiah. In Genesis 49:10, Jacob prophesied concerning the future ruler in Judah that "to him shall be the obedience of the peoples." Joel 2:32 says that *whoever* calls on the name of the Lord will be delivered." Zephaniah spoke on the Lord's behalf that there would come a time when "the peoples . . . call on the name of the LORD, to serve Him shoulder to shoulder" (Zeph 3:9). Isaiah prophesied several times that the nations would turn to Yahweh: "In the last day . . . all the nations will stream to [the house of the Lord]" (Isa 2:2). The servant of Yahweh will be used by God as "a light to the nations, to open blind eyes" (42:6b–7a; cf. 42:10–13; 49:6). In Isaiah 52:10, the prophet foretells that "all the ends of the earth may see the salvation of our God" (cf. 45:22–23; 52:4–5). Jeremiah similarly prophesies that the nations "shall know that my name is the LORD" (Jer 16:21). Even Simeon prophesied that God would save the Gentiles through the Lord Jesus Christ, who would be "a Light of revelation to the Gentiles, and the glory of Your people Israel." (Luke 2:32; cf. Matt 12:18; Luke 4:18).[72]

Though the nations turning to Yahweh may have seemed unlikely to the prophets' original audience, it provides the backdrop to the prophecy of Gentile salvation in Romans 9–11. Then again, certain aspects of the Gentiles' salvation in Christ were *not* revealed in the Old Testament. For instance, the connection between the Gentiles' salvation and the hardening of Israel is a New Testament mystery. The delay of the salvation of all Israel until the fullness of the Gentiles' conversion is another.

Hints of this surprising turn in God's plan, however, do appear in Jesus's words. One example is John 10:16, where Jesus says "I have other sheep, which are not of this fold; I must bring them also, and they will hear My voice." Another is Luke 21:24, "Jerusalem will be trampled under foot by the Gentiles until the times of the Gentiles are fulfilled."[73]

---

[71] Cranfield, *Romans*, 2:576; also see Moo, *Romans*, 718–79.

[72] A. J. Köstenberger, "Nations," in *New Dictionary of Biblical Theology*, ed. T. D. Alexander and B. S. Rosner (Downers Grove, IL: InterVarsity Press, 2000), 676.

[73] Interestingly, Luke 21:24 shares the use of the disputed ἄχρι οὗ ("until") with Romans 11:25.

All Israel Will Be Saved

The full number of Gentiles confessing Christ leads to the salvation of "all Israel." Paul posits that the partial hardening that leads to the great inclusion of Gentiles results in a great future blessing: "all Israel will be saved" (Rom 11:26). Two aspects of this promise require further exploration.

In this way. The interpretation of the phrase "in this way" has provoked spirited discussion. Amillennialist O. Palmer Robertson argues that these words cannot indicate time, but he concedes that if they did, then they imply a future for Israel. He suggests that the phrase addresses the manner Israel will be saved. So the phrase translated "in this way" (ESV, NIV) or "and so" (KJV, NKJV, NASB, NLT) does not look forward, but "looks into the past."[74] He argues that the word *thus* is never used temporally but often speaks of acts finalized with a separate event. For Robertson, *all Israel* means the "Israel of God," which comprises true believers in the body of Christ (Gal 6:16). Thus, when Paul says "in this way all Israel will be saved," he refers to the fullness of the Gentiles who receive salvation through faith in Christ:

> First, the promises and the Messiah were given to Israel. Then in God's mysterious plan, Israel rejected its Messiah and was cut off from its position of distinctive privilege. As a result, the coming of the Messiah was announced to the Gentiles. The nations then obtained by faith what Israel could not find by seeking in the strength of their own flesh. Frustrated over seeing the blessings of their messianic kingdom heaped on the Gentiles, individual Jews are moved to jealousy. Consequently, they too repent, believe, and share in the promises originally made to them. "And in this manner" (*kai houtōs*), by such a fantastic process which shall continue throughout the present age "up to" (*achris hou*) the point where the full number of the Gentiles is brought in, all Israel is saved.[75]

What of this argument? First, it should be noted that whether *kai houtōs* is temporal has relatively little bearing on the interpretation of Romans 11:26. The best clue concerning timing lies in the future tense verb "will be saved." The question of whether *kai houtōs* introduces a sequence has nothing

---

[74] Robertson, *Israel*, 182.

[75] Ibid. Also see Lenski, *Romans*, 724–30.

to do with whether the phrase is temporal.[76] The word *houtōs* is in a place of emphasis, expressing the only way Israel's salvation happens. Paul follows the phrase that opens with *kai houtōs* with "just as" (*kai kathōs*) to introduce "it is written" (*gegraptai*).[77]

The mystery of God's working in this age occurs in a triad: (1) hardening; (2) fullness of the Gentiles; and (3) the salvation of all Israel. The triad builds on itself. It culminates with the third statement concerning Israel's salvation.[78] The word *houtōs* signals an event that follows the fullness of the Gentiles coming in. Then Paul correlates his point with the citation from Isaiah 59. The fullness of Gentiles coming in is the end of the partial hardening, and when it is no longer hardened, all Israel is saved.[79]

If Robertson's interpretation were correct, it would mean that, for the first time in these three chapters and indeed in the book of Romans (with the sole doubtful exception of 2:28–29), Paul uses *Israel* or *Jew* to mean something other than the physical seed of Abraham. This point cannot be stressed too strongly. To take *Israel* in Romans 11:26 as the Christian church is to take it in a totally different sense than Paul has used it throughout chapters 9–11.[80] Indeed, this view overlooks the point of the explicit contrast between Gentiles and Israel sustained throughout the book of Romans.

It also damages the theodicy Paul has been writing in Romans 9–11. Paul's question in these chapters stems from the condemnation of Jewish people to a near-universal rejection of Christ, and he asks whether God has failed to keep his promises to Israel (9:4; 11:1, 11). Paul has been laboring to show God's justice in hardening the Israelites.

What is most troubling about Robertson's interpretation is that in his view God does *not* keep his promises to Israel but fulfills them in the church. In

---

[76] Schreiner, *Romans,* 618n16, 620–21; Hoehner, "Israel in Romans 9–11," 154, adds, "[I]t would seem best to consider that [οὕτως] introduces a logical consequence or inference, that is, the logical consequence of Israel's hardening until the fullness of the Gentiles comes in so that all Israel will be saved. This is the normal usage of [οὕτως] as seen in Romans 5:12."

[77] See BDAG s.v. "οὕτω/οὕτως;" Cranfield, *Romans,* 576. Several argue that οὕτως must be used *either* correlatively or denoting manner. See, for example, Schreiner, *Romans,* 621; and Moo, *Romans,* 720. But both Luke 24:24 and Phil 3:17 show that οὕτω/οὕτως can be used to denote manner and then raise a correlation with καθώς. Also see Ben Witherington III with Darlene Hyatt, *Paul's Letter to the Romans: A Socio-Rhetorical Commentary* (Grand Rapids: Eerdmans, 2004) 275–76.

[78] Cranfield, *Romans,* 2:574–75.

[79] Schreiner, *Romans,* 621.

[80] As Schreiner, *Romans,* 615, notes, "But what is remarkable here is the promise that Israel will be saved as a *people.*"

other words, for those Jews who were concerned about their fellow Israelites' rejection of Christ (Rom 9:3) and who pondered the status of God's promises to Israel in light of that rejection, the response is that the Jews as a whole will never accept Christ, despite Paul's words in Romans 11:15. When Paul speaks of the Jews as "natural branches" being "grafted back into their own olive tree" (11:24), he does not refer to a future, glorious turning of Israel to Christ. In Robertson's interpretation, the *telos* and apex of Paul's apologetic in Romans 9–11 comes to nothing.

All Israel. What does Paul mean that salvation will come to *all Israel*? Cranfield suggests four different interpretations.[81] One view is that *all Israel* refers to *"totus coetus electorum ex Israele,"* or the whole body of Jews saved throughout all history.[82] According to this view, "and in this manner all Israel will be saved" means that God will save all Israel because he is already saving his remnant throughout all time.[83] Witherington objects, "The problem with arguing that all the elect from Israel are meant is that such a view would be self-evident, even absurdly so in light of what Paul has already said. More importantly, he is speaking about something that transpires at the eschaton."[84]

The second view suggests that *all Israel* refers to the whole church, the elect of both Jews and Gentiles throughout the ages. John Calvin says, "I extend the word *Israel* to include all the people of God." Appealing to Galatians 6:16, he adds, "In the same way, in Gal. 6:16, [Paul] calls the Church which was composed equally of Jews and Gentiles, the Israel of God, setting the people, thus collected from their dispensation, in opposition to the carnal children of Abraham who had fallen away from faith."[85] In the same vein Robertson exclaims, "Believing Gentiles come *into Israel!*"[86] For Robertson, the church has now been grafted into the olive tree, Israel, and thus when the fullness of

---

[81] Cranfield, *Romans,* 576–77; Kruse, *Romans,* 448–51, counted six different interpretations, but his fourth and fifth views are nearly identical: Israel as a whole at the end of the age versus a large number of Israelites at the end of the age.

[82] Lenski, *Romans,* 725–26.

[83] Also see Kruse, *Romans,* 451; John Bengel, *Gnomon of the New Testament,* trans. Charlton T. Lewis (Philadelphia: Perkinpine and Higgins, 1860), 2:132; Louis Berkhof, *Systematic Theology,* 698–700; Ben L. Merkle, "Romans 11 and the Future of Ethnic Israel," *JETS* 43 (2000):709–721; Reymond, "Traditional Covenant View," 53; Storms, *Kingdom Come,* 326–29.

[84] Witherington, *Romans,* 275; cf. Hoehner, "Israel in Romans 9–11," 156.

[85] John Calvin, *The Epistles of Paul the Apostle to the Romans and the Thessalonians,* trans. Ross Mackenzie, ed. David W. Torrance and Thomas F. Torrance (Grand Rapids: Eerdmans, 1960), 255

[86] Robertson, *Israel,* 188; cf. Karl Barth, *The Epistle to the Romans,* trans. Edwyn C. Hoskyns (New York: Oxford, 1968), 416; Campbell, *Israel and the New Covenant,* 120–25.

the Gentiles come into Israel, all of Israel will be saved. Arguing for the same interpretation, N. T. Wright states that, "Paul is clearly offering a deliberately polemical redefinition of 'Israel', parallel to that in Galatians (6:16)."[87]

Nearly all adherents of this view appeal to the "Israel of God" in Galatians 6:16. Indeed, the view appears to be incoherent without that appeal. This interpretation of "the Israel of God," however, is suspect. For ample reasons, Galatians 6:16 can be applied to redeemed members of ethnic Israel itself.[88] The Jewish-Gentile tensions throughout Galatians suggest that Paul's "Israel of God" is not the church but the Jewish remnant he speaks of in Romans 11:4–6, viewed in prospect of the future restoration of Israel spoken of in 11:26.

David Wallace offers a similar view, arguing that *all Israel* means Jewish and Gentile believers, but appealing to Romans 2:29 and the identification of a true Jew as one who has experienced circumcision of the heart. To this he connects the citation from Isaiah in Romans 11:26–27, arguing that "reading 'all Israel' as the return of 'hardened' Israel shows sequence and how God works, but so does reading 'all Israel' as the aggregate of those who repent, both Jew and gentile, but not every Jew and gentile."[89] Like the foregoing views, however, Wallace's interpretation fails to account for Paul's repeated distinction between Jew and Gentile throughout Romans 9–11, specifically failing to account for Paul's explicit distinction between the "fullness of the Gentiles" (11:25) and "Israel" (11:26).

Others take the phrase *all Israel* quite literally, in the universalist sense (though here limited to the offspring of Abraham). According to this theory, *all Israel* is ethnic Israel but includes every ethnic child of Abraham, Isaac, and Jacob throughout all time. Richard Bell summarizes this view: "In view of Rom. 11.29 and Paul's general view of perseverance in Romans, it seems

---

[87] N. T. Wright, "Jerusalem in the New Testament," [8], accessed December 31, 2022, http://www.ntslibrary.com/PDF%20Books/Jerusalem%20in%20the%20NT.pdf.

[88] Horatius Bonar observed, "In the Epistle to the Galatians (vi. 16), the expression 'the Israel of God' has been generally interpreted as meaning the spiritual Israel, and as therefore giving countenance to the spiritualizing process by which the Old Testament predictions regarding Israel are robbed of all their peculiar and appropriate meaning. Now here, again, I should be inclined to suggest that the apostle may really be speaking of the literal Israel; and as throughout the whole epistle he has been contrasting and comparing the circumcision and the uncircumcision, the Jew and the Gentile, so here, he first prays for a blessing on the believing Gentiles, and then on the believing Jews," *Prophetical Landmarks: Containing Data for Helping to Determine the Question of Christ's Pre-Millennial Advent* (London: James Nisbet, 1847), 304; cf. Jonathan Pratt, "The 'Israel of God' in Galatians 6:16," *DBSJ* 23 (2018): 59–75; Horner, *Future Israel*, 228–34; *pace* Moo, *Romans*, 721.

[89] Wallace, *Election of the Lesser Son*, 208.

unthinkable that an Israelite could be excluded from salvation."[90] Bell's view can be quickly discarded in view of other Scriptures. Jesus himself strongly condemned the Jews who rejected him (Matt 11:23–24; John 8:42–47). Within Romans, Paul clearly teaches that not every Israelite will be saved. The "religious" Jew because of his "stubbornness and impenitent heart" against God and Christ is "storing up wrath" for himself (Rom 2:5). In 9:6–8, Paul plainly declared that "not all who are descended from Israel belong to Israel," and he was referring to ethnic Israelites.

Contrary to the above interpretations, the best understanding of Romans 11:26 is that a great turning of ethnic Israelites to Christ will occur near or after the close of the present age, after the Gentiles come in.[91] This view is not limited to dispensationalists: numerous others, including some committed amillennialists, espouse it.[92] For example, F. F. Bruce (a covenant premillennialist) says, "It is impossible to entertain an exegesis which understands 'Israel' here in a different sense from 'Israel' in verse 25."[93] Others agree that every mention of "Israel" and "Jews" in chapters 9–11, not to mention the entire book of Romans, refers to ethnic Jews.[94] This view asserts that Paul is speaking of a great mass conversion of ethnic Jews to Christ.

Wallace objects that such a reading "seems to hold rigidly to the constructs of the Old Testament idiom without any new sense given to the meaning of the phrase."[95] The hermeneutics underlying this statement are suspect in light of the consistent use of *Jew* and *Israel* throughout Romans and especially in chapters 9–11. If Paul has not elsewhere expanded the Old Testament sense of *Israel*, why should anyone assume that he is doing it here?[96]

---

[90] Richard H. Bell, *The Irrevocable Call of God: An Inquiry into Paul's Theology of Israel*, WUNT (Tubingen: Mohr Siebeck, 2005), 263.

[91] Pentecost, *Things to Come*, cites several OT passages that prophesy a salvation for Israel that is both national and individual: Jer 30:7; Ezek 20:37–38; Dan 12:1; Joel 2:31–32; Zech 13:1, 8–9.

[92] For some of the Reformed articulations of this view, see Jonathan Edwards, *An Humble Attempt*, in *Apocalyptic Writings*, vol. 5 of *The Works of Jonathan Edwards*, ed. Stephen J. Stein (New Haven, CT: Yale, 1977) 334; Charles Hodge, *A Commentary on the Epistle to the Romans* (New York: Hodder & Stoughton, 1882) 589, 598–99; Michael Horton, *The Christian Faith: A Systematic Theology for Pilgrims on the Way* (Grand Rapids: Zondervan, 2011) 949–50; Murray, *Romans*, 2:96–100; Kim Riddlebarger, *A Case for Amillennialism: Understanding the End Times* (Grand Rapids: Baker, 2003), 184–92. Even Martin Luther seems to have held this view, at least temporarily, *Commentary on the Romans*, trans. J. Theodore Mueller (1954; repr. Grand Rapids: Kregel, 1976), 161–62 (but also see editor's note on p. 162).

[93] Bruce, *Romans*, 218.

[94] For example, Moo makes this observation about Romans 9–11, *Romans*, 721.

[95] Wallace, *Election of the Lesser Son*, 202.

Still, an important question remains. If *Israel* means ethnic Israel, then in what sense is *all Israel* saved eschatologically? Are all Jews living at that time saved? So argues Lewis Sperry Chafer:

> The nation, but for certain rebels who are to be "purged out" (Ezek. 20:37–38), will be saved, and that by their own Messiah when He comes out of Zion (cf. Isa. 59:20–21; Matt. 23:37–39; Acts 15:16). "All Israel" of Romans 11:26 is evidently that separated and accepted Israel that will have stood the divine judgments which are yet to fall upon that nation (cf. Matt. 24:37–25:13). The Apostle distinguishes clearly between Israel the nation and a spiritual Israel.[97]

Chafer, however, must still make some allowance for those Israelites who will be purged (*not* saved) according to Ezekiel 20. All premillennialists agree: the Israel that will enter the millennial kingdom of Christ after the great tribulation will include only saved Israelites.

Burns helpfully observes that, since a remnant of Jews exists during the present widespread hardening of Israel, then a "representative, national mass" of converts before Christ at his second coming need not include every Jew alive at that time.[98] This suggestion seems to accord with Paul's specific emphasis in Romans 11. Moreover, the Old Testament offers precedent for *all Israel* comprising a great majority with a few exceptions. To cite one example, 1 Kings 12:1 describes *all Israel* coming to Shechem to crown Rehoboam king, though this number clearly excludes some of the nation (cf. Dan. 9:11; 2 Chron. 12:1).[99] Moo reminds his readers that Paul's actual words carry a "corporate significance, referring to the nation as a whole" and not "every single individual who is a part of that nation."[100] Paul is referring "to the last times, and to a very general conversion of [the people of the Jews] to the

---

[96] Although he seems uncomfortable with the idea, Wallace, *Election of the Lesser Son*, 203, does allow for the possibility that Paul means ethnic Israel. In this case, he rightly concludes that Paul's statement is not universalist but refers to "repentant" Jews.

[97] Lewis Sperry Chafer, *Systematic Theology* (Dallas: Dallas Seminary Press, 1948), 3:106. Chafer also cites Isaiah 66:8 in support of an instantaneous conversion of Israel at the second advent of Christ, a view shared by Pentecost, *Things to Come*, 266–67, 294; and Hoehner, "Israel in Romans 9–11," 155–56

[98] Burns, "Israel and the Church," 281–82; see Schreiner, *Romans*, 619; Johnson, "Evidence from Romans 9–11," 215 cites similar language from the Mishnah; Wallace, *Election of the Lesser Son*, 201.

[99] Bell, *Irrevocable Call*, 261; cf. Bruce, *Romans*, 218.

[100] Douglas Moo, *The Letter to the Romans*, 2nd ed., NICNT (Grand Rapids: Eerdmans, 2018) 737.

Messiah."[101] At that time, the veil that "lies over their heart" will be finally removed (2 Cor 3:15–16).

As it is written. The meaning of *all Israel* is further amplified by the Old Testament citations in Romans 11:26b–27.[102] Here Paul shows that the salvation of all Israel is prophesied in the Old Testament: "As it is written, 'The Deliverer will come from Zion, He will remove ungodliness from Jacob.' 'This is My covenant with them, when I take away their sins.'" This quotation presents some difficulty.

Many interpreters believe that the first three lines cite an altered form of the LXX for Isaiah 59:20–21a, and then the last line quotes a portion of Isaiah 27:9.[103] Some also suggest that a citation from Jeremiah 31:33–34 is included.[104] The most significant problem is the apparent change of preposition preceding *Zion*. Paul says "from Zion" (*ek*, cp. Ps 14:7) rather than following the LXX "on account of Zion" (*heneken*), which is itself slightly different from the Masoretic text "to Zion" (*ĕtsiōn*). The meaning of the prepositions *ek* and *heneken*, however, can overlap; *ek* can mean *on account of* (cp. Rom 11:6).[105] More importantly, Paul presents these four lines of prophecy as parallel and mutually supporting. In other words, the parallel lines lead the reader to understand *ek* as *on account of* or *for* rather than *from*. For the Deliverer to come *to* Zion (as the Hebrew reads) is not materially different from saying that the Deliverer will come *on behalf of* Zion. Read this way, the surface differences between the prepositions vanish.

Some have argued that *from Zion* indicates that Christ will come from a heavenly "Zion" when he delivers *all Israel*.[106] This interpretation, however, is not the best possibility. If the text must be read as *from Zion*, then it probably depicts the Deliverer of all Israel coming from David's royal house, for which Zion stands as a metonym (cp. Pss 14:7; 110:2; Isa 2:3). Still, the reading *for* or *because of Zion* (as found in the Septuagint and as accords with the sense

---

[101] John Gill, *An Exposition of the Old and New Testaments*, Baptist Commentary Series (London: Mathews and Leigh, 1809), 2:538–39; cp. Schreiner, *Romans*, 621.

[102] Burns, "Israel and the Church," 280–82.

[103] See, e.g., Seifrid, "Romans," 673–74; Moo, *Romans*, 727.

[104] Burns, "Israel and the Church," 280.

[105] Cp. BDAG, s.v. "ἐκ;" "ἕνεκα."

[106] Cranfield, *Romans*, 578; Moo, *Romans*, 727–28; Seifrid, "Romans," 674; Schreiner, *Romans*, 619. Those who hold this view offer as proof Ga. 4:26; Heb 12:22; and Rev 3:12, 21.

of Isa 59:20) fits nicely both the prophecy and the argument of Romans 11.

In Isaiah 59 the Deliverer is Yahweh himself (Isa 59:15b–19), who will come with salvation "on account of" or "for" all Israel, as promised in the Davidic Covenant. The center of future salvation is this Deliverer. Not surprisingly, given Paul's Christology (1 Cor 15:3–4; Eph 1:7; Col 1:13; 1 Tim 2:5–6; Titus 2:14; et al.), he identifies the "Deliverer" (Rom 11:26) with Jesus. This vision of Jesus as Yahweh the Deliverer is reinforced in multiple Scriptures (e.g., Isa 60:1–2, 19; cf. John 8:58; 12:41; 1 Cor 2:8; Phil 1:6).[107]

Paul's synthesis of Scripture prophecies in Romans 11:26b–27 portrays the sublime fulfillment of God's promises to his people. What is both striking and fitting is that Paul, after announcing that God will save all Israel in accordance with his promises, buttresses this declaration by appealing to New Covenant texts. Paul only mentions the New Covenant in three places.[108] Paul here connects the future salvation of all Israel to the New Covenant, particularly three New Covenant blessings. First is the future Deliverer ("the Deliverer will come"). Second is the cleansing sanctification of Israel through this Deliverer ("he will banish ungodliness from Jacob"). Third is the divine forgiveness of sins ("when I take away their sins"). As described by Paul, the covenant that God will make with Israel is nearly identical to the New Covenant prophesied in Jeremiah 31:33–34, where Yahweh promises to "put my law within them" and "forgive their iniquity."[109] Moreover, Paul sees these promises as being fulfilled literally.[110]

In Paul's understanding, the New Covenant blessings that await a saved Israel have already been secured through the atoning death of the Messiah. Salvation through atonement and spiritual renewal is central to Paul's theology of eschatological regeneration.[111] At the same time, Paul also sees a

---

[107] On Yahweh as Christ in Rom 11:26–27, see Cranfield, *Romans,* 2:577–78; Schreiner, *Romans,* 619–20; and Seifrid, "Romans," 674.

[108] See Bruce Compton, "Epilogue: Dispensationalism, the Church, and the New Covenant," in *Dispensational Understanding of the New Covenant,* ed. Mike Stallard (Schaumburg, IL: Regular Baptist Books, 2012), 258; cf. R. Bruce Compton, "Dispensationalism, the Church, and the New Covenant," *DBSJ* 8 (2003), 3–48; furthermore, Johnson, "Evidence from Romans 9–11," 215–16, observed that Paul has in view the Abrahamic, Davidic, and New Covenants—all three unconditional covenants—in Rom 11:26–27.

[109] See Burns, "Israel and the Church," 281–82.

[110] Michael Vlach, "What about Israel?" in *Christ's Prophetic Plans,* 118; *pace* Storms, *Kingdom Come,* 331–2.

[111] Cranfield, *Romans,* 579, nevertheless overstates things when he comments, "It is also to be noted that there is no trace of encouragement for any hopes entertained by Paul's Jewish contemporaries for the re-establishment of a national state in independence and political power, no—incidentally—anything which could feasibly be interpreted as a scriptural endorsement of the modern nation-state of Israel." Paul's silence regarding an eschatological politi-

future ratification of the New Covenant with Israel, occurring in conjunction with the nation's salvation. Undoubtedly he is also thinking of the promised outpouring of the Holy Spirit in Isaiah 59:21b, even though he skips these words to mention the forgiveness of sins from Isaiah 27:9. As Seifrid notes, "In this emphasis on God's giving of himself to Israel, Paul stands close to the Isaianic passage that he cites and echoes the very text of Isa. 59:21 that he omits."[112] In other words, Paul still has the broader message of Isaiah 59 in mind: God pours his Spirit on Israel and begins his permanent presence among his people in an eschatological kingdom of glory and salvation.[113]

The foregoing leads to an important conclusion: one should not limit Paul to saying that only these four lines of prophecy from Isaiah 59 and 27 will be fulfilled when "all Israel will be saved." Romans 9–11 has been a defense of God's faithfulness to his promises to Israel despite the current, widespread hardening of the nation. Romans 9 reiterates the rich blessings for those who are the "Israel of God," including "the adoption, the glory, the covenants, the giving of the law, the worship, and the promises" (Rom. 9:4). The question in 11:1, "Has God rejected his people?" is more than a vague concern for a restricted fulfillment of God's promises to Israel—it is tied to God's faithfulness to his word (cf. Matt 5:17–18). Paul's answer to this question is an emphatic negative. In other words, all the promises to the patriarchs and the people of Israel are a matter of concern for Paul. He is about to assert that the Jewish people are "beloved for the sake of their forefathers" (see below). Though the text does not mention every promise, one may rightly infer that the land, the reign, the kingdom, the blessings—all of it—is what Paul includes in the fulfillment when "all Israel will be saved."[114] Nevertheless, Paul's citation of the Isaiah prophecy shows that the

---

cal kingdom, does not imply that Paul denied such a kingdom; see 1 Cor 6:9–10; 15:24, 50; Gal 5:21; Eph 5:5; Col 1:13; 1 Thess 2:12; 2 Thess 1:5; 2 Tim 4:1, 18.

[112] Seifrid, "Romans," 677.

[113] Burns, "Future of Ethnic Israel," 214, observes, "Paul seems to be teaching that Messiah's eschatological Parousia will be the time of God's sovereign ratification of the new-covenant promise with Israel."

[114] Jonathan Edwards, who believed that God in his providence situated the Land of Promise in such a way as to make it the center of the universe (and thus the center of Christ's future kingdom), said, "[T]he Jews will return to their own land again, because they never yet possessed one quarter of that land, which was so often promised them, from the Red Sea to the river Euphrates (Ex. 23:31; Gen. 15:18; Deut. 11:24; Josh. 1:4). Indeed, it was partly fulfilled in Solomon's time, when he governed all within those bounds for a short time; but so short, that it is not to be thought that this is all the fulfillment of the promise that is to be. And besides, that was not a fulfillment of the promise, because they did not possess it, though they made the nations of it tributary," "Notes on the Apocalypse," in *Apocalyptic Writings,* 134; cp. Jonathan Edwards, *The Blank Bible,* vol. 24 of *The Works of Jonathan Edwards,* ed. Stephen J. Stein (New Haven, CT: Yale, 2006), 2:1028. Of course, Edwards was neither a dispensationalist nor a premillennialist.

center of the Old Testament prophecies is spiritual renewal of the people of Israel through the Deliverer, Jesus Christ.

This salvation through the Deliverer is an important point. Michael Horton claims, "Classic dispensationalism's pattern of two peoples and two programs requires two objects of fulfillment: Jesus Christ and the nation of Israel."[115] This claim misrepresents dispensationalism. Horton ignores dispensationalists' Christological emphasis in their vision of the millennial kingdom. For example, Alva J. McClain wrote, "All [the future kingdom's] spiritual blessings will be *centered in the royal Man*. . . . And since He will be King over all the nations, His spiritual blessings will be extended to all men."[116] Likewise, Charles Ryrie asserted, "There is no kingdom for Israel apart from the suffering Savior, as well as the reigning King. The Crucifixion was as necessary to the establishing of the kingdom as it was to the building of the church."[117] More importantly, Romans 11:26 shows that the future salvation of Israel is wrought by the Deliverer who comes to Zion to save Israel. The future salvation of Israel is centered in the Deliverer, in the Lord Jesus Christ, the coming Kingdom's King.

Beloved for the sake of their forefathers. Paul follows his explanation of Israel's future salvation with concluding remarks about the relationship of Israel's hardening to divine election. Paul says that the Jews are presently enemies because of their opposition to the gospel. He does not mean that the Jews are the enemies of the church but of God.[118] They are God's enemies (for now) because they reject the gospel (Rom 10:21; 11:15, 20). Yet their current opposition is not outside of God's plan because it is "for your sake," meaning that Israel's rejection of the gospel is for the benefit of Gentile believers who have come to Christ by grace during the present epoch (11:11, 25).

This status of enmity views Israel from the perspective of the gospel. The Jewish people, however, can also be viewed from the perspective of election. The parallel lines in 11:28 juxtapose these two sides of God's plan: "From the standpoint of God's choice they are beloved for the sake of the fathers." God still loves the Jewish people because of the promises he made to Abraham,

---

[115] Horton, *The Christian Faith*, 948–49.

[116] Alva J. McClain, *The Greatness of the Kingdom: An Inductive Study of the Kingdom of God* (Winona Lake, IN: BMH Books, 1959), 219.

[117] Ryrie, *Dispensationalism*, 150–51.

[118] Bruce, *Romans*, 218–19.

Isaac, and Jacob (11:16). The theme that Israel enjoys God's love because of the patriarchs is a constant one throughout the Old Testament.[119] Paul sees these promises not as void through spiritual fulfillment in the church but as real and abiding, awaiting fulfillment to Israel after God finishes his present work among Gentiles.

By invoking the patriarchs of Israel, Paul alludes to the promises given to them (Rom 11:1–2, 9:1–5).[120] Now, however, Paul connects these patriarchal promises with the future salvation of all Israel. This point is underlined in Romans 11:29, "For the gifts and calling of God are irrevocable." God's promises to the patriarchs are the root of the future salvation of all Israel. Such promises are unbreakable, made by God who cannot lie (Heb 6:18; Titus 1:2).

The chapter closes with a recapitulation of the ideas that have filled the argument of Romans 9–11. God, in the mystery of his will, hardens one people in order to bring mercy to another. Gentile believers were previously alienated from God through sin, but God hardened the people of Israel in order to show mercy to the Gentiles through Israel's disobedience (Rom 11:30). Paul continues, "So these also now have been disobedient, that because of the mercy shown to you they also may now be shown mercy." In God's purpose, the present disobedience of the Jews must give way to his mercy for Israel.

The text says that the mercy coming to the Jews will happen "now." The word *now* is a textual variant with strong evidence against its inclusion. Metzger comments that "a preponderance of early and diverse witnesses favors the shorter reading."[121] Textual critics include it because it is a hard reading. If it is genuine, perhaps Paul means that God's mercy to Israel is the next great step in the unfolding of God's sovereign grace.[122] God is at work, ordaining even the disobedience of humankind for the purpose of having mercy on all. The word *all* affirms that God sovereignly saves all kinds of people according to his purposes. These purposes will culminate in the salvation of "all Israel" (11:26).[123]

---

[119] Colin Kruse, *Romans*, 446n231, provides the following impressive list of OT citations concerning God's great love for the Jewish people: Deut 4:37; 7:7[–8]; 10:15; 14:2; 1 Kgs 3:8; Pss 33:12; 47:4; 65:4; 105:5; 106:5; 135:4; Isa 14:1; 41:8, 9; 42:1; 43:10, 20; 44:1, 2; 45:4; 49:7; 65:9.

[120] Moo, *Romans*, 731–32.

[121] Bruce M. Metzger, *A Textual Commentary on the Greek New Testament*, 2nd ed. (New York: United Bible Societies, 1998), 465.

[122] Cp. Moo, *Romans*, 735.

Humanity may not completely understand God's unconditional election, his sovereign purposes, or why he hardens. Christians, however, can be sure that even when God hardens and consigns men to disobedience, he has mercy somewhere in view.

Paul appropriately closes these great doctrines with a great doxology. God's wisdom and knowledge are deeper than finite knowledge could ever grasp. His judgments and ways are beyond humanity's comprehension. All things have been created by God, all continue sustained by God's mercy, and all exist for God's glory. Whether they are objects of mercy or hardening, recipients of severity or kindness, all things are ordered by God for his glory. "To him be the glory forever. Amen," (11:36).

Conclusion

I believe that Romans 9–11 disallows all forms of supersessionism. Paul lays the exegetical foundation of these chapters earlier in the book of Romans by consistently distinguishing Jews from Gentile. He carefully stresses that both Jews and Gentiles are sinners and that both Jews and Gentiles are saved exclusively through the righteousness of Christ received by faith. The church is made up of both Jews and Gentiles but not so as to obliterate the fact that some are Jews and others are Gentiles.

On this foundation Paul mounts an apologetic for God's faithfulness to his promises to Israel. He introduces the problem in Romans 9: while God is presently showing mercy to Gentiles, he is not unjust. God "has mercy on whom He desires, and He hardens whom He desires" (9:18). In 9:30–10:21, Paul notes the impotence of Jewish attempts to save themselves apart from Christ's righteousness. On the other hand, he notes God's mercy in sending them the good news about Jesus and his grace.

Romans 11 concludes Paul's defense of God's justice. He first emphasizes the remnant of Jews (including himself) who, by God's grace, have believed the gospel of Christ. Nevertheless, most Jews are currently being hardened according to God's sovereign will. Paul hastens to add that this Jewish hardening has resulted in salutary effects for Gentiles, whom God is currently bringing into his church. In time God intends the salvation of all Israel. He will save them by Jesus Christ, the Deliverer, and will establish his covenant with them. This commitment is grounded in the gracious, electing love of

---

[123] Moo, *Romans*, 736–37.

God for their forefathers in view of the patriarchal promises. In keeping with Paul's references to Jews and Israel throughout Romans, as well as the overarching argument of Romans 9–11, *all Israel* should be understood as the ethnic seed of Abraham, who will *en masse* believe in Jesus Christ after the full number of Gentiles has been saved.

Thus, Romans 9–11 is a crucial passage for understanding the distinction between Israel and the church. Paul holds out hope for the future salvation of Israel. He sees this salvation as the fulfillment of the Old Testament promises to ethnic Jews. This salvation preserves their identity as "his [God's] people" (11:1, 2), the "Israelites" or "Jews" (9:4; 11:14), Paul's "kinsmen according to the flesh" (9:3), and the "children of Abraham" (9:7). Furthermore, Burns's observation is worth repeating: "One can hardly overemphasize the fact that the church is never mentioned per se in this chapter."[124] Though Paul clearly emphasized the unity of Jews and Gentiles in the body of Christ (e.g., Gal 3:28; Eph 2:14, 18), he saw a future for Israel that fulfilled all God's promises through the Deliverer, Jesus Christ.

Paul understood the Old Testament promises to Israel to be binding in a way that necessitated a literal, future fulfillment. Without this presupposition, he would have had little reason to defend God's justice in Romans 9–11, let alone reason to defend it in the way he did. Jesus Christ will still save all Israel when all Israel turns to him after the times of the Gentiles are fulfilled.

---

[124] Burns, "Future of Ethnic Israel," 228.

Will Jesus Come Before the Millennium? A New Testament Answer from Revelation 20

W. Edward Glenny
University of Northwestern, St. Paul
St. Paul, Minnesota

One wag described the millennium as a thousand years of peace that Christians like to fight about. Some call the millennium the greatest controversy in the book of Revelation. Gregg writes, "Already in the second century, the watershed issue in the interpretation of the Apocalypse was defined in terms of one's understanding of the meaning of the 'thousand years' in Revelation 20."[1] He goes on to explain, "The term 'Millennium' (from the Latin: *mille* = thousand, and *annus* = years) has generally been adopted to refer to this period. In the Bible, only this one chapter near the end of Revelation mentions the thousand-year reign of the saints with Christ, and . . . it is no exaggeration to call this the most controversial chapter in the Bible."[2]

G. K. Chesterton famously said, "Though St. John the Evangelist saw many strange monsters in his vision, he saw no creatures so wild as one of his own commentators." This is an essay about the way that John's interpreters have understood the teaching concerning the thousand-year reign of Christ in Revelation 20. The three main views concerning the millennium are premillennialism, postmillennialism, and amillennialism. Proponents of these three views differ in their understanding of the relationship of Christ's return to his thousand-year reign and the nature of his reign. These two issues are closely related, as we will see. Premillennialism (sometimes called chiliasm) is the belief that Christ will return before the millennium and personally rule over an intermediate earthly kingdom for a thousand years before the new heavens and earth. Postmillennialism is the belief that, by their successful evangelism of the world, Christians will establish the millennial kingdom on this earth, which will be a thousand years of peace, and then Christ will

---

[1] Steve Gregg, *Revelation Four Views: A Parallel Commentary* (Nelson, TN: Thomas Nelson, 1997), 27.

[2] Ibid.

return. Some postmillennialists interpret the return and victory of Christ portrayed in Revelation 19 to be symbolic for the spread of the gospel in this age. Amillennialism is the belief that the millennium is in this age between Christ's first and second advents, either in heaven where believers rule with Christ or on this earth where Christ rules in the lives of believers; good and evil will coexist on this earth until Christ returns, ending the millennium and bringing in the eternal state. Amillennialism (like postmillennialism) is based on a two-age model, which has no place for an intermediate kingdom (millennium) after Christ's return and before the new heavens and earth, as premillennialists do.[3]

This essay is a survey of the content of Revelation 20, especially as it relates to the time of Christ's return in relationship to the thousand-year reign that is the dominant subject of the first ten verses in the chapter. The time of his return is the defining characteristic of the three views of the millennium mentioned above, and the various interpretations of proponents of those views will be discussed, as we survey the chapter section by section and interact primarily with premillennial and amillennial interpretations of Revelation 20; the postmillennial understanding of the passage is not as widely held as the other two views, and it is similar to amillennialism in regard to the return of Christ coming at the end of the thousand-year period. The goal of this essay is to defend and show the support for a premillennial return of Christ in Revelation 20.[4]

Outline of Revelation

Before we look at Revelation 20, it is helpful to summarize its location in the structure of the book and the arrangement of material bordering that chapter. Revelation contains four visions that provide the structure of the book.[5] They are preceded by a prologue and followed by an epilogue, and there

---

[3] The various proponents of these three views differ on many specific details, and it is difficult to give a description of any of the views in enough detail to satisfy all proponents of it. For more details on the three different views concerning the millennium in Rev 20, see Darrell L. Bock, ed., *Three Views on the Millennium and Beyond* (Grand Rapids: Zondervan, 1999); Mark Wilson, *Charts on the Book of Revelation: Literary, Historical, and Theological Perspectives* (Grand Rapids: Kregel, 2007), 100–101; and Gregg, *Revelation Four Views*, 458–84.

[4] I am honored to present this essay to Dr. Charles Hauser, my former colleague and dean at Central Baptist Seminary. This topic seems fitting for this occasion, since he is a staunch proponent of the premillennial return of Christ. For a more detailed defense of premillennialism, including the premillennial interpretation of Rev 20, see Matt Waymeyer, *Amillennialism and the Age to Come: A Premillennial Critique of the Two-Age Model* (The Woodlands, TX: Kress Biblical Resources, 2016).

[5] There are other ways Revelation could be outlined. See Brian J. Tabb, *All Things New: Revelation as Canonical Capstone*, New Studies in Biblical Theology 48 (Downers Grove, IL: IVP, 2019), 19–25.

are some intervening events between the third and fourth vision. This results in the following outline of the book:

Prologue (1:1-8)
First vision (1:9–3:22)
Second vision (4:1–16:21)
Third vision (17:1–19:10)
Intervening events (19:11–21:8)
Fourth vision (21:9–22:9)
Epilogue (22:10-21)[6]

Chapter 20 is placed strategically in the intervening section between the two angelic revelations found in 17:1–19:10 and 21:9–22:9,[7] and David Aune helpfully describes the contents of this intervening section as "the final defeat of God's remaining foes."[8] The contents of this section describe how God defeats the satanic rulers who control the satanic kingdom and establishes his eternal rule. Revelation 20 itself contains three visions that John sees, each marked by the words "and I saw" (*kai eidon*) in 20:1, 4, and 11. The first two visions are connected by the six-fold recurrence of the words "a thousand years" in 20:2, 3, 4, 5, 6, and 7, relating all of 20:1–10 to the thousand-year reign of Christ, which is presented in Revelation 20 as the essence of God's defeat of Satan.

The most important issue in this intervening section (19:11–21:8) concerning the time of Christ's return is whether the narrative of Revelation progresses and advances paragraph by paragraph through the section or whether there is a repetition of previous events. In 19:11–21, John narrates a vision of Jesus, the King of Kings and Lord of Lords, returning to earth on a white horse and defeating the beast, the false prophet, and the kings of the earth, who are gathered together to oppose the returning King. Jesus slays the kings of the earth and their armies with the sword coming out of his mouth, and he captures the beast and the false prophet, both of whom he throws alive into the lake of fire and brimstone.[9] The relationship of

---

[6] Buist M. Fanning, *Revelation*, ZECNT (Grand Rapids: Zondervan, 2020), 63–64.

[7] These angelic revelations in 17:1–19:10 and 21:9–22:9 are very similar in their beginnings and conclusions, and the main characters in them involve "antithetical female imagery": the whore Babylon in the first and the bride Jerusalem in the second. See David E. Aune, *Revelation*, WBC 52 (Nashville, 1998) 3:1068–69. The first angelic revelation is a vision of the destruction of Rome/Babylon, Satan's worldly kingdom, and the second is a vision of God's eternal order.

[8] Ibid., 1:civ. Aune divides the section into four subdivisions: (1) the divine warrior and His conquests (19:11–21), (2) the final defeat of Satan (20:1–10), (3) vision of the judgment of the dead (20:11–15), and (4) the transition to the new order (21:1–8).

[9] Premillennialists and amillennialists understand the return of Christ in 19:11–21 to refer to his second advent at the end of this age.

Revelation 20 to the events at the end of this age narrated in chapter 19 is integral to one's view of the millennium. Amillennialists believe that Revelation 20:1 takes the reader back to the beginning of the present age and that the binding of Satan in 20:2–3 is a recapitulation of events that happened at Christ's first advent; they also believe the reigning of believers described in 20:4–6 occurs in the present age in which they understand Jesus to be exercising his millennial reign in heaven over believers who have died.[10] On the other hand, premillennialists understand Revelation 20 to describe a progression in time beyond the return of Christ (19:11–21) at the end of this age. Thus, for premillennialists the narrative of Revelation progresses in chapter 20 to a summary description of an intermediate kingdom of a thousand years on this earth between this age (described in 2:1–19:21) and the eternal age to come in the new heavens and earth (described in 21:1–22:5).

Revelation 20:1–3

[1] Then I saw an angel coming down from heaven, holding the key of the abyss and a great chain in his hand. [2] And he laid hold of the dragon, the serpent of old, who is the devil and Satan, and bound him for a thousand years; [3] and he threw him into the abyss, and shut *it* and sealed *it* over him, so that he would not deceive the nations any longer, until the thousand years were completed; after these things he must be released for a short time.

In this passage God sends one unnamed angel from heaven to earth with the key to the bottomless pit and a chain to confine Satan. The angel seizes him, binds him for a thousand years, throws him into the bottomless pit, shuts the pit over him, and seals the pit. This is done so that Satan is not able to deceive the nations for the thousand years he is in the pit. It is hard to think of any way it could have been made clearer that Satan will not be allowed out of the pit and will not have influence on the "nations" (*ethnē*) during this thousand-year period. Then when those years are completed, he will be released again for a short time. The explanation of events emphasizes that Satan is to be completely sealed off and unable to leave the pit or have access to the earth in any way until the thousand-year period has ended. Fanning notes that the imagery of being placed in captivity "to prevent escape and to shut off even

---

[10] Some say his reign is in the hearts of believers on earth. Since this view is not as widely held, the more common amillennial view, that believers are reigning with Christ in heaven in this age, will be the main focus of attention.

contact or influence on the outside world is also a common motif in ancient Jewish and Christian texts."[11] The purpose for confining Satan in this way is "so that he would not deceive the nations any longer, until the thousand years were completed" (20:3), which is what he was doing before he was so confined (12:9; 16:13–14). The nine occurrences of *pit* (*abussos*) in the New Testament indicate that it refers to "an actual location in the spiritual realm where evil spirits are confined and prevented from roaming free on earth."[12]

There are several reasons why it is best to understand that there is no chronological break between chapters 19 and 20 but instead a progression of events and that the events described in chapter 20 follow the return of Christ in 19:11–21. The expression at the beginning of 20:1 (NASB), "Then I saw" (*kai eidon*), can indicate historical progression in Revelation (17:3; 19:19; 21:1), but it need not always do so since it commonly seems to indicate the order in which John sees the visions. However, what is important is that these words do not signify a major break in the structure of the sequence of visions in this section. They continue the structure begun in 19:11 (see also *kai eidon* in 19:17, 19; 20:1, 4, 11, 12; 21:1), and the visions (or different parts of one vision) seem to be structured in a "unified sequence"[13] moving from the return of Christ in chapter 19 to the new heavens and new earth in chapters 21–22, and the events of chapter 20 are placed between those chapters.

The content of chapter 20, especially the incarceration of Satan in 20:1–3, seems to require that the events of chapter 20 are a progression from the return of Christ in chapter 19 rather than a recapitulation of events in this age. It is unreasonable to try to reconcile the description of the binding of Satan (20:1–3) with the Bible's description of Satan's activities in this age: he has blinded the minds of unbelievers to keep them from coming to Christ (2 Cor 4:4); he goes about as a roaring lion (apparently with much freedom) seeking people to devour (1 Pet 5:8); he is deceiving the "whole world" (Rev 12:9; cf. 16:13–14; 19:20); the whole world (unbelievers) is in the power of the evil one (1 John 5:19); and Jesus describes Satan as "the ruler of this world" (John 12:31). These descriptions of Satan and his activity in this age

---

[11] Fanning, *Revelation*, 499–500. He mentions Isa 24:21–23; Luke 8:30–33; Rev 9:1–6; 1 En 10:4–6, 11–13; 18:13–16; 21:1–10; 54:1–5; Jub 10:5–6. Every detail, like the chain and key, need not be taken literally in order for this passage to refer to absolute restrictions on Satan.

[12] Waymeyer, *Amillennialism*, 183, 187; see BDAG, s.v. "ἄβυσσος."

[13] Craig A. Blaising, "Premillennialism," in Bock, *Three Views on the Millennium and Beyond*, 215.

indicate that the binding of Satan in Revelation 20:1-3 cannot refer to this age, as amillennialists believe, but must refer to a later time. This is confirmed by the words in 20:3 giving the purpose for Satan's imprisonment: "so that he would not deceive the nations any longer, until the thousand years were completed." The binding of Satan in Revelation 20:1-3 is not a time when Satan's powers on the earth are only limited; instead, it refers to a time when his power and influence will be stopped completely. This can hardly refer to the present age, as it does in an amillennialist interpretation.

Sometimes amillennialists attempt to place the events of Revelation 20:1–3 in the present age by connecting the angel's casting of Satan into the bottomless pit with events in Christ's ministry, especially with his victory on the cross. Passages used are especially Matthew 12:29, but also Luke 10:17, John 12:31–32, Colossians 2:15, Hebrews 2:14–15, 1 John 3:8, and Revelation 12:7–12.[14] In Matthew 12:29, Jesus refers to the necessity to "bind" a strong man before one can enter into his house and plunder it. The same word for "bind" is used in Revelation 20:2. However, since this reference in Matthew 12 is before Jesus's defeat of Satan on the cross and is simply a parable, it offers no real support for the amillennialists' use of it to connect the angel's work in Revelation 20:1–3 with Christ's work on the cross. Rather it illustrates Christ's power over Satan to exorcise a demon. A major obstacle amillennialists face in trying to directly connect Satan's incarceration in Revelation 20:1–3 with Christ's victory on the cross is the release of Satan after one thousand years in Revelation 20:7. Ladd explains that the victory Christ won over Satan on the cross was "once for all. Satan will never be released from bondage to Christ won by his death and resurrection."[15] To understand the binding of Satan in Revelation 20:1–3 as the redemptive work of Christ means the finished work of Christ "turns out to be the unfinished work of Christ when Satan is released."[16]

Amillennialists also often connect the incarceration of Satan in Revelation 20:1–3 with the casting down of Satan from heaven in Revelation 12:7–11. In chapter 12, the resurrected Christ ascends to heaven. Then a great battle commences as Michael and his angels battle against the dragon (Satan) and his angels, with the result that the dragon is cast from heaven

---

[14] See Waymeyer, *Amillennialism*, 198–205, for a discussion of this argument and these passages.

[15] George Eldon Ladd, *A Commentary on the Revelation of John* (Grand Rapids: Eerdmans, 1972), 263.

[16] Waymeyer, *Amillennialism*, 205.

down to earth. There are several verbal connections between the two passages, primarily related to the identity and names of Satan,[17] but the passages differ in important details and must refer to two different "falls" of this same Satan. First, the origin and destination of the casting down of Satan differ in the two passages. In chapter 12, Satan is cast down from heaven to earth, while in chapter 20 he is cast down from the earth into the pit (abyss). Second, the casting down of Satan in the two passages has opposite effects. In chapter 12, the casting down results in Satan proceeding with great wrath to persecute the people of God because he realizes his time is short. In chapter 20, however, the casting down of Satan results in Satan's confinement in the pit so that he is not able to deceive the nations for a thousand years.[18] Thus, the details of the casting down of Satan in chapter 12 do not agree with the details of the angel casting him into the bottomless pit in chapter 20.

It should now be clear that the content of Revelation 20:1–3 poses several severe challenges to the view that Revelation 19:11–21:8 does not contain a sequence of visions progressing from the return of Christ to the millennium to the new heavens and earth. The most natural way to understand the incarceration of Satan in 20:1–3 is that it follows the return of Christ in chapter 19 and is concurrent with the thousand-year reign of Christ on earth described in 20:4–6. Satan is confined so he cannot "deceive the nations any longer until the thousand years were ended" (20:3). As Michaels wrote, "*Within John's vision* there is little doubt that his perspective was premillennial."[19] In the narrative of Revelation the return of Christ precedes the thousand-year reign. But not only does it precede the thousand-year reign, the events of 20:1–3 are much more consistent with the premillennial interpretation of that view as a literal, glorious, earthly reign of Christ after his return that is free from any satanic influence rather than a reign in heaven in this age in which Satan is free to go about as a roaring lion deceiving the whole world.

---

[17] See G. K. Beale, *The Book of Revelation: A Commentary on the Greek Text*, NIGTC (Grand Rapids: Eerdmans, 1999), 992.

[18] See Waymeyer, *Amillennialism*, 278–82 on the differences between Rev 12:7–11 and 20:1–3. There are at least five "falls" of Satan in Scripture, and interpreters should not confuse them since they refer to different events in the career of Satan. Ezekiel 28:12–15 seems to symbolize his original fall in rebellion against God from his sinless state. Luke 10:18 refers to his defeat through the ministry of Jesus's disciples as they go out to serve him. Revelation 12:9 refers to his fall from heaven where God sometimes allowed him access to his throne to bring charges against God's people (cp. Job 1). Some premillennialists place this fall at the time of Christ's ascension, and others place it during the seven-year tribulation period at the end of this age. Revelation 20:2 refers to Satan's fall at the beginning of the millennium, when he is confined to the abyss for one thousand years. And Revelation 20:10 refers to his final subjugation when he is cast into the lake of fire and brimstone to be punished forever with the beast and the false prophet.

[19] J. Ramsey Michaels, *Revelation*, IVPNTC (Downers Grove, IL: IVP, 1997), 220. Michaels adds (220), "Different interpretations come into play when we read John's vision as the scenario for the end of the world . . . often because a literal premillennial reading is judged . . . to conflict with conclusions derived from other parts of the Bible."

Revelation 20:4–6

⁴ Then I saw thrones, and they sat on them, and judgment was given to them. And I *saw* the souls of those who had been beheaded because of their testimony of Jesus and because of the word of God, and those who had not worshiped the beast or his image, and had not received the mark on their forehead and on their hand; and they came to life and reigned with Christ for a thousand years. ⁵ The rest of the dead did not come to life until the thousand years were completed. This is the first resurrection. ⁶ Blessed and holy is the one who has a part in the first resurrection; over these the second death has no power, but they will be priests of God and of Christ and will reign with Him for a thousand years.

This part of John's vision is the most direct description of the millennium in all of Scripture, and it is the only passage that describes it as a thousand-year reign. It contains several issues related to the different views of the millennium. While the events of 20:1–3 appear to take place at the beginning of or immediately before the thousand years, these verses describe an activity that takes place during the whole period—the resurrection of believers to reign with Christ (20:5–6). The events in 20:7–10 are after the thousand-year reign of believers ("and when the thousand years are ended," 20:7).

There are several issues of contention between premillennialists and amillennialists (as well as postmillenialists) in these verses. Premillennialists believe these years are a literal future reign of Christ with believers on earth between the present age and the eternal state (new heavens and earth), and amillennialists understand this period to refer to the spiritual reign of believers in this age in heaven in an intermediate state awaiting their final resurrection.[20] The main issues in these verses are where the reigning takes place and exactly who the people are who are reigning with Christ. Of course, those issues factor into one's understanding of the time of Christ's return in relation to the millennium. If Christ's millennial reign is a reign of righteousness over all the earth and shared with believers who are resurrected from the dead,[21] then Christ must return first to establish that reign. If Christ's millennial reign is in

---

[20] Postmillennialists understand the thousand-year reign to be the reign of the redeemed in heaven and on the earth in this age; their reigning is a "spiritual reality." See Kenneth L. Gentry, Jr., "Postmillennialism," in Bock, *Three Views on the Millennium and Beyond*, 54.

[21] Postmillennialists believe Christ and Christians who have been regenerated and are on earth and in heaven establish a spiritual reign in this age, and Christ returns at the end of their period of reigning.

heaven during this age with believers in an intermediate state awaiting their resurrection, then his return is after that reign (amillennial view).

In Revelation 20:4, John sees two things: "thrones" and "souls." The "thrones" here are apparently on the earth; that is the location of the events in 20:1–3, where an angel came down from heaven to incarcerate Satan so that he could not deceive the "nations" until the thousand years had ended. It is also the location of the next passage (20:7–10), when the armies of the nations march "over the breadth of the earth" (20:9). Thus, it follows that the reign of Christ described in 20:4–6 during the thousand-year period that is mentioned six times in this passage (20:2–7) is in that same location unless there is compelling evidence to the contrary (see also 5:10, which promises believers will reign with Christ "on earth"). In the following lines John tells the reader that the people who are seated on these thrones are faithful Christians, who are given authority to judge and to rule with Jesus (see also 1 Cor 6:2–3; 2 Tim 2:12; Heb 2:5–9).

The second thing John sees is "souls." This English word is often understood in a Platonic sense as the immaterial part of a person, but the Greek word (ψυχή) is also often used in the New Testament to refer to the whole person. Here the souls belong to "those who had been beheaded."[22] These "souls" are "their immaterial, disembodied selves,"[23] and in that regard they are not a part of the people who have died but they represent the whole person in a disembodied, intermediate state, awaiting their resurrection. These "souls" in Revelation 20:4 are described in language very similar to that describing the saints who had died and were under the altar in 6:9–11 (cp. 6:9 and 20:4); they have died for their testimony for Jesus. However, their actions and experiences are different, apparently describing different phases in the lives of those who die for Jesus. In 6:9–11 they are calling out to God to avenge their deaths during a time of persecution on earth. However, in 20:4–6 that persecution of believers has ended, God has defeated their oppressors (19:11–20:3), and now they come to life and are resurrected to reign with Christ. The descriptions of these people (in 20:4 and 6:9) are nearly identical, but their experience is different because they are seen at different times in the

---

[22] I am understanding the genitive "of those who have been beheaded" to be a possessive genitive, thus the souls belong to these people and are not just a part of them (i.e., partitive genitive). See Daniel B. Wallace, *Greek Grammar Beyond the Basics* (Grand Rapids: Zondervan, 1996), 81–86, on the classifications of the genitives.

[23] Cf. Fanning, *Revelation*, 502. See BDAG, s.v. "ψυχή," for the range of meanings of the word.

narrative of the book of Revelation.[24]

The description of those who are seated on the thrones as "those who had been beheaded for the testimony of Jesus and for the word of God" does not mean only martyrs will rule with Jesus in the millennium. It is clear from elsewhere in Revelation (2:26–28; 3:21; 5:10) that others will also reign and rule with Jesus, and these martyrs are representative of all who reject the beast and are faithful to Jesus. The fact that they are described as being "beheaded" points to the high commitment of those who followed Jesus and "had not worshiped the beast or its image and had not received its mark on their foreheads or their hands."[25] This description of them in 20:4 leaves no doubt that they are believers.[26]

These "souls," or followers of Jesus, that John sees did two things in his vision: they "came to life and reigned with Christ for a thousand years."[27] The first verb "came to life" (ezēsan) is simply an aorist form of the verb (zaō), and the context requires that it be understood as an ingressive aorist, emphasizing the beginning of the state described by the verb (i.e., living).[28] They were dead and they lived, or actually "came to life." The second verb explains what these beheaded souls did after they came to life: they reigned with Christ for a thousand years. The first sentence in 20:5, referring to "the rest of the dead," indicates there are two groups of dead people in view and emphasizes that both groups are physically dead.

The form of the verb to live (zaō) in 20:4, describing the martyred believers who come to life, is the exact same form of the very same verb (ezēsan) that John uses to describe "the rest of the dead" in 20:5 who do not come to life until the end of the thousand years. The verse further explains this coming to life as "resurrection."[29] For premillennialists the coming to life in 20:4 describes

---

[24] On the basis of the similar description of believers in these passages, amillennialists like to argue that they both refer to the experience of believers during the present age in heaven; therefore, they argue that Rev 20:4–6 refers to the experience of believers in heaven reigning with Jesus in this age. However, the experience of the believers is not the same in the two passages, and the two passages refer to different times in the narrative of the book, one during a time of persecution for believers (6:9–11) and one during a time of victory, resurrection, and vindication for believers (20:4–6).

[25] The verb behead refers to beheading with an axe; BDAG, s.v. "πελεκίζω."

[26] See the further description of them in 20:6 and the discussion of that verse below.

[27] Fanning, Revelation, 503, notes that these two actions tie together in reverse order the two objects John saw at the beginning of 20:4.

[28] See Wallace, Greek Grammar Beyond the Basics, 558–59, for a summary of the ingressive aorist. He uses Rev 20:4 as an example of this usage of the aorist.

[29] Fanning, Revelation, 503, explains that in contexts referring to humans who have died the aorist of this verb often has an ingressive sense referring to either "resuscitation to physical life" (Mark 5:23) or "the restoration of the whole person in bodily resurrection" (Rev 2:8).

the experience of believers at the time of Christ's return and the beginning of his thousand-year reign when they are raised from physical death to share in his reign on earth for this period of time. And the description of the rest of the dead who come to life at the end of the thousand-year period in 20:5 refers to unbelievers who are not raised from the dead until the end of the thousand years at the time of the final judgment (20:11–15) and the second death (20:6). For amillennialists, the two references to believers coming to life (20:4, 6, with the exact same verbal form) refer to two different types of coming to life. For them, when believers come to life at the beginning of the thousand years as described in 20:4, it refers to the time of their death when their spirits are translated to heaven in an intermediate state to be with Christ until their bodies are raised at Christ's return at the end of the age.[30] Thus, they "typically explain 20:4 as describing the present experience of deceased believers who come to life spiritually and reign with Christ in heaven until his return."[31] However, amillennialists consider the exact same verb in 20:5 to refer to unbelievers coming to life, as a bodily resurrection of unbelievers at Christ's return at the end of the age, just as premillennialists do.[32] The natural and expected way to understand the two identical parallel verbs describing these contrasting groups, who come to life at different times for different fates, is that they refer to the same type of resurrection. The fact that the second group is described as "the rest of the dead" in 20:5 indicates clearly that both groups have died in the same way, and all understand the "rest of the dead" in the second group to be physically dead; this provides overwhelming evidence that those in the first group had suffered physical death and suggests they were "made alive" by being raised bodily to renewed life. This is one of the main problems for amillennial interpreters of this passage because they want to read the same verb form in two different ways, even though both occurrences are in the same context and apparently in parallel explanations.

Another major issue for amillennialist interpreters is the phrase *first resurrection* (20:5–6), which further clarifies the verb *came to life* as applied

---

[30] Some amillennialists understand the coming to life in 20:4 to refer to the regeneration of believers, but this understanding is not as widely held as the one mentioned above.

[31] Tabb, *All Things New*, 93; see Beale, *The Book of Revelation*, 991–1007.

[32] The first sentence in 20:5, which explains the parallel "coming to life" of unbelievers compared with believers at the end of 20:4, is placed in parentheses in the NRSV and NIV; these "parenthetical" words at the beginning of 20:5 appear to be explaining and clarifying the bodily resurrection of the unsaved dead, who are not among the group of those who come to life as described in 20:4 and whose fate would be an obvious question to the reader.

to the followers of Christ in 20:4. The second sentence in 20:5 says, "This is the first resurrection," and goes on to explain it in 20:6 as the resurrection of those who are "blessed," "holy," and do not experience the second death in the lake of fire (20:14) but "reign with Christ." This "first resurrection" is clearly for believers, and the descriptions of it in 20:5b–6 require it must be the experience of those who come to life to reign with Christ in 20:4. Furthermore, the demonstrative pronoun *this* in "this is the first resurrection" most naturally points back to the resurrection ("they came to life") that John had already described as accomplished in 20:4 and not to the coming to life he describes in 20:5, which is one thousand years later. Although there is no other mention of the "first resurrection" in Scripture, there are references to differentiations in the resurrection. Luke writes of the resurrection of the "just" and "unjust" (Acts 24:15; cf. the mention of the resurrection of the "just" in Luke 14:14), and John refers to resurrections to "life" and to "judgment" (John 5:29). Amillennialists do not dispute the application of "first resurrection" language to the believers who come to life (Rev 20:4), but they do have trouble explaining the experience of these believers as a "resurrection" since they interpret their coming to life as the transfer of the spirits of believers to an intermediate state of existence with Christ in heaven after physical death on earth. Their problem is that such a situation does not involve a resurrection; instead, in such a situation, people who are already spiritually alive die physically and are transferred to a new realm of existence. Resurrection in the Bible always involves a dying and being brought to life spiritually (non-bodily)[33] or a dying and being brought to life physically (bodily),[34] but it never involves dying physically and continuing to live spiritually.[35] N. T. Wright says, "to use the word 'resurrection' to *refer to* death in an attempt to invest it with a new meaning seems to me to strain usage beyond the breaking point."[36]

---

[33] Ladd, *Commentary on Revelation*, 265, calls this "entrance into spiritual life," as in John 5:25.

[34] See John 11:25; Rev 1:18; 2:8; 13:14.

[35] R. Fowler White, "Death and the First Resurrection in Revelation 20: A Response to Meredith G. Kline," unpublished paper presented at ETS, 1992, 8; Waymeyer, *Amillennialism*, 235–36. Both senses of the word are used in John 5:25–29, where the context clearly distinguishes between the two kinds of resurrection. However, Ladd, *Commentary on Revelation*, 266, explains that in Rev 20:4–6, "there is no such contextual clue for a similar variation of interpretation" as there is in John 5:25–29. It is noteworthy that for the minority of amillennialists who feel the believers' coming to life in 20:4 refers to their regeneration, the "first resurrection" refers to that regeneration, a use of resurrection language found elsewhere in Scripture. However, this view also intensifies other problems, such as the meaning of the thrones on which the believers judge and the fact that those who come to life are already beheaded in 20:4.

[36] N. T. Wright, *The Resurrection of the Son of God*, vol. 3, *Christian Origins and the Question of God* (Minneapolis: Fortress, 2003), 474.

So, if the verb *came to life*, which occurs in 20:4 and 20:5,[37] is translated consistently, and if the words *first resurrection* are read in a manner that is consistent with the meaning of *resurrection* elsewhere in the New Testament,[38] Revelation 20:4–5 refers to a bodily, physical resurrection. Those who partake in the "first resurrection" are raised bodily to reign with Christ for a thousand years on the earth, and "the rest of the dead" are raised bodily to face the second death, from which those who partake in the "first resurrection" are exempt.[39]

Revelation 20:6 is also important because the beatitude at the beginning supports the distinction between the blessedness of those who take part in the "first resurrection" and the fate of those who do not and are resurrected later to partake in the "second death" (20:14; 21:8). The "second death" has no power over those who are raised in the first resurrection and who reign with Christ for a thousand years. This verse is also important because it describes those who partake in the first resurrection in much broader terms than "those who were beheaded" (as in 20:4), clarifying that it is not only martyrs who participate in the first resurrection, described in 20:4, but all Christians. As described in 20:6, "they will be priests of God and of Christ, and they will reign with him for a thousand years." Revelation 1:6 and 5:10 describe all believers as "priests," and 5:10 promises that believers will "reign" on the earth. Thus, 20:6 concludes this short section by clarifying who the martyrs are that are described in 20:4, and by emphasizing the blessedness and different fate of those who are resurrected at the beginning of the thousand years in the "first resurrection" compared to the eternal loss of those who are resurrected at the end of the thousand years to face the Great White Throne Judgment.

---

[37] Premillennialists often quote the words of Henry Alford concerning the rendering of the verb *came to life* in 20:4–5,: "If, in a passage where *two resurrections* are mentioned . . . the first resurrection may be understood to mean *spiritual* rising with Christ, while the second means *literal* rising from the grave; then there is an end of all significance in language, and Scripture is wiped out as a definite testimony to anything." Henry Alford, "Apocalypse of John," *The Greek Testament* (Chicago: Moody, 1958), 4:732.

[38] One way amillennialists address the problem of identifying the "first resurrection" with the transfer of believers to an intermediate state in heaven at death is by defining *resurrection* in combination with its modifier *first*. This explanation of the meaning of *resurrection* goes back to Meredith G. Kline, "The First Resurrection," *WTJ* 37 (1975): 366–75. The problem with this explanation is that with it the adjective *first* gives the word it modifies, *resurrection*, a meaning that is not consistent with the meaning of the main noun elsewhere in Scripture. Also, as Harold Hoehner writes in "Evidence from Revelation 20," in *A Case for Premillennialism*, ed. Donald K. Campbell and Jeffrey L. Townsend (Chicago: Moody Press, 1992), 255, "The complexity of this view makes it suspect."

[39] The coming to life of unbelievers in 20:5 is not called a resurrection. The words *first resurrection* imply a second resurrection, which is apparently referred to by the mention of "the rest of the dead" coming to life after the thousand years (20:5).

Revelation 20:7–10

[7] When the thousand years are completed, Satan will be released from his prison, [8] and will come out to deceive the nations which are in the four corners of the earth, Gog and Magog, to gather them together for the war; the number of them is like the sand of the seashore. [9] And they came up on the broad plain of the earth and surrounded the camp of the saints and the beloved city, and fire came down from heaven and devoured them. [10] And the devil who deceived them was thrown into the lake of fire and brimstone, where the beast and the false prophet are also; and they will be tormented day and night forever and ever.

There are many issues in these verses, but we will limit ourselves to things related to the time of the return of Christ in relation to the millennium. Amillennialists usually understand the battle described in these verses to be another recounting of the battle at the end of chapter 19, which takes place when Christ returns. Premillennialists distinguish this battle, after the millennium, from the battle in 19:11–21, which they believe is one thousand years earlier. The crucial difference between the two battles is the absence of the false prophet and the beast in this battle (20:7–10). They were cast into the lake of fire at the end of chapter 19, and in these verses the last member of the satanic trinity, Satan himself, who was not mentioned in the battle in chapter 19, is finally completely vanquished.[40]

The omission of the false prophet and beast in 20:7–10 supports reading this whole section (19:11–21:8) chronologically, and not seeing this battle as a repetition of what happened in 19:11–21. As Michaels explains, "To John it is not a case of the same story being told twice, but of history repeating itself."[41] Furthermore, 20:7 could not be much clearer that the events are following each other in order in this chapter. The events in 20:7–10 take place "when the thousand years are ended" (20:7), and Satan was bound in 20:1–3 before the thousand-year period, not to be released until the end of that period. Thus, this event follows 20:1–3, which is before the thousand years described in 20:4–6. There is a clear sequence of events from 20:1 to 20:10.[42] This further supports the understanding that "the events

---

[40] These three enemies of God are destroyed by God in the opposite order that they were introduced (i.e., the introduction of Satan in 12:1–9, the beast in 13:1, and the false prophet in 13:11).

[41] Michaels, *Revelation*, 226.

[42] Also, the mention of Satan being "released" (λύω) and the reference to his "prison" in 20:7 both connect with ideas in 20:3 (same verb [λύω] and the "pit").

of all seven visions from 19:11–21:8 are chronologically sequenced."[43] That is clearly the natural way to read the section unless other Scripture passages are allowed to have more influence on the interpreter than the immediate context.

Revelation 20:11–15

[11] Then I saw a great white throne and Him who sat upon it, from whose presence earth and heaven fled away, and no place was found for them. [12] And I saw the dead, the great and the small, standing before the throne, and books were opened; and another book was opened, which is *the book* of life; and the dead were judged from the things which were written in the books, according to their deeds. [13] And the sea gave up the dead which were in it, and death and Hades gave up the dead which were in them; and they were judged, every one *of them* according to their deeds. [14] Then death and Hades were thrown into the lake of fire. This is the second death, the lake of fire. [15] And if anyone's name was not found written in the book of life, he was thrown into the lake of fire.

After God's purposes for this earth are fully accomplished in the millennium and the members of the satanic trinity have been cast into the lake of fire and brimstone, he judges the natural world (20:11), the rest of the dead who did not come to life in the first resurrection (20:12–13), and death and Hades (20:14–15). The destruction of all of these opens the way for the new heavens and earth, described in 21:1–22:5. One important implication for the millennium in 20:11–15 is the further insight into the identity of those who "came to life" after the thousand-year period; according to 20:5–6 and 20:12–13, they are the unsaved dead, who come to life after the thousand years are ended to stand before the Great White Throne Judgment to be condemned and cast into the lake of fire and brimstone.

Summary

As Waymeyer summarizes, "A straightforward reading of the events described in Revelation 19–21 is neither confusing nor difficult to follow."[44] On its face this section of Scripture teaches a premillennial return of Christ. This straightforward reading involves allowing the context to be the main

---

[43] Fanning, *Revelation*, 514.

[44] Waymeyer, *Amillennialism*, 8; see also 15–16.

factor in determining the meaning of the text rather than other passages or theological systems.[45] And this type of interpretation allows each text concerning the coming kingdom to speak for itself in its own context before the interpreter attempts to harmonize the meaning of all relevant texts into a theological system. Although many theologians understand the future age (new heavens and earth) to follow immediately after this age, Revelation 20 shows that such a reading is not a complete reading of the Scripture's teaching about the coming kingdom. On the basis of Revelation 20, we must make room in our theological systems for a thousand-year[46] intermediate kingdom on this present earth between the return of Christ and the new heavens and new earth, during which time Christ and his followers will reign on this earth and God's plans for this earth will be fulfilled.[47] Christ's premillennial return will usher in this thousand-year period.

---

[45] See Waymeyer, *Amillennialism*, 8–14.

[46] Premillennialists disagree whether the thousand years in Rev 20 should be taken literally or not (see Waymeyer, *Amillennialism*, 243–62). They seem to agree it refers to a "real period of time" (248), and most all take it as a long period of time. Fanning (*Revelation*, 508) feels the number "thousand" is "essentially literal" but also has connotative value.

[47] This reign of Christ in Rev 20 differs from his reign in Rev 21–22. See Michael J. Vlach, "The Kingdom of God and the Millennium," *TMSJ* (2012): 227–40. It is consistent with the reign of the Messiah "from Jerusalem on this existing earth prior to its complete transformation," as described in passages such as Isa 11 and Ps 72; see Fanning, *Revelation*, 504. In the same place Fanning also comments that, "The appropriateness of God restoring such a rule on the present earth as a vindication of his work in the history and politics of earthly nations is an important motif in the biblical story. The fact that this rule of God and his Messiah will continue in a new way in the new Jerusalem (21:5; 22:1, 3) does not mute this theme."

The Case for the Pretribulational Rapture

Jonathan Pratt
Central Baptist Theological Seminary
Plymouth, Minnesota

Even though only one clear text (1 Thess 4:13–17) and two implicit texts (1 Cor 15:51–52; John 14:1–3) teach the rapture, premillennialists agree that all those "in Christ" will be resurrected or translated in fulfillment of these passages.[1] They also agree on several other key points of eschatology related to the rapture: (1) the rapture is a separate event from the second coming of Christ to the earth;[2] (2) Daniel's seventieth week (Dan 9:27) is the seven-year tribulation period described in Revelation; (3) this seventieth week precedes the second coming of Christ to the earth; and (4) part (if not the entirety) of the seventieth week is a fulfillment of the Day of the Lord prophecies found in both the Old and New Testaments. But premillennialists are not unified with respect to the *timing* of the rapture, and it is here that we step into a minefield of options, which generally divide into three basic camps: pretribulationism, prewrath, and posttribulationism.[3]

---

[1] Alan Hultberg, "Introduction" in *Three Views on the Rapture*, ed. Alan Hultberg (Grand Rapids: Zondervan, 2010), 11, uses this language to describe these three texts, and most agree with him. For example, John F. Walvoord, *The Blessed Hope and the Tribulation: A Historical and Biblical Study of Posttribulationism* (Grand Rapids: Zondervan, 1976), 50; Douglas J. Moo, "A Case for the Posttribulation Rapture" in *Three Views on the Rapture*, ed. Alan Hultberg (Grand Rapids: Zondervan, 2010), 196.

[2] This does not suggest, however, that the rapture and the second coming do not occur at the same time. Most posttribulationists argue against a two-stage second advent and locate "the rapture after the final tribulation, at the same time as the final parousia" (Moo, "Posttribulation Rapture," 201). Also, some suggest that the rapture is one of several events that make up the second coming, but I am using these terms as two separate events (i.e., *rapture* refers to the gathering of resurrected and translated saints in the air while *second coming* refers to the return of Christ to the earth with his saints).

[3] Central Seminary's library has eight feet of shelf space dedicated to books on the rapture alone, and this does not include the numerous journal articles and book essays that could be provided. So a full listing of advocates for each of these positions is not possible here. Instead, please note two or three of the clearest articulations of each camp's view, as follows. *Pretribulationism*: Craig Blaising, "A Case for the Pretribulation Rapture" in *Three Views on the Rapture*, ed. Alan Hultberg, 25–73 (Grand Rapids: Zondervan, 2010); Paul D. Feinberg, "The Case for the Pretribulation Rapture Position" in *The Rapture: Pre-, Mid-, or Post-Tribulational*, ed. Richard Reiter, Paul D. Feinberg, Gleason L. Archer, and Douglas Moo, 45–86 (Grand Rapids: Zondervan, 1984); John F. Walvoord, *The Rapture Question*, rev. ed. (Grand Rapids: Zondervan, 1979). *Prewrath*: Alan Hultberg, "A Case for the Prewrath Rapture" in *Three Views on the Rapture*, ed. Alan Hultberg, 109–54 (Grand Rapids: Zondervan, 2010); Marvin J. Rosenthal, *The Pre-wrath Rapture of the Church: A New Understanding of the Rapture, the Tribulation, and the Second Coming* (Nashville: Nelson, 1990). Formerly, the prewrath position was labeled "midtribulationism," and there are slight differences between the two. I have chosen to use the prewrath label here since it is more recognizable than midtribulationism at present (see Alan Hultberg, "Introduction," 21–22), but throughout this essay I will use the two terms interchangeably. *Posttribulationism*: Moo, "Posttribulation Rapture," 185–241; Robert H. Gundry, *The Church and the Tribulation: A Biblical Examination of Posttribulationism* (Grand Rapids: Zondervan, 1973); George Eldon Ladd, *The Blessed Hope: A Biblical Study of the Second Advent and the Rapture* (Grand Rapids: Eerdmans, 1956).

Since much of the debate centers on the interpretation of the Olivet Discourse, the Thessalonian epistles, and several texts in Revelation, it will be necessary to deal with these and a few other relevant texts. My goal is to provide both exegetical and theological arguments in defense of the pretribulation rapture. Exegetically, I will consider John 14:1–3, 2 Thessalonians 2:6–7, and Revelation 12:5. Theologically, I will consider the issues of eschatological wrath, imminency, and arguments from the Thessalonian epistles. In this manner I hope to encourage the reader to accept the thesis that Jesus will rapture those "in Christ" prior to the start of the tribulation (i.e., Daniel's seventieth week).

Exegetical Support

Summarizing the opinions of opponents of the pretribulation rapture, Michael Svigel states,

> The perception among interested exegetes and theologians appears to be that rapture theology rests not on verifiable exegesis but on inferences drawn from ambiguous passages and on peculiar dispensational presuppositions. In short, many today believe that the doctrine of the church's rapture from the earth prior to the seven-year tribulation period simply has no clear exegetical basis.[4]

While such a belief may exist, I offer three texts from which legitimate exegetical proofs can be drawn.

John 14:1–3

Most premillennialists agree that Jesus is referring to the rapture when he tells his disciples, "I will come again and will take you to myself, that where I am you may be also" (John 14:3).[5] The parallels between John 14:1–3 and 1 Thessalonians 4:13–18 justify such an interpretation: (1) reference to the

---

[4] Michael J. Svigel, "'What Child Is This?' Darby's Early Exegetical Argument for the Pretribulation Rapture of the Church," *TrinJ* 35 (2014): 226.

[5] Moo, "Posttribulation Rapture," 197; Richard L. Mayhue, "Why a Pretribulational Rapture?" *TMSJ* 13 (Fall 2002): 246; John F. Walvoord, *The Blessed Hope and the Tribulation* (Grand Rapids: Zondervan, 1976), 91. Walvoord singles out J. Barton Payne as being an exception to this rule. Dr. Charles Hauser liked to pass along this story about J. Barton Payne. When Dr. Hauser taught at San Francisco Baptist Theological Seminary, Payne visited while taking a sabbatical so that he could do research for his book on prophecy. He had meetings with several of the faculty at the seminary especially because of their pretribulational position. During one of these sessions with Dr. Hauser, Payne, who was a posttribulationist, admitted to Hauser that in his mind, the most difficult text for the posttribulation position is John 14:1–3. Payne dealt with this passage in two of his books, arguing that "Jesus' promise to welcome men into His Father's heavenly house seems to refer to His coming to receive believers at their death." See J. Barton Payne, *Biblical Prophecy for Today* (Grand Rapids: Baker, 1978), 63; Payne, *The Imminent Appearing of Christ* (Grand Rapids: Eerdmans, 1962), 74.

coming of Christ ("I will come again" [John 14:3] and "the coming of the Lord" [1 Thess 4:15]); (2) being present with Christ ("where I am you may be also," [John 14:3] and "we shall always be with the Lord" [1 Thess 4:17]); (3) the promise of comfort ("do not let your heart be troubled" [John 14:1] and "comfort one another with these words" [1 Thess 4:18]); and (4) the language of translation from the earth to heaven ("will take you to myself" [John 14:3] and "caught up together . . . in the clouds" [1 Thess 4:17]).

But does this rapture predicted by Jesus in John 14 occur prior to or at the end of the tribulation period? I propose that Jesus's words point to a pretribulational gathering of believers with Christ in the Father's house. Two textual indicators support this assertion.

First, Jesus states that the destination of the rapture will be his "Father's house" which has "many dwelling places." While some, including Robert Gundry, understand this location as a metaphor for the Christian's spiritual position in Christ,[6] the text points in a more literal direction. The context of 14:2 calls for the natural reading of *monē*, which is "dwelling-place."[7] Specifically, the action of Jesus to "prepare a place" points to an actual location made ready by Jesus.[8] Thus, Jesus indicates that once he returns to heaven after his resurrection,[9] he will prepare a place where believers will dwell with him.[10]

Second, Jesus promises to take believers to "where I am." This phrase occurs several other times in John's gospel with clear eschatological overtones (7:34–36; 8:21–22; 13:33–36; 17:24).[11] The reality for the disciples is that

---

[6] Gundry, *The Church and the Tribulation,* 154–55; Gundry, "'In My Father's House Are Many Μοναὶ (John 14:2)," *ZNW* 58 (1967): 68–72. He uses John 14:23 as his main reason for taking the metaphorical view of μοναὶ, arguing that as the Father and Son have a dwelling place within the believer so also the believer will have a dwelling place "in Christ." Such a reciprocal reading does not mesh well with the context of 14:2 (i.e., are we to think that Jesus is saying that in heaven there are many in-Christ believers?). Walvoord, *The Blessed Hope,* 92, rightly calls Gundry's treatment "fanciful exegesis."

[7] BDAG, s.v. "μονή, ῆς, ἡ;" D. A. Carson, *The Gospel According to John,* PNTC (Grand Rapids: Eerdmans, 1991), 489.

[8] Notably, Gundry's suggestion that *place, prepare* and *house* all refer to spiritual realities rather than physical or actual realities in *The Church and the Tribulation,* 154, is based on Pauline notions ("in Christ" language) and other non-Johannine texts throughout the NT.

[9] George A. Gunn, "Jesus and the Rapture: John 14," in *Evidence for the Rapture: A Biblical Case for Pretribulationism,* ed. John F. Hart (Chicago: Moody Publishers, 2015), 108–9, argues that the concept of returning to one's "father's house" is common throughout Scripture and speaks of an actual place to which one returns after a sojourn away.

[10] John F. Walvoord, *The Return of the Lord* (Grand Rapids: Dunham, 1955), 55, provides a helpful distinction between John 14:1-3 and 1 Thessalonians 4:17. Whereas Paul describes the meeting of the church with Christ as taking place "in the air," Jesus provides clarity as to the destination of those who are taken to be with him—heaven.

[11] The Greek phrase shares the adverb (ὅπου) with either ὑπάγω ἐγὼ or εἰμὶ ἐγὼ to express the same connotation (i.e., the location of Christ after his resurrection with the Father in heaven). See Mayhue, "Why a Pretribulational Rapture," 246. In regard to the eschatological nature of this phrase, especially in 17:24, see Carson, *The Gospel According to John,* 570; and C. K. Barrett, *The Gospel According to St. John: An Introduction with Commentary and Notes on the Greek Text,* 2nd ed. (Philadelphia: Westminster, 1978), 514.

they will enjoy this blessing of presence with Jesus in glory at the point in time when Jesus takes them to be with him. Earlier in the Upper Room Discourse (13:36–37), Peter had asked why he could not join Jesus when he went away (13:33). Although Peter misunderstood the meaning of Jesus's words,[12] Jesus is clear that the opportunity to dwell with him in the place of his glory would eventually be afforded to all his followers (13:36). Thus, within the short space of five verses John twice records the promise of Jesus that his followers will enjoy dwelling with him in his "Father's house."

As a result of Jesus's instruction to his followers, we learn that Jesus promised to take the eleven along with all other believers to be with him in heaven. This is why Jesus's hope-filled words are comforting. Indeed, the pain of Jesus's physical absence in the present will be more than assuaged by the reality of his presence with his followers when he takes us to be with him. But the hope described in this passage is further enhanced by the reality that dwelling with Jesus in heaven during the tribulation keeps the believer from the "storms of divine wrath" as they "purge the earth and fit it for the millennial state."[13] While some seek to downplay this seven-year respite from the outpouring of divine wrath,[14] it still serves as a tremendous blessing to be exempted from this time period described as a "time of distress for Jacob" (Jer 30:7) and a "time of trouble, such as never has been since there was a nation" (Dan 12:1). Being with Christ in heavenly dwellings for just one day would be incalculably wonderful; how much more blessed will seven years be?

Finally, the significance of Jesus's promise of comfort to his disciples is *not* preceded by the mention of a time of tribulation.[15] While the expectation that such revelation should have been included by Jesus may seem a bit presumptuous, the question of why such information was kept from Jesus's hearers does seem to point to a glaring omission. It could even be considered cruel to promise comfort by means of a rapture that occurs only after the most intense period of human suffering ever seen on the earth.[16]

---

[12] Misunderstanding Jesus was not a problem for only Peter in John's gospel; several others demonstrated similar perplexity. See D. A. Carson, "Understanding Misunderstandings in the Fourth Gospel," *TynBul* 33 (1982): 59–89.
[13] Walvoord, *The Return of the Lord*, 55.

[14] Gundry, *The Church and the Tribulation*, 153.

[15] Blaising, "Pretribulation Rapture," 67; Walvoord, *The Rapture Question*, 73.

[16] Moo, "Posttribulation Rapture," 197, disagrees: "The 'blessed hope' of being reunited with the risen Lord is surely a comfort, no matter what believers have previously experienced." While this is certainly true, we believe that Christ offers far greater comfort to his hearers by promising to bring them to himself prior to the outpouring of divine wrath in the tribulation period.

2 Thessalonians 2:6–7

The main subject of 2 Thessalonians 2:1–15 is the Lord's second coming and the rapture of the church.[17] As we proceed through the passage, we learn that the Thessalonians have received false teaching regarding the presence of the Day of the Lord, and this information has deeply troubled them (2:2).[18]

But Paul urges his readers that they need not pay heed to such misinformation since the Day of the Lord has not yet begun because several events must take place prior to its occurrence. These events include the rebellion (*apostasia*) and the revelation of the lawless one (*anthrōpos anomias*) mentioned in 2:3, preceded by the ministry (*to katechon*) and removal of the restrainer (*ho katechōn*) in 2:6–7. So what is the meaning of these three events, all of which precede the Day of the Lord?

It appears that Paul is using a chiastic structure in 2:1–15 to develop his overall treatment of the coming of Christ.[19] The negative exhortation regarding the Thessalonians' disturbance by the false teaching about missing the salvation provided by the coming of the Lord in 2:1–3a is matched by the assurance of their salvation in 2:13–15. The second chiastic parallel concerns the rebellion (2:3b) which is explained in 2:10–12. Viewing the *apostasia* in this manner shows how the lawless one deceives unbelievers with his signs and wonders so that they rebel against God.[20]

The third level of the chiastic structure explains the revelation and activity

---

[17] The notion that these two terms, the *coming* (παρουσία) and the *assembling* (ἐπισυναγωγή), refer to the same eschatological event has been soundly refuted by Daniel B. Wallace, *Granville Sharp's Canon and Its Kin: Semantics and Significance*, Studies in Biblical Greek 14 (New York: Peter Lang, 2009), 193–97; Wallace, *Greek Grammar Beyond the Basics* (Grand Rapids: Zondervan, 1996), 270–90. While the grammar certainly indicates a relationship between the two terms, it neither supports nor affirms a particular eschatological position, whether pretribulationism or posttribulationism. Actually, the idea that the assembling of the church as a part of the larger complex event of the *parousia* is a very justifiable position with impersonal TSKS constructions.

[18] The mention of the Day of the Lord at this point in Paul's argument raises two questions: (1) how is the Day of the Lord connected to the Lord's coming and (2) why is the supposed presence of the Day of the Lord so troubling to the Thessalonians? Answering these questions in reverse order, the Thessalonians had ample reason to be alarmed by such teaching based on what Paul had already taught in his first letter to the church. In 1 Thess, Paul had stated that all Christians are delivered from the coming eschatological wrath (1:10; 5:9). The nature of this eschatological wrath is connected with the Day of the Lord judgments described in 5:1–8. Thus, if the false teachers are correct and the Day of the Lord has already begun, Paul's teaching about the avoidance of God's eschatological wrath appears to be incorrect. The first question is also answered in 1 Thess where Paul connects the Lord's coming, the rapture of the church, and the Day of the Lord in 4:13–5:11. Furthermore, Paul directly relates the coming of Christ with the Day of the Lord judgment in 2 Thess 1:9–10. See Gene L. Green, *The Letters to the Thessalonians*, PNTC (Grand Rapids: Eerdmans, 2002), 305. So we can see how the Day of the Lord fits under the broader umbrella of the discussion about the Lord's coming.

[19] Maarten J. J. Menken, *2 Thessalonians* (New York: Routledge, 1994), 71–73; Charles E. Powell, "The Identity of the 'Restrainer' in 2 Thessalonians 2:6–7," *BSac* 154 (July–September, 1997): 322–28.

[20] William W. Combs, "Is *Apostasia* in 2 Thessalonians 2:3 a Reference to the Rapture?" *DBSJ* 3 (Fall 1998): 63–87, comes to a similar conclusion, though the burden of his article is to demonstrate that the *apostasia* is not a reference to the rapture as some dispensationalists have argued.

of the lawless one (2:3c–4), described as the son of destruction, who exalts himself above every object of worship, takes up residence in the temple of God, and proclaims himself to be God. The parallel in the chiasm (2:8–9) gives further information about this *anthrōpos anomias*. He is energized by Satan, but his end comes definitively when Jesus destroys him at the time of his coming. There is little debate that this individual is the eschatological adversary of Christ typically referred to as the antichrist.[21]

The central element of the chiasm (2:5–7) focuses on the enigmatic restrainer and his work.[22] The interpretation of *to katechon* ("what restrains") and *ho katechōn* ("he who restrains") is key for the overall meaning of this section of Paul's letter not only because of its location in the chiastic structure but also because of its temporal connection to the lawless one and the Day of the Lord. To summarize, the false teaching about the Day of the Lord was causing the Thessalonians to question Paul's instruction about Christ's second coming and the rapture of the church. Paul combatted this error by showing that the Day of the Lord could not commence until the antichrist was revealed and had deceived his hearers to rebel against God. However, the manifestation of the antichrist could not take place until the restrainer was removed. Thus, the following order of events is required by the temporal indicators in the passage: the restrainer is removed; the lawless one is revealed and deceives; the rebellion occurs; the Day of the Lord commences.

Scholars have suggested numerous solutions to the identity of this restrainer,[23] but I focus here on several arguments which support the interpretation of *to katechon* as the gospel and *ho katechōn* as God the Holy Spirit. Romans 1:16–17 shows that the power of God for salvation comes through the gospel. This power in the gospel was evident in its delivery to and reception by the Thessalonians (1 Thess 1:5–6). That gospel message included repentance, service for God, and hope of deliverance from eschatological

---

[21] Gary S. Shogren, *1 & 2 Thessalonians*, ZECNT (Grand Rapids: Zondervan, 2012), 290–91, states, "Although it is not explicit within the canon, it is certainly implicit that the 'one abomination that causes desolation,' the 'Man of Lawlessness,' the 'antichrist,' and one 'beast' or the other from Rev 13 are intended as the same eschatological figure." G. K. Beale, *1–2 Thessalonians*, IVPNTC (Downers Grove, IL: Inter-Varsity Press, 2003), 205–7, draws several connections between the man of lawlessness in 2 Thess 2:3 and the "eschatological antagonist" who sets up the abomination of desolation and exalts himself above God in Daniel 11:30–45.

[22] Powell, "The Identity of the 'Restrainer'," 327–28, provides five reasons why this central portion of the chiasm relates to the subject of the gathering of the believers to Christ introduced in 2:1. As such, the teaching about the restrainer provides assurance to believers of their gathering to Christ and salvation in him.

[23] See Colin R. Nicholl, *From Hope to Despair in Thessalonica: Situating 1 and 2 Thessalonians* (Cambridge: Cambridge University Press, 2004), 228; Jeffrey A. D. Weima, *1–2 Thessalonians*, BECNT (Grand Rapids: Baker, 2014), 570–77, for a listing of these.

wrath (1:10). Not only is the gospel related to God's power, but it is vitally associated with the Word of God itself (2:13). God's Word is powerful to discern the thoughts and intents of the heart (Heb 4:12); it also defeats Satan as the sword of the Spirit (Eph 6:17), demonstrated by Christ's use of it against Satan (Matt 4:1–11). Hence, the gospel is the Word of God and the power of God used to combat lawlessness and Satan which is precisely what the *katechon* is doing in 2 Thessalonians 2:6.[24] As Powell states, "The association of the gospel with the coming of Christ in 1 Thessalonians 1:5–10 meshes well with the subject in 2 Thessalonians 2:1 and Paul's reminder in 2:5."[25]

If it is God's power and God's Word in the gospel that restrains the lawless one, then it is God himself who is the restrainer.[26] There are four reasons for identifying God as the restrainer, and several of these specify the Holy Spirit as the person of the Trinity who best functions in this role.[27] First, if the lawless one is supported by the power of Satan (2 Thess 2:9), then it would take the omnipotent power of God to restrain him.[28] Second, this interpretation gives the clearest force to the change in gender of the participles. Even though *pneuma* is neuter in gender, *ho katechōn* is masculine, confirming the personality of the Holy Spirit by *ad sensum* agreement.[29] Third, the Spirit strove against man and his sin (Gen 6:3) just as the restrainer contends with the lawless one in 2 Thessalonians 2; furthermore, part of the Spirit's ministry is to convict the world of sin, righteousness, and judgment (John 16:8–11).[30] Fourth, since the ministry of the Spirit includes indwelling and baptizing believers and working through those believers in the church, then the removal of the restrainer ("taken out of the way" [*ek mesou genētai*]) could refer to the

---

[24] Roger D. Aus, "God's Plan and God's Power: Isaiah 66 and the Restraining Factors of 2 Thess 2:6–7," *JBL* 96 (December 1977): 537–53, comes to a similar conclusion with regard to τὸ κατέχον by suggesting that Paul is drawing upon themes from Isa 66:18–21, where the gospel is preached to all nations before the end comes.

[25] Powell, "The Identity of the 'Restrainer'," 329. Much of the argument here comes from Powell.

[26] Aus, "God's Plan," 549, and Sigve K. Tonstad, "The Restrainer Removed: A Truly Alarming Thought (2 Thess 2:1–12)," *HBT* 29 (2007): 142–45, both argue for God as the restrainer by using OT passages in support (Isa 66:9 in Aus's case and Hab 2:3 in Tonstad's case). Both passages are eschatological in orientation, and both emphasize the significant and primary role God plays in restraining evil during the end times.

[27] Powell, "The Identity of the 'Restrainer'," 330.

[28] Charles Caldwell Ryrie, *First and Second Thessalonians*, EMBC (Chicago: Moody Press, 1959), 109–11.

[29] Gundry, *The Church and the Tribulation*, 125; D. Edmond Hiebert, *The Thessalonian Epistles* (Chicago: Moody Press, 1971), 314. See Wallace, *Greek Grammar Beyond the Basics*, 337, for a discussion of sense agreement between a pronoun and its antecedent.

[30] Ryrie, *First and Second Thessalonians*, 111; Powell, "The Identity of the 'Restrainer'," 330.

removal of the Holy Spirit through the removal of the church in the rapture.[31]

Paul's desire to encourage the Thessalonians in regard to their alarm about the presence of the Day of the Lord is accomplished with this interpretation since they knew that the rapture, the rebellion, and the appearance of the lawless one had not yet occurred. I will discuss the relationship between the Day of the Lord and the outpouring of God's eschatological wrath later in this essay, but Paul's argument clearly shows that the removal of the restrainer (i.e., the presence of the Spirit in the church) via the rapture precedes the rebellion, the appearance of the antichrist, and the commencement of the Day of the Lord. At minimum, a posttribulational rapture is ruled out by this interpretation, and a pretribulational rapture better fits these chronological parameters than does a prewrath rapture.[32]

Revelation 12:5

Though used as proof of the pretribulational rapture by several nineteenth- and early- twentieth-century interpreters including John Nelson Darby,[33] Revelation 12:5 has rarely appeared in any present-day defenses of this doctrine.[34] But I offer several reasons this text supports a pretribulational view of the rapture.[35]

First, I will establish that the rapture is being described in this verse. Second, I will show how this text demonstrates that the rapture will precede the seven-year tribulation.

Revelation 12:5 (ESV) states, "She gave birth to a male child, one who is to rule all the nations with a rod of iron, but her child was caught up to God and to his throne." I propose that the event spoken of here is the rapture

---

[31] Hiebert, *The Thessalonian Epistles,* 313; Robert L. Thomas, "2 Thessalonians," in *EBC,* ed. Frank E. Gaebelein, vol. 11 (Grand Rapids: Zondervan, 1978), 324–25; John F. Walvoord, *The Thessalonian Epistles* (Findlay, OH: Dunham Publishing Company, 1955), 125–26. Depending on one's interpretation of the timing of the appearance of the antichrist, this interpretation could support either a pretribulational or a prewrath rapture.

[32] Hiebert, *The Thessalonian Epistles,* 313. The difficult point for the prewrath advocate to answer relates to the appearance of the lawless one at the beginning of the seventieth week of Daniel. If the rapture occurs prior to this appearance, then the removal of the restrainer (i.e., the rapture) must take place prior to the tribulation.

[33] Svigel, "What Child Is This?" 229–45, provides a detailed discussion of the development of Darby's view in his lectures and writings; he follows this treatment with a listing of seven interpreters who also saw Rev 12:5 as teaching a pretribulational rapture.

[34] Dispensational interpreters have usually argued *against* using Rev 12:5 as a proof of the pretribulational rapture. See Keith H. Essex, "The Rapture and the Book of Revelation," *TMSJ* 13 (Fall 2002): 234–35; J. B. Smith, *A Revelation of Jesus Christ: A Commentary on the Book of Revelation,* ed. J. Otis Yoder (Scottdale, PA: Herald Press, 1961), 183–84; John F. Walvoord, *The Revelation of Jesus Christ* (Chicago: Moody Press, 1966), 189–91; Robert L. Thomas, *Revelation 8–22: An Exegetical Commentary* (Chicago: Moody Press, 1995), 125–26.

[35] I am relying heavily on Michael J. Svigel, "The Apocalypse of John and the Rapture of the Church: A Reevaluation," *TrinJ* 22 (2001): 53–67, for the argument presented here.

of the church. As with other visions in Revelation, the identification of the symbols is the prerequisite for a correct interpretation. Most agree that the woman (first introduced in 12:1) represents the elect and faithful remnant of Israel of both the Old and New Testaments[36] and that the dragon (12:3–4) who opposes the woman is Satan (12:9) and his earthly emissaries (seven heads and ten horns [12:3]).[37]

But the identity of the male child does not share such unanimity of opinion. Traditionally, most have interpreted the male child to be Jesus Christ.[38] However, there is good reason to see this symbol as having a double referent, an individual (Jesus) and a corporate entity (the church). Five arguments support this identification.

(1) The symbolism of the characters in Revelation 12:1–6 consistently demonstrates both a corporate and individual identification. The woman represents Israel primarily but also Mary secondarily; the dragon represents a corporate entity (the nations) as well as an individual (Satan); and the male child points to Jesus Christ and to his body, the church, united with him by means of the baptism of the Holy Spirit (1 Cor 12:13).[39]

(2) Identifying the male child as the body of Christ best explains the allusion to Isaiah 66:7. John intentionally employs a solecism, using the neuter adjective *arsen* as a modifier of the masculine *huion*, and it is likely that he does so to draw the reader's attention to Isaiah 66:7, where the same term (*arsen*) is used of the son born to the woman, Zion.[40] It is typical for John to use solecisms of this nature to point the reader back to the Old Testament context.[41] In Isaiah the child of the woman is a personification of Israel, a corporate body. In the same way, the male child of Revelation 12:5 represents

---

[36] Svigel, "The Apocalypse of John," 57; Grant R. Osborne, *Revelation*, BECNT (Grand Rapids: Baker, 2002), 456; G. K. Beale, *The Book of Revelation: A Commentary on the Greek Text*, NIGTC (Grand Rapids: Eerdmans, 1999), 628; Thomas, *Revelation 8–22*, 120–21.

[37] Robert H. Mounce, *The Book of Revelation*, rev. ed., NICNT (Grand Rapids: Eerdmans, 1997), 233; Svigel, "The Apocalypse of John," 59, agrees with this identification but suggests broadening the dragon symbol to stand for the world system as the great opponent of God's people throughout history.

[38] Beale, *Revelation*, 639; Osborne, *Revelation*, 462; Thomas, *Revelation 8–22*, 125–26.

[39] Svigel, "The Apocalypse of John," 60–61.

[40] G. K. Beale, *John's Use of the Old Testament in Revelation*, JSNTSup 166 (Sheffield: Sheffield Academic Press, 1998), 341–43, gives four textual reasons why the most likely OT allusion in Rev 12:5 is to Isa 66:7. Referring to John's grammatical ability, Beale states: "That John has not made a careless grammatical blunder is clear from 12:13, where the masculine τόν ἄρσενα *is correctly* used" (emphasis in original).

[41] Wallace, *Greek Grammar*, 62–64.

a corporate entity rather than an individual only.[42]

(3) Identifying the male child as the body of Christ takes seriously the language of Revelation 12:5. In particular, the verb, *harpadzō*, portrays the rapture of the church. Three lines of argument support this assertion: first, the unaffected meaning of *harpadzō* speaks of "snatching" rather than merely relocating from one physical place to another[43]; second, it appears that the New Testament authors never used *harpadzō* when describing Christ's ascension but rather used terms such as *epairō* (Acts 1:9), *anabainō* (John 20:17; Eph 4:8–10), *analambanō* (Luke 1:11), and *anapherō* (24:51) instead[44]; and third, the affected meaning of *harpadzō* often reflects the connotation of rescue from a violent attack which certainly meshes well with the scene described in Revelation 12:1–4 where the dragon waits to devour the male child.[45]

(4) Identifying the male child as the body of Christ best harmonizes with the quotation of Psalm 2:9 found at the beginning, middle, and end of Revelation. In Revelation 2:26–28 the promise of the psalm is extended to all believers, and the psalm is applied to Christ in Revelation 19:14–15. Thus, the dual application of the promise of Psalm 2:9 harmonizes with the identification of the male child as both Christ and his spiritual body of believers being symbolized in Revelation 12:5.[46]

(5) Identifying the male child as the body of Christ best explains the omission of the *sine qua non* of the gospel, namely, the death and resurrection of the Messiah. While the omission of the death and resurrection of Christ in this account is within the realm of possibility, especially given the symbolic nature of this account, the corporate identification of the male child as the body of Christ certainly alleviates the problem.[47]

Now that the rapture interpretation of Revelation 12:5 has been defended, I

---

[42] Svigel, "The Apocalypse of John," 61–62.

[43] Ibid. Svigel provides a lengthy and helpful word study. Also, BDAG, s.v. "ἁρπάζω."

[44] Ibid., 64. John describes the ascension of the two witnesses only twelve verses earlier in Rev 11:12 using ἀναβαίνω, the same word used in John 20:17 to describe Jesus's ascension.

[45] Ibid. "Jesus Christ was not snatched away to God to escape any threat, either real or imagined, either from Satan or from any other." Indeed, the nature of Jesus's ascension was quite different from the type of atmosphere described in Rev 12:1–4.

[46] Ibid., 65–66. John Nelson Darby, *Lectures on the Second Coming* (London: W. H. Broom, 1868), 61–62, connects the male child of Rev 12:5 with the church because of the connection to Ps 2:9 in Rev 2:26–28. He also finds this idea of eschatological judgment exercised by the church in 1 Cor 6:2–3 and Rev 20:4.

[47] Ibid., 66–67.

will show how this passage points to a pretribulational time frame for the rapture.[48] First, the woman, representing Israel, is clearly distinguished from the male child, representing Christ and the church. While the woman must go through the tribulation period (fleeing into the wilderness [12:6], protected by God [12:6, 14], and pursued by Satan [12:13]), the male child is protected from these same judgments because he is taken up to heaven.[49] Second, when the church is caught up to heaven, the spiritual warfare with Satan ensues, resulting in the casting down of Satan to the earth (Rev 12:5, 7–9).[50] Third, since these events take place in heaven during the first half of the seventieth week, the catching up of the church must occur prior to the start of the tribulation.[51] Thus, a chronological approach to the events of Rev 12–13 reveals the following: (1) the male child is caught up to heaven (12:5); (2) the first half of the tribulation involves war in heaven (12:7–8), the casting down of Satan (12:9), and an attack on Israel by Satan followed by her divine deliverance (12:13–16); and (3) the second half of the tribulation involves the protection of Israel in the wilderness for 1260 days (12:6, 14) during which the two beasts of Revelation 13 take their power and reign (12:17–13:18).[52] Understanding the vision of the woman, the dragon, and the male child in this way yields significant exegetical support for the teaching of a pretribulation rapture of the church.

Theological Support

Thus far I have provided exegetical support for the pretribulational rapture by investigating John 14:1–3; 2 Thessalonians 2:6–7; and Revelation 12:5. I have argued that the most straightforward reading of these verses yields a pretribulational understanding of the "taking" and "catching up" of

---

[48] Svigel, "What Child Is This?" 229–35, provides an overview of the development of John Nelson Darby's thought with regard to the pretribulational rapture interpretation of Rev 12:5. I will rely mostly on Darby's writings since he appears to be the progenitor of the arguments used to support this viewpoint.

[49] Darby, Lectures, 54–55, states: "In [Rev 12], you have first Christ Himself and the church, figured in the man-child; and then in the woman who flees from persecution for 1260 days you have the Jewish remnant, those who are spared in the time of judgment but are not yet brought into glory."

[50] Ibid., 65–67. Darby writes, "We find here, that while all the heavenly people, that is, the church of God . . . are called upon to rejoice that the accuser of the brethren is cast down . . . it is just the time when Satan comes down to earth, having great wrath, knowing that he has but a short time. Thus we get entire rejoicing in what is heavenly, and, at the same time, most desperate woe in what is earthly."

[51] Ibid., 68. Darby summarizes Rev 12, "While one class of persons—those associated with Christ—are caught up to God, and there is triumph and rejoicing and gladness amongst them when Satan is cast down, that is the very time when tribulation begins on the earth." A few pages prior to this statement, Darby affirms his belief that the seventieth week of Daniel's prophecy (Dan 9:27) cannot begin until the church is united with Christ in heaven (58–60).

[52] Svigel, "What Child Is This?" 234.

the church. Now I will pursue several theological arguments, lending further support for this doctrine. These include (1) the relationship of the church to God's wrath; (2) the doctrines of imminency, the rapture, and the Day of the Lord; and (3) the argument of the Thessalonian epistles.

The Church and Divine Wrath

The Bible speaks frequently about the wrath of God.[53] And "all agree that God has exempted the church from divine wrath."[54] The disagreement lies in the nature of that exemption from God's eschatological wrath. On the one hand, posttribulationists argue that texts such as 1 Thessalonians 1:10; 5:9 and Revelation 3:10 teach that Christians are protected from God's wrath even though they are on earth when the wrath is poured out.[55] Or they suggest that the outpouring of God's eschatological wrath does not truly begin until the Battle of Armageddon at the end of the tribulation when the church is raptured.[56] On the other hand, pretribulationists and prewrath advocates agree that such references to escaping from divine wrath indicate that the rapture of the church will occur prior to the outpouring of God's wrath during the seventieth week.[57] Pretribulationists and midtribulationists disagree, however, in regard to what constitutes divine wrath during the seventieth week. Pretribulationists understand all the judgments poured out during the tribulation to be demonstrations of divine wrath, while prewrath teachers believe that God's wrath is

---

[53] Wayne Grudem, *Systematic Theology: An Introduction to Biblical Doctrine* (Grand Rapids: Zondervan, 1994), 206, defines God's wrath as follows: "God's wrath means that he intensely hates all sin." This hatred for sin manifests itself in various ways throughout the Old and New Testaments. But Christians do not experience the wrath of God because Jesus satisfied God's wrath against sin when he bore the sins of the world upon himself in his death on the cross (Rom 3:25–26; Heb 2:17; 1 John 2:2; 4:10). The Bible also speaks about eschatological wrath that will be poured out on unbelievers particularly at the final judgment and that will result in their eternal separation from God (Rom 2:5, 8; 3:5; 5:9; Eph 5:6; Col 3:6). See Feinberg, "Pretribulation Rapture," 52–53. It is this last type of divine eschatological wrath that is the focus of the debate.

[54] Feinberg, "Pretribulation Rapture," 50, cites several posttribulationists, midtribulationists, and pretribulationists to support this statement. Even though the church does avoid God's wrath, this does not mean that the church never experiences persecution or suffering (e.g., John 16:33; Phil 1:27; 1 Pet 4:19) nor does it mean that the basis of the avoidance of God's wrath is Christ's death on the cross (see Feinberg, "Pretribulation Rapture," 51–52, for these two clarifications).

[55] Ladd, *The Blessed Hope*, 121; J. Barton Payne, *The Imminent Appearing of Christ* (Grand Rapids: Eerdmans, 1962), 143.

[56] Gundry, *The Church and the Tribulation,* 61–63. Gundry also argues that the types of distress described during the tribulation are *not* evidence of the outpouring of divine wrath but rather different manifestations of wrath from Satan and man (44–51).

[57] See James Oliver Buswell, Jr., *A Systematic Theology of the Christian Religion* (Grand Rapids, Zondervan, 1962), 2:389, and Hultberg, "Prewrath Rapture," 142–44, for the prewrath view. Pretribulation advocates will be mentioned below.

manifested only in the second half of the seventieth week.

I propose the Bible teaches that the church will not be present during *any* of the seventieth week because it will be raptured prior to its commencement. This assertion will be supported by considering (1) the connection of the seventieth week to the Day of the Lord in order to show that divine wrath is manifested during the *entirety* of the tribulation period and (2) the meaning of biblical texts that speak of the church escaping from divine eschatological wrath. Thus, as I show that all the judgments of the tribulation period are demonstrations of divine eschatological wrath and that the church will be kept from the outpouring of eschatological wrath, then the church must be raptured prior to the tribulation period.

The Seventieth Week and the Day of the Lord. Two lines of argument support the idea that God's wrath is poured out during the entirety of the seventieth week of Daniel's prophecy. First, all three cycles of divine judgments during the tribulation period (the seals, trumpets, and bowls) are referred to as demonstrations of God's wrath.[58] Of course, the most significant of these in regard to their connection to divine wrath are the seal judgments since they occur during the first half of the seventieth week.[59] A comparison of the seal judgments to the prophetic words of Jesus in the Olivet Discourse (Matt 24–25; Mark 13; Luke 21) indicates that the first six seals will be completed *before* the abomination of desolation at the midpoint of the seventieth week.[60]

Second, the seventieth week is part of the Day of the Lord which the Old Testament describes as an unprecedented manifestation of God's wrath on the inhabited world. To better understand Scripture's teaching on the Day of the Lord, we need to take an abbreviated look at the biblical progress of revelation about this subject.

Before commencing we must recognize the very common occurrence

---

[58] See Rev 6:16–17 (seals); Rev 11:18 (trumpets); and Rev 16:1 (bowls).

[59] This assumes a chronological progression of the three cycles of judgments in Revelation with the seal judgments occurring during the first half of the tribulation. For a contrary interpretation that views the three series of judgments as concurrently fulfilled, see Gundry, *The Church and the Tribulation,* 74–77.

[60] Robert L. Thomas, *Revelation 1–7: An Exegetical Commentary* (Chicago: Moody Press, 1992), 452–53; E. Schuyler English, *Studies in the Gospel According to Matthew* (New York: Our Hope Publications, 1935), 173–74, shows the following comparisons between Matt 24:4–14 and Rev 6:1–14: (1) false Christs (Matt 24:5 = Rev 6:1–2); (2) worldwide war (Matt 24:6–7 = Rev 6:3–4); (3) famine (Matt 24:7 = Rev 6:5–6); (4) pestilence (Matt 24:7 = Rev 6:8); (5) martyrdom (Matt 24:9 = Rev 6:9–11). To these a sixth comparison could be added: earthquakes in Matt 24:7 and Rev 6:12. This "beginning of birth pangs" in Matt 24:4–14 occurs prior to the "abomination of desolation" in 24:15. According to Dan 9:27, the "abomination of desolation" occurs in the middle of the seventieth week. Thus, the six seals of Rev 6:1–14, which correspond to the "beginning of birth pangs," occur prior to the middle of the seventieth week.

in prophetic literature of the complex structure of prophetic events.[61] Many promises which appear to be singular happenings when first mentioned in the Old Testament turn out to be a complex of events when discussed in the light of newer revelation. Two examples will suffice: (1) a single coming of Messiah in the Old Testament is actually two comings, each of which includes a multitude of events that can all be said to fulfill the promises related to the one coming; (2) the resurrection of the righteous and unrighteous, which appears to be a single event in Daniel 12:2, ends up as a complex of resurrections including the rapture of the church in 1 Thessalonians 4:16, the "first" resurrection of tribulation martyrs in Revelation 20:4 prior to the start of the millennium, and the resurrection of the "rest" of the unbelievers in 20:5 at the end of the millennium.

The Day of the Lord certainly fits into this category of "complex events." The Old Testament reveals that the Day of the Lord consists of at least three elements: (1) divine judgment associated with (2) a divine coming which leads to a time of (3) divine blessing. The preponderance of Day of the Lord texts refer to a time of divine eschatological judgment (e.g., Isa 3:16–24; 13:9–11; Jer 30:7; Ezek 38–39; Joel 2:1–2; Amos 5:18–20; Zeph 1:14–18). But the Day of the Lord is also described as a time of divine blessing (Isa 30:23–25; Joel 3:17–18; Zech 14:6–11). And what is it that advances the events of the Day of the Lord from judgment to blessing? Isaiah 2:19–21 and Zechariah 14:3–5 give the answer: the coming of the Lord.

Jesus provides further revelation about this day in his Olivet Discourse. He weaves teaching about the time of his second coming and the signs that precede it together with the Old Testament prophecies about Daniel's seventieth week, great tribulation, and the Day of the Lord.[62] Given what has already been stated with regard to the Day of the Lord as a complex event, Jesus shows that "the coming of the Son of Man in Matthew 24:36–

---

[61] Blaising, "Pretribulation Rapture," 50; Moo, "Posttribulation Rapture," 207; Gundry, *The Church and the Tribulation,* 75, writes, "The sweeping summary of a complex of events with later regressions to add more detail is a well-recognized feature of narratival style in Semitic literature." Kevin T. Bauder, "The Rapture," *In the Nick of Time,* Oct 2, 2015, "Complex events are not uncommon in biblical prophecy. They become apparent when later events or teachings distinguish details that were not disclosed in earlier prophecies. From a later perspective, these complexes can still be grouped under the rubric of the original event, but they can also be recognized as distinct, particular events that together compose the original event."

[62] Christ understands Daniel's seventieth week as part of the Day of the Lord, and hence, as a period of time during which God's wrath is poured out. Christ's language in the discourse clearly alludes to OT prophecies about the Day of the Lord (cp. Matt 24:21 with Jer 30:7; Dan 12:1; Joel 2:2). See Thomas, *Revelation 1–7,* 458. Blaising, "Pretribulation Rapture" 42–52, compares Jesus's teaching in the Olivet Discourse to Daniel's seventy-week prophetic structure, showing that when the Day of the Lord begins, the seventieth week begins.

25:46 is entirely the same thing as the coming of the Day of the Lord itself."[63]

Moving on to Paul's teaching in the Thessalonian epistles, we learn that the Day of the Lord is still a future event (1 Thess 5:2; 2 Thess 2:2–3) that includes the second coming of Christ (2 Thess 2:1). Furthermore, that second coming contains two elements: a rapture or gathering of the church (1 Thess 4:13–17; 2 Thess 2:1b) and a physical return of Christ to the earth (1 Thess 1:10; 2:19; 3:13; 5:23; 2 Thess 1:7–10; 2:1a).

So how should we assess this scriptural data about the Day of the Lord? First, the Day of the Lord is an unprecedented outpouring of divine wrath on the inhabitants of the earth. Second, the Day of the Lord is a complex of events that includes catastrophic judgments, divine blessing, and the second coming of Christ. Third, God's eschatological wrath revealed in the Day of the Lord events includes Daniel's seventieth week. Fourth, the Day of the Lord has not yet commenced so we must speak of it as a future time of eschatological, retributive wrath.

Biblical Texts That Support Escape from Wrath. Having demonstrated that the entirety of Daniel's seventieth week is a time of divine, retributive wrath, I now proceed to three texts which speak about the church's escape from that wrath. First Thessalonians 1:10 states that Jesus "delivers us from the wrath to come." There are three reasons this text speaks to the avoidance of God's eschatological wrath revealed in the tribulation. First, the general context of the Thessalonian correspondence deals with the Day of the Lord and the divine judgment associated with it. Thus, when Paul speaks about deliverance from wrath, avoidance of the Day of the Lord, which includes the tribulation, should be included.[64] Second, the first part of the verse speaks about the return of the Lord as the event that is related to the "coming wrath" from which Christians are exempted.[65] Third, the reference to deliverance from the coming wrath seems related to the portion of the epistle (5:1–11) where eschatological

---

[63] Blaising, "Pretribulation Rapture," 50.

[64] Feinberg, "Pretribulation Rapture," 53. Gary S. Shogren, *1 & 2 Thessalonians,* 76, offers an opposing perspective by pointing out that Christians are said to be on earth during the tribulation according to Matt 24 and Revelation though God protects them from his wrath during this time. While it is true that believers will be on earth during the tribulation, neither of these passages requires the presence of *church-age* believers in the tribulation. Additionally, the verb ῥύομαι with ἐκ more naturally speaks of rescue, deliverance, or salvation from coming wrath rather than protection from it while it is being meted out on the ungodly.

[65] Ibid.

woes are in view.[66]

First Thessalonians 5:9 provides even clearer evidence of the avoidance of retributive wrath during the tribulation. In 5:1–11, Paul discusses the arrival of the woes of the Day of the Lord (5:3), using language similar to Christ's in Matthew 24:8 ("beginning of the birth pains"). Paul states that the Day of the Lord will arrive unexpectedly (5:3a) and that no one will escape it (5:3b). However, the Thessalonian believers will not be overtaken by the Day of the Lord because they are children of the day rather than children of the night (5:5).[67] In accordance with his usual pattern, Paul exhorts his readers based on the indicatives he has just provided (5:6): they must not sleep (*mē katheudōmen*); they must be watchful (*grēgorōmen*); and they must be sober (*nēphōmen*).[68] Paul strengthens his emphasis on the imperatives by giving an explanatory basis (*gar*) for them (5:7):[69] sleeping and drunkenness are activities of children of the night. Contrariwise, (again, see 5:5) children of the day should be sober (5:8). So to this point in the paragraph Paul has established a contrast between believers who will escape the Day of the Lord because they are children of the light and unbelievers who will not escape the Day of the Lord because they are children of the night. He has also exhorted these believers to be spiritually alert and self-controlled considering their secure position.

Now in 5:9–10 Paul gives the theological reason the Thessalonians ought to be spiritually alert:[70] God has appointed them not to eschatological wrath but to salvation. This salvation comes through the cross work of

---

[66] Zane Hodges, "The Rapture in 1 Thessalonians 5:1–11," in *Walvoord: A Tribute,* ed. Donald K. Campbell (Chicago: Moody Press, 1982), 68–70, states, "If 1 Thessalonians 1:9b–10 offers an informal outline of the contents of the epistle, it might therefore be said that 'to wait for His Son from heaven, whom He raised from the dead, that is Jesus, who delivers us from the wrath to come' points toward the *future* and outlines the eschatological portion of the epistle in 4:13–5:11." See also Earl J. Richard, *First and Second Thessalonians* (Collegeville, MN: Liturgical Press, 1995), 58, and Green, *The Letters to the Thessalonians,* 110.

[67] Hultberg, "Prewrath Rapture," 119–20, argues that Paul's use of the phrase *as a thief* would be redundant if believers were not going to be present when the Day of the Lord begins. However, Hultberg's argument fails to account for the reality that even though believers will not be overtaken by the Day of the Lord because they will not be present, they must still be alert to the need for constant watchfulness. Yes, God has promised that believers will not be surprised by the sudden coming of the Lord, but he also exhorts them to be ever watchful. This manner of teaching is common in Paul as he supports the imperative with the indicative.

[68] Paul repeats this last imperative (νήφωμεν) in 5:8 to emphasize his point and to expand on their need for spiritual alertness by adding faith, love, and the hope of salvation to the equation.

[69] Charles A. Wanamaker, *The Epistles to the Thessalonians,* NIGTC (Grand Rapids: Eerdmans, 1990), 185, suggests that 5:7 is a parenthetical remark by Paul since the repetition of νήφωμεν in 5:8 shows he wants to emphasize the imperatival ideas of 5:6 and 5:8.

[70] He uses a ὅτι clause which governs 5:9–10.

Jesus Christ who died in the place of sinners (*huper hēmōn*) so that all believers will live with Him. The context shows that the wrath Paul is referring to relates to the Day of the Lord judgments (5:2, 4) spoken of in the earlier part of the paragraph. The subjects of this promise are the Thessalonians and all Christians who are "awake or asleep."[71] And this salvation is not only deliverance from eternal damnation but also speaks of life together with Christ in heaven.[72] When compared with the promise of 1 Thessalonians 1:10 (delivered from coming wrath), it would appear that 5:9 speaks of the same truth: Christians will escape God's eschatological wrath.

Thus, Paul mentions at least three realities that should have encouraged the Thessalonians as they dealt with the question of whether their present trials indicated that they had somehow stumbled into the Day of the Lord. First, he directly states that, as children of the day, they will not be overtaken by the Day of the Lord (5:5). Second, he assumes that they are children of the day rather than sleepy or drunken children of the night (5:8a).[73] Third, he says that God has decreed that they will be delivered from the eschatological wrath signified by the Day of the Lord judgments (5:9).

Even though 1 Thessalonians 1:10 and 5:9 provide the promise that Christians will escape God's eschatological wrath, posttribulationists and midtribulationists argue that the specific wrath that Christians avoid is not clarified in these verses.[74] So we turn to Revelation 3:10, where we find the promise that Christians will be kept from "the hour of trial that is coming on the whole world."

Most interpreters agree that the "hour of trial" is a reference to the tribulation period. Furthermore, they agree that the "hour" is not referring to a sixty-minute period but rather to a lengthier general time frame. The adjectival

---

[71] There is some debate regarding Paul's connotation for Christians who are "awake" or "asleep." I support the viewpoint that connects "asleep" with the sleeping believers of 1 Thess 4:15 so that Paul is suggesting that both living and physically dead believers are the focus (Wanamaker, 188–89). Another interpretation suggests that the contrast is between spiritually watchful ("awake") and unwatchful ("asleep") Christians. See Hodges, "The Rapture in 1 Thessalonians 5:1–11," 76–77.

[72] Feinberg, "Pretribulation Rapture," 54.

[73] Paul uses a causal participle (ὄντες) here, showing that the command to be sober is based on the reality that they are children of the day. See Shogren, *1 & 2 Thessalonians*, 208–9. The CSB, ESV, NASB, NIV, NET, and NRSV also concur.

[74] While prewrath advocates and posttribulationists do see a connection between these promises of escape from eschatological wrath and the Day of the Lord in 1 Thessalonians, they do not believe that Day of the Lord wrath occurs until the middle (prewrath proponents) or end (posttribulationists) of the tribulation. I have already tried to show that the Day of the Lord begins when Daniel's seventieth week begins. But Revelation 3:10 helps to establish a specific exegetical basis for the time when the church will escape eschatological wrath.

participle *melousēs* speaks to the eschatological nature of this hour.[75] The universal nature of this trial is clear in that the "whole world" is included; particularly affected are the earth-dwellers.[76]

But the big debate relates to Christ's promise: "I will keep you from the hour of trial." More specifically, what does the verb-preposition combination *tērēsō ek* mean? Is Christ promising to keep the church out of the tribulation entirely, or is he promising to keep the church through the tribulation?[77] I offer five reasons why Jesus's promise ought to be understood as keeping the church out of the tribulation.

The first reason relates to the only other New Testament passage where this verb-preposition combination is found: "I do not ask that you take them out of the world, but that you keep (*tērēsēs*) them from (*ek*) the evil one" (John 17:15). When we compare Revelation 3:10 with John 17:15, we find that the object of God's action in each case is distinct though similar in effect. In John, Christ asks that God will keep his followers from Satan, whereas in Revelation, Christ promises that God will keep his church from the hour of trial. Based on other Johannine passages (e.g., 1 John 5:18–19), it is clear that the church exists outside of Satan's domain.[78] Thus, when Christ asks that believers be kept from Satan, he does so based on the truth that the church is already outside of Satan's domain (i.e., the prayer for protection is a prayer for protection from without rather than protection from within).[79] Likewise in Revelation 3:10 the church is not

---

[75] Osborne, *Revelation*, 193, states that when John uses this participle in Revelation, it usually refers to the final eschatological events preceding the second coming (1:19; 8:13; 10:7; 12:5; 17:8).

[76] Schuyler Brown, "'The Hour of Trial' (Rev 3:10)," *JBL* 85 (1966): 309–10, notes that these people are the "persecutors against whom the martyrs cry out for vengeance." He supports this assertion by showing that this expression is used in Revelation it refers to the enemies of the Christian faith (6:10; 8:13; 11:10 [twice]; 13:8, 14 [twice]; 17:8). But Mounce, *Revelation*, 103–4, while agreeing with Brown on this point, still assumes that the church will remain on the earth though it will be protected from God's wrath. George Eldon Ladd, *A Commentary on the Revelation of John* (Grand Rapids: Eerdmans, 1972), 62, agrees. Despite opinions like those of Mounce and Ladd, the purpose of the hour of trial to try those who inhabit the whole earth indicates a reason why churches like the Philadelphian church will be kept from that hour entirely. While the posttribulational reading is possible, the pretribulational interpretation provides a more probable explanation of the church being kept from the hour of trial before it even begins.

[77] The posttribulational position that supports the idea of "emergence from within" for this verb-preposition combination is best represented by Gundry, *The Church and the Tribulation*, 54–61.

[78] John maintains a distinction between those born of God who are not touched by the devil (1 John 5:18) and those of the world who are under the power of the devil (5:19).

[79] Jeffrey L. Townsend, "The Rapture in Revelation 3:10," *BSac* 137 (July-September 1980): 259. This interpretation is in direct contrast (ἀλλά) with John 17:15a regarding Christ's request that Christians not be taken out of the world. Using a different verb-preposition combination (αἴρω + ἐκ), Christ asks that his followers not be taken out of the physical world in which they reside. Thus, Jesus is asking the Father not to take his disciples out of the physical world but to keep them out of the clutches of Satan, from which they have already been delivered spiritually (10:27–29). Blaising, "Pretribulational Rapture" 63, also notes that Jesus's qualification of his request for

yet in the hour of trial, and Christ's promise is one of protection from without.

Second, the combination of the stative verb *tēreō* with the transitive preposition *ek* yields the meaning "kept out of" rather than "protected from within."[80] At issue is how to determine the transitive versus the stative nature of the verbal action when transitive verbs are combined with stative prepositions and vice versa. Dan Wallace considers both kinds of verb-preposition constructions (e.g., stative verbs + transitive prepositions and transitive verbs + stative prepositions) and provides this general principle: "Stative verbs *override* the transitive force of prepositions. Almost always when a stative verb is used with a transitive preposition, the preposition's natural force is neutralized; all that remains is the stative idea" (emphasis original).[81] Applying this principle to the *tēreso ek* construction in Revelation 3:10, the stative nature of *tēreō* overrides the transitive force of *ek* resulting in the translation "keep from" the hour of trial.

Third, the way that the original promise to the Philadelphian church was fulfilled provides insight into how the promise will be fulfilled once the "hour of trial" finally begins. "They were *kept from* the time of the tribulation by being *kept away from* it (emphasis original)."[82] Of course, the way in which the Philadelphian church was kept from the tribulation was by means of physical death, and in this sense the Philadelphians serve "as a type, or illustration, of a true church," indicating that the "church will not go through this hour of trial."[83] Nevertheless, a *pre*tribulation rapture could have been a possible way God fulfilled this promise to the Philadelphians even though they died before the hour of trial. However, a *post*tribulation rapture could not have been a possible way for this promise to be fulfilled.[84]

---

protection away from Satan is provided in 17:15a. Here Jesus simply excludes from the prayer one possible option for "keeping them away from" Satan, namely, the option to be taken out of the world.

[80] See Gundry, *The Church and the Tribulation*, 55–59, for a detailed discussion supporting the notion of a "protection from within" meaning for τηρέω + ἐκ.

[81] *Stative* in this context means "non-transitive" or "non-motion" (e.g., *in* is a stative preposition while *into* is a transitive preposition). Wallace, 359, also states, "When a verb of motion is used with a stative preposition, again the verb is usually dominant: the entire construction indicates motion." Interestingly, verbs of motion (e.g., ῥύομαι) used with transitive prepositions (ἐκ) may result in a stative meaning (2 Cor 1:10; 1 Thess 1:10; 2 Tim 3:11). Also see Mayhue, "Why a Pretribulational Rapture?" 248, who notes the use of ἐκ in 2 Cor 1:10 and 1 Thess 1:10 to provide a stative idea.

[82] Blaising, "Pretribulation Rapture," 64.

[83] John F. Walvoord, *Major Bible Prophecies* (Grand Rapids: Zondervan, 1991), 278.

Fourth, if Jesus had wanted to be clearer about the church being protected while it went through the tribulation, he could have chosen several other prepositions to make his point. For example, he could have used *tēreō* + *en* as in John 17:11, 12; Acts 12:5; Eph 4:3; 1 Thess 5:23; 1 Pet 1:4; and Jude 1:21, where the idea of being kept in the midst of something is obvious. Similarly, *tēreō* + *eis* would have this same meaning (Acts 25:4, 21; 2 Pet 2:4, 9; 3:7; Jude 1:13). Though *tēreō* does not appear with *dia* anywhere in the New Testament, the idea of being kept through the hour of trial could also have been indicated by this preposition. But none of these prepositions was used.[85]

Fifth, the book of Revelation reveals that many saints will be martyred during the tribulation period. Apart from the divine protection of the 144,000 (Rev 7:4) and the woman (12:6), many believers will die (6:9–11; 7:14) during the seventieth week.[86] If Revelation 3:10 is promising protection for believers who are living through the tribulation, then these descriptions of martyrdom would indicate that Jesus's promise would not be fulfilled.

Imminency, Rapture, and the Day of the Lord

When considering the prophetic texts of the New Testament, the interpreter finds numerous texts that speak to two eschatological events as imminent: the return of Christ for his church and the return of Christ in judgment at the onset of the Day of the Lord. My goal here is to show how the New Testament teaching about the imminency of Christ's return for his church supports a pretribulational rapture. At the same time, we will consider those texts which speak about the imminency of the Day of the Lord. How are these two imminent events related?

The argument will proceed by first considering the teaching about imminency as given by Christ in the Olivet Discourse, by Paul in the Thessalonian epistles, and by James, Peter, and John. Second, we will consider the implications of the NT teaching on imminency as it relates to the pretribulational rapture.

New Testament Teaching about Imminency. In several accounts recorded in the Gospels, Jesus proclaimed the imminent (any moment

---

[84] Blaising, "Pretribulational Rapture," 64.

[85] Mayhue, "Why a Pretribulational Rapture?" 248.

[86] Ibid., 249; Walvoord, *The Blessed Hope*, 137.

nature) of his return by using the images of a master standing at the door knocking (Luke 12:36) and of the unexpected coming of a thief (12:39). Jesus indicated that his imminent second coming will bring blessing to the faithful and punishment to the unprepared.[87] A short time later Jesus used the coming of the flood in Noah's day and the destruction of Sodom in Lot's day to explain the imminency of his return (17:22–37) with an emphasis on the judgmental nature of that coming (17:27–29).

During the passion week Jesus delivered the Olivet Discourse, in which he indicated that no signs would precede the *parousia* (Matt 24:36–25:30).[88] He did so by using two illustrations (e.g., Noah in Matt 24:37–39 and the workers and grinders in Matt 24:40–41) that showed the uncertain timing of the Lord's coming in judgment. Furthermore, Jesus used five parables to enforce the surprising nature of his coming (the master on a journey in Mark 13:33–37, the householder and the thief in Matt 24:43–44, the faithful and wicked servants in 24:45–51, the wise and foolish virgins in 25:1–13, and the talents in 25:14–30). Thus, the two illustrations and five parables provide an emphasis on the imminent nature of Jesus's return to judge those who are unfaithful. As Thomas explains, "[Jesus] will return to begin the series of events that will mark Daniel's seventieth week, with no prior signals to herald His return. Since nothing remains to occur before His *parousia*, that *parousia* is imminent."[89]

In Jesus's final words to his disciples in the upper room, he suggested that his return to earth from his Father's house to take his own to be with him could occur at any time after his ascension (John 14:3). Since this promise of Christ's coming is presented with no mention of signs or a time of trouble preceding it,

---

[87] Robert L. Thomas, "Imminence in the NT, Especially Paul's Thessalonian Epistles," *TMSJ* 13 (Fall 2002): 192–93.

[88] Blaising, "Pretribulation Rapture," 48–49, shows that we could just as easily speak of the Day of the Lord as imminent in the same sense as we understand the coming of the Lord as imminent. When Jesus answers the question of the disciples in Matt 24:3, his language more specifically speaks about the Day of the Lord as imminent. Matthew, Mark, and Luke all record Jesus as speaking about "that day or that hour" (Matt 24:36; Mark 13:32), "the time" (Mark 13:33), and "that day" (Luke 21:34) as a comprehensive event that will be unexpected and, even in His case, unknown. As I argued above, the Day of the Lord is a complex event with a number of aspects including Daniel's seventieth week, the abomination of desolation, the great tribulation, the coming of Messiah, and the judgment of Israel and the nations. In the Olivet Discourse, some of these aspects are preceded by signs (particularly the second coming of Messiah [Matt 24:15–31]), but the *beginning* of this "day" or this "coming" (*parousia*) is not preceded by any signs at all (i.e. it is imminent). Blaising "Pretribulation Rapture," 50 summarizes: "[Jesus] speaks of 'his coming' or the coming of 'that day' as a surprise, occurring suddenly without any preceding signs. Yet he speaks of the sign of his appearing on the clouds of heaven as taking place after the abomination of desolation, which itself occurs in a context of false christs [*sic*], wars, and earthly and heavenly disturbances—all day of the Lord or time of the end features."

[89] Thomas, "Imminence in the NT," 196.

the prophecy is imminent.[90]

The imminency of the Day of the Lord and the rapture are also taught by Paul in his Thessalonian epistles. First, in 1 Thessalonians 1:10 believers are waiting for the Son from heaven, who is going to deliver them from the coming wrath. The implication is that Christ's return to keep the church from the coming wrath could be at any time.[91] Second, the clearest New Testament text on the rapture (1 Thess 4:13–17) indicates the imminence of this event. Paul includes himself as one expecting to be translated when he uses the first person plural pronoun in 4:15 and 17.[92] Third, Paul describes the beginning of the Day of the Lord as coming "like a thief in the night" (1 Thess 5:2).[93]

Not only do Jesus and Paul speak of the imminency of Jesus's return, but James, Peter, and John also mention this doctrine. For James the imminent coming of the Lord serves as an encouragement to persevere during times of suffering. Believers can be patient in their difficult circumstances because "the coming of the Lord is at hand" (Jas 5:8).[94] Even so, believers must avoid grumbling against one another because the Lord is also coming to judge sinners (5:9). Using language reminiscent of Jesus's words, James speaks of the

---

[90] Walvoord, *The Rapture Question,* 73; Wayne A. Brindle, "Biblical Evidence for the Imminence of the Rapture," *BSac* 158 (April–June 2001): 141.

[91] D. Edmond Hiebert, *1 and 2 Thessalonians,* rev ed. (Chicago: Moody Press, 1992), 218, comments on the incongruity of failing to read this text as supporting imminence: "If [the Thessalonians] had been taught that the Great Tribulation, in whole or in part, must first run its course, it is difficult to see how they could be described as expectantly awaiting Christ's return. Then they should rather have been described as bracing themselves for the Great Tribulation and the painful events connected with it."

[92] Thomas, "Imminence in the NT," 203; Hiebert, *1 and 2 Thessalonians,* 210.

[93] Hiebert, *1 and 2 Thessalonians,* 227. Some have noted a possible contradiction between Paul's statement in 1 Thess 5:2, which speaks of the onset of the Day of the Lord coming like a thief, and his words in 2 Thess 2:3 ("Let no one deceive you in any way. For that day will not come, unless the rebellion comes first, and the man of lawlessness is revealed, the son of destruction"). Based on most English translations, it appears that both the rebellion and the revealing of the man of lawlessness must take place *before* the Day of the Lord arrives. However, such is not the case. Robert L. Thomas, "The Rapture and the Biblical Teaching of Imminency," in *Evidence for the Rapture: A Biblical Case for Pretribulationism,* ed. John F. Hart (Chicago: Moody Publishers, 2015), 37–40, provides three helpful correctives to this interpretation. First, most English translations mistranslate the understood verb ἐνίστημι as "come" rather than its usual meaning, "is present" as it is translated in 2:2. Second, the ellipsis in 2:3 is usually supplied in English versions with something like "that day will not come," but this is not what Paul is addressing at this point. Rather, he is addressing the current non-presence of the Day of the Lord (e.g., "that day is not present"). Third, the adverb πρῶτον in 2:3 refers to the apostasy only and not to both the apostasy and the revelation of the man of lawlessness. So, the apostasy precedes the revelation of the man of lawlessness rather than the Day of the Lord (see John 7:51 for a similar construction with this adverb). Blaising, "Pretribulation Rapture," 56, provides a helpful summary: "Whatever the apostasy refers to, the activity of the Man of Lawlessness . . . actually belongs to the integrated day of the Lord/time of the end pattern taught by the Lord and recalled by Paul, not something that precedes it. The coming of the day of the Lord in both the Olivet Discourse and in 1 Thessalonians 5 is without signs, without warning."

[94] It would not be much of an encouragement if James were teaching his readers that Jesus's coming was at least seven years away and that during the interim they would have to endure tribulation that was far worse than their present circumstances.

Judge as "standing at the door."[95] Indeed, James is speaking of an imminent return of Christ as a time of blessing and judgment.[96]

Peter also writes about the imminency of the Day of the Lord in 2 Peter 3:10. Just as Jesus (Luke 12:39; Matt 24:43) and Paul (1 Thess 5:2) had before him,[97] Peter uses the imagery of the thief to emphasize the sudden and unexpected nature of the onset of the Day of the Lord.

Finally, John uses the same imagery of the thief as a metaphor for the imminent return of Christ in judgment (Rev 3:3; 16:15).[98] Furthermore, the language of imminence is used to describe the blessing provided for believers at Christ's coming in 2:25 and 3:11. The church in Thyatira is encouraged to persevere until Christ comes, indicating that Jesus will return to bless these believers (2:25). The Philadelphian church is also promised blessing if it holds fast to the truth since Christ is coming soon.[99]

We can summarize the teaching of Jesus, Paul, James, Peter, and John in three statements: (1) the unexpected coming of Christ results in both blessing and judgment; (2) the images of the thief coming in the night and the judge knocking on the door are first used by Jesus and then by the others to describe Christ's return;[100] and (3) imminency language is used to refer to the onset of the Day of the Lord and to the *parousia* of Christ.

Through the use of the images of the thief and the judge knocking on the door, we can also propose the following aspects about imminency generally: (1) people must be prepared at all times for these events to occur and (2) no

---

[95] Douglas J. Moo, *The Letter of James*, PNTC (Grand Rapids: Eerdmans, 2000), 225; Peter H. Davids, *The Epistle of James*, NIGTC (Grand Rapids: Eerdmans, 1982), 185; Thomas, "Imminence in the NT," 199.

[96] Davids, *The Epistle of James*, 185.

[97] Thomas R. Schreiner, *1, 2 Peter, Jude*, NAC (Nashville: Broadman & Holman, 2003), 383; Richard J. Bauckham, *Jude, 2 Peter*, WBC (Waco, TX: Word, 1983), 314–15, suggests that the source for the thief metaphor comes from Jesus's parable and conveys both unexpectedness and threat.

[98] Most commentators note that the thief language comes from Jesus's usage in Luke 12:39 and Matt 24:43 (see Osborne, *Revelation*, 177; Beale, *Revelation*, 837; Thomas, *Revelation 1–7*, 255). While all agree that Rev 16:15 refers to Christ's second coming, there is disagreement in regard to the identification of the coming predicted in Rev 3:3. For example, Beale and Osborne understand 3:3 to refer to a coming of Christ in present judgment upon the Sardis church as a "harbinger of the final coming in judgment" (Osborne, 177), whereas Thomas, 253–55, argues that 3:3 is speaking exclusively of Christ's second advent; his support includes (1) the simile of a thief is used exclusively of Christ's second advent in the rest of the NT; (2) this is the same language Jesus used earlier when telling the twelve to watch for His return; and (3) the history of Sardis, which had experienced several unexpected invasions in its history, speaks to the idea of an imminent return. In the end Thomas's arguments tip the scale toward seeing 3:3 as referring to the second coming.

[99] Mounce, *The Book of Revelation*, 104; Osborne, *Revelation*, 194: "Their anticipated reward, like the judgment of their adversaries (3:10), is imminent."

[100] Paul, Peter, and John used the image of the thief, and James used the picture of the judge standing at the door.

other prophecy in the Bible remains to be fulfilled before these imminent events can happen.[101]

Implications of Imminency for the Pretribulational Rapture. As our survey of New Testament prophecies about imminency has shown, a time of both blessing and judgment could occur at any time (i.e., there are no eschatological signs or events which have to happen before God's promises of blessing for believers and judgment for unbelievers take place). There is little question among students of these texts that the promises of imminent judgment relate to the onset of the Day of the Lord. The New Testament message is quite clear—the Day of the Lord and the judgments associated with it could begin at any time.

However, the promises about imminent blessing create some confusion due to their connection with the second coming of Christ, which clearly is preceded by certain signs. Two proposals have been suggested to resolve this confusion. First, we could stretch the meaning of imminency to include the idea that Christ's promises in regard to his return are merely near or "could take place soon, i.e., within a fairly brief period of time."[102] This stretching would allow advocates of a prewrath rapture and posttribulationalism to affirm the imminency texts related to the coming of Christ while still acknowledging the signs that precede the second coming of Christ to begin his millennial reign.[103] Second, we could review the complex nature of prophetic events such as resurrection and the Day of the Lord and acknowledge that the coming of Messiah fits into this same group of complex events. All agree that the prophecies about the Messiah's (apparently) singular coming in the Old Testament refer to a complex of events associated with two comings once the progress of revelation shows this to be true. Similarly, it should come as no surprise that the second coming of Christ also involves a number of aspects, some of which are preceded by signs and some of which are not.

---

[101] Thomas, "Imminency in the NT," 198.

[102] D. A. Carson, "Matthew," in *EBC,* ed. Frank E. Gaebelein, vol. 8, (Grand Rapids: Zondervan, 1984), 490.

[103] Blaising, "Pretribulation Rapture," 65–67, suggests that this way of understanding imminency fails properly to respect those texts which speak of the imminence of the rapture and which lack any signs. He argues that we should acknowledge two forms of imminency. On the one hand are texts which address the rapture and lack any previous signs. On the other hand, we can speak of the "imminence of the 'appearing of his coming'—which is his descent to earth to begin his millennial reign"; these texts are related to the "revealed structure of the tribulation and the signs that mark passage from its beginning to its end." Furthermore, these texts are "imminent in the sense that [Christ's coming] is known to be near as the revealed seven-year tribulation structure concludes." Blaising's summary is helpful: "Both posttribulationism and prewrath rapture views confuse these two forms of imminency, essentially replacing the imminency of the parousia (which is the imminency of the day of the Lord as a whole) with the imminency of the appearing of his coming."

From what we read in Matthew 24:15–35, the bodily return of Christ to set up the millennial kingdom at the end of the tribulation is preceded by signs and is thus not imminent.[104] Therefore, the aspect of Christ's *parousia* that is imminent must be the rapture of the church (and the start of the Day of the Lord).[105]

Assuming that the second of these proposals is preferred, I will show how both the judgment and blessing aspects of the imminency texts support a pretribulational rapture. It is possible that one could propose that the onset of the Day of the Lord judgment for unbelievers is separate from the promise of blessing for believers while maintaining a type of imminency for both. This is what midtribulationists and posttribulationists must do.[106] But if the meaning of imminency for both judgment and blessing is understood as occurring at any time without prior signs, the beginning of the Day of the Lord and the rapture must occur at the same time. This is precisely what Jesus indicates in Luke 12:35–40. Jesus promises blessing to those who are ready for him when he comes and knocks (12:37). On the other hand, Jesus uses the imagery of a thief to warn of the judgment pending for those who are not ready for his coming (12:39–40).

In James 5 we learn of promised blessing for those who are patiently awaiting the Lord's return. Just as the farmer receives the blessing of fruit from his labor (5:7), so the believer anticipates God's blessing when Christ returns (5:8).[107] At the same time, God promises judgment for sinners who fail to repent of their grumbling (5:9).

Paul encourages believers who are facing persecution in Thessalonica (2 Thess 1:3–4) by pointing to the righteous judgment of God against their persecutors (2 Thess 1:6; "it is only just for God to repay with affliction those who afflict you") while at the same time promising blessing for the Thessalonians who are enduring (2 Thess 1:7a; "to give relief to you who are

---

[104] This is the most difficult problem faced by posttribulationists with regard to the blessing-imminency texts. If the rapture does not take place until the end of the tribulation, it is not imminent because several events such as the abomination of desolation and the great tribulation would precede it.

[105] Blaising, "Pretribulation Rapture," 66, "All those who belong to Christ are in the position described in the second part of the Olivet Discourse; 1 Thessalonians 1:10; 4:13–5:10; and Acts 1:7. There are no signs that clearly indicate whether the Lord's coming will be sooner or later."

[106] Of course, these interpreters must stretch the meaning of imminency to include a period of time (see note 104 above). But in this way, they could envision the onset of the Day of the Lord judgments as distinct in time from the rapture which will take place in the middle or at the end of the tribulation.

[107] The imminence of Christ's return for blessing is substantiated by the fact that the Lord's coming is "at hand" (ἤγγικεν). See Moisés Silva, *New International Dictionary of New Testament Theology and Exegesis,* 2nd ed. (Grand Rapids: Zondervan, 2014), 2:76–78.

afflicted"). And both the judgment and blessing occur "when the Lord Jesus will be revealed from heaven with His mighty angels" (2 Thess 1:7b). The next two verses continue the description of judgment that God will bring "to those who do not know God and to those who do not obey the gospel of our Lord Jesus" (1:8). Particularly, they will experience "eternal destruction, away from the presence of the Lord and from the glory of His power" (1:9). Up to this point in Paul's discussion the timing of the judgment and blessing of God was explained as the revelation of Jesus from heaven with his angels (1:7). But now Paul becomes more specific by indicating that the judgment will occur "on that day" (1:10). This is clearly a reference to the Day of the Lord, which Paul discusses in 1 Thessalonians 5:2–3 and 2 Thessalonians 2:2.[108] And not only does judgment occur on that day, but Jesus receives glory from believers as well (1:10).[109] The connection of blessing and judgment occurring at the onset of the Day of the Lord shows that both are simultaneous and both are imminent.[110]

To summarize, Jesus taught about his imminent return by using the images of a thief in the night and a judge knocking on the door. Several New Testament writers picked up on these same images, prophesying that the Day of the Lord judgments as well as the blessing of the return of Christ could happen at any time. Since the return of Christ is a complex prophetic event and since the bodily coming of Christ is preceded by definite signs, the rapture must be the aspect of the coming of Christ that fits into the many prophetic expressions of imminent blessings promised to believers in the church. Furthermore, the rapture and the onset of the Day of the Lord judgments will occur at the same time, that is, at a time when they are not expected seven years prior to the second coming of Christ.

Theological Implications from the Thessalonian Epistles

When considering the teaching about the rapture and the Day of the Lord in

---

[108] Green, *The Letters to the Thessalonians*, 294; Wanamaker, *Epistles to the Thessalonians*, 232; Shogren, *1 & 2 Thessalonians*, 256.

[109] Paul describes the glorification of Christ by believers using two infinitive phrases (ἐνδοξασθῆναι ἐν τοῖς ἁγίοις αὐτοῦ and θαυμασθῆναι ἐν πᾶσιν τοῖς πιστεύσασιν), thus emphasizing both the action of worship ("glorified" and "marveled at") and the identity of the worshippers ("saints" and "all who believe"). Hiebert, 316, summarizes this event: "Christ will be glorified when it is openly displayed what He has wrought in His saints, now assembled with Him in glorified bodies and perfected in spirit."

[110] Thomas, "Imminence in the NT," 212–13, writes, "2 Thessalonians 1:10 . . . connects Christ's return to be glorified among believers with 'that day,' i.e. the day of the Lord. This is an event that will occur at the very beginning of the day of wrath. It is the same event referred to in 1 Thess 4:17 as a 'catching away,' in 2 Thess 1:7a as 'rest,' and in 2 Thess 2:1 as 'our gathering together to Him.' Here is a specific tie-in between the rapture of the church and the beginning of the day of the Lord."

the Thessalonian epistles, I find three implications that support a pretribulational rapture.[111]

Sorrow about loved ones. First Thessalonians 4:13 states that the believers were concerned about their dead loved ones missing out on the rapture. But if Paul had taught a posttribulational rapture to them initially, they would have been relieved that their relatives would not have to live through the horrors of the tribulation period.

Concern about the Day of the Lord. Second Thessalonians 2:1–2 speaks to the Thessalonians' concern that the Day of the Lord has begun. But if Paul had taught that the rapture would take place at the middle or end of the tribulation, the Thessalonians not only would *not* have been puzzled by reports that it had started but would also have expected the Day of the Lord to have begun prior to the rapture.[112]

Purpose of the translation of believers. One purpose of the rapture is the resurrection of saints "in Christ" (1 Thess 4:16). All agree that this must occur so that these believers can participate in the millennium on earth. However, what is the purpose for the translation of believers who are alive at the time of the rapture (4:17)? A posttribulational rapture falls short of providing any good answer. Why have a translation of believers if they have been divinely protected by God during the seven-year tribulation? Why should they be translated at the very end of that period only to be immediately brought back to earth? Would it not make more sense that they be permitted to stay on earth and enter the millennium in non-glorified bodies?

Conclusion

In this essay I have provided several lines of argument supporting a pretribulational rapture of the church. Exegetically, John 14:1–3, 2 Thessalonians 2:6–7, and Revelation 12:5 teach a rapture before the tribulation begins. Theologically, the avoidance of eschatological wrath, the imminency of the onset of the Day of the Lord and the rapture, and the implications of Paul's teaching about the pretribulational rapture in the Thessalonian epistles all serve to support this doctrine. So we say with Paul, "Maranatha" (1 Cor 16:22).

---

[111] These implications are predicated on the assumption that Paul had taught the concept of the pretribulational rapture to the Thessalonians during his three-week initial visit recorded in Acts 17:1–9. However, he did not have time to give some important details, which he later reveals in his two epistles to the church.

[112] This argument assumes that the Day of the Lord begins when the seventieth week of Daniel begins (see above).

Tributes to Charles Hauser, Jr., from Former Students and Colleagues

Charles A. Hauser: An Exegetical Giant
William D. Barrick

An exegetical giant among much taller men—that's how I remember my professor, my colleague, and my friend, Charles A. Hauser, Jr. When he taught the Gospel of Matthew as an English Bible course at San Francisco Conservative Baptist Seminary around 1970, I found his careful exegetical analysis of the Bible exactly what I needed to learn for my own study of Scripture. One of my fellow students (David Drullinger, currently serving as a missionary in Cape Town, South Africa) took extensive notes in shorthand to preserve Dr. Hauser's rich teaching. As students questioned a particular point of interpretation, our professor calmly presented detailed arguments supporting his conclusions. All the while his eyes twinkled, and his mouth formed a slight smile. Due to an early childhood speech problem, he had learned to think carefully before he spoke and then to calmly enunciate each statement with precision. It was obvious that he delighted in such interactions with his students—especially if the question had its origin in another class under a different professor. His joy in studying the Word of God was contagious. Although his physical stature was shorter than most, we all felt we came only to his knees as biblical expositors.

After my MDiv and ThM at San Francisco, I had the privilege to be his teaching colleague at Denver Baptist Theological Seminary from 1972 until 1978. It was then I finally yielded to his request to call him Charlie. Walking into Charlie's office, one was struck by three things: piles of papers, journals, and books on his desk, piles of books on the floor around his desk, and a sign that read, "If a cluttered desk is the sign of a cluttered mind, what is an empty desk the sign of?" Everyone soon learned that Charlie could locate any item quickly in his pile system, sometimes plucking the paper he wanted out of the middle of what appeared to be a disorganized stack. Just as with his teaching, he kept everything carefully filed away in his memory, where he could access it at will.

After the death of his first wife (Janet), Charlie accepted more speaking engagements and traveled often. During those years he developed a friendship with the seminary's registrar (Ann), who herself had also been widowed suddenly and painfully. While Charlie was away on one of his trips, she thought she could help him by organizing his office piles for him before he returned. She shelved the books in proper order and filed his papers in newly labeled file folders. I still remember Charlie sitting in his office at that unusually empty desk with a grim look on his face—his carefully organized world had been turned upside down. His terse declaration of dissatisfaction reduced Ann to tears. However, he soon returned to apologize for causing her grief, and she apologized for creating havoc in his carefully ordered office. It wasn't long before they were spending more time together as their romance bloomed, and there was a new twinkle in Charlie's eyes.

During my years as a student at the seminary in San Francisco, I sat under quite a cadre of very talented exegetes and expositors of God's Word. My colleagues at the seminary in Denver included three of those professors (Drs. Hauser, Myrant, and Muntz) as well as other men of great ability. Charlie, however, was the one man out of them all that I count as the best exegete. He, beyond all the others, taught me three aspects of interpreting Scripture and passing the fruit of that study on to others. First, he emphasized the need for exegetical accuracy. Accuracy can only be obtained by sticking to what the Scripture actually says—not by trying to read in the white spaces. "It's simple," he would say, "what does it say?" He always focused on what the text said in its original language—although he loved the New American Standard Bible (NASB) and used it in class, he insisted that we understand the Greek of Matthew's Gospel or the Hebrew of Isaiah even though he did not teach any of the Greek or Hebrew courses. He often admonished us (both as students under his teaching and colleagues with him in ministry) with the words of 2 Timothy 2:15, "Be diligent to present yourself approved to God as a workman who does not need to be ashamed, handling accurately the word of truth." For Charlie, there was no greater shame than to inaccurately handle God's precious, inerrant Word.

Second, Charlie demonstrated for us how to perform exhaustive research in order to identify the variety of potential interpretations, the arguments supposedly supporting those interpretations, and the theological background of the respective commentators, theologians, and expositors. From him I learned to love immersing myself in older commentators too often ignored by those who seemed to think that more recent biblical scholars must be better and more accurate than the older ones. He introduced me to John Peter Lange, W.

Robertson Nicoll, David Baron, John A. Broadus, A. T. Robertson, and E. J. Young among others. My library shelves testify to a determination to maintain an anchor in the past as well as a healthy interest in current scholarship. For this aspect of studying Scripture, he would sometimes smile and quote Proverbs 18:17, "The first to plead his case *seems* just, *until* another comes and examines him." For example, as he taught Matthew 16:18, he would discuss the view of someone like Leon Morris or Arnold Gaebelein and then ask, "Do you think these commentators have adequately responded to the arguments of Broadus on the identity of 'this rock'?" Of course, none of us had even looked at Broadus's commentary on Matthew and had no idea what view he held. After our awkward silence he would proceed to lay out Broadus's arguments before analyzing each one for us. He was a master teacher skillfully practicing his craft and showing us how to apply the hermeneutics we had been taught.

Third, some of my professors and colleagues helped stoke my passion for the Word and enthusiasm for teaching and preaching with passion. Charlie, however, modeled calmness and gentleness in teaching and preaching, together with passion. It's a lesson I'm still trying to learn and to practice—with varying degrees of success. At times he played the devil's advocate, doing so with a winsome spirit and quiet delight. When he had made his point and won the argument, he went on to the next point or the next verse without celebration. In other words, he taught with humility. Charlie embodied the apostle Paul's words in 1 Thessalonians 2:7–8, "But we proved to be gentle among you, as a nursing *mother* tenderly cares for her own children. Having thus a fond affection for you, we were well-pleased to impart to you not only the gospel of God but also our own lives, because you had become very dear to us."

Throughout his life Charlie remained dissatisfied with where he was in his personal growth in his knowledge of God's Word. His insistence on accuracy left him unwilling to submit his manuscript notes on the Gospel of Matthew for publication. Due to his reluctance to publish, none remains for us to pull off our shelves for reference and reading. For his students, that makes our class notes extremely valuable. Yes, I still have those notes and still refer to them, wishing I had had the ability to use shorthand to catch every detail. The greater privilege and joy, however, consists of having experienced at least a portion of Charlie's life and ministry. He left a significant impact on many, including myself.

Without a doubt, Dr. Hauser was one of my mentors and his faithful example set much of my trajectory in ministry as a seminary teacher. His humble attitude, quiet manner, and dogged determination to stick to the Scriptures in all matters of faith and practice set the tone for the years I enjoyed his teaching and friendship. Like Paul, he could say, "Brethren, join in following my example, and observe those who walk according to the pattern you have in us" (Phil 3:17). He truly stood as an exegetical giant among many who were taller than he, but whom he surpassed in excellence and humility.

Dr. Charles Hauser: New Testament Professor, Servant-Scholar, Personal Friend
Douglas R. McLachlan

Daniel J. Boorstin once pointed out that there is a great deal of difference between a celebrity and a hero, and these days celebrities often get a lot more attention. In our world of big names, curiously, our true heroes tend to be anonymous. The hero is known for his achievements; the celebrity for his well-knownness. The hero reveals the possibilities of human nature; the celebrity reveals the possibilities of the press and the media. Celebrities are people who make the news, but heroes are people who make a difference in the lives of real people. Boorstin unwittingly has described one of my heroes, Dr. Charles Hauser.

I first met Dr. and Mrs. Hauser while I was serving as pastor of Fourth Baptist Church and president of Central Baptist Theological Seminary in Minneapolis, Minnesota. He had accepted the call to become dean of Central Seminary. Before long, Marie and I became close friends with Charles and his wife Ann, who served as registrar of the seminary. Among other things, we enjoyed many birthday meals together over the years since the birthdays of our wives were in close proximity to one another as were Charles's and mine.

Dr. Hauser was a gifted New Testament scholar and exegete, who was passionate about truth, particular about his theology, and pastoral at heart. While his calling in life was professorial, he was concerned that our emphasis at Central should be on graduating an abundance of pastors who could function well as servant-leaders of New Testament local churches. Of course, a number of his students went on to serve in Christian institutions of higher education as professors, not the least of which was Dr. Kevin Bauder, but his heart was to equip young men to serve in the local church. As evidence of this heartbeat, Dr. Hauser served for several years on the pastoral staff of Fourth Baptist Church and was always a source of wise counsel to the pastoral team. On a personal level, I thought of Dr. Hauser as a trusted confidant and often appealed to him for counsel regarding delicate or difficult issues that might face our ministry from time to time.

What stands out most to me about Dr. Hauser's ministry is his "long obedience in the same direction," to use a familiar phrase that has become my favorite definition of faithfulness. I have always thought of faithfulness as the one indisputable evidence of success as defined by God. The apostle Paul said, "This is how one should regard us, as servants of Christ and stewards of the mysteries of God. Moreover, it is required of stewards that they be found faithful" (1 Cor 4:1-2 ESV). The term translated *steward* can be defined as "one who is entrusted with management in connection with transcendent matters."[1] In Dr. Hauser's case, the transcendent matters were "the mysteries of God"—the hitherto unrevealed secret counsels of God that have now been revealed through the apostolic pen in the New Testament documents. Of this treasured revelation, Dr. Hauser was a scrupulous, circumspect, and eminently faithful steward.

It seems to me that 1 Peter 4:10–11 is a fitting summary of Dr. Hauser's life and teaching ministry, and it represents the way I will best remember him:

> As each one has received a *special* gift, employ it in serving one another as good stewards of the manifold grace of God. Whoever speaks, *is to do so* as one who is speaking the utterances of God; whoever serves *is to do so* as one who is serving by the strength which God supplies; so that in all things God may be glorified through Jesus Christ, to whom belongs the glory and dominion forever and ever. Amen.

I believe this text is a clear affirmation of the driving force in Dr. Hauser's ministry—"that in everything God may be glorified through Jesus Christ." The authors of this book affirm that God is rightly the sole recipient of glory. They do, however, also affirm that Charles Hauser is rightly the recipient of honor. I agree with them. Therefore, I rejoice to be able to say of my good friend Charles—though it will mean much more to him coming from the lips of Jesus—"Well done, good and faithful servant!"

---

[1] BDAG, s.v. "οἰκονόμος."

Remembrance of Charles Hauser
Michael Grisanti

I joined the faculty of Central Baptist Seminary as a part-time instructor in July of 1985 and became a full-time professor the next year. I was part of the faculty team that interviewed Dr. Hauser before the seminary hired him to be part of our faculty. I served under him as an Old Testament professor until God directed me to The Master's Seminary in southern California.

Faithful servants who give their lives to the Lord for consistent ministry are always a blessing to others. The same was true for Dr. Charles Hauser and his wife Ann. I never was a student of Dr. Hauser's but had the privilege of serving with him for several years. When I summarize a person's life and impact, I like to think of key words that capture their core characteristics. Each person might have a different list of words to describe my beloved colleague, but here are mine:

Steady or consistent—Dr. Hauser was unflappable. His emotions did not seem to swing this way or that. He was as steady as a rock. As an academic dean who gives direction to a school, he is the kind of guy you want making or considering decisions. I would not go to Dr. Hauser for warm and passionate conversations, which was totally OK. I was thankful that Dr. Hauser stayed on the path he believed was right. Of course, that could also be frustrating at times (others might smile at that), but it was a long-term blessing.

Methodical—Dr. Hauser had a way of doing things, a system of sorts. He followed a regular pattern of life. Sometimes his method was disconcerting. If you worked with Dr. Hauser, you remember his "pile" approach to his desk and office. More times than I can remember, I went into his office to follow up on something I had sent him or something he asked me about. He would lift up a few layers of a pile and pull out the appropriate piece of paper that related to my question. Sure, this caused me and others some frustration, but I smile at what he could remember and find when I was confident that he had lost what I had given him. Each year, classes were scheduled, meetings were conducted, students received solid teaching, and things were stable. It was a lesson for me to learn. Not everyone gets things done in the same way!

Kind—Dr. Hauser and I had one especially challenging time in our relationship. I don't need to give any details. It was tough for both of us. We had some tense conversations and wondered about the heart motivation of the other person. In God's providence and goodness, we were able to reach a resolution, and I remained a faculty member at Central for another decade. Dr. Hauser came to where he embraced me as a faculty member he cared for and valued (as I did toward him). He would consistently ask how I or my wife and children were doing. He wanted me to flourish as a person and faculty member.

Faithful—This characteristic is similar to being steady but has some unique facets. Having spoken with his dear wife and Dr. Hauser at various times, I came to hear about some challenging times he faced in life. He modeled what it looked like to have core values based on Scripture that kept him going through good and challenging times. He is one of those poster examples of someone serving our great God faithfully in various ministry settings over a number of years.

A faithful husband of a loving wife—Dr. Hauser's wife Ann was a big part of his ministry effectiveness. Not only did she have strengths in areas of Dr. Hauser's weakness, she interacted with faculty and their wives and students and their wives in a way that added to Dr. Hauser's effectiveness as a seminary leader. Dr. Hauser and Ann modeled what I value in my marriage and long that our own children would experience—being more able to serve the Lord as a couple than we can on our own.

Honest and frank—In some ministry and work settings, there is too much intrigue and positioning for selfish purposes. Dr. Hauser, however, was a straight shooter. He did smile with some regularity, but his facial expression did not signal deeper thoughts. He could have been a deceiver and hidden what he really meant. The good news is that I never knew Dr. Hauser to knowingly deceive or misrepresent the truth. He would tell you what he thought without fanfare, but there was no question that he told you the way he saw things—unvarnished truth. Once I met with Dr. Hauser to hear his insight about an opportunity that came my way. He frankly shared his opinions with me and the reasons why he came to that conclusion. I was grateful for his care for me and openness with his wisdom. I valued the loving honesty of my brother in Christ.

Dr. Charles Hauser was a man who was not charismatic, flamboyant, or immediately impressive. On the other hand, he had character traits that are essential for any long-term ministry. Like me, he was imperfect and had weaknesses. Rest assured, we have lost a faithful friend and a man who modeled impactful gospel ministry. Our loss is heaven's gain.

Memories of Dr. Charles Hauser
L. Mark Bruffey

Dr. Charles Hauser listened far more than he spoke. He was a quiet man. He tended to address issues tersely, with utterances that went right to the point.

My First Teaching Review

I recall only one teaching review by Dr. Hauser, who was dean at the time. I had taught a course on research and writing in the fall and one called "logic for doing theology" in the spring (Dr. Hauser had tricked me into teaching the latter; I hadn't been smart enough to say no!). Both courses were heavily populated, and it was my first year teaching seminary students. Dr. Hauser had taken time to go through each of the many course evaluation forms. He had compiled the figures and also written down a host of student comments. He gave me a copy, which I still have somewhere in my files. I remember seeing an occasional accolade among the many pointed criticisms. I remember thinking, "This is seminary; all the students ought to appreciate the rigorous course that I set before them." Dr. Hauser looked across the pile of papers on his desk and said, "When I first started teaching, I discovered that my students were ready to lynch me." Oh! Dr. Hauser was nothing but fatherly and kind to me. I don't remember much else about that review, but I took the paper, highlighted the negative comments, inserted it at the front of my teaching binder, and consulted it many times in the ensuing years. If my teaching improved, it was due in large part to a single session with Dr. Hauser.

Loyalty to Staff, Faculty, and the Institution

Dr. Hauser was not a micromanager. I worked under his guidance both as librarian and as a member of the teaching faculty. I think that in his conversations with others above my pay grade, he must have been something like a tiger in defense of each of us to whom an area of responsibility had been assigned. With Dr. Charles Hauser, insubordination was not a thing. I enjoyed—but failed almost entirely to appreciate—the luxury of meaningful oversight within my purview as director of library services.

Someone close to Dr. Hauser recently remarked that Dr. Hauser felt that he was seldom heard. Perhaps we did not hear enough or well enough. His voice still reverberates and resonates within us, however, when we take time to reflect on the man and his ministry. Some of these reverberations are punctuated as we observe the consequences of actions against which he warned.

Managing faculty is like herding cats. It's just as impossible to herd five as fifty. Occasionally a new library policy would affect faculty, and I would be curious what the faculty might think. Dr. Hauser would say, "Don't ask the faculty. *Tell* the faculty. If you ask the faculty, all you'll get is a big discussion and no decision." Dr. Hauser valued highly the opinions and decision-making role of the faculty, of course. He also knew the kind of questions most suitable for faculty discussion. Dr. Hauser was especially concerned when the faculty took up the question of the relation between student beliefs and the doctrinal statement of the institution. At the time, graduating seniors were expected to indicate agreement with the entire statement. Someone had got the notion that students ought to be required only to agree with some lesser expression of the statement. Over the course of several faculty meetings, this question produced heated discussion. In my recollection Dr. Hauser ensured that everyone had opportunity—uninterrupted—to voice his opinion on this subject. Even his deeply personal and vested interest in this issue did not trump Dr. Hauser's commitment to Central Seminary as a faculty-run institution. Under Dr. Hauser, in those areas where a faculty ought to run an institution, it did.

Teaching Sunday School

I never took a seminary course from Dr. Hauser. Aside from an occasional sermon that he delivered at Fourth Baptist Church, my exposure to his teaching ministry came in connection with the church's Timothy Class. This adult Bible fellowship consisted mainly of senior citizens. My wife and I attended it for a decade, more or less. Dr. Hauser graciously requested that I substitute for him from time to time. We developed friendships with quite a few folks who came to hear Dr. Hauser teach; we were and are the richer for it.

Dr. Hauser was an expositor. He taught the Bible. In certain settings Dr. Hauser could become a little agitated. Whenever he taught, however, he delivered matter-of-fact, forthright lessons that evidenced serious study of the Scriptures and consideration of theological issues. His attitude, knowledge, and manner of delivery reminded me of the church where I had come to Christ.

He had these note cards. I never knew where he stored them or just how he organized them, but he always taught from a stack of these things. I've heard that he also taught his seminary courses using these legendary stacks. Methodically, he would work his way card by card with reading and commentary, putting each on the bottom until (I suppose) he realized that he was looking at the first again. I learned a lot from those cards.

Mentoring

As he was able and so long as he was dean, Dr. Hauser tried to spend a little informal time with me in various ways. I assume that many others could attest the same. He had these fancy-dangled, souped-up hearing aids. Periodically, he would ask that I accompany him to Starkey, a world-renowned company just down the road in Eden Prairie. While he and his devices were receiving maintenance, I would sit in the spacious guest lounge and look around at pictures of all the high-profile public figures who sported Starkey hearing aids. Of course, it wasn't about any of that or his need for a chauffeur; it was an opportunity to mentor. Seeing that he had no biological children, I suppose that I was one of many spiritual sons that God brought into his pathway. Dr. Hauser was no celebrity—at least not yet—but when we meet again there will be great celebration. No doubt he will be a highly decorated soldier of the cross.

More than a Seminary Education
Deborah R. Forteza

I went to a theological seminary to study the Bible for myself, but I left with many additional critical tools. A professor who was instrumental in my learning was the then dean, Charles A. Hauser, Jr. Dr. Hauser, everyone said, was tough. He expected excellent academic work, rarely gave As, and had a reputation for not changing grades when students appealed them. He was a wise, quiet, kind man, who always asked good questions and gave good advice.

My first class with Hauser was on the Gospel of Matthew. The course requirements included five short research papers summarizing different interpretations of verses in the Gospel and coming to a conclusion as to which was more probable in the light of all of Scripture. Because there were five papers, this gave students the opportunity to receive feedback on their work and try harder on the next paper. For me, getting an A turned into a goal with each successive paper that came back with something other than the highest grade written on the first page. My final paper was returned with an A-, and I guess my claim to fame is that when I reasonably appealed the grade, Hauser turned it into a solid A. I later learned that it had been years since he had changed a grade.

I've long since reflected on my drive to get good grades from professors who have a high academic standard as Hauser did. My conclusion is that I wanted to learn how to think critically and how to do hard academic work, especially what is required for sound theological interpretation; the professors with the high bar were the ones who actually pushed me to do that kind of work and ended up shaping not only my thinking but also my teaching. I don't think the problem was that I was merely interested in the grade so that easy grades consciously made me work less. Instead, his setting a high standard and encouraging students to attain it made me realize that there was a deeper level to explore if only I dedicated more time and energy to the task. After all, time and energy in seminary are limited, and often the urgency of other matters and work crowded out more in-depth study than some classes required. Moreover, getting an A from professors like Hauser meant something, and it offered the satisfaction of an arduous job well done, perhaps not unlike God's satisfaction when resting from the work of his good creation on the seventh day. Hauser was the kind of professor who would bring out the best work you could do, the most reflective of the image of God in human beings, and this, too, was very good.

In Hauser's classes I learned how deeply one could exegete a single verse while remaining true to the context and to the whole counsel of God. I was also taught how to offer a just description of all sides of an argument or a biblical interpretation and how to defend one point of view with sound reason and logic. More importantly, I was shown that within orthodoxy different theological interpretations are possible, and that charity is essential in any disagreement. Also, the role of the Holy Spirit in illumining God's Word was presented as fundamental. In my assignments, I learned to research thoroughly and to write clearly, which, in turn, led me to think more rigorously. All these tools still serve me well.

Were it not for professors like Hauser who believed the church needed women who carefully studied theology, I might not have finished my last seminary degree. During my studies, no one questioned that it was good for women to learn about biblical counseling, which is the program that led me to seminary. But when I considered studying the Bible further through an academic Master of Divinity, some people had misgivings because they believed that some levels of theological studies were reserved for men or that having a seminary degree makes women less submissive. My goal during my time in seminary was to have tools for personal biblical study, including the biblical languages, and I firmly believed then, as I do now, that God appoints men to be elders in his church and to lead in their homes. Nevertheless, since I was a student and wanted to be faithful to Scripture, I took the concerns seriously. Using the biblical study tools I had been given in conversation with the theological opinions of biblical scholars and mentors, I set out to study for myself the different views of the subject. I concluded that a woman's heart, not her restricted theological studies, is what makes her more or less submissive to God's plan for his church and the home, and therefore I finished my MDiv.

After seminary I went on to further graduate degrees in literature and eventually finished a PhD. As a first-generation college student who wrote her first paper in English in college, I never thought I could complete graduate work, much less doctoral work. But thanks in part to Hauser's teaching, I had most of the tools I needed. In addition to learning how to study the

Bible for myself, I had been taught in the classroom and by example to be a hard-working researcher and writer, to be dependent on God for help in my work, and to be sensitive to his leading.

I teach college students today much like Hauser and professors like him taught me. I strive to nurture three qualities that I believe are essential for successful teachers: the ability to make complex matters understandable and relevant; the willingness to offer intellectually demanding courses; and the vision to encourage students to use their minds and God-given gifts beyond the classroom for the benefit of the church and the world. As result, I hope to be to my students what Hauser was for me: someone to challenge, encourage, and inspire them.

Charles Hauser: A Friend and Mentor
Kevin T. Bauder

The Facts of His Life

The young Charles A. Hauser, Jr., suffered from a speech impediment. He struggled to make himself understood. Consequently, he intended to follow his father into the world of banking, where he would be working with ledgers and financial statements rather than with the public.

He might have enjoyed such a career except for one thing. The young Charles A. Hauser, Jr., was also a member of an independent Baptist church in Altoona, Pennsylvania—a church that produced multiple pastors and missionaries over the years. By the time Hauser had completed his BBA degree at the University of Pittsburg, he had become convinced that the Lord was calling him into vocational ministry.

He first attended the Pittsburg-Xenia seminary because it was near his home. His experience there was not happy. He was still troubled by the speech impediment, and one of his professors once told the young Charles that he ought to go into business because he would never be of any use as a minister. Hauser never forgot that discouragement, and it later gave him compassion for students who struggled to complete seminary.

Eventually, Hauser transferred to Dallas Theological Seminary, where he took his ThM degree. At Dallas he was strongly influenced by Charles Caldwell Ryrie. He then went on to study at Grace Theological Seminary under such luminaries as Ava J. McLain, Herman A. Hoyt, and John C. Whitcomb.

After receiving his ThD from Grace, Hauser taught briefly at the old Buffalo Bible Institute in Buffalo, New York. In 1962 he moved to California to join the faculty of the San Francisco Baptist Theological Seminary. While at San Francisco he became active in the so-called hard core of the conservative Baptist movement, eventually helping to frame the doctrinal statement for the New Testament Association of Independent Baptist Churches.

During those years, SFBTS was noted for its faculty. Hauser taught alongside individuals such as William Bellshaw, LaVern Shaeffer, and Bernard Northrup. These were men of strong and sometimes idiosyncratic opinions, and Hauser was forced to sharpen his thinking in conversation with his peers.

Along the way he had lost his speech impediment, though he could still stumble from time to time. Intemperate decisions by the seminary administration led to the exodus of nearly all the professors during the summer of 1972.

Hauser was invited by Bryce Augsburger to become a founding professor of a new seminary connected with Denver Baptist Bible College. In addition to teaching at Denver Baptist Theological Seminary, Hauser served as the academic vice president of both the college and seminary. The school struggled almost from the beginning, so the professors were perpetually behind in their salaries. Augsburger left the presidency in 1979, and Hauser continued to serve under William Fusco (the two men hailed from the same home church). After Fusco resigned in 1984, Hauser continued to serve under L. Duane Brown until the college and seminary closed in 1986.

After Denver, Hauser joined the faculty of Central Baptist Theological Seminary of Minneapolis. He also served as registrar and then dean of the institution. He taught at Central Seminary until his retirement in 2006, after which he became dean emeritus and served on the board. Central Seminary also awarded Charles Hauser the DHum degree, *causa honoris*. His career at Central Seminary mainly spanned the presidencies of Ernest Pickering, Douglas McLachlan, and Kevin Bauder.

Hauser was dean when the seminary was asked to teach courses in Romania during the early 1990s. Eventually Central Seminary opened a full branch campus in Arad, Romania, where it trained something like twenty percent of all Baptist pastors in that country. Hauser traveled frequently to that campus, and he oversaw its work until his retirement.

The wife of Charles Hauser's youth, Janet Melling, died while he was teaching at Denver. The registrar at Denver, Anna (Ann) Miller, had been widowed many years earlier. Their common experience of bereavement eventually drew them together. They married, and after Charles became the dean at Central Seminary, Ann took over the job of registrar.

Ann had three grown sons: Tim, Paul, and John. After Charles's retirement, the couple moved to Louisville, Kentucky, to be near one of her sons. They lived in Louisville until Ann's death in 2012. After Ann's death, Charles's health began to decline. Eventually he was diagnosed with Parkinson's disease, after which he moved into a care facility. His eyesight began to dim, and then his hearing began to fade. During the COVID lockdowns, he experienced profound loneliness. As his body weakened, he was eventually confined to a wheelchair.

Until near the end, Hauser would call his former coworkers for news about what was happening at Central Seminary. They would occasionally stop by to visit him when they were traveling near Louisville. For the last few months, however, he expressed bewilderment at why the Lord was leaving him on earth and not taking him to heaven. He was more than ready to go.

On Saturday evening, March 19, 2022, Charles A. Hauser, Jr., received his wish. He was permitted to lay aside the "earthly tent, which is our house," so as to be "absent from the body and to be at home with the Lord" (2 Cor 5:1, 8 NASB—a translation that Hauser loved). These are the facts of Charles Hauser's life.

I feel, however, that I cannot stop with this bare summation of biographical information. The influence of Charles Hauser was far greater than these words can hint. So I offer a description of Charles Hauser as a man of God.

The Influence of a Godly Man

I met Charles Hauser when I enrolled at Denver Baptist Theological Seminary in the fall of 1979. That semester I took two of his courses, one in theology and one on the Christian life. I can remember two statements that he made during that first semester. One was, "There is no such thing as a dispensational hermeneutic. There is only a literal hermeneutic, and if you interpret the Bible literally, you will be a dispensationalist." The other was, "Charles Finney was a figure from whose influence fundamentalism has yet to recover."

Unlike some theologians, Hauser wanted his theology to be driven mainly by the exegesis of the Bible. He also considered a right relationship with God to be critical theological preparation. He was willing to acknowledge some role for historical considerations, but he allowed virtually no place for philosophy, which he saw as a waste of time. His depreciation of philosophy had the potential to place us at loggerheads. What redeemed our relationship was his character.

Charles Hauser had suffered personal tragedy with the recent death of his wife. He and the rest of the faculty were experiencing financial hardship as their salaries were months in arrears. He had endured betrayal from the administration of his previous school, and this betrayal continued in the form of published personal attacks. These attacks were broadcast far and wide but were sent particularly to our seminary's library, where any student could read them.

We students had a close-up view of Hauser's reactions. He never betrayed a hint of impatience or anxiety. As nearly as we could tell, he was convinced that the Lord was completely in control of all his circumstances, and he was willing to leave their disposition to God. Day after day he stood before us with grace and equanimity. It was impossible to dismiss a man with that kind of character.

Charles Hauser loved the Bible. He relished teaching courses on biblical books. His expository courses on Matthew and Hebrews became legendary, and he continued to teach these courses even after his retirement. He thought that studying the Bible, developing a systematic theology, and living the Christian life all belonged together. He emphasized repeatedly that theology connects directly to life. He would warn, "Many people will be justified in placing their shattered lives at the feet of some preacher who taught them a bad theology."

For all that, Charles Hauser was no ivory-tower intellectual. He loved his Lord. He loved his wife Ann. He loved his coworkers and his students. He also loved sports, especially football.

At Denver, the seminary was attached to a Bible college that sponsored an annual college-versus-seminary flag football game. Hauser held credentials as a football official, and he always refereed this game. Later in Minneapolis, he would buy season tickets to watch the University of Minnesota's Golden Gophers on the gridiron. He regularly shared these tickets with his students. Pastor Andrew Hudson, one of the authors of this volume, testifies that this practice, and Hauser's ongoing personal attention, made a lasting impact on his life.

Charles Hauser cared deeply about his students. He never forgot that he was preparing them to be pastors, not professors (though many became professors). When student-related issues were discussed in faculty meetings, Hauser almost always took a student's position. He never forgot how difficult it had been for him to function in seminary with a speech impediment. He never forgot the humiliation of being told that the Lord could not use him in ministry. He was particularly compassionate toward students who had to struggle to learn. If a student had to appeal to the dean for help, he found that Hauser was on his side.

During his decades at Central Seminary, Hauser also served on the pastoral staff of Fourth Baptist Church. When Ernest Pickering resigned the pastorate at Fourth Baptist, Hauser became the interim pulpit supply. He taught a large adult Sunday school class, and he and Ann were involved with the Golden Agers group in the church.

Ann's first husband had died under the same kind of tragic circumstances as Charles Hauser's first wife. After his death, Ann had refused to think about marriage again until her sons were grown. When Charles and Ann eventually married, they seemed a bit of an odd couple. She was several years older than he and relatively tall, while he was quite short. Despite appearances, they were ideally suited for each other and became one of the most devoted couples I've ever seen. After his retirement, Hauser moved her to Louisville to be near one of her sons. Of course, this moved him out of his entire circle of acquaintances.

Ann died almost exactly ten years before Charles did. That last decade was the most difficult of his life. He felt lonely. He contracted Parkinson's Disease and lost the ability to live independently. He felt as if the Lord had set him on a shelf. He was eager for heaven, whether through death or through the rapture.

Only around fifteen people gathered for his funeral in Louisville. There were reasons. He had moved far from the circle of his acquaintances. He had outlived his generation. COVID had altered people's traveling habits. Still, the small gathering was wholly out of proportion to Hauser's influence in life.

He helped to prepare hundreds, perhaps thousands, of pastors in four institutions and on two continents. He helped to equip dozens of professors. He provided sound educational leadership at a time when many fundamentalist schools lacked that influence. He proved himself an able churchman, holding pastoral roles in multiple congregations. His was a life well spent.

Charles Hauser loved to read about those heroes of faith in Hebrews 11. In the process, he became like them: a man of faith, compassion, and perseverance. Measured either by theological acumen or by the stature of the fulness of Christ, Charles Hauser was a giant.

Made in the USA
Middletown, DE
12 December 2023

45383497R00166